Writing with Confidence

Third Edition

Writing with Confidence

Third Edition

Alan Meyers
Harry S Truman College

Scott, Foresman and Company
Glenview, Illinois

Boston
London

An instructor's manual with test bank and a separate answer key are available for this text. They may be obtained through your local Scott, Foresman representative or by writing to Skills Editor, College Division, Scott, Foresman and Company, 1900 East Lake Avenue, Glenview, Illinois 60025.

Acknowledgments

From *The World Almanac and Book of Facts 1987*. Copyright © 1986 by the Newspaper Enterprise Association, Inc., New York, New York 10166. Reprinted by permission.

From *The New Jewish Encyclopedia*, edited by David Bridger. Copyright © 1976 by David Bridger. Reprinted by permission of Behrman House, Inc.

Excerpts from pp. 116, 151, 159, and 276 from *The Book of Lists #3* by Amy Wallace, David Wallechinsky, and Irving Wallace. Copyright © 1983 by Amy Wallace, David Wallechinsky, and Irving Wallace. Abridged by permission of William Morrow & Company.

From *Anatomy of the Movies* by David Pirie. Reprinted by permission of Macmillan Publishing Company.

From *Cat Fancy*, September 1981. Reprinted by permission.

From *Chicago Tribune*, January 10, 1982. Copyright © 1982 by the Chicago Tribune Company. All Rights Reserved. Used with permission.

Excerpt from *The People's Almanac* by David Wallechinsky and Irving Wallace. Copyright © 1975 by David Wallechinsky and Irving Wallace. Reprinted by permission of Doubleday & Company, Inc.

Various excerpts selected from *The People's Almanac* by David Wallechinsky and Irving Wallace. Copyright © 1975 by David Wallechinsky and Irving Wallace. Reprinted by permission of Doubleday & Company, Inc.

From *The People's Almanac #2* by David Wallechinsky and Irving Wallace. Copyright © 1978 by David Wallechinsky and Irving Wallace. Adapted by permission of William Morrow & Company.

Sixteen excerpts from pp. 368–69, 609, 628, 240–41, 565–67, 805, 886–87, 151–52, 663, 692, 694, 676–77, 620, and 623–24 from *The People's Almanac #2* by David Wallechinsky and Irving Wallace. Copyright © 1978 by David Wallechinsky and Irving Wallace. Abridged by permission of William Morrow & Company.

From *The People's Almanac #3* by David Wallechinsky and Irving Wallace. Copyright © 1981 by David Wallechinsky and Irving Wallace. Adapted by permission of William Morrow & Company.

Excerpts from pp. 139–41, 153–54, 154–55, 160–61, 163, 290–92, 338–39, 535–37, 542–44, from *The People's Almanac #3* by David Wallechinsky and Irving Wallace. Copyright © 1981 by David Wallechinsky and Irving Wallace. Abridged by permission of William Morrow & Company.

Library of Congress Cataloging-in-Publication Data

Meyers, Alan.
    Writing with confidence.

    Includes index.
    1. English language—Rhetoric.   2. English language—Grammar—1950–   I. Title.
PE1408.M52   1988   808'.042   87-20500
ISBN 0-673-18728-4

ISBN 0-673-18728-4

1 2 3 4 5 6   92 91 90 89 88 87

Preface

This third edition of *Writing with Confidence*, like the first and second editions, is based on the premise that people write to communicate ideas, and if ideas are worth saying, they are worth saying well. Unlike many texts that stress grammar as an end in itself, this book recognizes that the study of grammar, syntax, spelling, and punctuation must clearly relate to the larger context and process of writing. As students read and then rewrite or revise the content of an exercise—whether it concerns Diamond Jim Brady, Ma Barker, or the history of the elevator—they discover that, through revision, ideas become clearer and more interesting. As students then complete the end-of-chapter writing and revising assignments, they are able to apply those same skills to their own writing.

CHANGES IN THIS EDITION

Based on suggestions from instructors who have used earlier editions of *Writing with Confidence*, this third edition offers the following new features:

• **New Chapter 1.** This opening chapter contains a full discussion of the writing process from prewriting through editing. It explores the similarities and differences between writing and speaking; the relationships among topic, audience, and purpose; the writer's own voice; and the writer's personal practices of composing and revising. It then examines and illustrates each stage of the writing process (from brainstorming and free writing to composing, revising, and editing), and leads the students through the planning, composing, and revising of their own paragraphs.

• **New Chapter on Paragraphs.** The completely revised Chapter 16 focuses on the purpose and form of a paragraph, its role within a composition, and its topic sentence and body. The section on the topic sentence guides students in limiting the sentence, ensuring that it states a point, and recasting it in the later stages of the writing process. The section on the body of a paragraph explores how a topic idea may be developed through facts, explanations, examples, and stories. A final section on paragraph unity offers practice in structuring and revising for unity throughout the writing process.

• **New Chapter on Style.** Chapter 17, entitled "Writing Concretely and Concisely," explores ways to make writing lively, vivid, and direct. It offers practice in pruning deadwood; writing strong verbs, adjectives, and expressions; eliminating unnecessary repetition of words and ideas; and avoiding clichés.

• **New Sequencing of Chapters.** Chapters 2 through 4, which examine writing complete sentences, using coordination, and using subordination, form a consecutive sequence on the treatment of sentence boundaries and sentence joining. The complete treatment of all punctuation marks has been moved to Chapter 11, closer to these earlier chapters.

• **More Sentence Combining and Sentence Writing.** Chapters 3, 4, and 17 offer more practice in sentence combining, first enabling students to combine or write sentences using one pattern and later enabling them to consider a variety of patterns based on content, context, and style.

• **More Explicit Directions in the Writing Assignments.** The directions for the writing assignments in Chapters 1 through 10 emphasize the consideration of audience, the steps in the composing process, and the formation of a topic sentence.

• **More Attention to Verbs.** Chapters 5, 6, and 12 have been revised and expanded to offer more practice with verb forms, both in single-word verbs and verb phrases. Chapter 12 not only patterns all the most important verb phrases but also explains how they are used.

• **Increased Coverage of Commonly Confused Words.** Chapter 15, "Writing the Right Word," has been expanded to include a number of additional sound-alike and look-alike word pairs.

• **New Subject Matter.** One quarter of the exercise content has been changed, incorporating material taken primarily from *The People's Almanac #2* and *#3*. The remaining exercises retain the most popular subject matter from earlier editions, although they have been revised for increased clarity and focus.

• **Increased Coverage of Prepositions.** A new section in Chapter 13 focuses on the most common meanings of the prepositions *in* and *on*.

CONTINUING FEATURES OF THE TEXT

While much has been changed in this new edition, those features that have proved most successful remain unchanged.

• **Flexible Organization.** Each of Chapters 2 through 10 is divided into two parts. Instructors may assign the first part of a chapter, evaluate students on the basis of the concluding *Editing* exercise, and then assign the second part of the chapter (entitled "Some Additional Help") to those students requiring further instruction and practice. Alternatively, instructors may assign any or all sections of each chapter according to the needs of their students.

• **Simple and Direct Explanations.** Simplified explanations of grammar and mechanics use a minimum of terminology and focus on what students need to know to generate effective sentences and paragraphs while eliminating errors. Occasional footnotes amplify more complex points of grammar and mechanics.

• **Attention to the Special Needs of Students.** Chapters 11 through 15 include material on punctuation, verb phrases, progressive tenses, indirect questions, double negatives, articles and prepositions, spelling, apostrophe use, hyphenation, capitalization, and sound-alike and look-alike words—all intended for students who require such instruction and practice, including those students whose first language is not English.

- **Flexible Testing Package.** *The Instructor's Manual to Writing with Confidence* contains three sets of tests for each chapter, allowing for great flexibility in evaluating and testing. The first two sets, Forms A and B, are parallel and can be administered as pretests and post-tests or can be utilized in a Mastery Learning approach (either in classrooms or writing laboratories). The third set, Form C, is paragraph-editing tests, allowing for a closer evaluation of the students' abilities to identify and correct errors. A set of mid-term and final paragraph-editing examinations has also been included.

- **Separate Answer Key.** To allow for greater flexibility, the answer key for the third edition has been published separately. Students can photocopy it if their instructors want them to check their own work.

I am again grateful to all those who have aided me in the preparation of this new edition. First, I thank the administrators of City Colleges of Chicago and of Truman College, who have provided me with an atmosphere in which I continue to explore my teaching and writing practices. Second, I thank my students, who have suggested ways of clarifying and improving the text. Third, I thank my editors, Anne Smith and Patricia Rossi, who guided me through the revision plan, and Elizabeth Smith-Eisenhauer, who blue-penciled my errors. Fourth, I thank the following users and reviewers who offered advice and encouragement: Mary Jo Berger, Community College of Denver—Auraria Campus; John M. Corley, Merced College; Joe Leonard, Southwestern College; Joanne Pinkston, Daytona Beach Community College; Mary Sue Ply, Southeastern Louisiana State University; Muriel Schultz, California State University—Fullerton; and Ellen Stukenberg, Columbus Technical Institute.

Finally, I thank my wife Ann and my children Sara and Bradley, for without their love and support any accomplishment of mine would be meaningless.

Alan Meyers

Contents

CHAPTER

6

Using the Past Tense and the Past Participle   121

CHAPTER

7

Using Modifiers (Descriptive Words, Phrases, and Clauses)   156

Guide to Writing Instruction

Writing with Confidence

Third Edition

CHAPTER 1

Exploring the Writing Process

This chapter will explore the writing process. You will see the relationship between writing and speaking—how in each you both discover and communicate your ideas. You will examine the goals of writing: *to inform, to persuade*, and *to entertain*. You will look at each stage in the writing process: *planning and discovering, composing* a first draft, and *revising and editing*. Then you will determine the best writing practices for you in each stage of the writing process. And finally, you will follow the development of a paper throughout the process.

COMPARING SPEAKING TO WRITING

When you speak, you don't just make sounds. You say *words* that *mean* something—to you and to your listeners. You speak because you want to share ideas, information, and opinions with specific people. You speak because you want those people to care about your ideas, understand your information, and be persuaded by your opinions. In short you speak because *you have a subject to discuss, a purpose for discussing it, and an audience to discuss it with*. Almost automatically—without really thinking about it—you adapt your message to fit your purpose and audience. You choose language that your audience most easily understands, present your ideas in a logical order, and try to be interesting and clear.

You also speak to address a second audience: yourself. Since you cannot know your thoughts exactly until you put them into words, you clarify, organize, and change your ideas as you say them aloud. If you listened to a tape recording of your informal speech, you would probably be surprised at how much you repeat yourself and drift from one subject to another. Such discovery and change, however, is a natural part of the communication process.

Writing and formal speaking are alike in many ways. Both involve discovering, shaping, and communicating ideas; both concern a subject, a purpose, and an audience. But in other ways, writing differs from speaking. When you speak, you can usually see and hear your listeners. As they respond to you, you respond to them. You answer their questions, re-explain ideas, and even change the subject if it bores them. When you speak, you can emphasize and clarify ideas through your voice and body language. You can raise or lower your voice, talk quickly or slowly, and pause for effect. You can point with your hands, shrug your shoulders, wink your eye, grin, or frown.

When you write, you lose all of these advantages because your audience is reading your words, not listening to them. You cannot see whether your readers are bored, confused, or unconvinced, and you cannot respond to their questions. Therefore you must try to anticipate and satisfy your audience's responses. You must choose an interesting subject for your readers and try to present it in an interesting way. Furthermore since you cannot use your voice and body to emphasize and clarify your ideas, you must pay greater attention to words, sentences, and the way you arrange them. You must read what you write and then rewrite until it says strongly and clearly just what you want it to say. You must choose, organize, and punctuate your language carefully.

EXAMINING THE WRITING PROCESS

A successful piece of writing, therefore, cannot and should not be done in one sitting. Anything you write should be written at least twice and often many more times. You should begin by exploring your ideas, finding out what you think as the words go down on paper. Then you should write, question, evaluate, and rewrite your first draft. You should revise and polish until you feel confident that your readers will clearly understand and be interested in your ideas. Writing, in short, is a *process* that involves *planning and discovering, writing a first draft, revising the paper through several drafts, and then editing and proofreading a final draft*. The page you are reading, for example, is the finished product—the last version—of many hours of work. You don't see the papers that went into the wastebasket along the way: the notes and false starts, the early drafts, and the later ones.

Prewriting, or Planning and Discovering

This first stage of writing is mostly for yourself, a time to explore your ideas and the way you express them. You choose a topic and then think and write freely about it, including whatever specific details come to mind. Sometimes you may list your ideas randomly in a process called *brainstorming;* sometimes you may explore your ideas in a process called *free writing.* (Both of these processes will be illustrated later in this chapter.) In either case, you write whatever comes to mind, putting the words on paper as fast as you can and not worrying about spelling, punctuation, or exact meanings—because you know you will change your mind and phrasing many times before you publish (that is, make public) the final draft. And in either case, you should plan, experiment, and play but not try to rewrite each line.

No two writers work in the same way, and the same writer may adopt different methods with each new task. Nevertheless, during the planning and discovering stage you should make some tentative decisions about what to say and the order in which to say it, although you will change your mind countless times as you rewrite and revise. Your preliminary decisions should be based on the answers to three general questions.

1. What is my subject, and what do I know about it? You should discuss something interesting, and the most interesting subjects to your audience are usually the most interesting ones to you. You may not think of yourself as an expert on any subject, but you are an expert on your own experiences. Choose a subject that you *care about* and *know about* (or can find out about). Then you will have more to say, and you will say it more clearly and confidently.

Occasionally in school assignments, you are given complete freedom to choose your subject. Most often, however, you must select a subject that fits within a larger, more general topic. For example, suppose you were asked to describe a skill, hobby, or some aspect of a job you know well. You would choose one you had feelings and opinions about, one you could describe in specific detail. Then you would search for that detail and explore your ideas. What tools or materials do you use in the hobby or job? How do you perform each task? What is most interesting or tedious in the task? What examples would best illustrate the task? You would make notes on your answers to these questions and refer to them later when you started to write.

2. Who is my audience? What you say about your subject depends greatly on your readers. For example, suppose you described how sales clerks are paid commissions in the shoe store where you work part-time. If you wrote for a general reading audience such as your classmates, you would probably give a general overview of the commission system and define the unfamiliar term *PM*, which in the jargon of the store means a bonus paid on certain merchandise, and you would illustrate this definition through examples. On the other hand, if you wrote about the same topic for a more specific audience (for example, other sales clerks), you would completely redirect the focus of your paper. You would not need to define PMs, but you could suggest ways that clerks could earn more money through commissions and PMs.

In most classroom situations you write for an audience of one: your instructor. How do you address the needs and concerns of that audience? If you write about a subject in your instructor's field of specialization (American history, zoology, data processing, marketing, and accounting), you need not define terms or provide a general overview of the subject matter—unless the instructor asks for such definitions and overviews. However, if you write on a subject that lies outside of your instructor's expertise, then you should address him or her as a general reader: someone curious to learn; happy to be entertained; or willing to be persuaded by a strong, logical argument. Since you know more than your instructor about the subject, you should define unfamiliar terms, give overviews, and provide examples.

A college instructor is also interested in your intellectual growth and achievement. Therefore, he or she will read your paper with a critical eye toward your knowledge about the subject; your ability to explain accurately, clearly, and logically; and your ability to write using standard methods of spelling, punctuation, and grammar. In these regards, however, an instructor is no different from any intelligent and thoughtful general reader who has similar expectations.

1 WARM-UP For each topic below, list two or three points you would include if you were writing to the various audiences specified. The lists for the first topic have been completed as an example, as will be the first part of every exercise throughout this book.

1. the value of popular music

   a. a general audience of people between the ages of eighteen and thirty

      lively beat and catchy melodies, great for dancing, great for

      background music while relaxing

   b. professional musicians

      profits from performing, enjoyment in performing, fame from

      performing

   c. parents of teenagers

      basically harmless entertainment for teenagers, socially acceptable

      way for teenagers to be rebellious, entertainment for adults

2. the benefits of controlled diets

   a. overweight adults

   _____

   _____

   b. professional athletes

   _____

   _____

   c. people with diabetes

   _____

   _____

   d. actors, actresses, and models

   _____

   _____

3. the pros and cons of freedom of speech

   a. publishers and journalists

   _____

   _____

   b. government officials

   _____

   _____

   c. ordinary citizens who wish to protest government policies

   _____

   _____

4. the advantages and disadvantages of tenure (virtually guaranteed employment) for teachers

   a. parents of students

   _____

   _____

   b. members of teachers' unions

   _____

   _____

   c. school administrators

   _____

   _____

   d. unemployed recent graduates of colleges of education

   _____

   _____

3. What is my purpose? You always communicate for a purpose—either *to inform, to persuade,* or *to entertain.* (In fact, your writing generally combines all of these.)

- When you *inform,* you are *explaining or describing an idea, a process, an event, a belief, a person, a place, or a thing.* You are giving your audience the facts and information about something, analyzing it in some way, defining terms, and explaining causes. An explanation of the commission system at the shoe store, for example, would be informative to your classmates. Informative writing is also called *expository* writing because it exposes the meaning of things.

- When you *persuade,* you are *trying to convince your audience that they should believe something or do something.* You are trying to make your readers change their minds or behave differently, so you appeal to their logic or emotion, or both. For example, a persuasive paper about the commission system might warn your classmates to beware of shoddy merchandise that greedy shoe clerks might try to foist on them.

- When you *entertain,* you are *trying to make your audience laugh, smile, be fascinated, be surprised, or even be angry.* Of course, everything you write should be entertaining, but sometimes that is your only purpose. In an entertaining paper about the commission system, you might describe the time you made one hundred dollars selling eight pairs of shoes to a man dressed in old work clothes.

Once you have tentatively answered these three questions, you can experiment with ways to communicate a subject to your audience and accomplish your purpose. You can consider what to say first, second, third, and tenth. You can consider what terms to define and when to define them.

You can consider what to include and what to leave out. In the limited space of a paragraph or composition, you cannot say everything, so you must settle on the most important, most relevant, and most interesting.

2 WARM-UP

After each of the following opening sentences of a paragraph, label its purpose *to inform, to entertain,* or *to persuade.* (There may be more than one possibility.) Be prepared to explain your choices.

1. Glassmaking began almost five thousand years ago in Egypt. ___to inform___

2. Beware of buying high-priced reproductions of antique bottles. _____

3. Coin collecting can be an enjoyable and profitable hobby. _____

4. Few sights are as magnificent as the setting of the orange-red sun as it disappears beneath the roaring waves of Florida's Atlantic seacoast. ____

_____

5. Smoking may be pleasurable to you, but can you continue to risk your health and life for the sake of that pleasure? _____

6. The United States began minting coins in 1792. _____

7. With no time remaining on the clock, Jordon stepped to the free-throw line. _____

8. Man is dog's best friend. _____

Composing a First Draft

During this second stage, your paper will begin to take a more formal shape. You now know more clearly what to say and what order to say it in—though doubtless you will change your mind later when you revise. In general you will write more slowly and cross out more often than you did during the planning and discovery stage. Nevertheless, you still needn't worry about getting things exactly right, for you will make additional changes in later drafts of the paper.

Revising and Editing

This last stage in the process involves making further discoveries, making further changes, and polishing your work. You will read your first draft, questioning organization, questioning word choice, and challenging yourself to supply more and more interesting details. Then you will rewrite the paper, removing some parts, adding others, and changing words and rephrasing sentences. You will reread it again, repeating the process until you are satisfied that it is interesting and clear. You must constantly ask yourself not, "Can this be understood?" but instead, "Can this be *mis*understood?" With that question in mind, you are more likely to find ideas that need clarification and phrases that need changing. Remember that you cannot sit next to your readers to tell them, "Well, what I meant was. . ."

Finally, because you want people to judge your ideas, not your mistakes, you must edit and proofread carefully. You must read what you have *actually* written—not what you *think* you have written. You must force yourself to look for misspelled words, words left out or repeated, grammatical errors, missing word endings, incomplete sentences, and incorrect punctuation.

BUILDING ON YOUR WRITING VOICE

Successful writers communicate ideas in their own words. Unfortunately, many students write unsuccessfully because they try to sound "literary," showing off their vocabulary instead of using it to communicate. You should write in your natural style, which many teachers call your *writing voice*. This is the voice you hear in your head while composing a paper. (Or it may be the voice you hear with your ears—many writers say their sentences aloud.)

To be sure, your writing voice is more formal (and grammatically more correct) than the one you use in casual speech. You must learn to build on this voice—strengthening, varying, and polishing it to make it graceful, confident, and clear. But such a voice can emerge only when you allow yourself the opportunity to *experiment with words and ideas*. You must *write with confidence*, trusting in your insights and your language, not censoring yourself and trying for perfection during your first attempt to put ideas on the page. Remember that the writing process is part discovery, part revision and restatement. You can change your ideas and your wording countless times—but first you must produce something to change. Then you can revise afterwards, cutting out what doesn't work, but reshaping and refining what does.

DEVELOPING YOUR PERSONAL WRITING PRACTICES

No two writers approach the writing process in the same way, so you should determine what works best for you. The choice of writing with a pencil, pen, or typewriter may seem trivial, but it isn't. Your physical comfort as you write increases your mental comfort and therefore your ability to compose. For example, if you change your mind and erase often during the first draft, then perhaps you should compose in pencil or pen with erasable ink. If you press down hard, a ball-point or felt-tip pen may suit you better. If you are impatient because your hand cannot keep pace with the speed of your mind, you should compose on a typewriter or word processor.

Consider some other matters, too. For example, do you write best in the morning or at night? Should you work at the library or in your room at home? Can you write with a radio on, or do you concentrate better in quiet surroundings? (Most people do need quiet.) Do you prefer to revise as you go along or after you have completed the first draft?

Regardless of what you decide about your writing practices, here is some advice to increase your efficiency.

In writing the first draft:
1. Write on only one side of the page so you can cut and paste sections you want to move or replace.
2. Leave wide margins on both sides of the page and write on every other line so you have room for changes and additions.
3. Say your sentences aloud as you write them, listening for what sounds natural, graceful, and clear.

4. Circle or underline words you think you have misspelled or might change later.
5. When an idea occurs to you that you should have mentioned earlier, write it on a separate page and then tape or staple it to the spot where it belongs.

In revising and editing the paper:

6. If possible, wait a few hours or days so you can approach your paper with fresh thoughts and eyes—more like the reader than the writer of the work.
7. Make small changes directly on the first draft, and write new sections on separate pieces of paper so you can tape or staple them to the original. (Recopy only when necessary—in the later stages of revision.)
8. Read your paper aloud, preferably to someone else. (You will be astonished at how many errors and awkward phrases you hear.)
9. Make a clean, neat copy of your final draft and then proofread it carefully.
10. Take pride in your work—it does, after all, carry your name.

ILLUSTRATING THE WRITING PROCESS

Let's examine how a paragraph might take shape during the writing process. Suppose, again, that you wanted to write an informative explanation about the commission system at the shoe store. There are at least two easy ways of discovering your ideas on the subject: listing them or writing them out more completely.

Getting Started Through *Brainstorming* and *Free Writing*

Using Brainstorming. One way to begin exploring your ideas—by making a random list—is called *brainstorming*. You simply put down whatever comes to mind about the subject and later choose what to include or leave out. Here's an example:

work at Mel's Shoes—a discount store

my working hours: 3:00–9:30 or 10:00 three nights a week, all day Saturday

work on commission but guaranteed the minimum hourly wage

commission includes PMs, also called *spiffs*

some selling time taken up with stock work: putting shoes back in boxes, replacing boxes in proper sections according to style and size

sell men's, women's, and children's shoes

store located downtown on Main Street

basic commission: 2% of selling price

also PMs—extra commissions

get $1.00 for hard-to-sell shoes or shoes purchased cheaply by store

get $1.00 extra when I sell two pairs to a customer

get $.50 extra for selling shoe polish

get $.25 extra for selling a pair of socks

get $10.00 extra for selling five pairs of shoes to a customer—but that rarely happens

things that slow me down so I can't make a lot in commissions: customers who want to try on every shoe in the store, stock work

Ralph, an older salesman, who tries to steal sales from the part-timers

Such a list includes too much information for one paragraph, so you should include only essential details. For example, although stock work, Ralph, and difficult customers may seem important to you because they lessen your opportunities to make commissions, these details are not essential because they don't explain how you are paid commissions. Therefore, you might return to the list, this time putting checkmarks next to the details that clearly belong:

✓ work on commission but guaranteed the minimum hourly wage
✓ commission includes PMs, also called *spiffs*
✓ basic commission: 2% of selling price
✓ also PMs—extra commissions
✓ get $1.00 for hard-to-sell shoes or shoes purchased cheaply by store
✓ get $1.00 extra when I sell two pairs to a customer
✓ get $.50 extra for selling shoe polish
✓ get $.25 extra for selling a pair of socks
✓ get $10.00 extra for selling five pairs of shoes to a customer—but that rarely happens

You might also put checkmarks next to the details that help establish the setting, but you needn't include too many:

✓ work at Mel's Shoes—a discount store
✓ located downtown on Main Street
✓ sell men's, women's, and children's shoes

Before you write the first draft, you could arrange details in the order you would present them. (The setting would probably come first.) Here is an informal outline.

I. Work at Mel's Shoes—a discount store
  A. Located downtown on Main Street
  B. Sell men's, women's, and children's shoes
II. Salary = commission plus PMs or minimum hourly wage, whichever is more
  A. Explanation of commission = 2% of selling price
  B. Explanation of PMs
    1. $1.00 on each hard-to-sell shoe or shoe the store bought cheaply
    2. $.50 on shoe polish and $.25 on each pair of socks
    3. $1.00 on each sale of two pairs of shoes
    4. $10.00 on each sale of five pairs of shoes

Using Free Writing. Another way to get started is through *free writing*. You simply jot down whatever comes to your mind about the subject, without worrying about spelling, complete sentences, and so on. Here is an example:

> Work part-time at Mel's Shoes, downtown on Main Street. Hours 9:00–9:30 or 10:00, three days a week, depending on how much stock work there is to do after we close. Also work all day Saturday. Stock work—hate it. Have to put all the shoes back in their boxes, then make sure all the boxes get back in the right spots according to style and size. Pay is good. I work on commission and PMs (we also call them *spiffs*). Commission is 2 percent. PMs run $1.00 on each pair of shoes the store is pushing, either because they bought them cheap or because they haven't sold well. I also get a $1.00 PM each time I sell a customer two pairs of shoes, and if I can sell five pairs at one time, I get $10.00. That happens once in a blue moon. Oh, yes, I also get a $.50 PM on shoe polish and a $.25 PM on socks, so all the PMs add up at the end of a day. Also, I'm guaranteed minimum wage if I have a poor day. Not a bad job really, although the customers' feet smell, and some jerks want to try on every shoe in the store. It beats digging ditches.

Free writing, like brainstorming, lets you discover specific details and ideas as they come to mind. Although the information is disorganized and much of it may be unusable, you will keep some phrasing for later drafts. First, however, you will have to narrow the topic and decide how to organize it, much like you do after brainstorming: you circle or put a checkmark next to the parts you want to keep and then choose the order in which they should appear.

3 WARM-UP

As in previous example, choose a job, hobby, or skill you are familiar with—and consider how it could make it an informative topic for most of your classmates. Then do some brainstorming, free writing, or both to explore your ideas. Afterward, narrow your focus, deciding on which parts to keep and on an order in which to present them.

Writing the First Draft

Once you have tentatively decided on your purpose and narrowed your focus, you can return to the ideas you gathered from brainstorming or free writing and compose a first draft. Don't worry about writing a perfect paper; you will revise it more than once. Also don't worry if you cannot think of a good attention-getting opening sentence; you can add it at any point in the writing process, even in your final draft. Here is an example of a first attempt:

> I sell shoes on commission. I can make as much as two hundred dollars working twenty hours a week. I work at Mel's Shoes, a discount shoe store located downtown on Main Street. Although I'm guaranteed the minimum hourly wage, I generally make much more from my commissions, which work this way. First, I get 2 percent of the selling price on each pair of shoes. So, for example, I receive one dollar on shoes that sell for fifty dollars. But I can make much more on the extra commissions called *PMs*. (We also call them *spiffs*.) The store pays the sales clerks a PM of $1.00 on each pair of shoes the store is pushing,

either because they bought them cheap or because they haven't sold enough of them. I also get a $1.00 PM each time I sell a customer two pairs of shoes, and if I can sell five pairs at one time, I get $10.00. That happens once in a blue moon. I also get a fifty-cent PM on shoe polish and a twenty-five-cent PM on socks, so all the spiffs add up at the end of a day. The customers' feet smell, and some customers want to try on every shoe in the store. It's really not a bad job. It beats digging ditches.

4 WRITING

Write a first draft based on the brainstorming or free writing you have done earlier. Make sure that you write on one side of the page only and that you leave yourself margins on both sides for changes. You may want to write on every other line of the paper so that you have room for changes.

Writing the Revisions

After you have taken a break, you can criticize and make changes on the first draft. You might notice these problems in the previous example (most of which will be discussed in later chapters):

1. The beginning of the paragraph doesn't attract interest in the subject.
2. The wording in several sentences is too informal (including too many contractions), repetitious, dull, or babyish.
3. The material should be rearranged so that relationships between ideas are clearer.
4. More details could be added in a few spots or taken out in others.
5. To create more formality, the pronoun *I* should be replaced with a third-person pronoun wherever possible.
6. The clichés could be eliminated.
7. Spelling, punctuation, and mechanical errors should be corrected, including the use of numerals where the numbers should be written out.

Here is a completely rewritten second version of the paper. Notice that there are even changes to the changes, which are added above the line, for the revision process does not stop with a single rewrite. The paper will be revised several more times.

If a sales clerk shows you some ugly shoes or ʌ_ill-fitting shoes_ ~~shoes that don't fit very well,~~ it may not be because ʌ_they are_ ~~they're~~ all he has but because he makes more commission on them. In many stores the commission system is good for the clerks but ʌ_unfortunate_ ~~bad~~ for customers. It not only encourages sales clerks to sell a lot of shoes but to sell certain kinds of shoes and merchandise that customers may not necessarily want or need. For example, ʌ_where I work,_ at Mel's Shoes, a shoe store located downtown on Main Street ~~where I work,~~ a part-time sales clerk can make as much as $200–300 weekly. The commission system ʌ_operates_ ~~works~~ this way. First, the clerk ʌ_receives 2 percent_ ~~gets %2~~ of the selling price on each pair of shoes. For example, he earns one dollar on shoes that sell for fifty dollars. But a good salesperson makes extra commissions called *PMs*. (We also called them *spiffs*.) The store pays the sales clerks a PM of _∧ a dollar ~~$1.00~~ on _∧ certain shoes it has bought cheaply or has overstocked. ~~each pair of shoes the store is pushing, either because they bought them cheap or because they haven't sold enough of.~~ They also receive another dollar for each sale of two pairs of shoes to a customer, and if they can sell five pairs at one time, _∧ make an extra bonus of ten dollars ~~they get $10.00,~~ although that happens rarely. The PMs also explain why sales clerks often ask you if you need shoe polish or socks; the clerks earn fifty cents on shoe polish and twenty-five cents on socks. Although such practices may _∧ occasionally seem annoying to you, they please the store owners and the sales clerks, who both benefit from them.

5 REVISING

Revise your first draft one or more times. You may need to rewrite the paper after you have made changes on the original version, and then to make further changes on the rewritten version. At various stages in the revising process, read your paper aloud—and read the last version to someone else.

Completing the Edited Final Draft

After you have revised your paper several times, look it over carefully for grammar, spelling, and punctuation. Such errors call attention to themselves and distract from your ideas. Let your reader judge you on what you have to say—and *not* on your errors in saying it. (In fact, the better you become at catching such errors during revisions, the better you will become at avoiding them in early drafts, but this latter skill is acquired with practice and usually doesn't happen immediately.) Finally, make a clean copy of the final draft according to the format your instructor recommends (and proofread it once more). Here is the final version of the sample paragraph, which has been changed further and edited carefully:

If a sales clerk shows you some ugly or ill-fitting shoes, it may not be because they are the only shoes left, but because the clerk makes a high commission on them. In many stores the commission system is good for the clerks but unfortunate for the customers. It not only encourages sales clerks to sell a lot of shoes but to sell certain shoes and merchandise that customers may not necessarily want or need. For example, at the discount shoe store where I work, sales clerks are paid two types of commissions. In addition to a two-percent straight commission on all sales, the clerks earn bonuses called *PMs* (also called *spiffs*) for special sales. Clerks receive a PM of one dollar for selling a certain style the store has bought cheaply or has overstocked. They receive another one-dollar PM each time they sell two pairs of shoes to the same customer and a ten-dollar PM on the rare occasions when they sell five pairs. These bonuses also explain why many sales clerks try to sell you shoe polish or socks—to earn the twenty-five-cent or fifty-cent spiffs on these items. Although such practices may annoy you, they obviously please the store owners and the sales clerks.

That, basically, is how the writing process works. You first discover and begin to organize your ideas. Then you write a first draft. And finally, you revise, edit, and proofread it as many times as necessary to make it clear, lively, logical, and legible. The exact methods you follow will be yours to decide—and, no doubt, you will change them with each writing task or as more efficient ones occur to you.

In Summary: In the writing process you should

1. consider your subject, your audience, and your purpose;
2. discover your ideas by putting them into words through brainstorming or free writing;
3. decide what to include and how to organize it;
4. write a first draft (and don't worry about making it perfect);
5. take a break and then criticize and revise the first draft several times, making changes in the margins and above the lines before rewriting;
6. read each version aloud, preferably to another person;
7. recopy the final draft legibly; and
8. proofread the final draft for spelling errors, repeated words, or words left out.

6 EDITING

Recopy your final draft and then proofread it for words left out, words repeated, spelling errors, and punctuation errors.

CHAPTER 2

Writing Complete Sentences

Chapter 1 urges you to develop your own habits and practices in exploring, planning, composing, and revising ideas for paragraphs and longer papers. You should attempt to discover what you have to say and then to say it clearly, convincingly, and interestingly. In this chapter and the ones that follow, you will continue to write paragraphs but will direct your attention to other concerns as well: grammar, punctuation, and spelling. Mastering them is important because you want readers to understand and respect *the content of your ideas,* not how you express (or misexpress) them. Nonstandard grammar, punctuation, and spelling call attention to themselves and lead some readers to believe you aren't "smart" (although using such nonstandard forms has nothing to do with a lack of intelligence). You must eliminate the errors so that you can be judged on what you have to say—not on what your errors might say about you.

If possible, the best time to search for and correct errors is *during revisions.* Too much attention to small matters in early drafts can freeze your creativity. You shouldn't have to stop and check the spelling of every word or the punctuation of every sentence in the heat of composing. When you revise, however, you can examine your work coldly and make necessary changes. With practice, these revising skills will become a natural part of your first drafting skills, although you will always need to revise and proofread.

This chapter will focus on one such revision skill: identifying and writing complete sentences. You will identify *subjects* and *verbs* of sentences, focus on two types of verbs—*action verbs* and *linking verbs*—and then work with sentences that contain more than one subject and verb. You will revise and correct incomplete sentences that others have written. And, you will look for complete sentences in paragraphs that you have written and revised, while paying special attention to *descriptive detail.*

DEFINING A FRAGMENT

A sentence *makes a complete statement;* its full meaning is clear.* Therefore you usually express ideas in sentences, even if you don't know a great deal about grammar. You probably do know that every sentence contains *at least one subject and one verb*, which together are called a *clause*. A *fragment*, however, is an *incomplete statement*, or only part of a sentence. Many fragments don't contain a complete clause; they are missing a subject or verb (or both). Some fragments contain a clause but are incomplete for other reasons we will explore shortly.

Fragments are not necessarily incorrect. In the give-and-take of conversations, listeners may understand a fragment ("that one" or "over there") in response to what they have said, especially when you accompany your words with gestures. In writing, however, you can't hear your readers, and they can't see your gestures. Many experienced writers employ occasional fragments for emphasis or variety—provided the meaning of the fragment is clear. The problem lies with unintentional fragments—those that confuse or annoy readers and muddle meanings.

Accidental fragments occur for two reasons: (1) some writers are not comfortable with their subjects, and (2) they punctuate by ear. In the first case, as writers struggle to express themselves, they don't listen to the sound of their writing voices. Their language becomes awkward and unnatural, so they put down half-thoughts and half-sentences. In the second case (again, usually when writers are struggling with ideas), they hear pauses and put periods at those spots, signaling the ends of sentences although the sentences haven't ended.

The first step in eliminating fragments, therefore, is to choose a subject you feel comfortable discussing and to revise your paper until the sentences flow naturally. Often you can best hear the flow by reading your papers aloud. The second step is more mechanical: to check each sentence during revisions, identifying complete statements and ensuring that you have punctuated them properly.

IDENTIFYING THE SUBJECTS OF CLAUSES

Since every sentence must contain at least one complete clause, you should be able to identify the subject and verb of every clause. And since subjects and verbs must go together, you can most easily identify the subject when you look for the verb at the same time. For a moment, however, just concentrate on the subject: *the word or words representing someone (who) or something (what) that the clause makes a statement about.* You will usually (but not always) find the subject *at or near the beginning of the sentence—before the verb*, which tells what the subject *does* or *is*.

> *subject* (who or what) + *verb*

*A sentence can also ask a question or make a command whose full meaning is clear.

The following sentence, for example, makes a statement about *Charles S. Stratton*. Notice that the verb *was born* begins the statement.

<u>Charles S. Stratton</u> was born in 1838.

Underline the subjects at the beginning of each of the following sentences. Just ask yourself: *Who or what does this sentence make a statement about?*

1. Charles weighed over nine pounds at birth.
2. He grew at a normal rate for the first six months.
3. However, his growth didn't progress very much after that.
4. P. T. Barnum and Charles met six years later.
5. Making money from midgets like Charles was the business of this famous showman and huckster.

Are these the subjects you underlined? Each one reveals an important trait about subjects.

1. <u>Charles</u> (this subject is a *noun*)
2. <u>He</u> (this is a *subject pronoun*)
3. <u>growth</u> (the word before this, *his*, is a possessive word and not part of the subject)
4. <u>P. T. Barnum and Charles</u> (these two subjects are joined by *and*)
5. <u>Making money</u> (this subject begins with an *-ing word*)

In Summary: The subject of a clause

1. is someone or something that the clause makes a statement about;
2. usually comes at or near the beginning of a clause—before the verb;
3. can be a noun (but not all nouns are subjects);
4. can be a subject pronoun (*I, we, you, he, she, it* or *they);*
5. *cannot* be a possessive word (such as *my, our, your, his, her, its,* or *their*) before a noun;
6. can be two or more subjects joined by *and;*
7. can be an *-ing word* (even though such a word may express an action).

---

1 WARM-UP   Underline the subject of each of the following sentences.

1. <u>P. T. Barnum</u> wanted to put Charles into a show.

2. Charles, however, was very shy.

3. Shyness was no problem for Barnum, though.

4. He hired the boy and his mother for three dollars a week and took them to New York.

5. Little Charles was given the stage name "General Tom Thumb."

6. On stage, he appeared in numerous costumes and played many roles.

7. He appeared as Cupid, a soldier, David against Goliath, and even Napoleon.

8. Acting soon became easy for him.

9. Within a short time, his performances were sold out.

10. Consequently, his salary was raised to fifty dollars a week.

11. General Tom Thumb traveled to London that same year.

12. His popularity there was enormous.

13. Even Queen Victoria saw him.

14. She asked him to give a second performance for her three-year-old son.

15. After that, Tom Thumb traveled to Paris.

16. The newspaper reporters there wrote about him daily.

17. A café was named for him.

18. His statue appeared in hundreds of shop windows.

19. He finished his European travels in Spain.

20. Everyone there wanted to meet him, too, including Queen Isabella.

    (Exercise 3 will tell you more about Tom Thumb.)

2 WRITING   Write a five- or six-sentence paragraph describing a person you know. Then underline the subject of each sentence.

SPOTTING ACTION VERBS (*DOES* VERBS)

Now you can turn your attention to the verbs in clauses. A verb *is one or more words that usually come after the subject and begin a statement about it.** Many verbs express action—they tell what the subject *does, did,* or *will do.* Notice in the following examples that many verbs also have *a tense* (past, present, future, etc.) and that some verbs can be *phrases—* they consist of more than one word.

Subject	Verb
Rochelle	helps
	played
	drives
	wanted
	is sleeping
	has left
	will try
	should have gone
	may have been working

*Of course, a verb can also begin a question about the subject. In that case the verb (or at least the first word of the verb) comes before the subject:

(a one-word verb)   *Is* Tom happy?
(the first word of a verb phrase) *Does* Tom *work?*
                           Can Tom *work?*
                           Could Tom *be working?*

Look again at some sentences about Tom Thumb. Circle the verbs of each. Just ask yourself: *What does (or did) the subject do?*

1. People in Europe loved Tom.
2. In England, large crowds would gather for each of his appearances.
3. The French people could not get enough of him.
4. He could have stayed in Europe for the rest of his life.
5. But Tom eventually grew homesick and returned to the United States.

Are these the words you circled? Each demonstrates a trait of action verbs.

1. (loved) (the verb has a tense—*past tense*)
2. (would gather) (a *two-word verb phrase*)
3. (could not get) (the adverb *not* comes between the words in the verb phrase)
4. could have stayed (a *three-word verb phrase*)
5. grew . . . and returned (the clause includes *two verbs* joined by *and*)

Notice that because each sentence is a statement and not a question, the verbs come after the subject.

In Summary: An action verb

1. usually comes after the subject;
2. states what the subject *does or did;*
3. frequently has a *tense* (past, present, future, etc.);
4. can be a *phrase* (more than one word) that may begin with the such helping verbs as *shall, should, may, might, must,* or *ought to;*
5. can include an *adverb* between the words of the phrase;
6. can be one of several verbs joined by *and.*

---

3 WARM-UP

Underline the subjects and circle the action verbs in each clause of the following sentences.

1. Tom Thumb (returned) to the United States after three years in Europe.
2. He learned much about the world.
3. He also earned a lot of money.
4. As a result, he bought himself a yacht and a miniature pool table.
5. Many people saw his performances over the next fourteen years.
6. At age twenty-three, he met another of P. T. Barnum's star midgets, twenty-year-old Lavinia Warren.
7. She stood only thirty-two inches tall, several inches shorter than Tom.

8. They fell madly in love at first sight.

9. Thousands of people attended their wedding soon afterward.

10. President Lincoln even invited them to the White House.

11. For the next twenty years, the couple would live happily together.

12. They owned racehorses and a private carriage.

13. They went everywhere and met everyone.

14. Then, suddenly, at age forty-three, Tom died.

15. At least ten thousand people came to his funeral.

16. As workmen were placing the life-sized statue of him over his grave, the people wept.

17. Lavinia later married again, and she lived to be seventy-eight years old.

18. However, at her death, she did not choose to be buried next to her second husband.

19. Instead, she found her final resting place beside Tom Thumb.

20. The words on her tombstone said simply, "His Wife."

4 WARM-UP

Complete the following paragraph by writing an action verb in each blank space.

Most people (1) _____ know _____ Fidel Castro, the leader of Cuba. However, most people (2) _____n't _____ his personal life and history. When he was in high school, the teachers (3) _____ him "the best all-around school athlete" in Cuba. In 1945, Castro (4) _____ the University of Havana to study law. He not only (5) _____ a law degree, but he later (6) _____ a Ph.D. in law. Although Castro soon (7) _____ revolutionary activities in Cuba, he (8) _____n't _____ his family. His wife Mirta (9) _____ Cuba for the United States and (10) _____ their young son with her. Castro's parents (11) _____n't _____ his political activities, either, and they (12) _____ him often. When Castro's father died, Fidel (13) _____ no emotion.

5 WRITING

Write a five- or six-sentence paragraph about something you did for the first time: your first bicycle trip, your first vacation trip, your first day in school, your first experience driving a car. Since this is a short paragraph, don't put in too many details. After you have written the paragraph, underline the subject(s) and circle the verb(s) in each sentence.

SPOTTING LINKING VERBS (*IS* VERBS)

Not all verbs show action. A second type of verb simply says that the subject *is* or *was* something. In other words, these verbs merely *link* the subject to words that describe or name the subject in some way. Here are several sentences with linking verbs.

Subject	Linking Verb	Description or Name
Walter	is	handsome and rich.
I	am	very happy.
Sonia	became	a doctor.
Cockroaches	are	terrible pets.
Your offer	sounds	wonderful.

The most important linking verb—and, for that matter, the most common verb in the English language—is *to be (is, am, are, was, were)*.* Place a line under the subject(s) and circle the *to be* verbs in the following sentences.

1. Macao is only six square miles in area.

2. Its inhabitants are Chinese.

3. But, oddly enough, it is a Portuguese territory.

4. At one time, many missionaries were in the little island country.

5. Today, its primary attraction is gambling.

Your answers should look like these:

1. <u>Macao</u> (is)

2. . . . <u>inhabitants</u> (are)

3. . . . <u>it</u> (is)

4. . . . <u>missionaries</u> (were)

5. . . . <u>attraction</u> (is)

Other than *to be*, the most common linking verbs are the following:

become	look*	feel*	get*
appear	smell*	sound*	act*
seem	taste*	remain*	stay*

---

*For advice on using the forms of *to be*, see Chapter 6 and Chapter 7.

*These often are action verbs, too.

Each one links a subject to the descriptive words *happy* or *good*.

Subject	*Linking Verb*	*Descriptive Word*
The woman	became	happy.
	appears	
	seems	
	looks	
	feels	
	sounds	
	remains	
	got	
	acts	
	stayed	
The food	tastes	good.
	smells	

In Summary: A linking verb

1. begins a statement of what a subject *is* or *was;*
2. is followed by words that describe the subject.

6 WARM-UP

Underline the subjects and circle the linking verbs in each clause of the following sentences. Not every verb is a linking verb.

1. <u>Simeon Styletes</u> (c. 388–459) (is) a Roman Catholic saint who believed in a life of suffering.
2. He is famous for his beliefs, but he is unusual for another reason.
3. He was the first flagpole sitter. (Actually, the "flagpole" was a pillar.)
4. At thirteen, Simeon got religion after hearing a sermon.
5. He soon became a monk and remained one for two years.
6. However, he was unhappy with the life of the monastery because it wasn't severe enough.
7. He seemed happier with a group of religious fanatics, but his actions were even too extreme for that group.
8. Once, for example, after he had wrapped a rope tightly around his body, his flesh became infected and it smelled foul.
9. After leaving this group, Simeon became a cave dweller, and later he chained himself to a rock on top of a mountain.
10. He got annoyed by the large crowds that came to visit him, so he built a ten-foot pillar to live on.
11. He remained a pillar sitter for the next thirty-six years until his death.
12. Over that time, he added stones to his pillar, and it grew taller—all the way to sixty feet in height.

7 WARM-UP
Write a linking verb in each of the following sentences. Try to use a different linking verb in each sentence.

1. Everything in the refrigerator _____looks_____ terrible.

2. The four-week-old sandwiches _____ green.

3. The taco with mayonnaise _____ odd.

4. The apples _____ like prunes.

5. The broken eggs _____ rotten.

6. In fact, some of the eggs _____ so old that they _____ like chickens.

7. That open bottle of Coke _____n't the real thing.

8. I _____ not _____ too happy about the condition of the refrigerator.

8 WRITING
Write a six- to eight-sentence paragraph describing the sights, sounds, smells, tastes, and feelings you perceive at this moment. Use a different linking verb in every sentence. ("The paper in front of me feels smooth. The rock music on the stereo sounds loud. My gum tastes sweet and fruity.") After you finish, circle the verb in every clause.

A Shorthand Way to Spot a Clause's Subject and Verb

You have seen that in every clause *someone* or *something does* or *is* something. One simple question should help you spot each clause's subject and verb:

Who or *what does* or *is?*

Who or *what*, of course, will tell you the subject of the clause. *Does* or *is* will tell you the verb.

Subject	*Verb*	
Who or *What*	*does* or *is*	something?

ELIMINATING SIMPLE FRAGMENTS

Remember that a fragment *is an incomplete sentence*. Since you can spot the subjects and verbs of sentences, you should have little trouble seeing when a sentence is *missing* a subject, a verb, or both. Such a sentence, of course, is a fragment, since it is incomplete.*

Commands ("Finish your breakfast." or "Give me that, please.") do not contain a stated subject. However, the subject *you* is understood to be part of the sentence.
   (You) finish your breakfast.
   (You) give me that, please.
Commands therefore are considered to be complete sentences. Expect to write commands when you are explaining how to do something. ("Take a cup of sugar and add it to the flour and water.")

9 WRITING   Each of the following groups of words is missing at least a subject, a verb, or part of a verb. Here is a challenge for you. Supply the missing words that will make complete sentences—and have the sentences tell a story.

1. A woman with three children.

   Rewritten: ___A woman with three children is having a difficult___ time today. ___

2. Destroying everything in the room.

   Rewritten: _____

   _____

3. Several of the children's toys.

   Rewritten: _____

   _____

4. From one end of the room to another.

   Rewritten: _____

   _____

5. The toys made out of plastic.

   Rewritten: _____

   _____

6. Broken into small pieces.

   Rewritten: _____

   _____

7. Pieces of crumpled paper, old socks, and dirty underwear.

   Rewritten: _____

   _____

8. On the wall, a photograph of the children.

   Rewritten: _____

   _____

9. Crying and shaking her head.

   Rewritten: _____

   _____

10. In cases like this.

    Rewritten: _____

    _____

WORKING WITH TWO OR MORE CLAUSES IN COMBINED SENTENCES

As you have already seen in this chapter, people often write more than one clause in a sentence. Here are a few more examples. Underline their subjects and circle their verbs.

1. Although John Camden Neild inherited a huge fortune in 1814, he spent almost none of it for the rest of his life.

2. His huge mansion had almost no furniture, and for a time it didn't even have a bed.

Is this what you found?

1. Although <u>John Camden Neild</u> (inherited) . . . <u>he</u> (spent)

2. His huge <u>mansion</u> (had) . . . , and <u>it</u> (didn't) even (have)

These examples are both combined sentences. That is, each example is actually two sentences that have been combined to make a single sentence with two clauses. Most adults often write combined sentences with two, three, or even four clauses. (For an example of what your writing would look like if you didn't write combined sentences, see Chapter 3, page 42.) Therefore, you should expect to include more than one clause in at least half of the sentences you write. Here are two more complicated examples of combined sentences. Underline the subject and circle the verbs in each clause.

3. His sole interest was to increase his fortune, which doubled during his lifetime.

4. However, after his death, his last will and testament specified that his entire estate should go to Queen Victoria.

You should have underlined and circled these subjects and verbs:

3. <u>interest</u> (was) . . . (fortune), <u>which</u> (doubled)

4. <u>last will and testament</u> (specified) (that) . . . <u>estate</u> (should go)

In sentence 3, *which*, the subject of the second clause, is a pronoun that refers to *fortune* in the first clause. In sentence 4, *that* joins the two clauses, although it does not function as the subject of the second clause. Two other pronouns—*who* and *that*—can also function like *which* in combined sentences:

Victoria took better care of the servants *who* suffered so much during Neild's lifetime.
She also restored an old church *that* was in bad repair.

A number of other words—*what, where, why, when,* and *how,* for instance—can join clauses in the same way:

He knew
- what he wanted to do.
- where he was going.
- why he was leaving.
- when he should leave.
- how he would get there.

You will learn more about forming these combined sentences in Chapters 3 and 4. Right now you should focus your attention on identifying such clauses.

10 WARM-UP

Underline the subject and circle the verb of each clause in the sentences below. Some sentences have one clause; others have two or three clauses.

1. In late 1971 <u>President Nixon</u> (ended) the jail sentence of ex-Teamsters' Union President Jimmy Hoffa, <u>who</u> (was) in jail for jury tampering.

2. Four years later Hoffa was attempting to regain his presidency when he suddenly disappeared.

3. On July 30, 1975, Hoffa went to a restaurant in suburban Detroit to meet Anthony "Tony Pro" Provenzano.

4. Tony Pro was a powerful opponent of Hoffa, and Hoffa wanted to make peace with him.

5. When Hoffa arrived at the restaurant, he called his wife to tell her that Tony Pro wasn't there yet.

6. That was the last time that anyone heard from Jimmy Hoffa.

7. The FBI later found a car that contained traces of Hoffa's blood and hair in the back seat.

8. Hoffa's stepson, "Chuckie" O'Brien, had been in the car with Hoffa, but the FBI didn't find enough evidence to convict O'Brien of anything.

9. A small-time hoodlum eventually told the FBI that Tony Pro had ordered Hoffa's death, but the FBI couldn't prove the hood's story.

10. To this day no one knows what happened to Jimmy Hoffa.

ELIMINATING DEPENDENT CLAUSE FRAGMENTS

Even though every clause has a subject and a verb, not every clause makes a complete statement. Therefore, not every clause is a sentence. Look at these examples of clause fragments:

If it rains tomorrow . . .
When the car went out of control . . .
Because the furnace broke down in the middle of winter . . .
Before this semester began . . .
Although salaries in the United States are at an all-time high . . .

These may sound like complete ideas in conversation, when they are in response to questions:

"Will you call off the picnic?"
"Only if it rains tomorrow."

In writing, however, these clauses are not responses to questions, so you expect something else to follow each clause.

If it rains tomorrow, *we'll have to call off the picnic.*

In this example, the *If* clause depends on the second clause to complete the statement, so the *If* clause is called a *dependent clause*. Complete the statement after each of the following examples.

When the car went out of control, _____

_____ .

Because the furnace broke down in the middle of winter, _____

_____ .

Although salaries in the United States are at an all-time high, _____

_____ .

What makes these clauses dependent? The answer is that they begin with the words *If, When, Because, Before,* and *Although*. These words require you to join two clauses into one sentence.*

Here is another group of incomplete sentences:

The man who said hello to us earlier . . . .

The team that won the most games this year . . . .

American automobiles, which usually cost more than cars from Japan,

. . .

Each has a subject *(The man, The team,* and *American automobiles),* and each has a dependent clause beginning with *who, that,* or *which.* Nevertheless the idea of each sentence isn't complete because nothing comes after the dependent clause to finish the statement about the subject. Notice how the first sentence could be completed:

The man who said hello to us earlier *is my math teacher.*

Complete the other two statements:

The team that won the most games this season _____

_____ .

American automobiles, which usually cost more than cars from Japan, _____

_____ .

> **In Summary:** A dependent clause fragment
>
> 1. contains a subject and a verb but doesn't make a complete statement;
> 2. needs another clause to complete the statement;
> 3. often begins with such words as *If, When, Because, Before,* and *Although;*
> 4. or begins with the words *who, that,* or *which.*

*For a more detailed explanation of dependent clauses and a longer list of such joining words, see Chapter 4.

11 WARM-UP

Label each of the following groups of words *S* (for sentence) or *F* (for fragment).

__F__ 1. Although the Revolutionary War actually began in 1775.

_____ 2. Because they felt the need for a formal document establishing their freedom from British rule, fifty-six rebels signed *The Declaration of Independence* the following year.

_____ 3. George Washington, who was commander-in-chief of the American army.

_____ 4. After both sides fought for seven years.

_____ 5. The thirteen colonies, which were now free to rule themselves, couldn't agree on a form of government.

_____ 6. The bigger states, which had more population.

_____ 7. Although every state wanted to unite behind a central government, no state wanted that government to be too strong.

_____ 8. The American people, who wanted a Bill of Rights guaranteeing their freedoms.

_____ 9. Before the states finally accepted our current Constitution in 1788, they tried out and rejected another form of central government.

_____ 10. The first ten amendments that were added to the Constitution.

12 WRITING

Make each of the following fragments a complete sentence.

1. Because you like cream pies so much, _I baked one for your birthday._

2. After you wipe that cream off your face, _____
   _____

3. A person who works hard _____
   _____

4. Most companies that hire hard-working people _____
   _____

5. When the bird flew into the house through the open window, _____
   _____

6. After we'd gotten rid of the bird and relaxed for a few minutes, _____
   _____

7. The newest video games, which do the most but cost the least, _____
   _____

8. If you want to watch television in my house, _____
   _____

9. Although most Americans watch the news on television, _____

_____

10. After the Sunday afternoon football games, which sometimes end at

7:00 P.M., _____

_____

13 EDITING

The following passage contains several fragments. Find and eliminate them by following this procedure.
1. Underline the subject(s) and verb(s) in every clause.
2. Make any changes that are necessary in sentences that are incomplete. These changes can include:
   a. supplying a missing subject or a missing (or incomplete) verb;
   b. joining an incomplete sentence to another sentence (usually by removing a period between the two sentences); and
   c. rewriting the fragment.
You don't have to rewrite the passage. Make all your changes above the line. The first several corrections are done for you.

Jack the Ripper

(1) On the last day of August, 1888, Mary Ann Nichols ∧*was walking* on the streets of London's East End. (2) She ∧*was* earning enough money to pay for a night's lodging. (3) Instead of a bed in a cheap hotel ✗ ∧*, her* (4) Her bed was a slab in the morgue. (5) Someone had mutilated her body ✗ ∧*and* (6) And cut her throat from ear to ear.

(7) Mary Ann Nichols was the first victim. (8) Of the man who later known as Jack the Ripper. (9) Four more murders followed hers. (10) Although each victim was a prostitute. (11) None of them assaulted sexually. (12) In the same way killed all five. (13) With their throats cut and their bodies mutilated. (14) Every killing occurred in the East End on the first or last weekend of the month. (15) Always happened in the early hours of the morning.

(16) Even though murder in the East End was commonplace. (17) These gruesome murders attracted great attention. (18) After the newspapers reported the second murder. (19) The Central News Agency received a letter. (20) This (in modern-day language) is what it said:

(21) I hear that the police have caught me, but they won't get me just yet. (22) I have laughed when they look so clever. (23)

And talk about being on the right track. . . . (24) I hate whores, and I won't quit ripping them till I do get caught. (25) . . . [During the last murder] the lady no time to squeal. (26) How can they catch me now? (27) I love my work and want to start again. . . . (28) [On] the next job . . . I shall clip the lady's ears off and send them to the police. . . .

(29) The note signed, "Yours truly, Jack the Ripper." (30) As a grim postscript he murdered two women in one night the next weekend. (31) Took Catherine Eddowes' left kidney with him.

(32) Writing seemed to amuse the Ripper. (33) Who sent at least two more letters to the newspapers. (34) One note arrived the morning after the night of the double murders. (35) The second note in a box that contained Miss Eddowes' kidney.

(36) On November 9, 1888, a man came to a small East End tenement. (37) Because he wanted to evict a prostitute from her apartment. (38) The man could not enter the apartment. (39) When he peeked through the window. (40) He saw Mary Kelley dead on her blood-soaked mattress. (41) She the last victim of Jack the Ripper. (42) He then vanished. (43) Leaving behind a trail of blood and terror. (44) He was never caught.

(45) To this day people about his identity.

SOME ADDITIONAL HELP IN ELIMINATING FRAGMENTS

A Clause Can Have More Than One Subject

Sometimes, you can become lost looking for the subject of a clause because the clause makes a statement about *more than one subject*. For example, read the following sentences and underline their subjects:

1. In October of 1971 the late Shah of Iran and his wife gave a little party in honor of the 2500th anniversary of the founding of the Persian Empire.
2. Three enormous tents and fifty-nine smaller ones were constructed (and air-conditioned) especially for the occasion.
3. Elaborate crystal, china, linens, Persian carpets, bidets, and even a marble bathtub for the Shah filled the tents.

4. Lavish refreshments and twenty-five thousand bottles of wine were supplied by Maxim's of Paris for the occasion.
5. Emperor Haile Selassie of Ethiopia, Marshall Tito of Yugoslavia, Princess Grace and Prince Ranier of Monaco, Vice-President Spiro Agnew, nine kings, five queens, sixteen presidents, and two sultans were among the five hundred guests at this modest affair.
6. The party and its related expenses cost the people of Iran only $100 million.

You should have underlined these subjects:

1. . . . the late <u>Shah of Iran</u> and <u>his wife</u>
2. <u>Three enormous tents</u> and <u>fifty-nine smaller ones</u>
3. <u>Elaborate crystal, china, linens, Persian carpets, bidets,</u> and <u>even a marble bathtub</u>
4. <u>Lavish refreshments</u> and <u>25,000 bottles of wine</u>
5. <u>Emperor Haile Selassie of Ethiopia, Marshall Tito of Yugoslavia, Princess Grace and Prince Ranier of Monaco, Vice-President Spiro Agnew, nine kings, five queens, sixteen presidents,</u> and <u>two sultans</u>
6. <u>The party</u> and <u>its related expenses</u>

In case you did not identify every subject of every sentence, here is a clue to help you: look for the word *and*, since it always joins two or more things.

A Clause Can Have More Than One Verb

You often write a clause in which the subject performs several actions, so the clause contains more than one verb. For example, circle the verbs in the following sentence:

Tom put the laundry in the washing machine, added detergent, closed the lid, and pushed the "start" button.

You should have circled *put, added, closed* and *pushed.* Again, notice that *and* appears before the final verb.

Be sure that you can identify multiple subjects and verbs in a clause. It is the first step in determining that the subjects and verbs are complete and the clause makes a complete statement.

14 WARM-UP

Underline the subject(s) and circle the verbs in the following groups of sentences.

1. On July 18, 1969, three American <u>astronauts</u> (took off) from Earth and (flew) to the moon.

2. Thirty-four hours later, they broadcast television pictures back to Earth and talked to the world's people.

3. As millions watched, the astronauts neared the moon and put their ship in orbit.

4. Later, the two halves of the ship separated. One half orbited the moon and sent signals back to Earth.

5. The other half landed on the moon and released two astronauts onto the moon's surface.

6. Astronaut Michael Collins stayed in one part of the ship and wished his partners well.

7. The other two men, Neil Armstrong and Buzz Aldrin, crawled through a tunnel, entered the other ship, and prepared for their descent to the moon.

(See Exercise 26 for more about the moon walk.)

15 WRITING   Fill in your own verbs and any other words necessary to complete the following sentences.

1. I _____ drove _____ to the store and _____ bought _____ a case of soda.

2. The halfback _____ and _____.

3. The bird _____ the tree and _____ the statue.

4. The singer _____ the stage, _____ the microphone, and _____.

5. I _____, _____, and _____.

Object Pronouns Cannot Be Subjects

You probably know that a pronoun is a word that takes the place of a noun. However, pronouns have several different forms, and *only subject pronouns* can function as subjects. Compare the subject pronouns to the object pronouns*:

	Subject Pronouns		Object Pronouns	
	Singular	*Plural*	*Singular*	*Plural*
1st person	I	we	me	us
2nd person	you	you	you	you
3rd person	he, she, it	they	him, her, it	them

Like all subjects, subject pronouns generally come before verbs. Object pronouns, on the other hand, can appear in a number of places, even after verbs. As you check your paper for complete sentences, always look for a subject *before* the verb. Don't mistake an object pronoun in a fragment for the subject pronoun in a complete statement.

Sentence: *He* made a huge impression in Europe.
Fragment: Made *him* a huge success in Europe.

*For a complete list of all pronoun forms as well as more practice with them, see Chapter 8.

16 WARM-UP

Label each of the following *S* (for sentence) or *F* (for fragment).

_____S_____ 1. Douglas Corrigan took off from New York on July 17, 1938 because he wanted to return to the West Coast.

_____ 2. He had arrived from California the day before.

_____ 3. Gave him the record for the fastest nonstop cross-country flight in his plane.

_____ 4. It was an old junker bought six years earlier for nine hundred dollars.

_____ 5. Failed it in safety inspections because it lacked basic equipment such as a radio and a beam finder to help him navigate.

_____ 6. In fact, he couldn't see out the window over some equipment in the cockpit of the plane.

_____ 7. Headed it west on takeoff and then, mysteriously, turned it in a wide arc over the Atlantic Ocean.

_____ 8. The ground crew stopped working and stared at it in disbelief.

_____ 9. It was going in the wrong direction.

_____ 10. Flying in the thick fog for the next twenty-four hours, he finally emerged and saw water—not land—below him.

_____ 11. Took him to Dublin, Ireland, where he informed officials of his "accidental" wrong-way flight.

_____ 12. Have called him "Wrong Way" Corrigan ever since.

Prepositional Phrases and Objects of Prepositions Cannot Be Subjects

Prepositions are the little words such as *in, of, to, off, above, on, over, with,* and *without.** When you write a preposition, you almost always write an object after it. The preposition and its object are called a *prepositional phrase.* Here are some examples:

to the store	by the house
from them	about us
for me	on the roof
with my friends	in a minute
above the trees	over the sea

Prepositional phrases often come *between* the subject and verb of a clause. Notice in the following sentences that the true subject precedes the prepositional phrase:

The route ~~to the store~~ is complicated.

The trees ~~along the road~~ look beautiful in the fall.

The story ~~about us~~ isn't true.

*For a complete list of prepositions, see Chapter 7.

Neither the prepositional phrase—nor the object within it—can function as a subject. Unfortunately, people sometimes write a fragment because they mistakenly think that the noun or pronoun object of the preposition is the subject. Here is an example:

On the top of the dresser has a lamp.

It must be rewritten to correct the error:

The top of the dresser has a lamp.
There is a lamp on top of the dresser.
On top of the dresser, there is a lamp.

17 WARM-UP

Draw a line through the prepositional phrases between the subjects and verbs in the following sentences. Then underline the subjects and circle the verbs.

1. One ~~of the world's richest men~~ (was born) in either 1900 (the date on his passport) or 1906 (the date he claimed was true).

2. The birthplace and first home of this Greek millionaire was the Turkish city of Smyrna.

3. The Turkish people in the city never got along with the Greek nationals, and soldiers from the Turkish army drove this young Greek and his family out and back to Greece in 1922.

4. The opportunities for success in Greece were very poor, so this young man without a job, hope, or money left for Argentina.

5. His first job in Buenos Aires was as a telephone operator at twenty-five cents an hour.

6. The business of importing tobacco soon attracted his interest, and he became quite successful in it.

7. He was a millionaire by 1930, and the size of his fortune grew quickly, mostly from his investments in the shipping industry.

8. Ships during the Depression were cheap, and he purchased six freighters in 1930 for twenty thousand dollars each.

9. By 1960 his fleet of ships had grown enormous.

10. The nickname of this famous man was "the Golden Greek," but his real name was Aristotle Onassis.

18 EDITING

Rewrite each fragment so that its subject is a noun or pronoun.

1. In the new stove has two ovens. ___There are two ovens in the new___ stove.

2. On a vacation is exciting. _____

3. On the botton of the refrigerator has little wheels. _____

4. In my back yard has some places for birds to build their nests. _____

_____

5. Under the counter holds several shelves. _____

_____

6. On the moon has no life. _____

_____

The Name of an Action Is Not an Action Verb

A *noun* names someone or something and therefore answers the question *who?* or *what?* In high school, you may have learned that a noun names "a person, place, or thing," but that is only partly true. A noun can also name an *idea* or even an *action*. (The *name* of an action isn't a verb, for unlike a verb, the name cannot have a tense.) Compare the following nouns and verbs:

Noun	*Verbs*
argument	argue, argued, will argue
discussion	discusses, discussed, will discuss
action	act, acted, will act
love	loves, loved, will love

Compare the nouns and verbs in the following sentences:

The <u>argument</u> lasted a long time.   We argued for a long time.

The <u>discussion</u> was interesting.   They discussed many issues.

The <u>action</u> was exciting.   Bill acts a little strange.

Real <u>love</u> is wonderful.   She loved him deeply.

As you check your paper for complete sentences, don't mistake a noun for a verb. Make sure that the action word begins a complete statement about the subject.

Sentence: Many people *exercise* (a verb) frequently and vigorously.
Fragment: Frequent and vigorous *exercise* (a noun) by many people.

19 WARM-UP

Label each of the following *S* (for sentence) or *F* (for fragment).

___F___ 1. A debate in the House of Representatives.

_____ 2. Thorough knowledge of the subject is very important.

_____ 3. An awkward arrangement of tables and chairs.

_____ 4. The disagreement was resolved peacefully.

_____ 5. The withdrawal of a large sum of money.

_____ 6. The election of 1980, in which Ronald Reagan defeated Jimmy Carter.

_____ 7. The investigation finally identified the criminal.

_____ 8. He made a wise decision.

Infinitives and *-ing* Words Can Be Nouns, but Usually Not Verbs

Underline the subject of the following sentence. (Warning: Don't underline the first noun or pronoun you see. Instead, ask: *What does this sentence make a statement about?* Then underline the word that answers the question.)

Running makes me tired.

You may have been tempted to underline *me*, but you should have underlined Running. It performs the action of the sentence.

Running makes. . . .

Try another sentence. This time, as you underline its subject, look for *more than one word*.

Getting a good job is difficult these days.

You should have underlined the phrase Getting a good job. The sentence says that it is difficult to get a good job. If only the words *a good job* were the subject of the sentence, the whole meaning of the sentence would change.

A good job is difficult these days.

Notice that the subject of both practice sentences above begins with an *-ing* word: *Running* and *Getting*.

> Most often, when the subject of a sentence is not a noun or pronoun, the subject is an *-ing word* or *a group of words that begins with an -ing word*.

Sometimes *-ing* words are verbs, but only when some form of *to be* comes before them.

am going	are seeing	were talking
is doing	was playing	have been working

Otherwise, *-ing* words are *not* verbs—even though they do show an action. Unless you write *am, is, are, was,* or *were* in front of an *-ing* word, you aren't using the *-ing* word as a verb.

Infinitives are formed from verbs but always begin with *to:*

to go   to see   to do   to be

Like *-ing* words in most circumstances, infinitives do not function as verbs, but they sometimes begin phrases that function as nouns, such as the subjects of these sentences:

To play a professional sport is the dream of many youngsters.
To pass biology seemed impossible.

As you check your paper for complete sentences, always look carefully at *-ing* words and infinitives. They may be the subjects of clauses in complete sentences; or they may erroneously be functioning as verbs in fragments.

20 WARM-UP

Underline the subject of each of the following sentences.

1. <u>Swimming</u> should build up your muscles.
2. Having a good time at one of John's parties is always simple.
3. To spend money is easy.
4. To make it is harder.
5. Being successful takes talent and hard work.

21 WRITING

Use these *-ing* words or infinitives as the subjects of your own sentences.

1. Dancing is good exercise. _____

   _____

2. Thinking _____

   _____

3. To cook well _____

   _____

4. Scratching _____

   _____

5. To work _____

   _____

Many Verbs Can Be Identified by Changing Their Tenses

One helpful way to identify the verb is to change its tense. If the clause doesn't make sense after the change, try looking elsewhere for a verb in the clause or consider the possibility that the clause is a fragment—perhaps it doesn't have a verb.

For example, you can change the tense of the verbs in the following clauses. (When the verb is a phrase, you can change the tense of only the *first word* in the phrase.)

Subject	Original Verb Tense	New Tense
He	*does*	*did*
She	*worked*	*works*
He	*is* working	*was* working
They	*were* working	*are* working
I	*have* worked	*had* worked
You	*have* been working	*had* been working
They	*don't* work	*didn't* work
I	*can* work	*could* work
We	*will* work	*would* work*

Would is the past tense of *will*, and *could* is the past tense of *can*. See Chapter 6 for more practice with these verbs.

Notice, however, that you cannot change the tense of the following action words because they don't function as verbs:

a *working* man

He is looking for *work.*

an *overworked* expression

to work for a company

Verb Phrases Often Begin with Key Words

You cannot change the tense of many verb phrases, but you can still identify them as verbs by looking for certain helping verbs. They always begin verb phrases:

Subject	Helping Verb	Possible Verb Phrase
I	*shall*	shall work
You	*should*	should work
We	*may*	may be working
He	*might*	might have worked
She	*must*	must have been working
They	*ought to*	ought to work

22 WARM-UP

Identify each verb in the following sentences by changing the tense of the verb and rewriting the change above the line.

1. Several witnesses ~~saw~~ (see) the thief run out of the building.

2. We always hear the rain tapping on the windowpane.

3. I felt the needle pierce the skin of my right arm.

4. You need enough money to make a down payment on a car.

5. He was looking for a good apartment to rent.

6. I'm filling out a very complicated application to send to a graduate school.

7. You can tell me how to fill it out.

8. I know that you will do well there.

23 WARM-UP

Circle the complete verb phrase in the following sentences. Look for the key words *shall, should, may, might, must,* or *ought to* at the beginning of each phrase as well as all the words that complete the phrase.

1. (Shall) I (send) you a letter of introduction?

2. You should receive the letter by next Tuesday.

3. Tomorrow may be a good time to see the movie.

4. He must have taken the bus to work.

5. You ought to see a lawyer for advice on how to file the suit.

6. He might have been sleeping during the afternoon.

A Verb Must Be Complete

A complete thought requires a *complete verb*. Remember, however, that a verb *can be a phrase with more than one word*. In fact, there can be as many as four words in a verb phrase. Here are a few examples:

is working	was done	could have come
has finished	will try	should have been studying
didn't want	doesn't know	may have been seen

Therefore, when you look for the verb in your sentences, don't always expect to find only one word. Look for *all the words* in a verb phrase. If you find that you left out some of the words in the verb phrase, put them in. Most of the words that people leave out of verb phrases are the forms of *to be: am, is, are, was,* or *were.* (See p. 101.)

24 WARM-UP

Circle the verbs in each of the following clauses, and write in any missing words in verb phrases. Some clauses are complete.

1. Astronauts Neil Armstrong and Buzz Aldrin are famous, but their fellow astronaut Michael Collins ∧did not receive much attention.
2. That's because he stayed behind in the ship and orbiting the moon while his partners were beginning their flight to the surface.
3. Consequently, they have received most of the attention and fame.
4. As they coming in for a landing, they discovered a big crater ahead of them.
5. Armstrong didn't panic but steered the ship past the crater.
6. In a few more seconds, he landing the ship on the moon's sandy surface.
7. Armstrong seemed calm.
8. However, his heart throbbing at 156 beats per second, twice its normal rate.
9. Armstrong and Aldrin should rested for the next eight hours.
10. But they feeling eager to complete their mission, and they couldn't sleep.
11. So, six and a half hours later, Neil Armstrong had finished his preparations and climbing down the ladder towards the moon's surface.
12. At 10:56 P.M., July 19, 1969, Neil Armstrong's size 9½ B boot touching the powdery sand of the moon.

25 EDITING

The following passage contains several fragments. Find and eliminate them by following this procedure:
1. Underline the subject(s) and circle the verb(s) in every sentence.
2. Make any changes that are necessary in sentences that are incomplete. These changes can include:
   a. supplying a missing subject or a missing (or incomplete) verb;

   b. joining an incomplete sentence to another sentence (usually by removing a period between the two sentences);
   c. rewriting the fragment.

You don't have to rewrite the passage. Make all your changes *above* the line. The first several corrections are done for you.

The Hindenburg Disaster

(1) Over the years, (2) 32,000 passengers had flown in German zeppelins—large passenger-carrying balloons—without a single accident. (3) But on May 6, 1937, (4) That perfect safety record ended.

(5) The flight of the zeppelin *Hindenburg* been normal. (6) Except for a storm delay of ten hours. (7) The big silver ship approached the Naval Air Station in Lakehurst, New Jersey. (8) And came in for its landing. (9) Passengers collected their belongings and prepared to leave the ship. (10) Crew members dropped the ship's mooring lines. (11) To naval and civilian workers who were on the ground. (12) While newspersons were photographing the arrival. (13) Radio commentators recording their remarks for later broadcast. (14) The landing was almost over.

(15) Suddenly, from the rear of the zeppelin was a puff of smoke. (16) Another puff of smoke followed. (17) Then came an explosion. (18) Herb Morrison of WLS radio described the next event: "It's burst into flames! . . . it's burning, bursting into flames! . . ."

(19) Many people on board the *Hindenburg* panicked. (20) Passengers broke through the windows. (21) And jumped one hundred feet to their death. (22) Thirty-four seconds later. (23) The ship lay on the ground. (24) Flames shot from it like a torch. (25) Many passengers who were badly burned. (26) Died within the next few days. (27) In all, thirty-five people on board died.

(28) What caused the disaster? (29) The ship was designed to use nonexplosive helium in its gas bags. (30) However, they filled instead with less expensive (and more dangerous) hydrogen gas. (31) The violent electrical storm that happened earlier in the day. (32) It may also have left static electricity in the air. (33) A spark from that electricity could have

started the fire. (34) However, another possibility. (35) Before it took off from Germany. (36) The *Hindenburg* had been carefully inspected for a bomb. (37) Was one overlooked and left on board? (38) To this day no one knows.

WRITING DESCRIPTION AND DETAIL

Good description is an essential part of all writing; it makes anything you say clearer, more interesting, and more vivid. It creates a sharp, specific image that looks, sounds, and feels like the real thing. A good description is like a good movie. Instead of merely *telling* readers that something is good, or interesting, or unusual, it *shows* the readers a picture that they can see for themselves. Through careful attention to detail and word choice, good description projects a picture on a large screen in technicolor with stereophonic sound.

Writing clear and lively description doesn't require a large vocabulary or any special talent. Instead it requires only a good eye and enough patience to revise and revise again. First, you must carefully observe the object you want to describe, noting details and taking notes to remember them. Then you must arrange the details in some logical order. Your organization can be *spatial*—moving in space from top to bottom or right to left—or it can be *chronological*—moving in time from start to finish. Finally, you must write the description and revise it several times, always trying to include specific details and words that vividly portray your observations.

As you read the following example of a description, pay special attention to the verbs: *revolve, observe, sways, climbs, whistles, sobs, hurry,* and *rock*. None of them are especially unusual or fancy; they are just more precise and lively than such verbs as *move, go, make, get,* and *have*.

If you enter the Prater, a famous city park in Vienna, Austria, you will encounter the world's most exciting ferris wheel. It is the world's tallest, rising 209 feet above the ground—as high as a twenty-story building. Fifteen enormous, glass-enclosed cages, each holding at least ten people, revolve slowly around the hub of this 230-ton mass of steel girders and cable. Unlike the passengers on a typical ferris wheel, who sit strapped in their seats, the passengers on the Prater wheel are free to walk around inside the carriage and observe the scenery from every angle. Your ride on the wheel is unhurried and majestic—up to a point. Your carriage sways gently back and forth as it slowly climbs. The only sound you hear is the wind that whistles and sobs through the great web of cables supporting your carriage. Then, as you reach the top, there is a sudden change. All of the passengers, who have been looking away from the center of the wheel, now hurry to the opposite side to catch the view as they descend. This sudden shift in weight causes the carriage to rock violently, taking your stomach on a ride it won't appreciate. Once the swinging slows down, so does your accelerated heartbeat, and you can relax again and enjoy the view of Vienna.

Discussion Questions

1. What is the topic sentence—the sentence that states the general idea or theme of the paragraph? Where is the topic sentence located? Why is it located there?

2. About midway in the paragraph, a description of your ride on the ferris wheel begins. Could any of the details about the ride be introduced earlier? Why or why not?
3. How many of the five senses does the description of the ferris wheel use? Which words and phrases refer to each of these senses?

PARAGRAPH WRITING AND REVISING ASSIGNMENT

Choose an object you find interesting—a piece of furniture, a building, a painting, a favorite toy that you still have from your childhood, or any unusual object at school or at home that you can observe carefully. Write a one-paragraph description of the object so that a person who has never seen it before can visualize it clearly and understand why you find it interesting.

Follow these steps in writing your paragraph.

1. Examine the object closely. Look at it from every angle and note specific details, colors, shapes, and any sounds it makes. If it moves, notice how it changes in different positions. Take notes of what you observe.

2. Arrange your observations in some sort of logical order. Think about how you can most clearly present all your information. Your first sentence—the topic sentence—ought to state what the object is and provide a short summary of the information that will follow in the rest of the paragraph. Here is an example: "The stereo component system in my bedroom isn't very large, but it delivers a powerful and clear sound." Now the other sentences in the paragraph should describe, first, the size and appearance of the stereo system, and second, the sound of the system. Perhaps as you mention each component of the system, you could describe it from top to bottom, or from right to left. Think about the organization, and take some notes or make a short outline to help you remember your ideas as you write the paragraph.

3. Write a first draft. Concentrate on getting your ideas down on paper. Don't worry about the exact language you use; you will change it many times in revisions. Just relax and let the words flow out. In fact, say your sentences aloud to see how they sound before you write them. After you have finished your first draft, put it aside for a while.

4. Revise your first draft. Read your paragraph aloud, looking for sentences that aren't clear, parts that need more detail, wording that falls flat. Rearrange the paragraph by cutting it up with a scissors if necessary.

Then return to this revised paragraph and revise it again, paying special attention to writing complete sentences. Edit the next-to-final draft carefully, perhaps underlining subjects and circling verbs as you look for incomplete clauses. Don't stop there, however. Check for dependent clause fragments. (Look for their marker words such as *if, because, before, although, who, that,* or *which.*) Then check your paragraph for spelling, punctuation, and grammatical errors before writing a clean final copy to hand in. Be sure to proofread the final copy, too; careless errors often appear at this stage.

CHAPTER 3

Joining Your Sentences: Coordination

As you write, you frequently join two or more sentences into one. That is no accident, and it is not bad writing. You *should* join sentences. If you don't, here is what can happen:

I write like a first grader. My sentences are short. They are choppy. They are too simple. They can't express complex thoughts. Short sentences get boring. They become repetitious. I had better stop now. You might not read much more.

Unfortunately, when people join sentences they sometimes make errors that result in unclear or incomplete ideas. You already saw such errors in Chapter 2, which discussed dependent clause fragments. (You will return to dependent clauses in Chapter 4.) This chapter focuses on two different ways to join independent clauses (which by themselves can be complete sentences): with a *coordinating conjunction* or with a *semicolon*. You will also learn how words and phrases called *conjunctive adverbs* explain the relationship between clauses joined by a semicolon. And finally, you will examine another method of developing a paragraph: by describing a place.

JOINING EQUAL STRUCTURES WITH COORDINATING CONJUNCTIONS

A word that joins other words is called a *conjunction* (like a *junction* that joins two roads). Look at the following pairs of words joined by conjunctions.

John and *I* (two subjects)
tripped or *fell* (two past-tense verbs)
a *fat* yet *athletic* man (two words describing *man*)
moved *quickly* but *carefully* (two words describing *moved*)

Notice that each pair of words is grammatically equal, or *coordinate* (*co* = equal; *ordinate* = level). The conjunctions joining them (*and, or, yet, but*) are therefore called coordinating conjunctions since they join grammatically equal things. There are seven coordinating conjunctions: *and, but, yet, or, nor, so,* and *for.*

> The coordinating conjunctions (*and, but, yet, or, nor, so, for*) join grammatically equal things.

JOINING TWO INDEPENDENT CLAUSES WITH COORDINATING CONJUNCTIONS

A *clause* is simply a group of words with a subject and a verb. (See Chapter 2.) Since every sentence has at least one subject and one verb, every sentence then has at least one *independent clause* (a clause that can be a sentence by itself). However, suppose you use a coordinating conjunction to join two sentences into one. That sentence will have two clauses—each of which is an independent clause because it can be a sentence by itself. A sentence with two independent clauses is called a *compound sentence.*

Here are some examples of compound sentences. To prove that each sentence has two clauses, underline the subject and circle the verb of each clause.

1. Male babies often wear blue, *and* female babies wear pink.

2. Years ago, people wanted to protect their infant boys from evil spirits, *so* they dressed the boys in blue.

3. People associated blue with good spirits, *for* those spirits lived in the blue sky.

4. People probably cared about their female children, *yet* people did not care enough to dress them in blue.

5. Many years later, people still dressed the males in blue, *but* they chose pink for the females.

6. The superstition about evil spirits had disappeared, *or* people might have dressed their girls in blue also.

7. Nowadays, few parents know the original reasons behind these traditional colors, nor do parents care.

Here is what you should have underlined and circled.

1. male babies (wear) . . . female babies (wear)

2. people (wanted) . . . they (dressed)

3. people (associated) . . . those spirits (lived)

4. people (cared) . . . people (did [not] care)

5. people (dressed) . . . they (chose)

6. superstition (had disappeared) . . . people (might have dressed)

7. few parents (know) . . . (do) parents (care.)

Look at the examples again. You will see that each of the seven conjunctions explains a particular relationship between the two clauses.

and shows *addition*

but shows *contrast*

yet shows an unexpected *contrast* (similar to the one expressed by *although*)

or shows an *alternative*

so shows a *result* (the first clause results in the second)

for shows a *reason* (the second clause gives a reason for the first)

nor shows a *negative alternative* (it is the negative form of *or*)

Compound Sentences

    independent clause, *and* independent clause
                  , *but*
                  , *yet*
                  , *or*
                  , *so*
                  , *for*
                  , *nor*

In Summary: To join two sentences (two independent clauses) into one compound sentence.

place *a comma and a coordinating conjunction* between the two clauses. The coordinating conjunctions are *and, so, for, yet, but, or,* and *nor*.

> **A Special Warning:** Many people think that *then* is a coordinating conjunction. But it is not.
>
> *Incorrect:*   I finished studying, *then* I took a break.
> *Correct:*   I finished studying, *and then* I took a break.
> *Incorrect:*   First we're going out for dinner, *then* we're going to a movie.
> *Correct:*   First we're going out for dinner, *and then* we're going to a movie.
>
> Be sure to put a coordinating conjunction before *then* when you join two sentences.

1 WARM-UP

Using the words provided, write two sentences that imitate the pattern of each sentence below.

1. Most American women work, and many of them have challenging jobs.

    (college graduates/graduate school) Most college graduates have enjoyed their education, and many of them go on to graduate school.

    (high school athletes/scholarships) _____

    _____

2. Many elderly people drive slowly, but they have very few accidents.

    (pre-med students/doctors) _____

    _____

    (babies) _____

    _____

3. Cats can be very friendly, yet they are very independent.

    (dogs) _____

    _____

    (rock stars) _____

    _____

4. Don't drive when you're drunk, or you might have an accident.

    (drugs) _____

    _____

    (stay up late) _____

    _____

5. Bill must pay his college tuition, so he has to find a good summer job.

    (pass final exams) _____

    _____

    (owes money) _____

    _____

6. Many students want to get a master's degree in business administration, for most people with M.B.A.'s earn a lot of money.

(teachers) _____

_____

(sports cars) _____

_____

7. I don't own a motorcycle, nor do I want one.

(pets) _____

_____

(foreign language) _____

_____

2 COMBINING

Join each of the following pairs of sentences with a coordinating conjunction. Place a comma before the conjunction, and use each conjunction at least once.

1. Jay Gould (1836–1892) supposedly began to make his fortune by inventing and selling a mousetrap. He went on to connive, cheat, and steal with such ruthless zest that he can truly be called the ultimate robber baron. Jay Gould supposedly began to make his fortune by inventing and selling a mousetrap, but he went on to connive, cheat, and steal with such ruthless ambition that he can truly be called the ultimate robber baron.

2. He became a multimillionaire by monopolizing the railroad industry. He left countless ruined businessmen in his wake. _____

_____

_____

3. He was primarily interested in money and power. He had relatively few indulgences and left the serious spending to his heirs. _____

_____

_____

4. He did have a few habits worthy of mention. He accumulated the largest collection of orchids in the world, and he loved yachts. _____

_____

_____

5. Gould was a sickly man and was on a strict diet. He kept a Viennese pastry cook on his prize yacht *Atalanta* to prepare ladyfingers for Gould. _____

_____

_____

6. Gould could drink only the milk from a special cow, which traveled with him in her own railroad car. He would damage his ulcerated stomach.

   _____

   _____

7. The blue bloods of the New York Yacht Club would not let a robber baron like Gould adulterate their ranks. Gould started his own organization, the American Yacht Club. _____

   _____

   _____

8. The members of high society weren't threatened too much by Gould's first rebellion. They certainly were after his coup staged against the Academy of Music, New York's finest opera house and the staunchest barricade of exclusive old money and old snobbery. _____

   _____

   _____

9. Gould and many other robber barons such as the Astors, Rockefellers, Morgans, and Vanderbilts couldn't buy a box at the Academy for any price. They couldn't even be invited to attend the operas. _____

   _____

   _____

10. Gould joined forces with the other snubbed millionaires to build the Metropolitan Opera. In less than two seasons the Academy was ruined and forced to close down. _____

    _____

    _____

11. The members of high society had tried to dominate Jay Gould. It was Gould who forced them to their knees. _____

    _____

    _____

3 WRITING

Complete each of the following compound sentences with an independent clause.

1. In today's world computers are becoming more and more important, and _more industries are relying on them._____

2. Computers can do most jobs faster and more accurately than people, so _____

3. Computer manufacturing companies in California and elsewhere are expanding rapidly, for _____

   _____

4. Older companies with old-fashioned production methods must adapt to the ways of the computer revolution, or _____

_____

5. Many businesses know that they must change, yet _____

_____

6. Computer-designed robots are revolutionizing the automobile industry, but _____

_____

7. Computer chips are in all sorts of household appliances, for the chips don't cost much to manufacture, nor _____

_____

4 WRITING

Write seven compound sentences, using a different coordinating conjunction in each sentence.

1. _____ ,and
_____

2. _____ ,but
_____

3. _____ ,or
_____

4. _____ ,yet
_____

5. _____ ,so
_____

6. _____ ,for
_____

7. _____ ,nor
_____

The Run-on Sentence

You should use a coordinating conjunction and a comma to join two independent clauses, but many people make a common error when joining independent clauses. Read the following.

1. I have always liked old movies my favorite is *Gone with the Wind*.
2. We ate a very early dinner later we ordered a pizza.

These are *run-on sentences*—two independent clauses joined with no comma and no conjunction. Rewrite them below to join them correctly.

1. _____

_____

2. _____

_____

The Comma-spliced Sentence*

There is another common error writers make when joining sentences. Read the following.

1. I think the weather is changing, the winters seem much colder.
2. Caffeine may not be healthy, many people have stopped drinking coffee.

These are *comma-spliced sentences*—two independent clauses joined with only a comma but no conjunction. Correct them below.

1. _____

_____

2. _____

_____

5 WARM-UP

Label each of the following sentences as a comma-spliced sentence (C.S.) or a run-on sentence (R.O.) Then join each sentence by inserting, in the space above, the proper conjunction (*and, but, or, for, so,* or *yet*) and a comma where necessary.

C.S.　　 1. She was born Myra Belle Shirley, ∧but she became a legendary criminal under a different name, Belle Starr.

R.O.　　 2. Her older brother Ed Shirley was always in trouble ∧, and he soon joined the Cole Younger–Jesse James gang from Missouri.

_____ 3. Myra Belle was hardly old enough to wear a dress, she also joined the gang.

_____ 4. During the Civil War, the gang didn't join the army, they fought as civilians for the South.

_____ 5. In 1863 these so-called heroes attacked the town of Lawrenceville, Kansas, they slaughtered as many as 182 innocent civilians.

_____ 6. After the war's end the gang still needed some excitement, they robbed a bank in February 1866.

_____ 7. This first robbery gave them a taste for more crime they killed, robbed, and beat people.

*If your native language is not English, you may need to pay special attention to comma-spliced sentences. In other languages (for example, Spanish) joining two independent clauses with a comma is common practice. In English it is not.

_____ 8. Then Myra Belle decided to quit the gang, she wanted to start her own business.

_____ 9. She went south to Dallas, Texas, she set up a "ranch" with many female cowhands and male "visitors."

_____ 10. Later, Cole Younger was forced to flee the law he went to Belle's ranch.

_____ 11. She had become a beautiful twenty-year-old woman, apparently Cole liked the way his friend's sister had developed since he last saw her.

_____ 12. At any rate Belle and Cole soon became more than friends, Belle gave birth to an illegitimate child named Pearl.

_____ 13. Although she had many other lovers, she still had to support herself she stole horses, rustled cattle, and (according to rumor) worked as a prostitute.

_____ 14. She probably only planned the robberies others carried them out.

_____ 15. In the 1870s the local authorities began to lose patience with Belle and her enterprises, she moved to Oklahoma.

_____ 16. She had many outlaw lovers, then she developed an interest in Native Americans.

_____ 17. She lived several years with a handsome brave named Blue Duck, this arrangement broke up before she married a Cherokee named Sam S. Starr.

_____ 18. She and Sam were soon divorced, she continued to go by the name of Belle Starr.

_____ 19. In 1881 even Jesse James turned to Belle for help, she was delighted to provide a hideout for him and his associates.

_____ 20. Poor Jesse left but should have stayed he was shot in the back by "that dirty little coward" Robert Ford.

_____ 21. A few years later when Belle was only forty-one, she met the same fate, she too was shot in the back and killed.

_____ 22. A neighbor was charged with murder, the charges were later dropped.

_____ 23. No one else was ever charged with her murder her death went unpunished.

_____ 24. Perhaps her eighteen-year-old son killed her, he was angry over a whipping she had given him for riding her horse without permission.

6 EDITING

Some—but not all—of the following are run-on or comma-spliced sentences. Above each line, insert the proper conjunction and a comma where necessary. Otherwise, leave the sentence as is.

The Lizzie Borden Case

(1) On the morning of August 4, 1892, in Fall River, Massachusetts, Lizzie Borden entered her elderly parents' bedroom, ∧ₐₙ𝒹 there she found them viciously axed to death. (2) Her wealthy father Andrew had a crushed skull, her stepmother Abby had received nineteen hatchet blows. (3) The murders were bloody, but the death notice in the newspapers was quiet and understated. (4) Soon, however, news of the murders spread through the community, people bolted their doors and avoided the streets.

(5) Lizzie, who was thirty-three and the younger of two girls, had lived with her father all of her life, she had rarely spoken to him or her stepmother during the previous two years. (6) The members of the family shared the same house but shut themselves up in separate rooms and came together only at mealtimes. (7) After all the publicity about the murders, a member of the police department stayed on duty at the house to protect Lizzie and her sister.

(8) The investigation of the crime was very careless nobody took fingerprints or made chemical tests for bloodstains. (9) A list of Lizzie's dresses were made but later lost. (10) A list of all the blood spatters was also lost, it had to be rewritten from memory. (11) In a corner of the cellar a police officer found a brand-new small hatchet its handle had just been broken. (12) He put the hatchet back, then the police chief ordered it to be examined. (13) The hatchet head fit the wounds exactly, but there were no blood stains on it, it had been cleaned with ashes.

(14) At the inquest when suspicion fell on Lizzie, she admitted having tried to buy a type of acid before the murders, she wanted to "clean a sealskin coat." (15) The acid was known to be useless as a cleaning fluid, it was very poisonous and impossible to trace in a human body. (16) The Bordens did not die of poisoning, Lizzie's admissions could not be used as

evidence in the trial. (17) The day before the murders, Lizzie had purchased a small ax, but there were many axes in the basement. (18) A neighbor's testimony was also interesting. (19) She had seen Lizzie burn a dress just before going to jail, Lizzie claimed it had paint on it.

(20) During the trial Lizzie sat quietly, like a good innocent Christian lady in her blue suit, black hat, and short white gloves. (21) She first claimed to be eating pears in the backyard during the time of the murders, then later she claimed to have been in the attic getting her fishing equipment. (22) There was no evidence that anyone else entered the house. (23) However, the defense attorney said that Lizzie had no blood on her dress or body, she couldn't have killed her parents. (24) She would have had only nine minutes to bathe and get rid of her bloody clothes between the time of the crime and her discovery of the bodies. (25) The attorney was obviously very convincing, the jury returned after only an hour and one-half of deliberation with a verdict of not guilty.

(26) Lizzie lived peacefully in her home until she died at the age of sixty-six, her will left thirty thousand dollars to the Animal Rescue League. (27) (Footnote: (28) Years later, methods used in a similar case proved that an ax murderer may not get blood on his or her clothing. (29) Today most believe Lizzie was guilty, children chant this rhyme as they skip rope:

> Lizzie Borden took an ax
>
> And gave her mother forty whacks;
>
> When she saw what she had done,
>
> She gave her father forty-one.)

7 WRITING   Write a paragraph about an unusual incident you once saw or were involved in (an accident, a bad storm, a crime that happened to you or someone else, or a time when something disappeared without explanation). Be sure to include specific detail describing the incident. Join independent clauses with coordinating conjunctions, and try to use all seven of the conjunctions if possible.

JOINING TWO INDEPENDENT CLAUSES WITH SEMICOLONS

You can also join two independent clauses without using a conjunction. Instead, join them with a *semicolon* (;). Notice that the semicolon is a combination of a period and a comma. Think of the period as signifying the end of the first sentence, and think of the comma as joining it to the second sentence.

> The accident caused no serious injuries; no one involved required hospitalization.
>
> California is our country's most populous state; one out of every ten Americans lives there.
>
> Joel generally acts shy in a large crowd; his girlfriend is more outgoing.

The first word after the semicolon is not capitalized (unless it is a name or the pronoun *I*) because the word doesn't begin a new sentence.

The semicolon is a rather formal device for joining independent clauses; it creates a longer pause than does the comma, thereby emphasizing the logical relationship between the clauses. Too many semicolons in a paper create an awkward and stilted style, so you shouldn't overuse them. Don't try to substitute semicolons for commas whenever you write comma-spliced sentences. Reserve the semicolon for formal writing, and use it only when you want to stress the logical connection between ideas.

8 WRITING

Using the words provided, write a sentence that imitates the pattern of each sentence below.

1. An amphibian can breathe with lungs or gills; it can live in water or on land.

   (fish) A fish can breathe only with gills; it can live only in water.

2. A mammal does not lay eggs; it gives birth to live infants.

   (bird) _____

   _____

3. An ostrich does not have usable wings; it cannot fly but must walk everywhere.

   (snake/legs) _____

   _____

4. A whale has lungs but no legs; it can live in water but not on land.

   (turtle) _____

5. Males do not have a uterus; they cannot give birth.

   (females) _____

9 WRITING   Complete each of the following compound sentences by adding a second independent clause after the semicolon.

1.   The biggest source of income for professional sports is TV; most teams make millions of dollars from TV.

2.   Football draws the largest television-viewing audiences; _____

_____

3.   However, baseball stars are much more highly paid than most football players; _____

_____

4.   Not all professional sports attract big TV audiences; _____

_____

5.   In recent years basketball has lost some of its popularity; _____

_____

Conjunctive Adverbs After Semicolons

Joining two independent clauses with a semicolon is often not enough. You must explain the relationship between the clauses.

Tom said he was so full that he could burst; he ate a second piece of cake. (Don't these two clauses seem illogical together?)

To make the relationship clearer, add a word directly after the semicolon.

Tom said he was so full that he could burst; *nevertheless,* he ate a second piece of cake.

This word is called a *conjunctive adverb* because it is partly a conjunction and partly an adverb.* Unlike a coordinating conjunction, it doesn't actually join two clauses; the semicolon joins them. However, it does explain how the clauses are related. Here are some other examples of conjunctive adverbs that follow the semicolons between clauses. Notice that a comma comes after each conjunctive adverb.

1. Math was never easy for me in high school; *however,* my grades in college math courses have been good. (*However* shows contrast.)
2. Competition among the various telephone companies has increased over the last few years; *consequently,* long-distance rates have been steadily dropping. (*Consequently* shows that the first clause causes the second clause.)
3. Our sports program produces a number of fine athletes; *moreover,* its stress on academic achievement has produced a number of fine scholars. (*Moreover* shows addition.)

Here is a list of the most common conjunctive adverbs, which may be single words or short phrases.

*For a definition and discussion of adverbs, see Chapter 7.

to express addition: additionally, in addition, also, furthermore, moreover

to express contrast: however, nevertheless, on the other hand, still, even so

to express result: consequently, therefore, thus

to express an alternative: otherwise, instead

to express a time relationship: then, later, earlier, meanwhile

to express emphasis: indeed, in fact, to be sure

Be Careful. People often make errors when they begin to use semicolons and conjunctive adverbs.

- Because a conjunctive adverb is an *explaining* word, *not* a joining word, any of the previous examples can be written as two separate sentences—without a semicolon.

  Math was never easy for me in high school. *However,* my grades in college courses have been good.

Furthermore the conjunctive adverb does not have to begin the second sentence but can be placed in other positions.

  My grades in college courses have been good, *however.*
  My grades in college courses, *however,* have been good.

- Therefore you shouldn't automatically place a semicolon before a conjunctive adverb. Use the semicolon *only when it joins two independent clauses.*

Incorrect: The course; *nevertheless,* is required for graduation.
Correct: The course, *nevertheless,* is required for graduation.
Correct: The course is required for graduation; *nevertheless,* it rarely fills to capacity.

In Summary: To join two sentences with a semicolon,

1. place the semicolon between the two sentences, making them independent clauses;
2. do not capitalize the first word of the second clause;
3. if you want to explain the relationship between the two clauses, place a conjunctive adverb after the semicolon, and place a comma after the conjunctive adverb.

  independent clause; *nevertheless,*   independent clause
                    ; *however,*
                    ; *therefore,*
                    ; *thus,*

10 WRITING

Using the words provided, write two sentences that imitate the pattern of each sentence below.

1. Many people want to know the sodium content of foods; therefore, they are carefully reading the labels on cans and packages.

(sugar) _Many people want to cut down on the amount of sugar they eat; therefore, they are buying products with artificial sweeteners._

(weight) _____

_____

2. Bill's hospitalization was very expensive; however, his medical insurance paid for most of the charges.

(examination/passed) _____

_____

(automobile accident/injured) _____

3. There are more women than men in college today; furthermore, most of these women want to enter professions once dominated by men.

(cars safer than cars ten years ago/mileage) _____

_____

(nonsmokers) _____

_____

4. Education about drug abuse is widespread; nevertheless, thousands of people die from overdoses every year.

(heart disease) _____

_____

(guns) _____

_____

5. There are very few quiet study areas in the dormitories; consequently, many students study in the library.

(inexpensive houses) _____

_____

(movies) _____

_____

11 WRITING

Complete the following sentences by adding a conjunctive adverb after the semicolon and then a second independent clause. Use a different conjunctive adverb for each sentence.

1. I find schoolwork extremely exciting and challenging; _therefore, I always work hard at it._

2. Money isn't everything; _____

_____

3. Marijuana is illegal; _____

_____

4. Most students want to major in business; _____

_____

5. European and Japanese cars sell very well in the United States; _____

_____

In Summary: To join two independent clauses,

1. place a comma and a coordinating conjunction *(and, but, or, nor, for, so,* and *yet)* between the two independent clauses;
2. place a semicolon between the two independent clauses. If necessary, after the semicolon, use a conjunctive adverb *(however, therefore, nevertheless, thus,* and so forth.) followed by a comma.

---

12 COMBINING

Combine each of the following pairs of sentences by writing either a coordinating conjunction or a semicolon (and a conjunctive adverb if necessary) above the lines. At least half of the sentences should be joined with semicolons.

Robert F. Stroud (1890–1963): The Birdman of Alcatraz

1. Robert F. Stroud became a self-taught expert on birds. ~~He~~ *; moreover, he* was the best-known example of self-improvement in the American prison system.
2. He dropped out of school in third grade. He drifted into Alaska in 1908.
3. Another man beat up Stroud's girl friend there. She pleaded with Stroud to kill him, which he did.
4. Since Alaska was a wild place in those days, it was reasonable to expect that Stroud would get off with a short sentence. A new judge gave him the maximum sentence—twelve years—in a federal penitentiary.
5. Soon he fought with another prisoner. Six months were added to his sentence.
6. Stroud was transferred to the new Leavenworth, Kansas, prison in 1912. He discovered there that books could make life in prison more bearable.

7. Stroud couldn't stay out of trouble. He got into a fight with a guard and stabbed him to death.

8. After another trial Stroud was sentenced to death. President Wilson commuted his sentence to life imprisonment after Stroud's appeal.

9. One day Stroud found two baby sparrows in the prison exercise yard. He took them back to his cell.

10. His interest in birds grew quickly. He soon became a regular contributor to journals on birds and was an acknowledged expert on the subject.

11. His expertise in curing bird diseases was greatly in demand. He wrote *Stroud's Digest on Diseases of Birds*, which is still in public libraries.

12. At one point the prison authorities gave him an extra cell and let him fill it with birds, books, a typewriter, and a microscope. At other times they threatened to take away his privileges.

13. In the twenty-sixth year of his sentence, he was transferred to Alcatraz Island. He had to leave his birds behind.

14. Deprived of real birds, "The Birdman of Alcatraz" poured into reading and research with a passion. He eventually expanded his interests into law and French, which he taught himself.

15. He was in prison for fifty-four years, always hoping for a parole. It never came, and he died in Alcatraz in 1963.

13 EDITING   Some—but not all—of the sentences in the following passage are run-on or comma-spliced sentences. Correct them by adding coordinating conjunctions above the line or by adding semicolons and conjunctive adverbs (if necessary) above the line.

The Collyer Brothers: Strange Hermits

(1) Homer Collyer was found dead in March, 1947, ∧ his death fascinated New Yorkers. (2) This blind and paralyzed ex-lawyer had starved to death among so much junk that the police spent several hours getting into his house. (3) Neighbors crowded around, they hoped to get a glimpse of the millions of dollars that he and his brother Langley, a former engineer and concert pianist, had supposedly stashed away. (4) Police officials were more concerned with the question of where Homer's brother Langley had gone.

(5) The Collyer brothers weren't always so strange. (6) They had lived in

their house with their mother for twenty years, she died in 1939. (7) At that point the brothers gave up their careers and didn't talk to anyone in fact they allowed all the utilities to be shut off. (8) Homer went blind and became paralyzed around 1940, but he never saw a doctor, he was completely dependent on Langley. (9) Langley thought that he could cure his brother's blindness by feeding him one hundred oranges a week. (10) Homer never left the house, Langley fetched water from the park four blocks away and roamed the streets at night looking for food and supplies.

(11) Langley was terrified of burglars, so he barricaded the house's doors and windows and piled up mountains of junk filled with tunnels for him and booby traps for intruders. (12) After Homer's death, sanitation officers slowly cleared away the clutter in the house, they removed 120 tons of material in the two weeks it took them to reach the second floor. (13) They found fourteen grand pianos, the chassis of a Model T Ford, old toys, boxes of rotting clothing, thousands of books, tons of newspapers, many bicycles, several sewing machines, a coil of barbed wire, thirty-four bank books (totaling only $3007), many weapons, the jawbone of a horse, two large sections of a tree, and endless other items that Langley must have dragged home from back alleys and garbage cans.

(14) Finally, officials reached a pile of rubble only ten feet from where Homer's body had been and found the body of Langley beneath it. (15) He must have been crawling through a tunnel of junk on his way to feed Homer, he had been crushed by one of his own booby traps. (16) Nobody found millions of dollars, the Collyer's attorney valued their property at only $100,000.

SOME ADDITIONAL HELP WITH COORDINATION

Don't Mistake a Subject and Two Verbs for Two Separate Clauses

Remember the seven coordinating conjunctions.

and	yet	so	nor
but	or	for	

Remember, too, that they can join any two grammatically equal things—such as two verbs in the same tense.

> ran *and* played
> came *but* then left
> will sink *or* swim

Notice that these conjunctions have no comma before them, although the conjunction between two independent clauses does. To avoid mistaking a subject and two verbs for two independent clauses, remove the conjunction between them for a moment. Then see if both remaining groups of words are complete ideas by themselves. Try this with the following sentence to check if the , *and* is joining two independent clauses.

> John vacuumed the rugs in every room, and then cleaned the bathroom.
> (Without, *and*) John vacuumed the rugs in every room. Then cleaned the bathroom.

The second group of words is not a complete thought. Since it has a verb but no subject, it is a fragment, not an independent clause.

There are two ways to correct the original sentence.

1. Remove the comma. "John vacuumed the rugs in every room and then cleaned the bathroom."
2. Add a subject to make two clauses. "John vacuumed the rugs in every room, *and* then *he* cleaned the bathroom."

14 EDITING   Some—but not all—of the following sentences contain an error in comma usage. Correct the errors, either by crossing out the comma or by adding a subject above the line.

Edward Payson Weston (1839–1929): The Great Pedestrian

(1) Hundreds of people were gathered at the Chicago city limits in 1909, and they were straining for a glimpse of him. (2) Then the great athlete came into view, and the crowd cheered for seventy-one-year-old Edward Weston, the greatest pedestrian of all time. (3) Weston was dressed a little more heavily than usual, for he had been walking through blizzards and even crawling through snowbanks ever since reaching upstate New York.

(4) Weston had been a weak and sick boy, and began walking to improve his health. (5) He took his first long walk at the age of twenty-two, and covered 443 miles from Boston to Washington in 208 hours. (6) He gained national attention from a walk six years later in 1867, when he hiked from

Portland, Maine, to Chicago—1326 miles in just under 25 days.

(7) He accomplished several such feats in America, so the British invited him to England for a competition. (8) He walked 550 miles in under 142 hours, and won the competition, of course.

(9) Weston's most famous trip was his first journey all the way across the United States, and he completed it at the age of seventy-one. (10) He walked 3895 miles in 105 days, but arrived 5 days later than planned due to bad weather. (11) This wasn't even his last walk. (12) He made that walk when he was seventy-five, but he lived to be ninety.

Don't Mistake Conjunctive Adverbs for Coordinating Conjunctions

Remember that when you place a comma between two independent clauses, you must follow the comma with one of the six coordinating conjunctions. Here is an example.

Our dog barks at strangers, *but* he is friendly to everyone he knows.

However, when you place a semicolon between two independent clauses, you may follow the semicolon with a conjunctive adverb.

Our dog barks at strangers; *however,* he is friendly to everyone he knows.

Here is a list of coordinating conjunctions and conjunctive adverbs that have approximately the same meaning. Compare the way each is punctuated.

Coordinating Conjunctions	*Conjunctive Adverbs*
,and	; also, ; additionally, ; furthermore, ; moreover,
,but	; however,
,yet	; nevertheless, ; still, ; even so,
,so	; consequently ; therefore, ; thus,
,or	; otherwise, ; instead,

15 TRANSFORMING   Rewrite each of the following sentences, either changing the comma and coordinating conjunction to a semicolon and conjunctive adverb or vice versa.

,coordinating conjunction

1. In 1833 Horatio Greenough made a colossal marble statue of George Washington, but he discovered that the floor of the Capitol could not hold it.

2. _____
_____
_____
_____

3. Everything else had failed, so the statue was put inside the Smithsonian Institution.

4. _____
_____
_____
_____

5. Washington was dressed in a Greek toga, and half of his body was naked.

6. _____
_____
_____

;conjunctive adverb,

1. In 1833 Horatio Greenough made a colossal marble statue of George Washington; however, he discovered that the floor of the Capitol could not hold it.

2. He hoped to solve the problem by placing the statue outdoors; however, the weather soon deteriorated it.

3. _____
_____
_____

4. Greenough had wanted the statue to be impressive; therefore, he made it in the classical style.

5. _____
_____
_____

6. Purists complained that the statue was obscene; presidents shouldn't be shown half-naked.

16 EDITING   Some—but not all—of the sentences in the following passage are run-on or comma-spliced sentences. Correct them by adding coordinating conjunctions above the line or by adding semicolons and conjunctive adverbs (if necessary) above the line.

Mary Mallon (1868–1938): "Typhoid Mary"

(1) In 1906 in the elegant summer home of a New York City resident, the recently hired cook prepared a special hot-weather meal, then she served it to the guests. (2) Ten days later several of them became sick and feverish they were admitted to a hospital with typhoid fever, a highly contagious disease. (3) Shortly afterward the owner of the summer home complained to the New York City Health Department, and the department

assigned Dr. George Soper, sanitary engineer for the city, to the case. (4) He wasn't Sherlock Holmes, but he did finally decide that the cause of the minor epidemic was the hired cook, Miss Mary Mallon.

(5) Mary had changed jobs by then, in fact, she had disappeared. (6) As he tried to track her down, Soper discovered that Mary changed jobs frequently and in each place that she worked a case of typhoid was reported. (7) He finally found her and explained that, as far as he could determine, she was the first known typhoid carrier in the United States. (8) He begged her to submit to a physical examination and tests, but, waving a rolling pin, she chased him down the stairs and slammed the door after him.

(9) The city sent a doctor and several police officers to her living quarters, they took her into custody and placed her in the isolation ward of a hospital. (10) Tests proved that she was indeed a carrier she had been the cause of at least seven outbreaks of typhoid involving twenty-six cases of fever. (11) Mary Mallon was a stubborn woman she refused any form of treatment. (12) She was finally transferred to another hospital and was given an ultimatum: submit to treatment or spend the rest of her life in the hospital.

(13) After a court battle the city health department agreed that Mary could have her freedom if she gave up cooking and handling food. (14) However, Mary took a new identity and disappeared again for five years she avoided authorities. (15) Finally, at the Sloane hospital for women, twenty-five nurses contracted typhoid and two died, Dr. Soper discovered that Mary Mallon was working in the kitchen. (16) She was arrested and spent the rest of her life in confinement on North Brother Island.

DESCRIPTION OF A PLACE

Like any description, a description of a place must concentrate on specific details, employ several of the five senses, and arrange its details in some logical order, usually a spatial order. However, describing a place is somewhat complicated because most places contain activity: people, animals, or things in motion. Your task as a writer is to establish the physical setting first. (Where is it? What is it like?) Then you can describe what goes on within the setting. One way to describe the activity is in habitual terms—what usually or often happens.

The following description of Mt. Fuji accomplishes both of those tasks. First it focuses on the place and then on the people who visit Mt. Fuji.

(1) Standing fifty miles southwest of Tokyo, Japan, is Mt. Fuji (or Fujiyama), the most climbed and probably the most beautiful mountain in the world. (2) The mountain, adjacent to a lake-filled plain, is an almost perfect volcano cone; it rises 12,388 feet from its broad base to a pointed summit that is capped with snow nine months of the year. (3) The volcano is now dormant, but part of its attractiveness lies in the certain air of mystery surrounding it. (4) Some day it will erupt again, for it has done so eighteen times in recorded history. (5) Looking into the cone of the volcano is an irresistible temptation for the hundreds of thousands of people who climb the mountain each year. (6) Many of the visitors are Buddhist pilgrims on their way to a temple that was built near the top almost one thousand years ago. (7) Buddhists receive great honor for undertaking these journeys; in fact, their thirty-third and eighty-eighth ascents are considered special achievements. (8) However, the well-traveled trail to the summit is now so commercialized that it has lost some of its holy aura. (9) Not only is there a post office along the trail, but there are numerous fast-food stands as well. (10) Despite this descent into commercialism, Mt. Fuji rises majestically above the city of Tokyo. (11) It remains one of the world's most beautiful sights and is an irresistible temptation to mountain climbers of every sort.

Discussion Questions

1. What is the topic sentence of the paragraph? Another sentence restates the main topic of the paragraph. Where does this occur and why?
2. Which sentences discuss the physical setting? Which ones discuss the activities of the people? Which sentence serves as the transition between the two parts of the description?
3. Look at the conjunctions *and*, *but*, and *for* in the middle of sentences; what relationships between ideas do they establish? Also look at the two uses of semicolons (;). Could conjunctions be easily substituted for these semicolons? Why or why not?

PARAGRAPH WRITING AND REVISING ASSIGNMENT

Write a one-paragraph description of a place in your school (your classroom, the library, the cafeteria, or the quadrangle) and the typical activity that occurs there each day. Establish the setting first and then describe what people usually do within that setting. In your final draft (but not necessarily in your early drafts) include a topic sentence that makes these ideas clear, such as: *During lunch hour, the cafeteria at my school overflows with students who are eating, socializing, and even studying.*

The best way to gather material for the paragraph is to go to the place and take notes on what you see: Where is it located? What is its shape? What are its dimensions? Where are the people? What are they doing?

Take notes for perhaps fifteen minutes; if you stay longer, you will observe too much to discuss in one paragraph. Afterwards, explore and organize your ideas through brainstorming, free writing, or outlining. Then write a first draft of the paragraph and revise it.

Return to the paragraph later and revise it again, making sure that your description is clear and specific. Edit the next-to-final-draft carefully, checking for the following matters:

1. complete sentences and clauses;
2. correct use of coordination to join sentences; and
3. correctly spelled words.

Write a clean copy to hand in, and don't forget to proofread the final copy.

CHAPTER 4

Joining Your Sentences: Subordination

Often one of the clauses in a combined sentence cannot be a sentence by itself. It depends on the other clause to complete its meaning and therefore is called a *dependent clause*. (See Chapter 2.) There are three main types of dependent clauses.

1. *when-why-where* (adverb) clauses
2. *who-which-that* (adjective, or relative) clauses
3. *what-that* (noun) clauses

Why do you join sentences and make one of them a dependent clause? There are two reasons. First, you can best express the logical relationship between certain ideas by making one of the ideas dependent. Second, dependent clauses add variety and sophistication to your writing, making it more interesting. In this chapter you will examine these reasons further as you practice joining sentences and creating dependent clauses. You will begin with adverb clauses, move on to adjective clauses, and finish with noun clauses. Finally, you will practice another method of paragraph development: narration.

FORMING *WHEN-WHY-WHERE* (ADVERB) CLAUSES

Adverbs usually answer the questions *when, why, where,* or *how* in a sentence. Therefore *when-why-where* clauses function as adverbs. They are different from the independent clauses discussed in Chapter 4, as the following illustration should explain.

You may recall that an independent clause can be a complete sentence by itself. Here are two examples.

1. I was downtown today.
2. I saw a serious automobile accident.

As you saw in the previous chapter, you can combine them with coordinating conjunctions such as *and* or with semicolons.

I was downtown today, and I saw a serious automobile accident.

I was downtown today; I saw a serious automobile accident.

Either method of combining the clauses suggests that the two ideas are equally important (remember that *coordinate* means *equal-level*). However, isn't the idea in the second clause far more important than the idea in the first?

You should therefore join the clauses in another way. Make the first clause *subordinate (sub = lower)* to the second clause by placing a *subordinating conjunction—when*—at the beginning of the first clause.

When I was downtown today, I saw a serious automobile accident.

Now the joining word *when* establishes a different logical relationship between the two clauses: the first clause tells *when the action of the second clause occurred*. The first clause has no other function; in fact, it *depends* on the second clause to complete the meaning and so is called a *dependent clause*. By itself, it cannot be a complete sentence.

When I was downtown today . . . (What happened?)

A combined sentence with a dependent clause and an independent clause is called a *complex sentence*. Look at the following two clauses:

I lost a day's pay yesterday.

I couldn't come to work.

Try joining them. Make the less important idea subordinate by placing the subordinating conjunction *because* in front of it.

_____ I lost a day's pay yesterday.

_____ I couldn't come to work.

You probably put *because* in front of the second clause, "I couldn't come to work." Now the clause explains *why* you lost a day's pay, and, by itself, it cannot exist as a sentence.

(What happened?) . . . because I couldn't come to work.

Join these two clauses with the subordinating conjunction *where*.

_____ there is smoke

_____ there is fire.

Notice that the clause beginning with *where* cannot be a sentence by itself.

Complex sentences using such words as *when, because,* and *where* are necessary not only because they add variety to your writing, but because the coordinating conjunctions *(and, but, or, nor, for, so,* and *yet)* usually cannot establish the same logical relationships between ideas. If you combine too many sentences with the coordinating conjunctions, you probably aren't thinking carefully about how your ideas relate logically. Therefore your writing may be unclear, forcing your readers to draw the connections between ideas that you should have drawn for them.

> **Complex Sentences**
>
> A *when-why-where* (adverb) dependent clause depends on an independent clause to complete its meaning
>
> > *When-why-where* dependent clause + independent clause = complete sentence

The Most Common Subordinating Conjunctions

The following subordinating conjunctions provide many options for expressing logical relationships between ideas.

When conjunctions (expressing a time relationship)

After	After I left . . .
As	As I was walking down the street . . .
Before	Before the lights go out . . .
Once	Once you have finished the cleaning . . .
Since	Since I left my baby . . .
Until	Until the car needs a tune-up . . .
When	When the semester is over . . .
While	While the music was playing . . .

Why conjunctions (expressing a cause-effect relationship)

Because	Because you are studying to be an attorney . . .
Since	Since the water in the lake is so warm . . .

Where conjunctions (expressing a relationship of location)

Where	Where there is smoke . . .
Wherever	Wherever you can find a job . . .

Conjunctions expressing a contrasting or conditional relationship between ideas

Although	Although you look honest . . .
Even though	Even though you look honest . . .
If	If I have the opportunity . . .
Unless	Unless he stops playing that music so loudly . . .

> **In Summary:** An adverb dependent clause
>
> 1. begins with a subordinating conjunction such as *when, because,* or *where;*
> 2. is less important than the independent clause it is joined to. It usually only establishes *when, why,* or *where* the action of the independent clause occurs;
> 3. depends on the independent clause to complete its meaning and so cannot be a complete sentence by itself.

1 WARM-UP   All of the following are combined sentences containing at least two clauses. Circle each conjunction that joins the clauses and then, above the lines, label each clause *D* (for *dependent*) or *I* (for *independent*).

The Real Alice in Wonderland

1. On July 4, 1862, the Rev. Charles Lutwidge Dodgson, a thirty-year-old college mathematics teacher, took three little girls on a rowboat trip up the Thames River to Godstow, England, (where) they planned to have a picnic.

2. As they journeyed down the river, Dodgson told a fanciful tale about a girl falling down a rabbit hole into a strange land.

3. The outing was a great success, and the three girls—Alice, Lorine, and Edith Liddell—were held spellbound by the Reverend Dodgson's story.

4. When they returned home, Alice asked Dodgson to write it down.

5. He did so under the pen name of Lewis Carroll, and today *Alice's Adventures in Wonderland* is considered by many people as the greatest children's book ever written.

6. Ten-year-old Alice Liddell was Dodgson's favorite of the three girls, so he named the heroine after her.

7. She was the daughter of George Liddell, the dean of the college, and she had large blue eyes and a beautiful oval face.

8. Although the Liddell girls were practically the only children in the vicinity of the college, Charles Dodgson was always available as their playmate.

9. Since the scholarly Dodgson was extremely shy and a lifelong bachelor, taking photographs of little girls, especially Alice, was his only expression of love.

10. However, as the years passed, Mrs. Liddell grew suspicious of "Uncle" Charles' attention toward her daughter, so Alice's mother discouraged the relationship.

11. If Mrs. Liddell hadn't stopped Dodgson from seeing Alice, his own inclinations would have done so, for he generally lost interest in girls when they reached puberty.

2 COMBINING   Combine each of the following pairs of clauses. Make one clause dependent by writing an appropriate subordinating conjunction from the list on page 68.

1. _____ When _____ the umbrella was invented in 1771 to protect people from the sun, people in Philadelphia laughed at the idea.

2. _____ average people opposed it, doctors thought it would prevent sore eyes, fever, dizziness, and epilepsy.

3. _____ a drunk waved at some tail feathers on the wall behind a bar and asked for a glassful "of those cocktails," Betsy Flanagan gave him a drink with one of the feathers in it. This was the first cocktail, invented in 1776.

4. In 1776 _____ Congress adopted the Declaration of Independence, the *London Morning Post* reported the event in a six-line article placed beneath the notice for a new play.

5. In Massachusetts a slave named Quork Walker won his freedom in 1781 _____ he argued that the state constitution said, "All men are born free and equal."

6. In South Carolina in 1781, Rebecca Motte asked patriots to shoot flaming arrows into her home _____ the British were using it as a fort.

7. _____ Deborah Sampson spent seventeen months disguised as a man so she could serve in the army, she married in 1782 and had three children.

8. Deer hunting by night was made illegal in the Carolinas in 1784 _____ farmers complained that cows and horses were being shot by mistake.

9. _____ Benjamin Franklin handed a letter to one of two men traveling from England to France in a balloon in 1785, he posted the first airmail letter.

10. _____ the balloon began to lose altitude over the English Channel, the men cast away everything unnecessary—including all their clothes—and barely made it to France.

Punctuation of Adverb Clauses

You may have noticed that some adverb dependent clauses are followed by a comma and some are not. The rules for placing the comma are simple.

1. If the adverb clause comes first, place a comma after it.

When the alarm clock rings in the morning, I call it dirty names.

2. If the adverb clause comes last, use no comma, except before the words *unless, although,* or *since.* (These commas are optional.)

I call the alarm clock dirty names when it rings in the morning.
I always manage to make it to work on time, although my hair may not be combed or my shirt buttoned.

> ### A Warning About Adverb Clause Fragments
>
> Because each adverb clause has a subject and a verb, you can easily mistake the clause for a complete sentence. Remember, however, that a clause beginning with a subordinating conjunction *must* be joined to an independent clause.
>
> | | |
> |---|---|
> | *incorrect:* | When Jerry opened the present. His eyes lit up. |
> | *correct:* | When Jerry opened the present, his eyes lit up. |
> | *incorrect:* | Angela will become a doctor. After she finishes medical school. |
> | *correct:* | Angela will become a doctor after she finishes medical school. |
> | *incorrect:* | Many people were angry. Because the concert started two hours late. |
> | *correct:* | Many people were angry because the concert started late. |
>
> The easiest way to avoid writing adverb clause fragments is to *read your first draft aloud* before you revise it. You should be able to hear when one clause should be joined to another. You may also want to review pages 25–29 in Chapter 2 for additional practice in avoiding adverb clause fragments.

3 COMBINING

Combine each of the following pairs of sentences in the most appropriate way. Make one clause subordinate by writing a subordinating conjunction above the line, and make any other necessary changes in capitalization or punctuation above the line.

1. The hamburger's history began in the Middle Ages in Russia. _{when} The Tartars (natives of Tartury) ate chopped raw meat seasoned with salt, pepper, and onion juice.

2. The Tartars invented this delicacy. We call seasoned raw chopped steak *steak tartar.*

3. German sailors picked up this new food at ports in the Baltic Sea. They took it home to Hamburg, Germany.

4. The Hamburg residents, or Hamburgers, weren't used to eating meat raw like savages. They broiled it, and the hamburg steak was born.

5. German immigrants brought the hamburg steak to America. They came here in the nineteenth century, and in 1900 Louis Lasser introduced it at his lunch wagon in New Haven, Connecticut.

6. He put the patty between two pieces of bread, following the practice of the fourth earl of Sandwich. Lasser carried the evolution of the hamburger one step forward.

7. The hamburg steak became truly popular. A cook slapped broiled beef patties between the halves of a bun at the St. Louis Fair in 1904.

8. Word reached this country that an English nutritionist named J. H. Salisbury was prescribing hamburg steaks without buns to his patients. Americans adopted them, too, and called them Salisbury steaks.

9. For a long time hamburg steaks, or hamburgers, were made from beef scraps and bad cuts of meat. The hamburger-loving public demanded the best part of the cows under the bun.

10. The hamburger began its greatest period of popularity. McDonald's and a host of other stands spread throughout the country in the 1950s.

4 WARM-UP

Label each of the following groups of words *S* (for *sentence*) or *F* (for *fragment*).

_____F_____   1. When you are in the neighborhood.

_____   2. If I can be of help, let me know.

_____   3. Although it looks like rain and the weather service predicts it.

_____   4. In 1782, after the United States had won the Revolutionary War.

_____   5. A place where most people want to see and be seen.

_____   6. Since many psychics and religious groups have warned of the end of the earth.

_____   7. However, until the world does end in fire and rain.

_____   8. We'll get together again before you leave.

_____   9. Unless professional soccer receives more public support in America.

_____ 10. Because Esperanza hates fried food.

5 WRITING

Using the words provided, write two sentences that imitate the pattern of each sentence below.

1. After students go through the ordeal of registration, they deserve medals for bravery in the face of unmentionable horrors.

(final exams)_ After students take final exams, they are entitled to a break between terms.

(school cafeteria) _____

_____

2. Although most students enjoy discussions about politics, last night's lecture was poorly attended.

(athletics) _____

_____

(beauty contest) _____

_____

3. Because college is so expensive, most students have to work to pay their tuition.

(financial aid) _____

_____

(science courses) _____

_____

4. Most of my friends go to Mother's Cafe if they want to relax and have a good time.

(home) _____

_____

(library) _____

_____

5. Don't take Professor Sanderson's class unless you want to study hard and learn a lot.

(drink) _____

_____

(married) _____

_____

6 WRITING   Complete each of the following sentences, using a comma where necessary.

1. When you are in the neighborhood , please come to my place and _____
visit me.

2. _____ if I can help you.

3. After the United States had won the Revolutionary War _____

_____

4. Since many people predict that a large earthquake will hit California before the end of the century _____

_____

5. _____

before it happens.

6. Students at many colleges _____

_____ because _____

_____

7. If _____

_____

8. _____ unless

_____

9. Although _____

_____

10. _____ after

_____

In Summary: To join two clauses, use one of these methods:

1. Coordination

Independent clause , and independent clause.
                     , but
                     , for
                     , or
                     , so
                     , yet
Independent clause ; independent clause.
Independent clause ; additionally, independent clause.
                     ; also,
                     ; consequently,
                     ; furthermore,
                     ; however,
                     ; indeed,
                     ; instead,
                     ; meanwhile,
                     ; moreover,
                     ; nevertheless,
                     ; nonetheless,
                     ; still
                     ; then,
                     ; therefore,
                     ; thus,

2. Subordination

After dependent clause, independent clause.
Although
As
Because
Before
If
Once
Since
Unless

Until
When
Whenever
Where
Wherever
While

Independent clause after dependent clause.

although
as
because
before
if
once
since
unless
until
when
where
wherever
while

Note the types of conjunctions and punctuation marks used in each method.

FORMING *WHO-WHICH-THAT* (ADJECTIVE, OR RELATIVE) CLAUSES

A second kind of dependent clause is the *who-which-that* clause. Suppose you wrote these two sentences.

1. For many years, I've been friends with a girl.
2. She lives next door to me.

These are so short and simple that you will probably want to combine them. Notice that sentence 2 begins with the pronoun *she*, which refers to *a girl*. If you replace *she* with another pronoun, *who*, you can combine the two sentences:

For many years, I've been friends with a girl *who lives next door to me*.

The pronoun *who*, which also refers to *a girl* and is the subject of the italicized clause, *relates* the rest of the clause "lives next door to me" to "a girl." In other words, the *who* clause describes the noun "girl," so the clause functions as an adjective. It is a dependent clause in a complex sentence.

Suppose you want to join these two sentences.

3. I bought three chairs.
4. They look beautiful in my living room.

You can make sentence 4 into a *that* clause.

I bought three chairs *that look beautiful in my living room.*

The word *that* relates the rest of the clause, "look beautiful in my living room," to "three chairs." In other words, the *that* clause describes "three chairs."

. . . three chairs that look beautiful in my living room.

Look at one more example.

5. That sewing machine works better than the newer machines.
6. It is ten years old.

You can make sentence 6 into a *which* clause.

That sewing machine, *which is ten years old,* works better than the newer machines.

What two things does the word *which* relate?

1. _____

2. _____

Since the *who-which-that* adjective clauses *relate* two things, they are also called *relative clauses,* and *who, which,* and *that* are called *relative pronouns.* You should place relative clauses directly after the words they describe. Otherwise, the sentence may not say what you intend.

poor: I bought a chair for *my mother that looks beautiful.* (Does the chair or your mother look beautiful?)

better: I bought my mother *a chair that looks beautiful.*

Note these rules about relative pronouns.

1. When you describe people, use *who, that,* or *whom.**
2. When you describe things, use *which* or *that.*†
3. But use *whose* before a noun to show possession, referring to either people or things.

*Use *whom* when it is the *object* of the clause: The man *whom* $\overset{\text{s}}{\text{you}}$ $\overset{\text{v}}{\text{met}}$ last week. . . .

However, most of the time you can drop *whom* from the clause completely: The man you met last week. . . .

†Don't confuse *what* with *that.* *What* begins direct questions: *What* do you want?

It also begins *indirect questions* that are part of a combined sentence: I know *what you want.*

Notice that you cannot substitute *that* for *what* in the indirect question above. ("I know that you want" isn't a complete sentence.) Similarly, you cannot substitute *what* for *that.* ("I see the chair what I want" doesn't make any sense.) For more on *what* in indirect questions, see Chapter 12.

Notice how *whose* replaces a possessive word when sentences are combined.

> Ms. Gleason is a teacher. *Her class* is very popular.
>
> Ms. Gleason is a teacher *whose class* is very popular.

You can occasionally substitute a few other words for *that* as relative pronouns.

> During the summer the beach is *the place where* you'll find me most of the time.
>
> I want to talk to the parent whose son broke that window.
>
> Nobody knows *the reason why* Sammy dropped out of school.
>
> *The time when* I study best is late at night.

A *Who-Which-That* (Relative) dependent clause depends on an independent clause to complete its meaning:

Who-Which-That dependent clause

+ independent clause = complete sentence

In Summary: Relative clauses

1. describe people or things;
2. begin with *who* (or *whom*) or *that* when they describe people;
3. begin with *which* or *that* when they describe things (or *whose* for possession, *where* for places, *why* for reasons, or *when* for times);
4. should follow directly after the words they describe.

---

7 COMBINING

Combine each of the following pairs of sentences by making the second sentence into a relative clause. Begin the relative clause with *who, whom, which,* or *that.*

1. a. The Declaration of Independence was written in 1776 by Thomas Jefferson. b. He was only thirty-three.

   The Declaration of Independence was written in 1776 by Thomas

   Jefferson, who was only thirty-three.

2. a. In 1819 a reward of six cents was offered in the *New York Evening Post* for a nineteen-year-old apprentice blacksmith. b. He was either "lost, stolen, or strayed."

_____

_____

_____

3. a. The two authors of the Declaration of Independence, Thomas Jefferson and John Adams, died on July 4, 1826. b. That date was the fiftieth anniversary of the Declaration's signing.

_____

_____

_____

4. a. Maryland announced in 1826 that any public offices could now be held by Jews. b. Public offices had previously been limited to Christians.

_____

_____

_____

5. a. In 1827 Sarah J. (Buell) Hale promoted the idea of Thanksgiving as a national holiday. b. She started the first women's magazine.

_____

_____

6. a. Noah Webster published *The American Dictionary of the English Language* in 1828. b. He is called the "father of his country's language."

_____

_____

_____

7. a. Webster spent twenty years working on the dictionary. b. He wrote it in longhand.

_____

_____

_____

8. a. In 1829 postage on an individual letter cost from six cents to twenty-five cents. b. The rate depended on the distance the letter traveled.

_____

_____

_____

9. a. In 1830 President Jackson signed a law. b. It required all eastern Native Americans to be resettled west of the Mississippi River.

_____

_____

_____

10. a. Robert Dale Owen's *Moral Physiology* sold 25,000 copies in 1830. b. It was the first American book on birth control.

_____

_____

_____

8 WRITING

Complete each of the following sentences with a relative clause beginning with *when, why,* or *where.*

1. Thanksgiving is a time _when the family gets together._

2. The library is a place _____

3. No one knows the reason _____

4. Summer is the season _____

5. I will meet you at the restaurant _____

6. We can meet on any night _____

Punctuation of Relative Clauses

Sometimes you should enclose a relative clause in two commas, and sometimes you should use no commas at all. Here is how you decide. Read the following sentence that discusses an object.

1. A car $\begin{cases} that\ has\ a\ dead\ battery \\ which\ has\ a\ dead\ battery \end{cases}$ can't be driven.

If you remove the relative clause from the sentence, which car do you mean?

A car . . . can't be driven right now.

The sentence doesn't say which car. The relative clause you removed provides essential information in the sentence; *it identifies the car (or restricts its meaning to that particular car).* The sentence discusses *only* a car that has a dead battery, not just any car.

However, look at this next sentence.

2. My new car, *which has a dead battery,* is causing me nothing but trouble.

If you remove the relative clause from this sentence, you will see that the identity of the car is still clear.

My new car . . . is causing me nothing but trouble.

Therefore the relative clause in sentence 2 doesn't restrict the meaning of the word *car;* the words *my new car* make that meaning clear. The information in the clause is not essential, so you should enclose it in two commas, which function almost like parentheses.

My new car *(which has a dead battery)* has caused me nothing but trouble.

Notice that you put commas only around a clause that begins with *which.* If the clause begins with either *which* or *that,* commas will make the sentence sound strange or confusing.

Correct: I just got a new car { *that* cost a lot of money.
                                     { *which* cost a lot of money.

Incorrect: I just got a new car, *that* cost a lot of money. (This seems to be a comma-spliced sentence.*)

Now compare the following two sentences. Which sentence suggests that the writer has *more than one brother?*

3. My brother who lives in Texas has a very good job.
4. My brother, who lives in Texas, has a very good job.

You should have chosen sentence 3. The relative clause restricts the meaning of my brother to *only the brother who lives in Texas*—not another brother who lives somewhere else. In sentence 3 the relative clause provides nonrestrictive information and is therefore enclosed in commas.

Finally, since deciding when or when not to use commas isn't always easy, keep this advice in mind: *When in doubt, leave the commas out.*

In Summary: To punctuate relative clauses,

1. do not put commas around a clause that restricts the meaning of a word to a particular person or thing—a clause limiting the choice to *only* that person or thing and not any other one;
2. put two commas around a clause that does not restrict the meaning of a word, and put the commas in the same locations where you would put parentheses;
3. if a clause can begin with either *that* or *which,* do not enclose it in commas;
4. if a clause can begin only with *which,* enclose it in commas;
5. when in doubt, leave the commas out.

---

9 WARM-UP

Underline the relative clauses in the following groups of sentences. Then place commas around the relative clauses that need punctuation.

1. There have been many athletes who overcame severe handicaps and later excelled in professional sports. These handicaps‸ which ranged

---

*I am indebted to my student Brigitte Grabs, who suggested this method of determining when to punctuate such clauses.

from the loss of an arm or a leg to illnesses like polio, would have made most people permanent cripples.

2. Rocky Blier who played for the Pittsburgh Steelers football team had been badly injured in the right foot and leg during the Vietnam War. However, he spent years on exercise and rehabilitation before rejoining the team that later played in four Super Bowl championship games.

3. Charley Boswell went blind while he was rescuing a friend from a tank that was under fire in World War II. In 1947, however, he won the National Blind Golf Tournament, a feat which he repeated thirteen times.

4. At the age of six Peter Gray was involved in an accident that resulted in the amputation of his arm. Nevertheless in 1945 he played in seventy-seven games for the St. Louis Browns which was a major league baseball team at that time.

5. Ray Ewry who developed a form of paralysis in childhood was confined first to bed and later to a wheelchair. He regained the use of his legs through daily exercise and won Olympic gold medals in various standing jumps during four Olympics which were in 1900, 1904, 1906, and 1908. The total number of medals that he won (ten) is still an Olympic record.

6. John Hiller who was the best relief pitcher for the Detroit Tigers baseball team suffered a heart attack in January 1971. He rejoined the team in the middle of the next year, and in his first full season after that which was 1972 he set a league record for the most saves by a relief pitcher.

7. In 1949 the famous golfer Ben Hogan was in an automobile accident that nearly killed him. Severe blood clots that remained in his legs badly limited his circulation. Nevertheless he returned to golf and several times won all the major tournaments which included the U.S. Open, the Masters, and British Open.

8. Wilma Rudolph developed scarlet fever and double pneumonia at the age of four, diseases that caused her to lose the use of her left leg. She learned to walk at the age of seven and took up track five years later. In 1960 she won three Olympic gold medals, including one for her performance that set an Olympic record in the 100-meter dash.

9. As a youth, O. J. Simpson had rickets which is a disease that is caused by too little calcium in the bones. He wore leg braces for years, and the disease left his leg permanently bowed. Simpson went on to play in the National Football League, and he once ran for 2003 yards in a year.

10. Bill Talbert developed diabetes at the age of nine. When he was thirteen, however, he ignored his doctor's advice which was to avoid all physical activity and took up tennis. He went on to win thirty-three national tennis championships which included thirty doubles championships.

10 WRITING

Using the words provided, write two sentences that imitate the pattern of each sentence below.

1. Medicine and law are professions that pay very well.

   (test-piloting airplanes) _Test-piloting airplanes is a job that would be exciting._

   (sweeping floors) _____

2. Yesterday I met a man who knows you.

   (woman) _____

   (baby) _____

3. Every student must take freshman composition, which is required for graduation.

   (foreign language) _____

   (advanced psychology) _____

4. My new microwave oven, which has a built-in turntable, is a wonderful convenience.

   (pocket calculator) _____

   (Mercedes Benz) _____

5. The president of the university is a woman whom most students admire.

                          or

   The president of the university is a woman most students admire.

   (best friend) _____

   (Robert Redford) _____

11 WRITING

Complete each of the following sentences. Use commas where they are necessary.

1. The thing that I want to do most in the next few years <u>is to finish my</u> <u>college education and get a good job.</u>

2. Soybeans which have twice as much protein as meat and are much cheaper in cost _____
_____

3. In northern states the weather which has become increasingly more severe _____
_____

4. _____ which many students major in _____
_____

5. The older chairs and desks that are falling apart _____
_____
_____

6. The third-world countries that need the most development and industry
_____
_____

7. _____
who make the most money.

8. _____
that _____
_____

9. _____
which _____
_____

10. _____
who _____
_____

FORMING *WHAT-THAT* (NOUN) CLAUSES

The third kind of dependent clause is a noun clause. Notice the nouns in the following sentences:

I am interested in *the answer*.
His behavior annoyed me.
He told me *the truth*.

You can substitute clauses for these nouns, and these clauses will begin with the words *what or that*.

I am interested in *what you said.*
What he did annoyed me.
He told me *that I was beautiful.**

Noun clauses usually begin with *what* or *that*, but you may use other words, too

He told me $\left\{\begin{array}{l} \textit{where} \\ \textit{how} \\ \textit{when} \\ \textit{why} \end{array}\right.$ I should go.

He asked me $\left\{\begin{array}{l} \textit{if} \\ \textit{whether} \end{array}\right.$ he should go.

Don't place a comma before or after noun clauses.

In Summary: Noun Clauses

1. usually begin with the words *what* or *that* (although *that* may be omitted from the clause);
2. may also begin with words such as *where, why, how, when, if,* or *whether.*

A Warning About Relative-clause and Noun-clause Fragments

People sometimes write relative-clause or noun-clause fragments, thinking that these clauses are complete sentences.† Notice, however, that the following groups of words are not complete ideas:

1. The cat that sleeps on top of the television set. . . (*does* or *is* what?).
2. . . . Which always makes you angry. (*Who* or *what does* or *is* something that makes you angry?)
3. The pen (that) I lost . . . (*does* or *is* what?)
4. Mrs. Everly, who lives in the apartment above me, . . . (*does* or *is* what?)
5. What I need to know . . . (is what?)

To avoid these fragments, look for the signal words *who, that, which,* or *what.* They usually signal the beginning of a relative clause (unless, of course, they signal the beginning of a question). Also, look at each of your sentences and ask: Is this a complete thought? (See pages 25–26 in Chapter 2 for more practice in eliminating relative-clause fragments.)

---

*The word *that* can often be omitted from a noun clause: He told me (that) I was beautiful.

†Like adverb-dependent-clause fragments, relative-clause fragments are quite common in speech when someone responds to a question.

12 WRITING

Complete each of the following sentences with a noun clause.

1. Peter asked me where ___I was going.___

2. The doctor determined that _____

3. Everyone wants to know how _____

4. Please inform me about when _____

5. Can you tell us if _____

6. No one can explain why _____

7. Do you know where _____

8. Whatever _____ will be all right with me.

9. What _____ was the long trip in the car.

10. What _____ is what you get.

13 WARM-UP

Label the following groups of words *S* (for *sentence*) or *F* (for *fragment*).

___F___ 1. The thing that I want to do most in the next few years.

_____ 2. Cereal manufacturers claim they can produce vegetable foods that look and taste just like meat.

_____ 3. Unemployment, which was the highest during the Great Depression and was much lower in the 1970s.

_____ 4. Which one of the apartments looks best?

_____ 5. The lamp you see on the table over there.

_____ 6. That course is very popular among the athletes.

_____ 7. Summers, which are becoming hotter, and winters, which are becoming colder.

_____ 8. The third-world countries that need the most development in industry.

_____ 9. Rabbit meat, which is very popular in rural areas.

_____ 10. We will replace each of these old desks, which are scratched and falling apart.

_____ 11. Whenever they choose to finish their work, which could be months.

_____ 12. Whatever you want to have lunch is fine with me.

14 WRITING

Write a paragraph about an injury or serious illness you once had. Tell what happened and how you recovered from the problem. Use subordination to join clauses in several of the sentences you write.

15 EDITING

The following passage contains many errors related to joining sentences. Some sentences use coordination where they should use subordination. Some sentences use an inappropriate subordinating conjunction or relative pronoun to join clauses. Some sentences are actually fragments. Some sentences contain incorrect punctuation or are missing commas. Correct each error by making any necessary changes above the line. You may need to read an entire paragraph before you decide where to make corrections.

Captain William Kidd (1645?–1701), Pirate

(1) Songs and legends have pictured Captain William Kidd as a cruel, cutlass-wielding pirate. (2) Biographers portray him as a person _{who} ~~which~~ you wouldn't want to meet on a dark night. (3) In recent years researchers have fitted together the pieces of the puzzle of Kidd's life and discovered a more accurate portrait. (4) While Kidd was no saint. (5) He was the victim of a bad press.

(6) Born in Scotland, he went to sea as a young man and settled in New York in 1690. (7) Because he was an unmannered man who used salty language. (8) He no doubt felt most at home among the pirates, who wore scarlet sashes and strutted around the docks. (9) However, he also made friends among the town's leading citizens, served the English crown well in various battles with France, married a wealthy widow, joined the Trinity Church, participated in local politics, and gained a reputation for honesty in business dealings.

(10) Then in 1695 on a trip to London, Kidd met an English Earl whom explained that British vessels were being seized by pirates in the Indian Ocean and asked Kidd, if he would work for a private syndicate as a pirate hunter. (11) Kidd agreed and was given a ship, a crew, and a royal commission. (12) Which authorized him to seize French vessels and to capture pirates legally. (13) Kidd was to bring any confiscated cargoes to the earl in Boston by the spring of 1697.

(14) Right from the start, everything went wrong for the new captain. (15) His ship leaked and became fouled with weeds and worms; furthermore, many of his men died from cholera. (16) After nine frustrating months without capturing any pirates, the crew who was made up mostly of drifters, wharf rats, and cutthroats, wanted to plunder every

ship in sight. (17) Kidd's men mutinied. (18) Because he refused to attack any ships except those manned by pirates or French. (19) Finally when William Moore, the leader of the rebellion, threatened Kidd; the captain threw a bucket at the man and hit him in the head. (20) Moore died the next day either from the blow or a recent illness.

(21) Because this action probably saved Kidd's life, he lost control of the crew, and he had no money for food or repair of his rapidly deteriorating ship. (22) At this point he began seizing ships; although, the only two vessels it could be proved he took sailed under French passes and were legal prey according to his commission. (23) But in England deserters from his crew and other men spread gory tales about him.

(24) As a result Kidd became a political football. (25) One political party, the Tories, accused several members of the other party, the Whigs, of backing a syndicate of pirates headed by Kidd. (26) Since he had become a liability, so the Whigs decided to make him the villain. (27) When the captain returned to Boston, the earl, who had been his sponsor had him arrested. (28) After Kidd spent months chained to the walls of a damp, cold prison. (29) He was sent to Newgate Prison in London. (30) The Tories would have gotten him either a pardon or a light sentence, if he had turned against the Whigs. (31) But Kidd insisted on his own honesty and that of his backers, which led to his trial for the murder of Moore and another trial on five counts of piracy. (32) Although he continued to claim he was innocent of any crime, but he was hanged on May 23, 1701.

SOME ADDITIONAL HELP WITH SUBORDINATION

Don't Join Two Clauses with Both a Subordinating Conjunction and a Coordinating Conjunction

Sometimes people write fragments that contain two clauses, like the following example:

When the night is young *and* I am feeling good. . . .

You can make the fragment into a complete sentence in one of two ways. You can drop one of the conjunctions.

When the night is young, I am feeling good. (*and* dropped)

The night is young, *and* I am feeling good. (*when* dropped)

Or you can add an independent clause.

When the night is young and I am feeling good, *I go dancing in all the hot spots.*

16 WARM-UP   Eliminate one of the conjunctions in each of the following fragments by drawing a line through it.

1. When King Louis VII of France was married to Queen Eleanor, ~~and~~ her father gave the King a dowry of two provinces in southern France.

2. After he had come back from fighting in the Crusades in 1152, and he shaved off his beard.

3. Although Eleanor said he was ugly without the beard, but he refused to grow the whiskers back.

4. After they argued violently and Eleanor divorced him, and she married King Henry II of England.

5. Because she wanted back the two provinces her father had given Louis, and she asked Henry to demand that they be returned.

6. When Louis refused, so Henry declared war on France.

7. After the war had gone on for 301 years, and it finally ended in 1453.

Don't Confuse a Conjunctive Adverb with a Subordinating Conjunction*

Semicolons join two independent clauses. (See Chapter 4.) Semicolons cannot join an independent clause to a dependent clause.

incorrect: The twins look exactly alike; *although* their behavior is quite different.

correct: The twins look exactly alike *although* their behavior is quite different.

Similarly, you cannot use a comma instead of a semicolon to join independent clauses.

incorrect: The twins look exactly alike, *however* their behavior is quite different.

correct: The twins look exactly alike; *however,* their behavior is quite different.

You might make these errors if you confuse subordinating conjunctions with conjunctive adverbs. To determine the difference between the two,

*See Chapter 3.

see if the clause beginning with the connector can stand by itself as a complete sentence.

> *Although* their behavior is quite different. . . . (The clause cannot stand by itself as a sentence; the connector *although* is a subordinating conjunction.)
>
> *However,* their behavior is quite different. (The clause can stand by itself as a sentence; the connector *however* is a conjunctive adverb.)

If you are still unsure after this test, try moving the connector within the clause. When you cannot move it, the connector is a subordinating conjunction. When you can move it, it is a conjunctive adverb.

> *Although* their behavior is quite different. . . . (*Although* cannot be moved; it is a subordinating conjunction.)
>
> *However,* their behavior is quite different.

or

> Their behavior, *however,* is quite different.

or

> Their behavior is quite different, *however.*
> (*However* can be moved; it is a conjunctive adverb.)

17 WARM-UP

Punctuate each of the following groups of sentences.

1. In 1840 the East India Company of England was not exporting enough goods to China∧ therefore∧ it began to ship illegal opium into the country for some quick profits.

2. China ordered all the opium destroyed consequently England declared war.

3. British gunboats smashed the Chinese ports until China surrendered in 1842.

4. China had to give Britain the island of Hong Kong although it also paid Britain twenty-one million dollars.

5. The British continued to pour opium into China however the Chinese started another battle, called the Boxer Rebellion, in 1900.

6. Six countries, including the United States, sent troops to China to crush the rebellion. After China was defeated it again paid huge sums of money to each country.

7. The Chinese finally got even during the Vietnam War when they planted large opium crops to sell to American soldiers.

8. Premier Chou En-lai said that he was merely returning the favor since the West had always fought China with opium.

18 EDITING The following passage contains many errors related to joining sentences. Some sentences use coordination where they should use subordination. Some sentences use inappropriate subordinating conjunctions or relative pronouns to join clauses. Some sentences are actually fragments. Some sentences contain incorrect punctuation or are missing commas. Correct each error by making any necessary changes above the line.

The Death of Julius Caesar

(1) Julius Caesar, the leader of the Roman Empire, was due to leave Rome on March 18, 44 B.C., to fight the Persians. (2) Cleopatra, who was his lover, was living in Rome, but there were rumors that he planned to return with her to Egypt and rule the empire from there. (3) Relations between the Roman senators and Caesar were strained because of these rumors and other rumors that Caesar wanted to be made king. (4) Especially after a "prophesy" had been discovered that said only a king could defeat the Persians.

(5) Caesar scheduled a meeting of the senate for March 15, because he wanted to discuss some routine business. (6) However, Caesar's major opponent in the senate, a man named Cassius, was sure that Caesar was going to ask the senators to make him king. (7) After he had convinced Marcus Brutus who was a respected senator and Caesar's brother-in-law. (8) The two senators agreed that the only honorable solution to the problem of Caesar's ambition was to assassinate him.

(9) Since a respected figure like Brutus headed the conspiracy. (10) About sixty men agreed to the plan, including twenty senators which would carry out the murder. (11) The meeting on March 15 seemed an ideal time, because the Senators could then immediately transfer power to themselves. (12) They planned to hide daggers in their robes and stab Caesar in turn.

(13) During the night before the meeting, Caesar's wife Calpurnia had a nightmare. (14) In which she dreamed that Caesar was assassinated. (15) Although Caesar was usually not superstitious; Calpurnia's dream disturbed him, so he planned to cancel the meeting. (16) The next day,

however, the senators sent a messenger to his house, and he asked Caesar to attend the meeting. (17) Caesar agreed.

(18) At 11:00 Caesar entered the hall, and sat down. (19) A senator immediately approached him with a petition, and the other senators crowded around. (20) The man what was assigned to strike the first blow, Casca, sneaked up behind Caesar and stabbed him. (21) He aimed for the throat but only grazed his chest. (22) Caesar fought him off, but the other senators began stabbing him in the body. (23) Caesar fought back, lunging at each senator, as he made loud cries. (24) Finally, Marcus Brutus advanced on him. (25) When Caesar recognized his brother-in-law. (26) He gave up the fight. (27) His last words supposedly were, "Et tu, Brute? [You, too, Brutus?]—Then fall Caesar."

NARRATION

Narration is simply *telling a story*. It involves setting a scene (establishing where and when the story happened and who were the main characters) and then letting the action unfold. A good narrative paragraph or paper usually requires the following elements:

1. It must be *unified* around one main idea. All the action should develop that idea.
2. It must be *detailed*, so that the readers feel as if they were there observing the action.
3. It should begin at the beginning and end at the end. Most stories therefore follow a *chronological order* (an order in which events occur consecutively over a period of time). Only the most skillful storyteller can jump back and forth in time without confusing readers.

Here is an example of a one-paragraph narration.

(1) On a cold, gray Thursday in December, 1903, a small two-winged plane nicknamed *The Flyer* rested unsteadily on a rolling platform that was attached to a rail anchored in the sandy beach near Kitty Hawk, North Carolina. (2) The plane's engine roared while the wind whistled through the wires that held the double wings together. (3) Orville Wright lay face down in the middle of the lower wing. (4) When his brother Wilbur released the cable that held the plane in place, the plane moved slowly forward into the strong wind. (5) As it neared the end of the monorail, *The Flyer* rose smoothly into the air and climbed to about ten feet above the sand. (6) It flew for several seconds, rising and falling, and then made a nose dive toward the ground. (7) It slapped hard against the sand and skidded to a stop. (8) The flight had lasted

about twelve seconds, and the plane had traveled only about 120 feet. (9) Altogether, the Wrights made three more flights before *The Flyer* was damaged by a sudden gust of wind. (10) Although the events of the day received little publicity outside Kitty Hawk at the time, almost every school child today knows that these two brothers gave wings to mankind.

Discussion Questions

1. Does the paragraph begin with a topic sentence? Which sentence establishes the importance of the events?
2. Which sentences establish the setting? Where does the action of the story begin?
3. Pay special attention to the verbs. Which ones are most colorful?
4. Look carefully at each sentence. Where do you find clauses beginning with the words *while, when, as, although, that,* or *who?* Can any of these clauses function as complete sentences by themselves? What is the logical relationship between ideas established by each of these clauses?

PARAGRAPH WRITING AND REVISING ASSIGNMENT

Write a paragraph narrating an important event in your life that affected you greatly. ("Firsts" often make good subjects for such narratives: your first day at school, your first date, your first job, the first time you drove a car, or the birth of a first child.) Assume that the audience is a group of general readers, such as your classmates, who do not know you and would be interested in what the story reveals about you. After a revision or two, the paragraph should include the following elements:

1. a topic sentence that makes the point of the narrative clear, such as: "My first time behind the wheel was an adventure for me and my father";
2. some details that establish the setting: where, when, and who;
3. sufficient detail to develop the topic idea convincingly and clearly; and
4. an arrangement of the details in chronological order.

Return to the paragraph a few hours or days later and revise it further, again making sure that your narration is specific and follows a clear chronological order. Edit the next-to-final-draft carefully, checking for the following matters:

1. complete sentences and clauses;
2. correct use of coordination to join sentences;
3. correct use of subordination to join sentences;
4. correctly spelled words.

Write a clean final copy, and proofread it before handing it in.

SUPPLEMENTARY WRITING AND REVISING ASSIGNMENT

When most families get together on holidays or special occasions, they hear the same stories year after year. Write a three- or four-paragraph account of one of the legends from your family. Assume that your audience is a group of people who do not know you, and shape the story so it reveals something important about your family or one of its members. If you cannot recall a family legend, write a story about a pleasant event from your childhood.

It isn't necessary to include a formal introduction and conclusion in your story. However, be sure to establish the setting in the first paragraph. Also, at the beginning or the end of the story, make the significance of the story clear.

Again, try to be specific as you write. Include as many details as you can, but make sure that all the details are important. For example, don't describe your uncle and aunt's little store if that information doesn't affect the story. On the other hand, if the point of your story is how your uncle and aunt suffered a great loss when a fire destroyed the store where they had worked all of their lives, then you ought to take your readers on a short tour of the store.

Making Subjects and Verbs Agree

The following two sentences are written in the *present tense*, which discusses *habitual states or actions* or *actions that are happening now*.

I *are* looking at television.

He *am* happy most of the time.

They sound odd and a bit unclear because they do not have subject-verb agreement; the verb in each sentence does not agree with its subject. You expect to see *I am* and *He is*, not *I are* and *He am*. Read the sentences again with normal subject-verb agreement.

I *am* looking at television.

He *is* happy most of the time.

Now you can concentrate on the meanings of the sentences; nothing in either one distracts or puzzles you.

Look at one more sentence.

One of the dogs are sleeping.

According to this sentence, how many dogs are sleeping? The sentence probably confused you for a moment because the verb *are* agrees with the wrong word, *students*. Correct subject-verb agreement clears up the problem.

One of the dogs *is sleeping*.

It should be apparent why subject-verb agreement is important. As a writer, you want readers to pay full attention to *your ideas*—not to unexpected or confusing word forms. During revisions you should check for errors in matters related to subject-verb agreement; and with practice, you will make these errors less often in first drafts.

This chapter will examine subject-verb agreement. You will work with *noun subjects*, *pronoun subjects*, and *compound subjects*. You will work with three important present-tense verbs—*to be, to do,* and *to have*—and their contractions. You will also work with special problems in subject-verb agreement: collective nouns, sentences beginning with *there,* phrases between the subject and verb, and phrases representing a part of the subject. And finally, you will explore another method of developing a paragraph: process analysis.

USING NOUNS AS SUBJECTS

Almost every present-tense verb has two different forms: one without final *-s* and another with final *-s.* Here are some examples.

see sees	try tries	pay pays
speak speaks	do does	determine determines
have has	sneeze sneezes	demonstrate demonstrates

A verb takes a final *-s* or *no -s* according to its subject, which can be singular or plural. *Singular,* as you know, means *only one,* so *nouns that name only one person or thing are singular.* A singular noun almost never ends in *-s,** but *the present-tense verb* after every singular noun subject *ends in -s:*

John works as a disc jockey.

The *sun is* 110 times larger than the earth.

My *aunt makes* jewelry from colored stones.

Ice cream contains several ingredients and 50 percent air.

The *competition* for high-salaried jobs *is* difficult.

On the other hand, plural means *more than one.* You already know that most plural nouns end in *-s,* such as *toys, chairs, coins, bicycles, pigeons,* and *plants.* In the following sentences notice that the plural noun-subjects end in *-s,* but the verbs that follow do not end in *-s.*

Two million *comets are* in the solar system.

The *astronauts weigh* only about thirty pounds on the moon.

Sizzling hot *meteors enter* the earth's atmosphere at the rate of one million an hour.

Only about *150 meteors break* through the atmosphere and *hit* the earth's surface each year.

The *-s* ending on plural nouns is important; it tells the readers that you mean *more than one.* Remember, too, that a noun can be a subject or an object, so a plural noun can occur anywhere in a sentence.

The Rule of One -s

Plural verbs *never* end in *-s,* but most plural nouns do. Therefore if the noun-subject ends in *-s,* most of the time the verb should not. And if the verb ends in *-s,* most of the time the noun subject should not.

*There are only a few singular nouns that end in *-s,* such as *news* and *bus,* and a few more that end in *-ss,* such as *kiss, mess,* and *dress.* These, however, are exceptions.

> **The Rule of One -s for Nouns and Verbs**
>
> *Singular:*   noun (no -s) + verb with -s
>   (The *student studies* in the library.)
> *Plural:*   noun with -s + verb (no -s)
>   (The *students study* in the library.)

1 WARM-UP

Write the appropriate present-tense form of the verb supplied in each of the following sentences.

1. The Nile River (share) _____shares_____ the distinction with the Amazon of being perhaps the world's longest river.

2. No person (have) _____ ever been able to measure it exactly.

3. According to M. Devroey of Belgium, its length (measure) _____ 4145 miles.

4. Other sources (give) _____ the length as 3500 miles, the distance from Mediterranean Sea to Lake Victoria.

5. However, Devroey (contend) _____ that the Nile (begin) _____ at the head of the Kagera river in Rwanda, which (feed) _____ Lake Victoria.

6. Several countries (depend) _____ on the Nile for transportation, irrigation, drinking water, and electric power.

7. Egypt, for example, (need) _____ the river for its very existence—as it has for the past 6000 years.

8. The recently built Aswan Dam (provide) _____ Egypt with two million acres of irrigated land.

9. But scientists (claim) _____ that the dam also (cause) _____ problems.

10. These problems (include) _____ holding back the rich watery soil called silt that (fertilize) _____ the Nile Valley.

11. Furthermore the water (flow) _____ faster without silt and (erode) _____ the bed of the Nile, which may someday lead to the collapse of the banks along the river.

2 EDITING

Some of the nouns in the following sentences should be plural. Change them by adding -s or -es endings.*

1. There are more than a billion starˢ in the various galaxyⁱᵉˢ of the universe.

*See Chapter 15 for the spelling rules on final -s or -es.

2. Compared to the other star in our galaxy, the sun is average-sized, although its mass is 330,000 time the earth's.

3. Once every 225 million year, the sun travels completely around the galaxy.

4. The distance between the sun and the earth is 93 million mile, but heat from the sun reaches the earth in eight minute.

5. Nuclear explosion within the sun cause its tremendous heat, eleven thousand degree Fahrenheit.

6. Every gram of material in the sun produces twenty-two trillion calorie.

7. In term of mass those calorie amount to four million ton.

8. However, the sun loses only 7 percent of its total mass every trillion year.

9. The sun has always had mystical significance.

10. Astrologer from the West believe that the sun is a good influence.

11. On the other hand, Easterner think that the sun is a bad influence.

Some Irregular Plural Nouns

A few nouns do not form their plurals in the regular way. Here is a list of most (but not all) of those nouns.

Singular	Plural
child	children (not childrens)
man	men (not mens)
woman	women (not womens)
mouse	mice
goose	geese
medium	media
referendum	referenda
_____	people (not peoples)*
foot	feet (not feets)

A few other nouns have the same form in the singular and the plural. Here is a list of most (but not all) of these nouns.

Singular	Plural
deer	deer
fish	fish (or fishes)
moose	moose

3 WARM-UP

Change the following singular nouns to plural nouns.

1. child _____children_____   3. deer _____

2. man _____   4. woman _____

*Peoples is correct when you use it to mean *more than one group of people*, as, "The peoples of many countries are members of the United Nations."

5. mouse _____   7. medium _____

6. goose _____   8. fish _____

4 WARM-UP   For each of the following sentences, fill in a present-tense verb.

1. Some deer_____ run _____through the woods.

2. Three fish _____ in the pool.

3. Several sheep _____ in the pasture.

4. My clothes _____ fine.

5. His pants _____ right.

6. The bus _____ at this corner every day.

7. Some people _____ too much.

8. My glasses _____ to be wiped clean.

USING PRONOUNS AS SUBJECTS

A pronoun takes the place of a noun and can thus serve as the subject of a sentence. Notice the forms of the verb *to play* when you combine the verb with each of the subject pronouns.

	Singular	*Plural*
1st person	I play	we play
2nd person	you play	you play
3rd person	he plays	they play
	she plays	
	it plays	

Which pronouns take a verb ending in *-s?* Which pronouns take a verb without *-s?* You can then see the rule for present-tense, subject-verb agreement.

Only the *third-person singular pronouns (he, she,* and *it)* require a verb ending in *-s.* The other pronouns don't require a verb with an *-s* ending.

I
we   } verb without *-s*
you
they

he
she   } verb with *-s*
it

5 WARM-UP   Replace the following noun-subjects with pronoun-subjects.

1. Liz and Dick _____they_____   11. my father's sister _____

2. the puppies _____   12. George _____

3. Juanita _____   13. a hair _____

4. spelling _____   14. his hair _____

5. my brother _____   15. love and marriage _____

6. our mother _____   16. working _____

7. his grandparents _____   17. Coach Gibbs _____

8. Mr. Washington _____   18. January _____

9. the nun _____   19. their house _____

10. the pope _____   20. their cars _____

6 WARM-UP   Fill in the proper present-tense form of the verb after each pronoun.

1. I (type) _____type_____ my homework assignments.

2. She (run) _____ two miles every morning.

3. They (grunt) _____ loudly.

4. It (move) _____ slowly.

5. You (grin) _____ at people too much.

6. He (wiggle) _____ his nose all the time.

7. We (dance) _____ on Saturday nights.

8. She always (agree) _____ with me.

9. He (sleep) _____ in class every day.

10. They (trip) _____ when they walk.

USING COMPOUND SUBJECTS

Remember that plural means *more than one*. Another kind of plural subject is a *compound subject*—two or more subjects combined by *and*, whether they contain nouns, pronouns, or both. For example, look at the following phrases:

Angela and Susan	an apple and a pear
Angela and I	love and marriage
a flower, a bush, and a tree	ice cream, cake, candy, and Alka Selzer

Since these plural subjects contain the word *and*, they will not be followed by verbs with -*s*.

> The Rule of *And* for Nouns and Pronouns
>
> subject *and* subject + verb without -*s*.

7 WARM-UP

Write the appropriate present-tense verb form after each subject in the following sentences.

1. That nut and that bolt (fit) _____fit_____ together.

2. You and your sister (look) _____ alike.

3. My coat and scarf (need) _____ to be replaced.

4. Harry and Belinda (fight) _____ like cats and dogs.

5. A hot dog with catsup (taste) _____ better than a hot dog with peanut butter.

6. That hammer and that stethoscope (belong) _____ to me.

7. The man in the green coat (look) _____ like a Russian spy.

8. John, Jill, and Jerry (live) _____ in the same dorm.

9. The bracelet with the diamonds and rubies (cost) _____ a lot of money.

10. You and I (understand) _____ the concept of compound subjects.

8 COMBINING

Combine each group of sentences into one, making a compound subject and changing the form of the verb as necessary.

1. Tom likes dancing. Gloria likes dancing, too.
   Tom and Gloria like dancing.

2. My roommate cleans the apartment regularly. I also clean the apartment regularly.

   _____

3. You deserve a break today. Everyone in class deserves a break today, too.

   _____

4. She studies hard. Her boyfriend studies hard, too.

   _____

5. One fish looks weird. The other fish also looks weird.

   _____

9 TRANSFORMING

Make each sentence below into two sentences, each with a separate subject, and change the verb form as necessary.

1. Maria and Mario come from Mexico.
   Maria comes from Mexico. Mario also comes from Mexico.

2. The plate and the cup belong in the cabinet.

   _____

   _____

3. You and Juan know some interesting people.

   _____

   _____

4. My parents own a house.

_____

_____

5. My brother and I live together.

_____

_____

> **In Summary:**   In Present-Tense Subject-Verb Agreement
>
> 1. the pronouns *he*, *she*, and *it* and all *singular* nouns agree with verbs ending in *-s;*
> 2. all other subject pronouns (*I*, *we*, *you*, and *they*) and all *plural* nouns agree with verbs that do not end in *-s;*
> 3. almost all plural nouns end in *-s*, but the verbs that agree with them do not; almost all singular nouns do not end in *-s*, but the verbs that agree with them do.
> 4. all compound subjects (two or more subjects joined by *and*) are plural and agree with verbs that do not end in *-s*.

10 WRITING

Write a paragraph describing your family's normal activities every morning or evening after dinner. Write about what they do together and individually. After you finish writing, underline the nouns in each sentence and circle every verb. Then check the nouns and verbs for *-s* endings; remember the rule about one *-s*.

USING IMPORTANT VERBS IN THE PRESENT TENSE

The verbs *to be*, *to do*, and *to have* are especially important for two reasons: they occur more often than most other verbs, and they occur in verb phrases as *helping verbs*—that is, as verbs that come before the main verbs. As a reminder, here are a few examples of verb phrases: *are going*, *has gone*, and *doesn't go.*

To Be

To be is the most common verb in the English language. You will find it everywhere in your writing. It always precedes verbs ending in *-ing* in a verb phrase.

> I *am looking* for an honest man.
> Arnie *is smoking* a foul cigar.

Further, it is often a linking verb. (See Chapter 2.)

> They *are* beautiful.
> I *am* a genius.

In the present tense, *to be* has three forms—*am*, *is*, and *are*. The form you use depends on the subject with which it agrees.

I	am
he, she, it (or singular noun)	is
we, you, they (or plural noun)	are

11 WARM-UP

Fill in the appropriate present-tense form of the verb *to be*.

1. He ___is___ talking to Mr. Williams.

2. We _____ are so hungry we could eat a buffalo.

3. I _____ both smart and good looking.

4. School _____ a pleasure and a joy for me.

5. My dog _____ is smarter than my brother.

6. Their house _____ old.

7. I _____ happy to meet you.

8. My sister and I _____ very similar in appearance.

9. Trudy _____ tall and slender.

10. You _____ in the right room.

11. O. J. Simpson and Walter Payton _____ two of the best running backs in pro-football history.

12. My pen _____ always leaking.

13. _____ Kim and you are getting along well?

14. _____ you feeling all right?

15. _____ we finished with this exercise?

The Contractions of *To Be*. Note the contractions of *to be* with various subjects.

I am = I'm	it is = it's
you are = you're	we are = we're
he is = he's	you are = you're
she is = she's	they are = they're

Notice that the apostrophe is each contraction replaces the letter that has been left out.*

You can easily make two types of errors when you mean to write these contractions:

1. You can leave off the -'s, the -'m, or the -'re. Look at your sentences, and if you see, for example, "*He* a good man," change it to "*He's* a good man."

2. You can confuse *we're* with *were*, *you're* with *your*, *it's* with *its*, and *they're* with *their* or *there*. Since the words sound or look similar, you

*Apostrophes are also used with possessive nouns. See Chapter 14.

may write one when you mean the other. Look carefully at your sentences to make sure that each contraction contains an apostrophe and that words which are not contractions do not have apostrophes.

12 WARM-UP

Fill in the appropriate present-tense *contraction* of *to be.*

1. You're_____ the one who wanted to go on this roller coaster!

2. It _____ going too fast.

3. I can't stand those turns; they _____ making me dizzy.

4. I _____ feeling sick.

5. We _____ never doing this again.

6. Next time ask your friend Willie to go on this ride with you. He _____ dumb enough.

13 WRITING

Write a paragraph describing what is happening around you at this moment. Focus on what individual people or things are doing: "The man next to me is writing furiously" or "The clock on my desk is ticking away." All of the verbs in your sentences should be in the present continuous tense: that is, they should use *to be (is, am,* or *are)* + an *-ing* word. After you have finished writing, check your paper for correct use of *to be.*

14 EDITING

Here is a challenge. The following passage contains many sentences missing some present-tense form of *to be.* Above each line, write in the proper form—either the full form or the contraction—where it is needed.

Lloyd's of London

(1) Most people think that Lloyd's of London is an insurance company, but it's not. (2) It a group of 5500 people who put up their own money as security against any default that likely to occur.

(3) They each personally responsible for liabilities of at least $35,000. (4) Yet there great benefits they can receive from their investment. (5) A total of three million dollars daily in premiums taken in by Lloyd's. (6) Its main customers the owners of large ocean ships.

(7) Although the company not in the long-term life-insurance business, it always insuring other things. (8) It responsible for some very unusual policies. (9) For example, it insured Jimmy Durante's nose for $140,000, Fred Astaire's legs for $650,000, and an unnamed English actress' forty-two-inch bust for $250,000.

(10) However, large sums of money paid out by the company, too. (11) When the *Titanic* sank, the company paid over $3 million. (12) When San Francisco had its earthquake, the company paid $1½ million.

(13) If you in the market for an unusual policy, you might be interested in some others that the company has issued. (14) If you a model, the company willing to insure that your face will not develop lines. (15) You afraid that satellites will fall from the sky on you? (16) For seventy-four dollars, Lloyd's will insure you for $22,400 against it. (17) Yet the company not willing to insure everything. (18) It would not insure an acrobat's back teeth since she hung from them in her act. (19) It also turned down the request of one European man to insure his daughter's virginity.

To Do

You use *to do (do, does)* frequently since it is a helping verb in most present-tense questions.

Do you *play* the guitar?

It is also a helping verb in most present-tense negative statements.

He *doesn't work* on Sundays.*

As a quick reminder, here are the forms of *to do*.

I			he		
we	}	*do*	she	}	*does* (not *dose*)
you			it		
they					

Few people have difficulty with these forms, but pay close attention to the negative forms of *to do*.

I			he		
we	}	*do not* or *don't*	she	}	*does not* or *doesn't* (not *dosen't*)
you			it		
they					

Doesn't is the verb form that creates problems. Many people say and write "He don't" instead of "He doesn't." If you are one of these people, the following exercises may be helpful.

*If your native language is not English, you might take careful note that *only the helping verb changes* form to agree with its subject. The verb following the helping verb *never* changes.
Do you *play* . . . ?   You *don't work*.
Does he *play* . . . ?   He *doesn't work*.

15 **WARM-UP**

Write the appropriate negative form of *to do* (*doesn't* or *don't*) in each of the following sentences.

1. Lions may be frightening to their prey, but they generally _____don't_____ bother each other.

2. They're actually rather social animals. A lion _____ live alone but in a group of two to forty others called a *pride*.

3. However, the pride is ruled by one dominant male, and the rest of the animals certainly _____ share equal rights with him.

4. He is first in mating, and the other lions _____ eat until he's had his portion.

5. He sets up his territory (about forty or fifty square miles) by spraying bushes with a heavily scented urine and then announces his claim with a monstrous roar. Other prides _____ enter this area.

6. Lions _____ hunt during the day because their twitching ears can tip off a quarry; instead, the pride tracks down herbivorous animals in darkness.

7. Lionesses are chiefly responsible for providing food. This, it seems, _____ stem from the male's laziness but because his mane is to easily detected.

8. In a heavily stocked game preserve, a 350-pound lion will eat 45 pounds of food daily. However, a lion _____ eat nearly as much in captivity, usually only 10 to 15 pounds a day.

9. In fact lions _____ have to eat regularly; they have been known to go for several weeks without food.

10. Lions _____ run great distances, but their speed in short spurts reaches sixty miles per hour.

11. The biggest threat to lions _____ come from other animals; it comes from human hunters and poachers.

16 **TRANSFORMING**

Rewrite each sentence below, making it negative.

1. He hates it. _He doesn't hate it._____

2. She usually helps. _____

3. You have to see it. _____

_____

4. It operates well. _____

5. We like to talk for hours. _____

_____

6. They eat breakfast early. _____

_____

7. Helen works in a jewelry store. _____

_____

8. Terry usually sits over there. _____

_____

9. I want help. _____

_____

10. Ralph does everything slowly. _____

_____

To Have

The verb *to have* also appears in writing often. You use it as a simple verb.

I *have* homework to do.
In his self-portrait Vincent Van Gogh *has* only one ear.

You also use it as a helping verb.

We *have lost* a fortune in Las Vegas on this trip.
Alfred *hasn't* ever *failed* an examination.

It has only two present-tense forms.

I we you they	}	*have*	or	I've we've you've they've
he she it	}	*has**	or	he's she's it's

17 WARM-UP

Fill in the proper present-tense form of *to have* in each of the following sentences.

1. The word intelligence _____ has _____ no good definition.

2. People who _____ identical IQ's often do not think the same way.

3. For example, creativity _____ nothing to do with IQ.

4. Studies _____ shown that creative children with average IQs do as well in school as children with high intelligence but low creativity.

*Don't confuse these present-tense forms with the past-tense form of *to have*, which is *had*.

5. Creative children _____ scored lower on IQ tests because they have answered questions "incorrectly" for good reasons that the test writer had not thought of.

6. The brain grows and _____ various stages of development, during which IQ changes.

7. Some mental abilities _____ to be developed early or they will disappear forever.

8. For instance, if a rat _____ been petted or played with when it was five to ten days old, it will be an explorer the rest of its life.

9. Other things _____ an influence on intelligence, too.

10. Intelligent people often _____ more wrinkles on the surface of their brains.

11. Breast-feeding _____ also been associated with high IQ.

12. Many intelligent people _____ been only children or oldest children.

13. It _____ been shown that intelligent people sleep less.

14. During sleep their eyes _____ more movement, showing that the brain is more active.

The Negative Forms of *To Have*. For more practice with *to have*, use its negative forms, which look like this.

$$
\left.\begin{array}{l} \text{I} \\ \text{we} \\ \text{you} \\ \text{they} \end{array}\right\} \quad \textit{have not} \text{ or } \textit{haven't} \text{ (or } \textit{do not have)}
$$

$$
\left.\begin{array}{l} \text{he} \\ \text{she} \\ \text{it} \end{array}\right\} \quad \textit{has not} \text{ or } \textit{hasn't} \text{ (or } \textit{does not have)}
$$

18 WARM-UP

In each of the following sentences, fill in a present-tense negative form of *to have: doesn't have, don't have, hasn't,* or *haven't,* whichever is appropriate.

1. In our solar system eight planets ___don't have___ any rings around them, but Saturn does.

2. Uranus _____ ever been seen by the naked eye, although it has been seen through a telescope.

3. New York and New Jersey _____ destroyed the wild marijuana growing inside their borders—fifteen million cigarettes' worth.

4. You probably _____ heard of the South American water hog, which, at 150 pounds, is the world's largest rodent.

5. Jaguars _____ many fears, but they are afraid of dogs—even small ones.

6. An ostrich egg _____ much chance of becoming an ostrich since most of the eggs are eaten by baby ostriches.

19 WARM-UP

As a way of summing up this section on the verbs *to be, to do,* and *to have,* read the following sentences and circle the proper verb form in the parentheses.

1. The Earth (has/have) a life expectancy of another seven and one-half billion years.

2. It (is/are) the heaviest planet in the solar system.

3. And its weight (is/are) constantly increasing as ten tons of meteors fall to its surface each day.

4. The Earth (doesn't/don't) have a round shape, as many people think.

5. It actually (have/has) a pearlike shape.

6. The surface area of the Earth (is/are) 196,950,000 square miles.

7. Most of that area—72 percent—(is/are) water.

8. But only 1 percent of the Earth (is/are) fresh, drinkable water.

9. Despite what many people think, the oceans (isn't/aren't) full of life.

10. They (doesn't/don't) have any living things in 90 percent of their waters.

11. Similarly, one out of every seven square miles of the land surface on Earth (is/are) desert.

12. In fact the Sahara Desert in Africa (has/have) expanded in recent years.

13. So life (isn't/aren't) everywhere on Earth.

14. It (doesn't/don't) exist in any place where water is boiling or frozen—as in volcanoes or glaciers.

15. One place where life certainly (doesn't/don't) exist (is/are) the Earth's core—the center of the Earth.

16. It (has/have) extremely high temperatures.

17. At present scientists (doesn't/don't) know whether those temperatures (is/are) rising or falling.

HANDLING SPECIAL PROBLEMS WITH SUBJECT-VERB AGREEMENT

Collective Nouns

A collective noun represents a collection of two or more persons, things, or ideas.

committee	group	company
audience	team	the French

Deciding whether a collective noun is singular or plural is a problem for even the most experienced writer. Therefore when you spot a collective noun in your proofreading, see if one of the following rules applies.

Rule 1. Most of the time collective nouns are *singular when they represent the whole group of persons, things, or ideas acting together.*

The *band is playing* (together) "Norwegian Wood."
A *jury decides* (together) a person's guilt or innocence.
The football *team* (together) *has won* all its games.*

Rule 2. A few collective nouns are always plural.

The *police are* increasing the size of their force.
The *Dallas Cowboys* usually *have* a good team.
The *Spanish enjoy* bullfights.

20 WARM-UP

Write in the proper present-tense verb form.

1. During the last week of the term, the class usually (review)
   _____reviews_____ the most important lessons.

2. The tribe (meet) _____ at the old reservation every year.

3. The Boston Celtics (play) _____ exciting basketball most of the time.

4. The police (be) _____ sponsoring a neighborhood youth program.

5. The city (control) _____ the funds for the program.

6. The English (like) _____ tea with their breakfast.

---

*Occasionally, collective nouns are plural when they represent a group of people, things, or ideas acting *individually*.

The *band are turning their* (individual) instruments.

The *jury have* not *seen their* (individual) families for a month.

However, these situations don't occur very often. When they do, the best way to treat such situations is to rewrite the sentences with plural subjects.

The *members* of the band *are* tuning their instruments.

The *jurors have* not seen their families for a month.

Indefinite Pronouns   *Indefinite pronouns* (pronouns that don't refer to a definite person, place, or thing) are *always singular*. There are four categories of indefinite pronouns.

some	*every*	*any*	*no*
somebody	everybody	anybody	nobody
someone	everyone	anyone	no one
something	everything	anything	nothing

21 WRITING   Complete each of the following sentences, using a present-tense verb.

1. Everyone _likes hot fudge sundaes._ _____

2. _____ anyone _____

3. There _____ n't anything _____

4. Somebody _____

5. There _____ nothing _____

_____

There Are or *There Is*   When you begin a sentence with *There* and have to decide whether to use *are* or *is* after it, look at the subject that follows the verb. If it is singular, use *is*. If it is plural, use *are*.

There *is something* that you should know.
There *are* several *things* that you should know.
There *are a table* and a *sofa* that you should fix.

Notice that in the last example above there are *two* subjects after *are*.

> There + is + singular subject
> There + are + plural subject

22 WARM-UP   Fill in the proper form of *to be.*

1. There __are__ a man and three children waiting for you outside.

2. There _____ a class in biology scheduled for two o'clock.

3. There _____ many things to learn about subject-verb agreement.

4. There _____ not much that you can do.

5. There _____ some shopping and other chores to do.

Phrases Between the Subject and the Verb

Sometimes you write a clause that contains a prepositional phrase or other type of phrase between the subject and the verb. (See Chapter 2, p. 32.) As a result, you may accidentally make the verb agree with a noun or pronoun in the phrase and not with the actual subject of the sentence. For example, what verb form should you use in the following sentences?

That woman over there with those children (is/are) a friend of mine.

The shape and size of the ring (is/are) unusual.

You should have chosen (1) *is* and (2) *are*. Here are the sentences again, with the prepositional phrases removed.

That woman . . . is a friend of mine.

The shape and size . . . are unusual.

To find the subject and therefore the right verb form, remember once again to ask yourself:

Who or *what* is this sentence about?

or

Who or *what* does or is?

23 WARM-UP

Fill in the proper present-tense verb form and cross out the prepositional phrase between the subject and the verb.

1. The reason for all those fires (be) _____is_____ faulty wiring.

2. The report on violence and crimes (show) _____ that crime is increasing.

3. Most people from Mexico (be) _____ Catholic.

4. The woman next to the two men over there (breed) _____ race horses.

5. The government of the people, by the people, and for the people (represent) _____ us all.

Phrases with *of* Between the Subject and the Verb

Certain expressions with *of* are an important exception to the rule about prepositional phrases.

Some of the wine . . .
All of the requirements . . .
Most of the lesson . . .

These sentences discuss *a part of the subject* (or even *all* of it), so the subject-verb agreement depends on whether the true subject is singular or plural.

Some of the wine is spoiled.
All of the requirements are fair.
Most of the lesson is interesting.

In Summary: To determine subject-verb agreement with phrases expressing part or whole of the subject, use this formula.

1. some of
none of
most of
all of
part of
} + singular subject + verb with -*s*

2. some of
none of
most of
all of
part of
} + plural subject + verb without -*s*

24 WARM-UP

In each of the following sentences, fill in the proper present-tense form of the verb in parentheses.

1. A lot of the maple syrup you put on your pancakes (come)
_____comes_____ from sugar maple trees.

2. All of the tapping of the trees (happen) _____ during the last snowfall of the spring.

3. A great deal of the sap (have) _____ moved from the roots up to the branches by then.

4. But most of the movement (stop) _____ when the snow arrives.

5. Maple syrup is delicious, but most of it (be) _____ very fattening sugar.

6. Some people (buy) _____ maple-*flavored* syrup and think it is the real thing.

7. But most of these flavored syrups (contain) _____ only 2 percent real syrup.

8. All of the bottles marked 100-percent pure (be) _____ the ones to buy.

25 EDITING

The following passage contains a variety of errors: incorrect subject-verb agreement, incorrect noun plurals, missing verbs, and incorrect contractions of pronouns with *to be*. To correct these errors, make any changes that are necessary above the lines.

Palmistry: How to Do It

(1) Palmistry is what peoples do when they read hands. (2) According to

hand readers, or palmist△, it△ a way to gain knowledge about someone's personality, history, and future. (3) Serious hand readers spend a lifetime studying their art, and they usually combines their skill with some spiritual talent. (4) Here's the general rules for reading hands.

(5) First, the position of the hands in relation to the rest of the body are the key to personality. (6) For example, worried people often clenches their hands or hold them tight. (7) A person who don't have a strong character often have an open, floppy, dangling hand.

(8) Second, the size of the hands supposedly reveal things about a person. (9) Very small hands tends to reveal a person who immature. (10) A person with large hands are logical and can do delicate, intricate work.

(11) The third important characteristic of the hands are the palms. (12) The left palm shows qualities that your born with. (13) The right palm reveals what you has done with those quality. (14) Anything that show up clearly on both palms is a very strong quality.

(15) There's four important line in the palm: the *life line*, the *head line*, the *heart line*, and the *fate line*. (16) The *life line* tell how long you going to live. (17) Breaks in it shows periods of illness or period when you has great personal problem. (18) The *head line* either goes straight, or it curve. (19) A straight line mean that you practical. (20) A curved line shows that you are artistic and sensitive. (21) Breaks in this line is a sign that your judgment aren't good.

(22) Anyone who care about love wants to know about the *heart line*. (23) A long heart line with a lot of branches say that you're going to have a lot of love affair. (24) A lot of small lines that cross the heart line means that you going to have many disappointments in love.

(25) For palm readers, the most important line is the *fate line*. (26) There's a lot of breaks in it that show major changes in your life. (27) Some of the lines that cross the fate line tells about important obstacles that you has to overcome. (28) Does the palm and all of its lines actually mean anything? (29) That for you to decide.

SOME ADDITIONAL HELP IN SUBJECT-VERB AGREEMENT

Listen for -s Endings   People often leave off -*s* endings on plural nouns or on verbs because they *don't hear* those endings. The sound of final -*s* is too close to the sound of the letter before it. In fact final -*s* can have any one of three different sounds, determined by the following rules.

Rule 1. When the last sound before final -*s* does not require the use of the vocal cords (sounds such as *f*, *k*, *p*, and *t*—try pronouncing each; you'll hear only air passing across your lips), the final -*s* is pronounced like *s*.

guest*s*   walk*s*
chef*s*   hope*s*
laugh*s*   hit*s*
  (pronounced
  laffs)

Rule 2. When the last sound before final -*s* requires the use of the vocal cords (sounds such as *b*, *g*, *m*, *r*, *v*,*w*, and all the vowels—try pronouncing each; you'll hear an *uh* sound with the consonants), the final -*s* is pronounced like *z*.

rob*s*   law*s*
bug*s*   day*s*
leave*s*   toe*s*

Rule 3. When the last sound before final -*s* is like *s* (*ce*, *sh*, *ch*, *x*, *z*, *ss*, and *s* spellings make these sounds), you must create another syllable to pronounce the final -*s* sound: *es* (pronounced *ez*).

plac*es*   wish*es*   buzz*es*   bus*es*
rich*es*   box*es*   kiss*es*

Practice pronouncing these words and any others you can add to the lists until you associate final -*s* spellings with the *s*, *z*, and *ez* sounds. You might read aloud a story written in the present tense and emphasize each -*s* ending.

Don't Be Fooled by Possessive Words

What is the subject of each of the following sentences?

My friends are here.
Their car is expensive.
Juan's fingers are cold.
The children's education is difficult.

You should have answered *friends*, *car*, *fingers*, and *education*, but you could easily have confused these words with the possessive words that come before them: *My*, *Their*, *Juan's*, and *children's*. Be careful with a possessive word. It is not the subject but is merely a word that *describes the subject* by telling who owns or has it. Therefore, although a possessive word can be singular or plural, it *cannot affect subject-verb agreement*.

Notice these examples.

My book (singular) is brown.
My books (plural) are brown.
Their book (singular) is brown.
Their books (plural) are brown.
Sam's book (singular) is brown.
Sam's books (plural) are brown.
John and Sally's book (singular) is brown.
John and Sally's books (plural) are brown.

26 WARM-UP

Fill in the proper present-tense verb form in each of the following sentences.

1. My checkbook (balance) _____balances_____.

2. Their sister (owe) _____ me money.

3. Jocko's plaid pants (look) _____ great.

4. Her sister's best friend (do) _____ not need help.

5. What (be) _____ their friend's sister going to do?

6. The teacher's apples (need) _____ polishing.

7. The teachers' apples (need) _____ polishing.

8. That girl's clothes (be) _____ expensive.

9. Smith Farm's cows' milk (do) _____ not taste good.

10. Our house (have) _____ eight rooms.

Don't Be Fooled When You Ask a Question

Locating the subject of a sentence that makes a statement isn't difficult.

Tom has stopped seeing Gerry.
Robby and Sam have done all their work.

But locating the subject—especially if it is plural—can be confusing when you ask a question.

Has Tom stopped seeing Gerry?
Have Robby and Sam done all their work?

Notice that in the second question you almost automatically want to say "*Has* Robby and Sam done all their work?" because the word directly after *Has* is Robby. You might easily ignore poor Sam, leaving him without a verb, so be careful. Look for the noun-subject(s) and pronoun-subject(s) following the verb, just as you did for sentences beginning with *There.*

27 WARM-UP

Fill in the proper present-tense form of *to have* in each of the following sentences.

1. _____Have_____ I done a good job?

2. _____ you got a spare nickel?

3. _____ Carlos and Linda seen each other lately?

4. _____ we got time to take a nap?

5. _____ Sam seen the doctor?

6. _____n't he seen the light?

7. _____n't it been a great day?

8. _____n't Linda and her sister gotten along this week?

28 WARM-UP

Fill in the proper present-tense form of *to be* in each of the following sentences.

1. _____Are_____ you enjoying these exercises?

2. _____ he making money?

3. _____ Clara and Lourdes here today?

4. _____ Long Nam and the other Vietnamese settled in the United States?

5. _____ I the best-looking person in this room?

6. _____ you busy all day?

7. _____n't he and his wife angry over the rent increase?

8. _____n't we going to need some skim milk?

29 EDITING

The following passage contains a variety of errors: incorrect subject-verb agreement, incorrect noun plurals, missing verbs, and incorrect contractions of pronouns with *to be*. To correct the errors, write any changes that are necessary *above* the lines.

Some Facts About Cats

(1) Ever since the Egyptian$_\wedge^s$ made cats their pets 4000 years ago, cat$_\wedge^s$ have always been important to mankind as rodent killers. (2) Today some cat still earn their living as rat exterminators, and a few other stars such as Morris makes good money on TV. (3) However, the primary job of cats these days are to be good companions—and kind owners—of their pet humans.

(4) A cat is very smart, but it don't learn the way a dog does. (5) Some tests of intelligence shows that the cat is brighter than a dog. (6) Nevertheless a cat don't allow itself to be trained. (7) It a proud, independent animal that obey only because it likes its owner or because its in the mood.

(8) There's thirty-six different breeds of cats, but all the breeds is basically the same in physical structure. (9) They are different only in the texture of their hair and in their coloring. (10) Cat are unusual in several way. (11) Their the only animals—other than camels and giraffes—that walks by moving their front and hind legs on one side, then the other. (12) The cat's skeleton is very much like a human's, but even though humans are fifteen time larger than cats, peoples each have only 206 bones, and cats have 230.

(13) Cats are exceptionally clean, and they has a strong sense of balance. (14) The cat's eyesight (especially at night) is its strongest sense, but a cat also hear well. (15) Cats are the only animal that purr—that is, they makes a low rumbling sound when there pleased.

(16) How much like people is the female cat and male cat? (17) Most mother cats are tender and protecting, but unlike people, they can give birth several time a year. (18) Tom cats (male cat) are like rolling stones. (19) They never stays around to take care of the kittens. (20) Maybe their just too catty.

PROCESS ANALYSIS

When you describe or analyze a *process*, you explain *how something works* or *how to do something*. A description of how an egg develops into a mature chicken is process analysis. So is a description of how an automobile carburetor mixes gasoline with air. Recipes in a cookbook and instruction sheets with new appliances explain how to make or use something, so they analyze a process, too. Of course every worthwhile process analysis gives readers information or instruction that they want or need to know.

Process analysis combines the elements of both description and narration. It describes the process carefully and arranges the steps of the process in chronological order. However, unlike narration, which is usually written in the past tense, process analysis is usually written in the present tense because it describes an activity that people do again and again. Of course any paragraph or theme of process analysis must be carefully worded and specific in its details. Its organization usually follows these two steps.

1. It introduces the process and lists the materials (tools, parts, or ingredients) involved in the process. It also defines any terms that the audience needs to understand.

2. It describes the process in a step-by-step, chronological order so that the readers can visualize the process or do it themselves.

Here is an example of a paragraph that explains how to do something.

(1) Anyone who wants a hobby that is easy, fun, and even profitable should try collecting autographs. (2) A valuable autograph isn't just a signature; it can be a letter, note, document, or any other object that has been signed by a famous person. (3) Its value depends on the person who signed it and the circumstances under which it was signed. (4) While thank-you notes are a dime a dozen, a letter with unusual or interesting content can be worth hundreds of dollars. (5) For example, Bess Holmes of Philadelphia received not only a signature from the astronaut Buzz Aldren but also received a brief, vivid account of his 1969 walk on the moon. (6) People will pay a lot of money for such a letter. (7) How then should someone begin to gather autographs? (8) It doesn't require much effort, and a person can build a good collection for the price of a few postage stamps. (9) She merely writes to famous people and asks them questions that are provocative enough for them to answer in a reply. (10) The first step in collecting autographs is for someone to think of people she would like to write—people she knows something about and can therefore ask interesting questions. (11) Next she finds their addresses in the latest edition of *Who's Who*—a book that gives short biographies of prominent people. (12) Finally, she writes letters (keeping them short) and waits for the replies. (13) When she has collected a number of autographs and wants to sell them, she should join the Manuscript Society, 429 North Daisy Avenue, Pasadena, California 91107. (14) Membership is ten dollars, and with it she receives the Society's quarterly magazine, *Manuscripts*. (15) It is filled with information about where to buy and sell autographs.

Discussion Questions

1. What is the topic sentence? Does the rest of the paragraph develop its main idea?
2. Does the paragraph define any terms? Does it illustrate any concepts by giving specific examples?
3. Where does the step-by-step explanation of the process begin? How many steps are involved in the process?
4. Why do you think the paragraph suggests that a collector write short letters to famous people?
5. In what tense is the paragraph written? Why?
6. What person (first, second, or third) and number (singular or plural) are used to describe the process?

PARAGRAPH WRITING AND REVISING ASSIGNMENT

Choose a process that you know how to do (or you can find out how to do)—something that you think would be interesting or useful to your classmates. Be sure to choose a subject that you can explain thoroughly in one paragraph—not a subject that is too complicated and requires more development. For example, you could write about making a great pizza, shooting a free throw, or performing a task on your job. In the prewriting stages, begin by brainstorming several lists (and add to them as more ideas occur to you).

1. all the materials needed to perform the task
2. all the steps in the process
3. any terms that need to be defined or explained

Then write the paper, using a third-person-singular subject so that you can practice subject-verb agreement. After a few revisions you should have written a paragraph that includes all of these elements:

1. a topic sentence that generally outlines the process for the readers, such as: "If a person wants to make a great pizza, all he needs are a few fresh ingredients, a hot oven, a few cooking utensils, and a little creativity";
2. a sentence or two that lists the materials needed in the process;
3. a specific description of each step in the process, arranged in logical order; and
4. transitional words such as *first, second, next,* and *finally,* showing the movement from step to step.

After some time has elapsed, reread the paragraph from the audience's point of view, asking if anything else needs to be explained for them to understand the process fully. Rewrite the paragraph again, and as you edit make sure that you have been consistent in person and number—that you haven't switched from *he* (or *she*) to *you* or *they.* Also, check each of the following matters:

1. complete sentences and clauses;
2. correct use of coordination to join sentences;
3. correct use of subordination to join sentences;
4. correct subject-verb agreement and noun-plural forms; and
5. correctly spelled words.

Finally, write a clean copy to hand in, and don't forget to proofread.

SUPPLEMENTARY WRITING AND REVISING ASSIGNMENT

Choose a machine or a natural process your classmates would find interesting. You can explain how a computer stores information, how photosynthesis works, how a sewing machine makes a stitch, or how a carburetor mixes fuel and air. Observe the process carefully, and read about it if necessary. Take notes on what you find, but be careful not to copy from any book, manual, or magazine. Begin by making several brainstorming lists such as those described in "Paragraph Writing and Revising Assignment," and then write a three- or four-paragraph description of the process. Revise the paper until it clearly follows a logical format such as the following:

1. an opening paragraph that introduces the subject, summarizes the process, and mentions the materials or parts involved;
2. a middle section (one or two paragraphs) that describes each step in the process;
3. a summary of the process in the final paragraph.

Be sure to include appropriate transitional words to show the movement between steps. Revise and edit your paper according to the guidelines mentioned in "Paragraph Writing and Revising Assignment."

CHAPTER 6

Using the Past Tense and the Past Participle

You often write about actions that have already happened, especially if you write about one of your own experiences—something you have done, seen, or heard. In these cases you write in the *past tense,* which of course *describes completed actions or events before the present.*

Writing in the past tense isn't difficult. Verbs do not change to agree with their subjects (except for one verb, *to be*), and most verbs share the same form: they simply end in *-ed.* However, in your first drafts you may make errors that can be cleared up in revisions: you may leave off *-ed* endings, you may confuse that past tense with other tenses, and you may not write the most commonly recognized forms of the irregular verbs (verbs whose past-tense forms do not end in *-ed*). This chapter examines these matters so that you can be sensitive to them when revising. You will work with the past tense of regular verbs and with the irregular verbs *be, could,* and *would.* You will see how a related verb form called the *past participle* is used in two other tenses: *the present-perfect tense* and *the past-perfect tense.* You will examine past-tense and past-participle forms of the remaining *irregular verbs,* and you will explore the remaining uses of the past participle as it appears in a verb phrase after *have,* in the *passive voice,* and as an *adjective* after a linking verb or before a noun. Finally, you will look at another method of paragraph development that often relies heavily on the past tense: *causal analysis.*

USING THE PAST TENSE WITH REGULAR VERBS

Here are some past-tense sentences.

S   V
Mario painted his bedroom yesterday.

S   V
The question confused me.

S   V

Jill tumbled down the hill after Jack.

S   V

The strong brew warmed my insides.

Notice the ending of each verb: *-ed*. As you probably know, this is the most common past-tense ending, and verbs that have it are called *regular verbs*. No matter what the subject of the sentence is, the past tense of regular verbs will always end in *-ed*. Therefore a regular verb changes from the present to the past tense following a simple rule.

Present-tense verb (without *-s*) + *-ed* = Past Tense

   Examples: walk + *-ed* = walked
                  seem + *-ed* = seemed
                  sew + *-ed* = sewed

Note: if the present-tense verb ends in *-e*, the past tense merely adds *-d*.*

   Examples: like + *-d* = liked
                  smoke + *-d* = smoked

---

1 WARM-UP

Write *Pr* after each present-tense sentence and *P* after each past-tense sentence.

1. Howard slipped. ____P____

2. Sims kicks the ball well. _____

3. I earn my money. _____

4. They walk together. _____

5. She played a trick. _____

6. The turtle burped. _____

7. I wanted to see you. _____

8. We feel happy. _____

9. He sewed on a button. _____

10. The road turns to the right. _____

11. The flower pot looked fine. _____

12. The squirrel climbed the tree. _____

13. He talked a lot. _____

14. You owe me a favor. _____

15. They jump up and down. _____

---

*If a verb ends in *-y* or a single consonant, its spelling may change slightly when it adds *-ed* (for example, *try* becomes *tried*, and *refer* becomes *referred*). The rules explaining these spelling changes are in Chapter 13.

16. The hippopotamuses dance. _____

17. We reach the top floor by elevator. _____

18. He preached about being good. _____

19. We wait for the bus on the corner. _____

20. This concludes the exercise. _____

2 TRANSFORMING

In the left column are present-tense verbs. In the right column are past-tense verbs. Fill in the missing present-tense or past-tense verb.

Present Tense	*Past Tense*
1. They work.	1. They ___worked___.
2. He _____ in Texas.	2. He lived in Texas.
3. I need some help.	3. I _____ some help.
4. It follows in a straight line.	4. It _____ in a straight line.
5. The rain _____ down.	5. The rain rushed down.
6. You hate bananas.	6. You _____ bananas.
7. The audience applauds.	7. The audience _____ .
8. She _____ up her coat.	8. She zipped up her coat.
9. I dread taking tests.	9. I _____ taking the test.
10. The buses pass by here.	10. The buses _____ by here.
11. He smells like a goat.	11. He _____ like a goat.
12. Jabbar _____ the ball.	12. Jabbar dribbled the ball.
13. We love that book.	13. We _____ that book.
14. They try to explain.	14. They _____ to explain.
15. I want to see you.	15. I _____ to see you.

3 TRANSFORMING

The following passage is written in the present tense. Change the passage to the past tense by writing the proper past-tense form of each verb above the line.

America Gets Its Name

(1) Christopher Columbus supposedly ∧discovers the New World in 1492. [discovered]

(2) Nevertheless Columbus refuses to believe that he lands on an unknown continent. (3) To the day he dies, he persists in the belief that he reaches a new part of Asia.

(4) Meanwhile a Florentine merchant named Amerigo Vespucci sails on four voyages to the west. (5) The first one occurs in 1497—five years after Columbus touches the New World. (6) Vespucci lands on a continent now

called South America, and he claims that no European walks on that soil before. (7) He calls it the *New World*.

(8) Vespucci never once suggests that the New World should be named after him. (9) But an unusual chain of events causes that naming to occur. (10) While he travels, Vespucci composes many letters to friends about what he observes. (11) Somehow, somebody else learns of the letters, forges copies of them, and publishes them as a book called *Four Voyages*. (12) The book carries Vespucci's name as author, without his knowledge or approval.

(13) One of these forged letters inspires a mapmaker to name the New World after Vespucci. (14) The mapmaker, a German, includes the letter in his book and states his belief that Vespucci discovers the New World. (15) Therefore the mapmaker insists that people should call the land *America*— a Latin respelling of *Amerigo*. (16) The idea soon gains great popularity, even though Vespucci never claims credit for the discovery and the mapmaker later learns of Columbus' voyages and retracts his suggestion.

(17) So the naming of America happens accidentally and against the will of both Columbus and Vespucci, who remain good friends and always respect and praise each other.

USING *TO BE* IN THE PAST TENSE

Only one verb in the past tense changes its form to agree with the subject of a sentence: the verb *to be*.

Subject	Verb
I he she it singular nouns	was or wasn't
we you they plural nouns	were or weren't

Notice that the past tense of *to be* acts much like a present-tense verb. The verb form ending in *-s (was)* agrees with *he, she, it,* and singular nouns; it also agrees with *I.*

All of the rules for subject-verb agreement in Chapter 5 apply to *was* and *were.* You may want to review that chapter before you do the following exercises (or consult the chapter if you have any problems with the exercises).

4 WARM-UP

Write in the proper past-tense form of *to be* in each of the following sentences.

1. I _____was_____ glad.
2. You _____ right.
3. Tonto _____ the Lone Ranger's companion.
4. There _____ a big truck parked in front of the building.
5. It _____n't bad.
6. A lot of activity _____n't necessary.
7. The pants _____ too tight.
8. Harry and I _____ too tired to notice.
9. _____ Juan and his friend speaking to you earlier?
10. _____n't that too bad?
11. There _____ a lot of people here.
12. _____ you done?
13. A table and a lamp _____ sitting in the corner a minute ago.
14. Those fish_____n't very large.
15. There _____ two people who didn't finish.
16. _____n't their apartment beautiful?

5 COMBINING

Combine each of the following sentences into one sentence with a compound subject, and change the form of *to be* if necessary.

1. The food was excellent. The service was excellent. __The food and the__ __service were excellent.__

2. The weather was beautiful. The scenery was beautiful. _____

3. Tom wasn't happy. Bill wasn't happy, either. _____

4. There was a desk in the corner. There was a tall lamp in the corner. ____

5. Where was Mr. Smith? Where was Mr. Williams? _____

6. Were the pants too small? Was the shirt too small? _____

_____

6 TRANSFORMING

In the following paragraph, change *a person* to *people,* and make any other changes in pronouns or verb forms that are necessary. Write all your changes above the line.

A Short, Colorful History

(1) The color red has a long and colorful history. (2) In ancient Egypt a person who considered himself part of "the red race" (another name for Egyptians) was always using red dye in his clothing. (3) During the Roman times a person in the army was always looking for red flags that told him a war was starting. (4) During the French Revolution a person who saw a red flag was sure to know that it represented revolution. (5) Then, in the Russian Revolution a person who was a Communist thought of the red flag as his banner.

[handwritten edits above the text: "people" above "a person"; "themselves" above "himself"; "were" above "was"; "their" above "his"]

USING *COULD* AND *WOULD* IN THE PAST TENSE

Could is the past tense of *can.* Use *could* when you want to discuss ability in the past (just as you would use *was able* or *were able*). Compare *could* and *can* in these sentences.

Lilia *could play* the piano as a child, but she *can't play* well now.
Four years ago Rodolfo *couldn't speak* any English, but now he *can speak* fluently.

Would is the past tense of *will.* Use *would* when you want to discuss the future from a point in the past. Compare *would* and *will* in these sentences:

Last week, Albert *said* that he *would start* his new job soon.
He can't begin his job today, but he *will begin* soon.

7 TRANSFORMING

Rewrite the following sentences, changing them from the present tense to the past tense, or vice versa.

Present Tense	*Past Tense*
1. I know that I can pass the test on Friday.	I knew that I could pass the test last Friday.

2. He says that he will be late today.

_____

_____ the next day.

3. _____

_____

Bill wanted to know if he could borrow your car.

4. _____

_____ today.

His car wouldn't start yesterday.

5. Can you swim well?

_____

_____ as a child?

6. _____

_____

Jeannette thought that she would graduate in two years.

7. No one can answer my question.

_____

_____

8. Do you know when the test will be given?

_____

_____

8 WRITING

Complete each of the following sentences, using *can, could, will,* or *would.*

1. Ralph asked the teacher if _she would pick up the books he dropped._

2. We're sure that we _____

soon.

3. When I was a child, _____

_____

4. Ballplayers have to retire when they _____

the things that they _____ when they were younger.

5. In high school did you think that you _____

_____?

6. Susan asked me if I _____

9 WRITING

Write a paragraph describing something you did yesterday, using the past tense of any of the following verbs: *be, can, will, walk, watch, look, use, study, learn, play, carry, enjoy, help, talk, need, show, stop, ask, open, close,* or *change.*

USING THE PRESENT-PERFECT TENSE WITH REGULAR VERBS

Compare these two sentences.

Conrad lived in California in 1965.

Conrad has lived in California since 1965.

Which sentence tells you that Conrad still lives in California?

Your answer should have been the second sentence. It is an example of the *present-perfect tense,* which describes an action that *began in the past but continues up to the present.* Whenever you use the present-perfect tense, you relate something in the past to the present time.

To make sure that you see the difference between the past tense and the present-perfect tense, let's examine the present-perfect tense further.

How to Form the Present-Perfect Tense

Circle the verbs in these present-perfect-tense sentences.

Susan has played the piano since 1972.

They have not called me for three days.

I have owned this car since December.

You haven't traveled anywhere for centuries.

He has needed a new coat all winter.

In each sentence you should have found two words that make one verb: (1) the present-tense helping verb *has* or *have* and (2) a verb form called the *past participle,* which for regular verbs looks exactly like its past-tense form ending in *-ed.*

Past Tense	*Past Participle*
opened	opened
cooked	cooked
discussed	discussed

Notice that the helping verb—*has* or *have*—changes to agree with its subject but that the past participle does not change.

Present-perfect tense of regular verbs:

$$\left.\begin{array}{c} have \\ or \\ has \end{array}\right\} \; + \quad \text{past participle} \\ \text{(verb ending in } \textit{-ed)}$$

10 TRANSFORMING

Change the following past-tense sentences into present-perfect-tense sentences.

1. He typed the letter. _He has typed the letter._____

2. I noticed the new stoplight on the corner. _____

_____

3. He worked in this area. _____

_____

4. She and I talked for hours. _____

_____

5. The new movie theater opened. _____

_____

6. The rope slipped off the hook. _____

_____

7. They changed their whole life-styles. _____

_____

8. The city just increased bus fares. _____

_____

9. I fulfilled some of my childhood dreams. _____

_____

Two Uses of the Present-Perfect Tense

You can use the present-perfect tense in two ways.

1. **To describe an action that began in the past but continues into the present.** If you mention the specific time when the action began, you usually will use the word *for* or *since*.

   Jeannie has stirred that batter *for two minutes*.
   I have listened to this lecture *since two o'clock*.
   You have looked tired *for several days*.
   It has snowed *since yesterday*.

2. **To describe an action in the indefinite past** (you don't mention a specific time) **that relates to the present.** When you discuss something happening now, you often relate that idea to the past. And most often, you discuss that past incident in the present-perfect tense.

Present Perfect	*Present*
We've watched that movie many times,	but *we* still *love* it.
He's called me twice this week,	and *he's calling* me again later.
I've never *traveled* to Spain,	so *I want* to go there.

   Frequently, the past action ended just before the present. Sentences using the present-perfect tense with this meaning often contain such words as *just, recently, already,* or *yet*.

   She has *recently* returned from the hospital.
   I have *just* swallowed a toad.
   He has *already* changed the light bulb.
   Have you sliced the turkey *yet?*
   I haven't finished this lesson *yet*.*

*Use *yet* for questions and negative statements, but use *already* for affirmative statements.

11 TRANSFORMING   In each of the following sentences, write the appropriate past-tense or present-perfect form of the verb in parentheses.

1. In the 1870s three men (tell) _____told_____ a German named Jake Waltzer about a gold mine in a mountain sacred to the Apache Indians of Arizona.

2. The unprincipled Waltzer promptly (kill) _____ the men, taking the mine for himself.

3. He (protect) _____ its location until he died in 1891, leaving a map to his mistress, although she never found the mine, which may have been buried in an earthquake.

4. Since then, people (call) _____ it the Lost Dutchman Mine after the "Dutchman" Waltzer.

5. For a century, at least a thousand fortune hunters (search) _____ Arizona's Superstition Mountains looking for the sacred gold mine, but all in vain.

6. The Phelps-Dodge Corporation once (back) _____ an exhaustive hunt for the mine by a group of geologists and prospectors, but with no significant results.

7. To date, twenty people in all (die) _____ as a result of accidents or murders while seeking the gold, giving rise to the legend that the Indians (curse) _____ all who might try to desecrate their mountain.

8. Others say that pigmies or an old prospector (guard) _____ the entrance to the mine, shooting anyone approaching it.

9. According to one treasure hunter, the secret of finding the mine lies in the symbols that Mexican miners (carve) _____ on cliffs within a five-mile radius of a peak called El Sombrero.

10. If you can interpret the symbols, you'll find the gold, but so far no one (decipher) _____ them.

USING THE PAST-PERFECT TENSE WITH REGULAR VERBS

Like the present-perfect tense, the past-perfect tense is a combination of two words.

Past-perfect tense:

had + past participle

The past-perfect tense, however, is purely a *past* tense. It describes an action that occurred *before* another past-tense action.

Columbus *had discovered* America before Copernicus was born.

Notice that the first clause—in the past-perfect tense—occurred before the second clause—in the past tense. The word *before* also shows that the actions took place at different times, so the past-perfect tense isn't absolutely necessary to make the meaning of the sentence clear. But compare the following two sentences. Which one means that Ann *did not live in New York* at the time she spoke?

Ann told me that she *lived* in New York.
Ann told me that she *had lived* in New York.

You should have answered the second sentence, for the past-perfect tense shows the difference in time. In this case the past-perfect tense is absolutely essential; nothing else tells the reader that the actions took place at separate times.

> **In Summary:**   Use the past perfect tense
>
> to discuss an action in the past that occurred before another action or time—especially when there are no words such as *before, after,* or *as soon as* in the sentence to distinguish between the times.

Since the present-perfect tense and the past-perfect tense are so similar, they are easy to confuse. Remember the following important differences.

1. The present-perfect relates something in the past to something in the present. Its helping verbs are *has* and *have.*
2. The past-perfect tense occurs in past-tense writing. Its helping verb is *had.*

12 WARM-UP

In each of the following sentences, write either the present-perfect or the past-perfect verb form—whichever is appropriate.

1. After I (travel)___*had traveled*___ for several hours, I stopped to eat lunch.

2. After I (travel) _____ for several hours, I usually stop to eat lunch.

3. We (live) _____ in California since 1971, and we intend to stay.

4. We (live) _____ in California since 1971, but we moved in 1978.

5. Jim already (talk) _____ to Lisa before he decided.

6. Jim (talk) _____ to Lisa, and now he is ready to decide.

7. You (study) _____ violin for nine years and you still can't play!

8. You (study) _____ violin for nine years, and you still couldn't play when I asked you!

The Past Participle of *To Be*

The past participle of *to be* is *been*. Sentences in the present-perfect tense that use *to be* look like the examples below.

> I *have been* here before.
> He *has been* sick for a week.

Be careful to use *have* or *has* (or their contractions *'ve* or *'s* with pronouns) before *been* in the present-perfect tense. *Been* by itself cannot be a verb.

> He's *been* busy this week.
> They*'ve been* on vacation for a month.

13 WARM-UP

In each of the following sentences, write the present-perfect tense or the past-perfect tense, using *been.*

1. Matthew _____had been_____ absent a lot, but then his attendance improved.

2. I _____ thinking lately about trying out for the basketball team.

3. We _____n't _____ home to see our parents yet this year.

4. Maria _____ involved in three or four different clubs until she became ill.

5. Working and going to school this semester _____n't _____ easy.

14 WRITING

Complete each of the following sentences in the past-perfect tense, using the verb in parentheses when it is supplied.

1. The doctor told me that I (contract) _had contracted a rare disease._

2. The instructor asked the students if they (complete) _____

_____

3. Most of the orchestra (rehearse) _____ their parts before they performed.

4. The woman screamed when she saw that the dog _____

_____

5. After the car _____

the passengers cheered.

6. We _____ that _____

_____

USING THE PAST TENSE AND PAST PARTICIPLE OF IRREGULAR VERBS

More than one hundred verbs have *irregular* past-tense and past-participle forms—that is, their past-tense and past-participle forms do not end in *-ed*. Fortunately, these verbs are easy to memorize because they can be grouped into seven categories.

Category 1. The final *-d* in the present tense changes to *-t* in the past tense and past participle.

Present Tense	Past Tense	Past Participle
bend	bent	bent
build	built	built
lend	lent	lent
send	sent	sent
spend	spent	spent

15 WARM-UP

Fill in the proper past-tense or past-participle form of the verb in parentheses. Some sentences may require *had* and the past participle.

1. William Beckford (1759–1844) (build) _____built_____ some of the strangest structures in the world.

2. His father died and left Beckford a large fortune when Beckford was ten, and he (spend) _____ the money in rather odd ways.

3. His mother (send) _____ him around the world as a young boy to learn languages and to acquire culture.

4. He (lend) _____ himself to many activities: writing books, playing the piano, and making love with a variety of people.

5. By 1790 he (spend) _____ time managing his own business affairs.

(To find out more about Beckford, do Exercise 16.)

Category 2. The final consonant becomes *-d*.

A. No vowel change before the final consonant.

have	had	had
make	made	made

B. Vowel change before the final consonant.

flee	fled	fled
hear	heard*	heard*
lay	laid	laid†
pay	paid	paid
say	said	said
sell	sold	sold
tell	told	told

16 WARM-UP

Fill in the proper past-tense or past-participle form of the verb in parentheses. Some sentences may require *had* and the past participle.

1. Beckford (lay) _____laid_____ plans to build himself a magnificent home in England.

2. In fact he (tell) _____ a woman friend that he intended to construct a huge tower worthy of his importance and wealth.

3. As a first step, he hired workers away from other projects and (pay) _____ them large sums to erect a twelve-foot wall around his property—seven miles in circumference.

4. To complete his great tower, he (make) _____ five hundred men work around the clock, rain or shine.

5. He (tell) _____ the men to complete the tower in record time, so they (have) _____ to slap its wood-and-concrete foundation together carelessly.

6. Many people (hear) _____ of the project and (be) _____ convinced that the man (be) _____ insane.

7. Nevertheless the crew soon (make) _____ the tower. It (be) _____ three hundred feet high but extremely narrow, like a candied apple on a stick.

8. Before the finishing touches could be added, a gentle wind snapped it in two. It fell in a heap as workers (flee) _____ the area.

9. A sensible man would have (sell) _____ the property and left, but not Beckford.

10. He (tell) _____ his men, "Build me a new tower—at once." (To find out even more about Beckford, do Exercise 17.)

*The *sound* of the vowel changes.

†See Chapter 15 for a discussion of the difference between *lay* and *lie*.

Category 3. Final -*t* is added.

A. Vowel change before the final consonant.

creep	crept	crept
feel	felt	felt
keep	kept	kept
leave	left	left*
lose	lost	lost†
mean	meant†	meant†
sleep	slept	slept
sweep	swept	swept

B. Vowel change, and change to -*ght* at end of word.

bring	brought	brought
buy	bought	bought
catch	caught	caught
teach	taught	taught
think	thought	thought

17 WARM-UP

Fill in the proper past-tense or past-participle form of the verb in parentheses. Some sentences may require *had* and the past participle.

1. The tower's collapse should have (teach) _____taught_____ Beckford that the foundation (be) _____ too narrow, but he (leave) _____ it essentially unchanged.

2. He would not make changes because he (mean) _____ to finish quickly.

3. Instead, he (buy) _____ huge amounts of stone and (think) _____ that adding them to the wood and cement (will) _____ strengthen the building enough for it to stand.

4. After his workers (sweep) _____ away the wreckage, they (lose) _____ no time beginning again.

5. They (feel) _____ they (will) _____ waste time if they rested, so they rarely (sleep) _____ .

6. They finally (catch) _____ up with their schedule and completed the tower on December 20, 1800. Beckford named it Fonthill Abbey.

7. To celebrate its completion, Beckford (bring) _____ in another crew to decorate the Abbey.

   (Beckford's story continues in Exercise 18.)

*Note the change from -*ve* to -*ft*.

†The *sound* of the vowel changes.

Category 4. Only the vowel changes.

A. The same past tense and the past participle.

bind	bound	bound
bleed	bled	bled
breed	bred	bred
dig	dug	dug
feed	fed	fed
find	found	found
fight	fought	fought
grind	ground	ground
hang	hung	hung
hold	held	held
lead	led	led
meet	met	met
read	read*	read*
shoot	shot	shot
sit	sat	sat
slide	slid	slid
speed	sped	sped
spin	spun	spun
stand	stood	stood
stick	stuck	stuck
strike	struck	struck†
swing	swung	swung
wind	wound	wound
wring	wrung	wrung

B. The same present tense and the past participle.

become	became	become
come	came	come
run	ran	run

18 WARM-UP

Fill in the proper past-tense or past-participle form of the verb in parentheses. Some sentences may require *had* and the past participle.

1. The crew (dig) _____ dug _____ into the thick underbrush surrounding the Abbey and (stick) _____ thousands of colored lanterns everywhere.

2. They (hang) _____ huge tapestries on the walls and (run) _____ purple curtains from one end of the huge windows to the other.

*The sound of the vowel changes.

†Note the additional spelling change. Also, in passive voice (see p. 142), the past participle is *stricken*.

3. They (speed) _____ through the house and (stand) _____ hand-carved furniture everywhere they (can) _____ .

4. Then, Beckford had a party. When the guests (come) _____ into the tower, the sight of its fancy decorations (strike) _____ them dumb.

5. Beckford (meet) _____ them and (lead) _____ them through the Abbey, where they (find) _____ one treasure after another.

6. After they (sit) _____ at a fifty-foot table, Beckford (feed) _____ them a huge meal.

7. Beckford had promised them a nice intimate party, which instead (become) _____ a huge affair.

8. The guests weren't thrilled, but they (hold) _____ their tongues and enjoyed themselves.

(Still more about Beckford follows in Exercise 19.)

Category 5. The vowel changes in each form.

begin	began	begun
drink	drank	drunk
ring	rang	rung
sink	sank (*or* sunk)	sunk
spring	sprang (*or* sprung)	sprung
swim	swam	swum

19 WARM-UP

Fill in the proper past-tense or past-participle form of the verb in parentheses. Some sentences may require *had* and the past participle.

1. The party lasted for days, and on Christmas Eve Beckford (spring) _____sprang_____ another surprise.

2. He announced that the next meal (will) _____ be cooked inside the Abbey—although there (be) _____ no kitchen. That same night, workers (begin) _____ to slap together a kitchen and completed it by daybreak.

3. As the guests ate and (drink) _____ in the dining room that evening, a large crash (ring) _____ out.

4. The heat from the kitchen fires had weakened the still-wet mortar of the bricks. As a result, the walls had (sink) _____ and then collapsed.

(Do Exercise 20 to find out what happened next.)

Category 6. The verb ends in *-t* or *-d* and does not change for the past tense or the past participle.

bet	bet	bet
burst	burst	burst
cast	cast	cast
cut	cut	cut
fit	fit (*or* fitted)	fit (*or* fitted)
hit	hit	hit
hurt	hurt	hurt
let	let	let
put	put	put
quit	quit	quit
rid	rid	rid
set	set	set
shed	shed	shed
shut	shut	shut
slit	slit	slit
spread	spread	spread
thrust	thrust	thrust

20 WARM-UP

Fill in the proper past-tense or past-participle form of the verb in parentheses. Some sentences may require *had* and the past participle.

1. A servant (burst) _____burst_____ into the room to inform Beckford of the disaster.

2. Beckford (cast) _____ aside the man's news, shrugged, and (put) _____ the men to work building a new kitchen immediately.

3. He (let) _____ nothing interrupt his meal.

4. So the men (set) _____ about the task of restoring the kitchen.

5. After a few days they (fit) _____ the new bricks in place and (quit) _____ their labors.

(Beckford's story ends with Exercise 21.)

Category 7. The past participle ends in *-n* or *-en*.

beat	beat	beaten
bite	bit	bitten*
blow	blew	blown
break	broke	broken
choose	chose	chosen
do	did	done†
draw	drew	drawn
drive	drove	driven

*Note the spelling change.

†Note the end-spelling is *-ne*.

eat	ate	eaten
fall	fell	fallen
fly	flew	flown
forget	forgot	forgotten*
forgive	forgave	forgiven
freeze	froze	frozen
get	got	gotten*
give	gave	given
go	went	gone†
grow	grew	grown
hide	hid	hidden*
know	knew	known
lie	lay	lain
ride	rode	ridden*
rise	rose	risen
see	saw	seen
shake	shook	shaken
shine	shone (or shined)	shone
slay	slew	slain*
speak	spoke	spoken
steal	stole	stolen
strive	strove	striven
swear	swore	sworn
take	took	taken
tear	tore	torn
throw	threw	thrown
wake	woke	woken
wear	wore	worn
weave	wove	woven
write	wrote	written*

21 WARM-UP

Fill in the proper past-tense or past-participle form of the verb in parentheses. Some sentences may require *had* and the past participle.

1. After the party (draw) __had drawn__ to a close, Beckford (take) _____ up residence in the Abbey.

2. The badly ventilated building (freeze) _____ in winter, (get) _____ unbearably hot in summer, and (shake) _____ in the slightest breeze.

3. But Beckford (choose) _____ to live there for many years even though he must have (know) _____ that the building was unsafe.

4. As time (go) _____ by, it also (steal) _____ away his fortune.

*Note the spelling change.

†Note the end-spelling is -ne.

5. Finally, he (give) _____ up on the Abbey and (sell) _____ it for a huge sum of money.

6. He then (become) _____ involved in another project and soon (break) _____ ground on a new tower in the town of Bath.

7. The tower eventually (rise) _____ 130 feet above ground.

8. By this time Beckford (become) _____ completely mad.

9. He (swear) _____ that he (will) _____ never look at another mirror or a woman.

10. So he (see) _____ that all the corridors had little compartments.

11. Whenever he (awake) _____ and started down the corridors, the women servants (throw) _____ themselves into these compartments and (hide) _____ .

12. He lived out his life in this new tower. One day the news arrived that a bad storm (blow) _____ down the Abbey a few days earlier.

13. He (fly) _____ into a fit of laughter.

14. He (beat) _____ the odds, and so he (do) _____ n't mind that his monumental tower (break) _____ apart.

22 WRITING   Choose five past-tense forms of the verbs in Category 7 and write a sentence using each form. Then, rewrite each of these sentences in the present-perfect tense, rewording the sentence if necessary.

1. (past tense) _I spoke to my aunt last night._

   (present-perfect tense) _I have spoken to her a lot recently._

2. (past tense) _____

   _____

   (present-perfect tense) _____

   _____

3. (past tense) _____

   _____

   (present-perfect tense) _____

   _____

4. (past tense) _____

   _____

   (present-perfect tense) _____

   _____

5. (past tense) _____

_____

(present-perfect tense) _____

_____

6. (past tense) _____

_____

(present-perfect tense) _____

_____

A STUDY HINT

You probably don't need to memorize all of the irregular verbs since you already know many of them. Therefore make your studying more efficient by preparing your own list of the irregular verbs in each category that you do need to memorize.

23 WRITING   Write a paragraph about something important that you did last week. Use any past-tense verbs that you want.

24 WRITING   Write a paragraph about a hobby or favorite pastime you have had for a long time. Describe what you have done and how you have done it.

USING THE PAST PARTICIPLE IN OTHER WAYS

The Past Participle After *Have* in Three-Word Verb Phrases

The exercises in the previous section have shown that many three-word verb phrases contain *have* + the past participle.

could have done	may have seen
should have gone	might have taken
must have been	would have thought*

Remember this simple rule: when *have* is a helping verb, the main verb after it *must* be a past participle.†

> $\left.\begin{array}{l} could,\ should,\ would, \\ may,\ might,\ must \end{array}\right\}$ + *have* + past participle

*In four-word verb phrases the third word is always the past participle *been*.

I should have *been* studying. They could have *been* stolen.

Be careful not to confuse *have* with *of* in three- and four-word verb phrases. See Chapter 15, p. 348–49.

†The only exception to this rule is *have to*, as in "I have to go now."

25 WRITING

Complete each of the following sentences, using *have* and an appropriate past participle.

1. I didn't do well on the examination. I should _have done better_____

_____

2. Yesterday was a holiday, and we could _____

_____

3. If I had listened to your advice, I would _____

_____

4. Mr. Williams wasn't at work yesterday. He must _____

_____

5. I don't know if Bill wants to have lunch with us. He may

_____ already.

6. Many people thought that they saw a flying saucer, but they might

_____ a balloon.

The Past Participle After *To Be* (Passive Voice)

You can also place a past participle after some form of *to be* when the *subject of your sentence does not perform an action*. Instead of performing an action, the *subject receives the action*.

The secret **was told** to me by a genie.

Notice that the sentence's subject—*the secret*—did nothing. The *genie* did the telling. In other words, the subject is *passive*. It does not act but is acted upon.

When writing a sentence with a passive subject, you write in the *passive voice*. Here are more examples of passive-voice sentences.

The tickets **are sold** by three vendors. (Three vendors perform the action.)

The papers **were blown** across the yard by a fierce wind. (The wind performed the action.)

The meal **was cooked** by Janis. (Janis performed the action.)

> Passive Voice (the subject is acted upon):
>
> Subject + *to be* + past participle

The opposite of the passive voice is the *active voice*, in which the subject *acts*—it *does* something. Compare the two voices.

active: A *genie* told me the secret.
passive: *The secret* was told to me by a genie.

Rewrite the other three passive-voice sentences above in the active voice.

1. Three vendors _____
2. A fierce wind _____
3. Janis _____

Is your first sentence in the present tense? Are your next two sentences in the past tense? If not, check them against the passive-voice sentences.

26 TRANSFORMING Change the sentences on the left to the active voice and the sentences on the right to the passive voice. When you change a sentence, make sure to keep the original tense.

Passive Voice

1. _Yesterday, I was beaten up_ _by three big thugs._

2. That Cadillac is driven by a chauffeur.

3. The oak tree _____ _____

4. The boat is powered by an outboard motor.

5. The city streets _____ _____

6. The cat was spoiled by its owners.

7. _____ _____

8. _____ _____

9. Her nails are bitten to the bone.

10. _____ _____

Active Voice

1. Yesterday, three big thugs beat me up.

2. A chauffeur _____ _____

3. Lightning struck the oak tree behind our house.

4. An outboard motor _____ _____

5. Huge machines clean the city streets.

6. _____ _____

7. Jackson slammed the ball past the infielders.

8. Wing Young's serves excellent Chinese food.

9. _____ _____

10. The car's brakes made that terrible screeching sound.

The Past Participle as an Adjective After Linking Verbs

Sometimes a past participle shows no action at all. It functions instead as an adjective describing a noun. For example, a past participle often comes after a linking verb (*is, seem, become,* or *sound*—see Chapter 1) and describes the subject of the sentence.

Subject	Linking Verb	Past Participle
I	feel	tired.
The eggs	seem	done.
The child	is	lost.
The blender	was	broken.

Notice that nothing *happens* in these sentences. The past participle does not act on the subject. Fill in a word (ending in *-ed*) that describes the subject of the following sentence:

Tom seemed _____ ed when he heard the announcement.

Did you write *surprised, amazed, annoyed, overjoyed, excited,* or any other word that describes how he seemed? These words are all past participles.

27 **WARM-UP**   Change the following verbs to their past-participle forms.

Verb	*Past Participle*
1. strengthen	strengthened
2. know	
3. interest	
4. overdo	
5. convince	
6. involve	
7. use	
8. scare	
9. annoy	
10. overwhelm	
11. prejudice	
12. warn	
13. sleep	
14. wear	

Now, insert one of these past-participle forms in each of the following sentences.

1. My muscles got _____ strengthened _____ after months of exercise.

2. The bed looks _____ in.

3. I was _____ against seeing that horror movie.

4. But I went anyway and got _____ out of my mind.

5. You might be _____ in the film.

6. That fellow seems _____ that he is brilliant.

7. We became _____ to his odd behavior.

8. The chicken tasted _____ .

9. Please don't get _____ with me.

10. That old radio looks _____ out.

11. When I have too much to do, I feel _____ .

12. Don't disturb Sue; she is very _____ in a book she is reading.

13. I am _____ against conceited people.

14. That actor is well-_____ .

28 WRITING   Write a paragraph describing a good meal you recently had. Use linking verbs to describe the sights, sounds, smells, tastes, and feelings you experienced during the meal. Several of the adjectives after the linking verbs should be past participles.

The Past Participle Before Nouns

Past participles can also be adjectives before nouns.

> A *frightened dog* hid under the table.
> He's a *well-known actor*.

When you write, look carefully at the words before nouns. An incorrect past-participle form can be confusing and distracting. Read this sentence, for example:

> There's a tire man resting on the couch.

Does the sentence mean that the man sells tires or that the man is tired? It probably means the latter idea, but we can't be sure. Here's another example:

> I like devil eggs.

Does that mean that you like eggs that the devil lays or that you like eggs that are deviled (seasoned heavily)? The odds are that you mean deviled, but again we can't be sure.

29 WRITING   Write an appropriate past participle in each of the following sentences.

1. He sells _____used_____ cars.

2. I've just put on a freshly _____ shirt.

3. When Grubbs caught the ball, 60,000 _____ fans leaped to their feet.

4. I like _____ eggs for breakfast.

5. The police caught the man selling _____ goods.

6. _____ cars are cheaper than new ones, but they usually aren't as reliable.

7. Several players were hurt during the game: Lopez had a _____ nose; Johnson suffered a _____ leg muscle; and Hansen limped off with a _____ ankle.

8. He's still an un_____ writer.

The Past Participle After Nouns

A past participle can also come after a noun when the participle begins an *adjective phrase* (two or more words that function as an adjective):

	Phrase	
A woman	*named Melinda*	just asked to see you.
I've always liked books	*written by Hemingway.*	

30 WRITING

Complete each of the following sentences with a phrase that begins with a past participle.

1. Do you know a man _____named_____ Harry Leggs?

2. The food _____ by our chefs at La Gourmet is among the finest you will ever taste.

3. You will see the new dishes _____ on the table.

4. Always buy a car from a dealership _____ for a reliable service department.

5. Try not to go to places _____ by too many tourists.

6. Don't taste food _____.

In Summary: A past participle

1. comes after *have* or *has* in the present-perfect tense or after *had* in the past-perfect tense;
2. comes after *have* in three-word verb phrases, such as *might have done* or *could have been working;*
3. comes after *to be* in the passive voice;
4. comes after a linking verb;
5. comes before a noun; and
6. comes at the beginning of a phrase after a noun.

---

31 EDITING

The following passage contains many errors in past-tense and past-participle verb forms. To correct these errors, make the necessary changes above the line.

The Story of Cleopatra (69 B.C.–30 B.C.)

(1) In 51 B.C. Egypt was a powerful country and the enemy of Rome. (2) Then the king die^d, and Cleopatra became ruler of Egypt, along with her ten-year-old brother Ptolemy, whom she marry^ied, according to Egyptian custom. (3) Ptolemy's guardians seen that Cleopatra was ambitious and clever, and they made things so dangerous for her that she was force to flee to Syria in 49 B.C. (4) She gathered an army there and fighted her

brother's troops. (5) In the meantime the Roman leader Julius Caesar lead his army into Egypt and conquer the country. (6) After he had came into the Egyptian palace, he demanded to see both Ptolemy and Cleopatra because he want them to make peace.

(7) Cleopatra arrived secretly. (8) She was brung into the palace by a servant, who had wrap her in a rug. (9) The servant unrolled the rug in front of Caesar, a dramatic entrance that must have surprise and impress him. (10) Cleopatra and Caesar possibly become lovers that night, although Cleopatra have probably been a virgin up to that point.

(11) The next morning Ptolemy refuse to make peace with his sister and throwed his crown on the floor. (12) Eventually, the young boy fighted Caesar again and was slay in battle. (13) Cleopatra then was marry to another brother, also name Ptolemy, but he later died from poisoning.

(14) Caesar and Cleopatra spent two years together, and they had a child call Caeserion. (15) When Caesar went back to Rome, he was declare Emperor, and Cleopatra soon followed him there but didn't live with him. (16) Caesar had many enemies among the Roman senators, who was afraid of his affair with the queen of a strong country like Egypt. (17) Finally, several senators, including one named Mark Anthony, stab Caesar to death on the floor of the Senate.

(18) Cleopatra went back to Egypt, where she builded a strong navy and ran the country. (19) Meanwhile, in Rome, Mark Anthony was officially gave control of Egypt. (20) In 42 B.C. he summoned Cleopatra to Rome. (21) With her usual great sense of style, she sailed into the city aboard a purple-sail ship with silver oars. (22) She wear a costume that made her look like Venus, and women who look like sea nymphs surrounded her. (23) She gave an enormous banquet for Anthony, with gold plates and a floor that was cover with roses.

(24) Of course she and Anthony soon was lovers. (25) They went to Egypt and gambled, drunk, and go to orgies for a year. (26) After that, Anthony returned to Rome and married the sister of his enemy, Octavian,

so that the two men could make peace. (27) However, Cleopatra won him back, and she married him in 37 B.C. under Egyptian law (making him a bigamist under Roman law).

(28) Anthony's actions made Octavian furious, and he started a war with Egypt. (29) By this point Anthony had became a drunk, and Cleopatra controlled him. (30) She convince him to fight Rome at sea—a good strategy—but the Egyptian army was soundly beat, except for the ships that was commanded by Cleopatra. (31) Soon, however, these ships were setted on fire, and false rumors spreaded that Cleopatra was dead.

(32) When Anthony heard the rumors, he threw himself on his sword. (33) He was quickly took to Cleopatra's room, where he die in her arms. (34) She soon grew depress, lost hope, and allow the Romans to capture her. (35) Rather than be a prisoner, Cleopatra committed suicide when she letted a snake bite her.

(36) Cleopatra died after she had try the impossible—to make Egypt free from Roman rule and a powerful kingdom by itself. (37) She had hoped to make an alliance with Rome by marrying an important Roman ruler. (38) She failed, but after her death she become a legend.

SOME ADDITIONAL HELP IN USING THE PAST TENSE AND PAST PARTICIPLE

Listen for -ed Endings

Some people often leave off -ed endings on past-tense or past-participle verb forms because they *don't hear* these endings. Although many words are spelled with a final -ed, those words are often pronounced with a final t or d sound. The last sound before the final -ed determines the pronunciation.

Category 1. A t or d sound precedes final -ed, and the -ed is pronounced as a full syllable.

wan*t*ed	wai*t*ed	plea*d*ed
ha*t*ed	nee*d*ed	no*dd*ed

Category 2. The last sound before final -ed does not require the use of the vocal cords (sounds such as s, ch, k, p, th, sh, f, or h). The final -ed is pronounced like t.

	pronounced		*pronounced*
lea*p*ed	(leapt)	hi*k*ed	(hikt)
rea*ch*ed	(reacht)	ra*c*ed	(ract)
wi*sh*ed	(wisht)	wor*k*ed	(workt)
lea*f*ed	(leaft)	lau*gh*ed	(laught)

Category 3. The last sound before final *-ed* requires the use of the vocal cords (sounds such as *b, g, m, n, r, v, w,* or *z*). The final *-ed* is pronounced like *d*.

	pronounced		*pronounced*
ro*bb*ed	(robbd)	pu*rr*ed	(purrd)
be*gg*ed	(beggd)	hea*v*ed	(heavd)
hu*mm*ed	(hummd)	se*w*ed	(sewd)
stu*nn*ed	(stunnd)	bu*zz*ed	(buzzd)

Try the same procedure recommended in Chapter 5 for becoming more aware of word endings. Practice pronouncing aloud the words on the above lists and any others you can add to the lists until you associate the final *-ed* spelling with the *ed, t,* and *d* sounds. You might read aloud a story written in the past tense and emphasize each verb ending.

Don't Be Fooled by Words Between *Have* and the Past Participle in Verb Phrases

Remember that some form of *have (have, has,* or *had)* almost always triggers a past participle.

I *have seen* the new Woody Allen film.
We *had left* before you arrived.
They *could have spoken* to Mr. Williams.

But you often put another word between *have* and the past participle.

I *have* **just** *seen* the new Woody Allen film.
We *had* **already** *gone* before you arrived.
They *could have* **already** *spoken* to Mr. Williams.

Don't let these descriptive words trick you into ignoring the *have, has,* or *had* that comes before them. If you are tricked, you may end up writing something like *have just saw, has always grew,* or *had already went.* So when you proofread during revisions, look for any form of *have* and see if it triggers a past participle.

32 WARM-UP

Some of the following sentences contain inappropriate verb forms. Above each line, change the verb forms when necessary.

1. I could have _∧ <del>did</del> a better job. *[above: done]*

2. They have never ran that far before.

3. We have finally and completely become accustomed to city life.

4. They have sometimes went to the ocean to swim.

5. We haven't really ate anything since breakfast.

6. He hasn't ever swam that far before.

7. I have just written a fine paper!

8. We really gave it all we had.

9. She has simply worn, torn, and beat us down.

10. I just seen a man with carrots in his ears.

33 EDITING   The following passage contains many errors in past-tense and past-participle forms. To correct these errors, make any necessary changes above the line.

Mutiny on the Bounty, 1789

(1) In 1787 William Bligh was a thirty-four-year-old lieutenant in the British navy. (2) He was ∧ c̶h̶o̶s̶e̶ [chosen] by his superior officers to command *The Bounty*, a 250-ton ship that have been made ready for a voyage to Tahiti to complete Operation Breadfruit. (3) This scheme had been began by wealthy investors to transplant breadfruit trees from South Pacific islands to the West Indies as a cheap food for slave labor. (4) With a crew of forty-three, including First Mate Fletcher Christian, *The Bounty* lefted England on December 23, 1788. (5) Ten months and 27,086 miles later, it dropped anchor at Tahiti. (6) After six months on the island, the crew of *The Bounty* putted to sea again for the West Indies on April 4, 1789 with 1500 plants in 774 pots, 39 tubs, and 24 boxes.

(7) Ship captains was emperors of their vessels with the power to enforce any discipline necessary for the safety of ship and crew, but Bligh's brand of discipline was unique. (8) He felted no sympathy for anyone and demanded absolute obedience. (9) On the way to Tahiti, for example, Bligh had make up a story that someone had stold a supply of cheese. (10) The reason behind this deception was to get rid of some spoil pumpkins. (11) Instead of cheese, each man was gave a pound of rottened pumpkin and two pounds of dry biscuits. (12) When the men complained, he tolded them that if they didn't like it he will feed them grass.

(13) Mate Fletcher Christian, always in the middle between Bligh and the crew, take more abuse from the captain than anyone else. (14) After *The Bounty* had went to sea again from Tahiti, Christian planned to jump ship some dark night. (15) On April 27 Bligh throwed a tantrum over some missing coconuts and blamed Christian. (16) When darkness fall and Christian had took his watch, he decide to assume command of the ship. (17) At sunrise he and his followers caughted Bligh unawares and forced the captain into a small boat with eighteen loyal supporters and a tiny supply of food and water. (18) Before they was casted adrift, Bligh begged for mercy. (19) Christian say: "No, Captain Bligh, if you had any honor, things would not have came to this; and if you had any regard for your wife and family, you should have thought of them before and not act so much like a villain."

(20) The twenty-three-foot boat, design for use in quiet water between the ship and the shore, was pack tightly with men, bags, tools, containers of water, bread, and salt pork. (21) With this three-ton cargo, the boat rided dangerously low in the choppy Pacific as it drifted away from *The Bounty*. (22) Bligh immediately begun round-the-clock watches and determined the daily food ration—one ounce of bread and a half of a pint of water. (23) A course was setted for Tahiti, the nearest island, where they arrive three days later. (24) The natives attacked them before they can find any water, so Bligh and his men head for Timor, an island 3600 miles away across the open sea.

(25) Each day they fighted the elements. (26) One storm come after another. (27) Wet food spoil, and the undernourish men growed weary. (28) But miraculously, Bligh's seamanship brung them to their destination on July 14, where the party was transfer to a small ship and returned to England. (29) Only Bligh and twelve men survive the impossible journey.

(30) Most of the mutineers was caught, but Fletcher Christian and some others returned in *The Bounty* to Tahiti, where sixteen choose to stay. (31) However, Christian and eight others leaved for Pitcairn Island to begin a

colony, accompany by nine native women and seven boys. (32) A year later Christian was kill in a fight over a woman, and then the women massacred all of the mutineers except two.

(33) The colony remained undiscover until 1814. (34) Alexander Smith, who had change his name to John Adams, was the head of the colony and the single survivor among the mutineers. (35) He died on March 29, 1829, but the colony still survives in the descendents of Fletcher Christian and his eight followers.

CAUSAL ANALYSIS

A *causal analysis* is an explanation of *why something happened or is happening*. For example, when a car won't start, you or a mechanic will look for the cause or causes of the problem. Is the battery dead? Is some part broken, such as the fuel pump? Is a wire loose or worn out? Is there any gas in the fuel tank? It could be any one of these causes or a combination of several. Similarly, when many students fail an examination, the instructor must look for the causes. Did the students study enough? Were the instructor's lectures clear? Was the examination too difficult, or were the directions on the examination too confusing? Causal analysis is often a combination of process analysis and narration; it explains how things happened, usually in chronological order.

Because few things in life are simple, there is often more than one cause for an event. Therefore writing about causes takes careful thought and planning. In the prewriting stage list the various causes that occur to you, consider the probability of each one (testing the probability if you can), and decide on the most likely explanation or explanations. In the writing stage subordinate the less important causes in favor of the more important ones. Additionally, when you aren't positive that your explanation is right, use such terms as *maybe*, *possibly*, or *probably*.

Typically, a paragraph or theme that uses causal analysis begins by naming and perhaps describing the event. Then it lists and analyzes the causes of the event. Here is an example of a paragraph that traces a series of causes as they occurred over a period of time.

(1) Most children will drink anything—even medicine—if they can drink it through a flexible straw, which bends to any angle and is so fascinating to use. (2) The invention of this wonderful device came about through a chain of events that ended when a thoughtful father decided to make drinking easier for his daughter. (3) Here is how the story unfolded. (4) The first drinking tubes were made of glass, but they were impractical because they were both hard to clean and easily breakable. (5) To eliminate these problems, someone invented the artificial drinking straw, which was made from paper coated with wax. (6) However, this new straw had its drawbacks, too. (7) The paper bent easily, cracked easily, and was generally unclean. (8) Finally, one day in 1938, Joseph B. Friedman watched as his daughter became frustrated with a paper straw. (9) Because she had bent it over the rim of her glass, nothing would pass

through the straw. (10) Friedman thought that a corrugated straw would solve the problem, so he set out to invent one. Eventually he succeeded. (11) His finished product was plastic, disposable, and appropriate for both hot and cold drinks. (12) Thus this unsung hero made the life of his daughter and of countless other children richer, fuller, and a lot more fun.

Discussion Questions

1. The topic sentence is not the first sentence of the paragraph. Where is the topic sentence? What is the function of the first sentence?
2. What caused Joseph B. Friedman to invent a flexible straw? Was there more than one reason? Which sentences or parts of sentences give those reasons?
3. Which sentences or parts of sentences serve as *transitional devices*, which show the movement from one idea to another?
4. Most of the paragraph is written in the past tense. Which sentences are in the present tense? Why?

PARAGRAPH WRITING AND REVISING ASSIGNMENT

Write a paragraph analyzing the reasons behind a fairly important decision you recently made: to major in a particular field, to work part-time, to move, to buy a car, and so on. Assume that you are writing for a general reading audience who will be interested in your topic because of the advice and insights you can share with them. Explore your ideas first by making a brainstorming list of the reasons and then ranking them from the strongest to the weakest. (You may choose to include only the strongest reasons.) When you write your topic sentence, introduce or summarize the reasons for making the decision: "I decided to major in accounting for several reasons" or "I decided to major in accounting because of my interest in business and because of the great job opportunities it will offer me." Later drafts of the paragraph should explain those reasons specifically and clearly, with explicit transitions between ideas.

After waiting awhile, revise the paragraph, seeing if your cause-effect relationships are logical and clearly explained. As you edit the paragraph, pay special attention to all of the following matters:

1. complete sentences and clauses;
2. correct use of coordination to join sentences;
3. correct use of subordination to join sentences;
4. correct past-tense and past-participle forms;
5. noun-plural forms and correct subject-verb agreement (especially with *was* and *were* but also with any present-tense sentences);
6. correctly spelled words.

As always, hand in a clean, proofread copy.

SUPPLEMENTARY WRITING AND REVISING ASSIGNMENT

Choose another important event in your life, one for which the causes were complex and deep: for example, ending a long friendship (or marriage), having a child, changing careers, or giving up smoking.

Assume that your audience is a group of people who know you now but didn't know you at the time of the event. Write the paper so that these people can understand you better. If, however, you prefer not to write about yourself, then write about an event in the life of someone you know well.

Analyze the reasons behind that change or decision, perhaps by making a brainstorming list of the reasons and then ranking them from strongest to weakest, as described in "Paragraph Writing and Revising Assignment." Think about and explore various incidents that illustrate each reason. (Free writing may be useful here.)

Take the paper through several drafts. Later versions should devote a separate paragraph to each reason so that you can explain and illustrate each one fully. Be sure to criticize and edit the paper according to the guidelines mentioned in the "Paragraph Writing and Revising Assignment."

Here is an example of a full theme that discusses the causes of a terrible defeat in battle.

The Mystery of Custer's Last Stand

Probably no single battle in U.S. history has generated more controversy than the Battle of Little Bighorn River. On June 25, 1876, General George Armstrong Custer made his famous last stand. Three thousand warriors of the Great Sioux Nation, led by their chief Sitting Bull, killed Custer and every one of his seven hundred soldiers in the Seventh Cavalry. No one will ever know why Custer ordered his troops into such a one-sided fight in which they had no chance for survival. No one will ever know why he didn't retreat once the battle had begun. The answers can't be known because no one from Custer's side lived to tell the story. However, some bits of information about the battle suggest four reasons.

First, Custer ignored the orders of his commanding officer. He was supposed to bring his troops to the valley of the Little Bighorn River and wait there until another company of troops, together with additional and better arms, could join him. Custer decided to attack without them. He rode his troops right into the valley, traveling by night and well past dawn, and his men and horses were exhausted.

Second, Custer apparently ignored the advice of his own Indian scouts. Two men, Mitch Bouyer and Bloody Knife, warned him that there were too many Sioux warriors at the campsite to be captured with just 700 men. Custer probably thought that his Seventh Cavalry could whip any Indian party and dismissed their warnings.

Third, Custer probably misinterpreted the movements of the Indians. He divided his troops into three groups, who were to attack the campsite from different sides. After the first group, led by Major Marcus Reno, charged the village, a messenger informed Custer that the number of warriors they were fighting was indeed much larger than they had expected. Apparently, Custer assumed that, large in number or not, the Sioux were fleeing, so he and his men rushed to the far end of the campsite to cut off the escape. He rode hard and fast, further wearing down his men and their horses.

Fourth, when the three groups of Custer's men separated, they probably soon lost communication with each other. Major Reno attacked the campsite, expecting Custer to follow him from the rear. However,

Custer himself was trapped on the far end of the camp and couldn't come to Reno's aid. Reno finally retreated to a wooded spot near the village, where he was forced to make a stand. His Indian opponents not only outnumbered him, but they had better weapons. By the time the third group of the Seventh Cavalry could arrive, Reno's men were dead, and this last group was trapped as well. In the meantime Custer and the men he led were being slaughtered.

To this day the name Custer has become synonymous with headstrong behavior and stupidity. Although no one knows exactly why Custer and his men lost their lives, that headstrong behavior and that stupidity are likely reasons.

Discussion Questions

1. Why doesn't this theme give definite reasons for Custer's defeat and the death of his soldiers?
2. How many reasons does the theme suggest? What in the organization of the theme makes these reasons easy to locate?
3. What is the function of the first paragraph of the theme? What is the function of the last paragraph?
4. Look carefully at each paragraph for words and phrases that show a lack of certainty. Which words and phrases do you find? Where do you find them?
5. When does the composition depart from past-tense explanation? Why?

CHAPTER 7

Using Modifiers (Descriptive Words, Phrases, and Clauses)

One of the important matters to consider as you revise is the placement of *modifiers*—words, phrases, or clauses that describe a variety of ideas in sentences. Because incorrectly placed modifiers can confuse readers, this chapter offers you advice in placing them correctly. The chapter begins with an explanation of the types of modifiers, including single words, phrases, and dependent clauses. Then it examines the placement of modifiers so you can avoid two common errors: *misplaced modifiers* and *dangling modifiers*. Finally, you will practice yet another method of paragraph development: *definition*.

IDENTIFYING MODIFIERS

A *modifier is a word, phrase, or clause that describes something in a sentence and therefore modifies (that is, changes) the meaning of what it describes.* Modifiers can describe almost anything in a sentence. If they describe *nouns,* they function as *adjectives;* if they describe *verbs or words formed from verbs such as -ing words or past participles,* they function as *adverbs.* Suppose, for example, that you want to describe the noun *book.* You can place adjectives before the word.

> a *new* book
> a *lost* book
> an *interesting new* book

You can add *adjective phrases* after the word.

> a book *with a complicated plot*
> a book *causing a lot of controversy*
> a book *written by Steven King*
> a book *to read at the beach*
> a book, *The Revenge of the Dragonfly* (actually a noun phrase called an appositive)*

Or, as you might recall from Chapter 4, you can add *adjective (relative) clauses* after the word.

> a book *that I enjoyed*
> a book *which doesn't cost a lot*

You may also recall from Chapter 4 that adverbs generally describe *when, where,* or *why* an action occurred. They can also explain *how.* For example, if you want to describe the verb in the clause *I studied,* you can use single-word adverbs.

> I studied *yesterday.*
> I studied *diligently.*
> I studied *diligently yesterday.*
> *Yesterday* I studied *diligently.*

You can also use adverb phrases.

> I studied *for an hour.*
> I studied *lying on the couch.*
> *Bored with biology,* I studied my math instead.
> I studied *to pass my math test.*

Or you can use adverb clauses.

> I studied *because I wanted to pass my math test.*
> I studied *when I finished dinner.*

In short, modifiers can be placed *before or after* the words they describe, and they can be single words, phrases, or clauses. Examine the modifiers in the previous examples and you will notice the similarity between adjective and adverb phrases. In both cases many of the phrases can begin with a preposition (*with* a complicated plot, *for* an hour), an *-ing* word (*causing* a lot of controversy, *lying* on the couch), a past participle (*written* by Steven King, *Bored* with biology), or an infinitive (*to read* at the beach, *to pass* my math test). Of course adjective clauses begin with such words as *that, which,* or *who,* and adverb clauses begin with such words as *when, if,* and *because.*

*See Chapter 11 for more on appositives and how to punctuate them.

> **In Summary:**   A modifying phrase can begin with
>
> 1. *a preposition*, such as *over, from, with, by, after,* or *in;*
> 2. *an -ing word*, such as *sitting, doing,* or *building;*
> 3. *a past participle*, such as *known, torn,* or *ripped;*
> 4. *an infinitive*, such as *to know, to have,* or *to buy;* or
> 5. *a noun*, such as in these examples: my friend *John* and the movie *Teenage Vampires.*
>
> A modifying clause can begin with
>
> 1. *who, that, which, whom,* or *whose* for *adjectives;* or
> 2. *because, while, as, if, unless, although, after,* and so on for *adverbs.*

1 WARM-UP

Each sentence below contains one or two adjective phrases or clauses. Underline the modifier and draw an arrow to the noun it describes.

1. "Yankee Doodle" is an irreverent Revolutionary War song that inspired General Washington's troops.

2. However, its composer was a British army surgeon who intended to ridicule the colonials during the French and Indian War.

3. Dr. Richard Shuckburgh, who wrote the first version of "Yankee Doodle," was camped with some British and American troops during the French and Indian War.

4. The colonials, dressed in an assortment of nonmilitary garments, were a motley group compared to the uniformed British troops.

5. Shuckburgh wrote a song ridiculing the colonials' lack of style and sophistication.

6. His lyrics, full of army-camp humor, were also quite bawdy.

7. Infuriated by the insult, the colonials eventually adopted "Yankee Doodle" and changed the words so that it became their own defiant rebel song.

8. Edward Bangs, who was a Harvard student, wrote a version for the army to sing after George Washington took command on July 3, 1775.

2 WARM-UP

Each sentence below contains one or two adverb phrases or clauses. Underline the modifier and draw an arrow to the verb it describes. (Remember that adverbs generally answer the questions *when, where, why,* or *how.*)

1. Noah Webster had seen the need for an American dictionary long before he began work on one.

2. Although the Americans were independent of the British, English language dictionaries ignored American words and used English spellings and pronunciations almost exclusively.

3. Convinced that a national language would help unify the country, the multitalented and intensely patriotic Webster began a rigorous schedule of research in 1803.

4. After three years of effort Webster published *A Compendious Dictionary of the American Language*.

5. Webster then plunged into the preparation of a much longer dictonary, which consumed his energies for the next two decades.

6. Finally, in November 1828 the two-volume, seventy-thousand-word *American Dictionary of the English Language* came off the press.

7. George and Charles Merriam of Springfield, Massachusetts, acquired the rights to Webster's dictionary upon his death in 1843.

8. The Merriam brothers published their own dictionaries to update and continue Webster's work.

9. They brought out the first *Merriam-Webster Unabridged Dictionary* in 1847 and revised it in 1964.

10. In 1890 they published the *First International Dictionary* and in 1898 the *First Collegiate Dictionary*.

PLACING MODIFIERS CORRECTLY

Many modifiers seem to describe more than one item in a clause. Therefore, to avoid confusion, you should place the modifier close to the word it describes, usually—but not always—*directly before or after that word*. For example, notice how the following sentences change when you move the word *only*.

I *only* want to give Harry Schnozzle a nose job.
Only I want to give Harry Schnozzle a nose job.
I want *only* to give Harry Schnozzle a nose job.
I want to give *only* Harry Schnozzle a nose job.
I want to give Harry Schnozzle *only* a nose job.

You can also move longer modifiers around to change the meanings of certain sentences. However, unless you are careful how you place them, the sentences may not say what you want them to say.

poor: Yesterday I shot an elephant in my pajamas. (What was it doing in your pajamas?)
better: *In my pajamas yesterday*, I shot an elephant.

poor: I baked a cake for my friends *covered with chocolate frosting.*
(What did you do for your friends who were covered with
vanilla frosting?)

better: I baked my friends a cake *covered with chocolate frosting.*

poor: We discussed why the whales are endangered *in school today.*
(Was somebody harpooning whales in school today?)

better: *In school today* we discussed why whales are endangered.

Here is another way to check for a correctly placed modifying phrase.
Ask yourself: Would the word nearest the phrase be included if the phrase
were made into a dependent clause? Note these examples.

correct placement
(When **I** was) in my pajamas yesterday, **I**. . . .

incorrect placement
Yesterday, I shot an **elephant** (when **the elephant** was) in my pajamas.

In Summary: To correct misplaced phrases and clauses,

1. as you proofread your paper, each time you see a modifier,
   ask yourself: Does this clearly describe what I want it to
   describe?
2. if not, move it to another place in the sentence where its
   meaning is clear;
3. or, if that won't work, rewrite the whole sentence so that its
   meaning is clear.

---

3 EDITING

Each of the following sentences contains a misplaced modifying phrase or
clause. Underline the problem phrase and then draw an arrow to the spot
where it belongs.

1. The second president of the United States, <u>after living to be ninety,</u>
   John Adams, died in his Braintree, Massachusetts, home.

2. This lifelong hypochondriac lived longer than any other president,
   always fearing an early death.

3. Adams complained to everyone at the age of thirty-five that his health
   was feeble.

4. During the eighty-ninth year of his life, his son John Quincy Adams's
   inauguration as our sixth president gave John Adams great pleasure.

5. Ironically, John Adams died on the fiftieth anniversary of the signing of
   the Declaration of Independence, which he helped write at six o'clock in
   the evening.

6. Earlier that same day, July 4, 1826, the other author of the Declaration
   of Independence, Thomas Jefferson, unknown to Adams, had died.

4 EDITING   Rewrite each of the following sentences, placing the modifying phrase or clause where it fits most logically.

1. *(modifier)* a man unknown to most Americans

   (sentence) Not George Washington, but John Hanson was the real first president of the United States.

   Not George Washington, but John Hanson, a man unknown to most Americans, was the real first president of the United States.

   _____

2. *(modifier)* for the first time

   (sentence) In 1781, while Washington was fighting the last battles of the Revolution, representatives from the thirteen American colonies met in the Continental Congress.

   _____

   _____

   _____

3. *(modifier)* after the debate

   (sentence) They wrote the Articles of Confederation, our first constitution.

   _____

   _____

   _____

4. *(modifier)* from Maryland

   (sentence) In November 1781 John Hanson was elected "President of the United States in Congress Assembled."

   _____

   _____

   _____

5. *(modifier)* although having virtually no other duties

   (sentence) Hanson chaired the meetings of Congress.

   _____

   _____

   _____

6. *(modifier)* because of ill health

   (sentence) He served as president for one year, and then he resigned.

   _____

   _____

   _____

7. *(modifier)* by the thirteen states

   (sentence) Six men followed him as president before the new constitution was approved and Washington became president.

   _____

   _____

   _____

8. *(modifier)* because it intended to create more recognition for him

   (sentence) In 1973 Maryland made April 14 of each year John Hanson Day.

   _____

   _____

   _____

Dangling Modifiers

Sometimes a modifier describes nothing at all in a sentence. It dangles unattached because the word it should describe is not in the sentence.

Walking down the street on a windy day, my hat blew off. (*Who* was walking down the street? It wasn't your hat—which in this sentence is the only thing the phrase could describe.)

Turning the rock over, its underside was wet and dark. (*Who* turned the rock over? Its underside couldn't have done it to itself, unless the rock had magical powers.)

To score high on the quiz, studying is important. (*Studying* won't score high on the quiz, yet the sentence doesn't mention any person.)

You cannot eliminate a dangling modifier merely by moving it around in a sentence since the phrase describes nothing in the sentence. Instead, you must rewrite the sentence and add the word the modifier describes.

As I was walking down the street on a windy day, my hat blew off.

Turning the rock over, Professor Dirtdigger discovered that its underside was wet and dark.

To score high on the quiz, you must study.

In Summary: To eliminate dangling modifiers,

1. as you proofread your paper, each time you see a modifier, ask yourself: Does this clearly describe what I want it to?
2. if the word it should describe is not included in the sentence, rewrite the sentence to include the word and place the descriptive phrase where its meaning is clear;
3. or, if necessary, rewrite the sentence and the modifier to clarify the meaning of both.

5 EDITING

Each of the following sentences contains a dangling modifier. Underline the problem phrase and then rewrite the sentence to eliminate the problem. If necessary, you may change a phrase to a dependent clause.

1. Upon graduation from Harvard University at the age of nineteen, a job of teaching at a school became available to John Adams. After John Adams had graduated from Harvard University at the age of nineteen, a job of teaching at a school became available to him.

2. After a few years of teaching, his parents hoped that he would enter the ministry. _____

_____

_____

3. However, unhappy with both teaching and the Massachusetts clergy, the law was his chosen profession. _____

_____

_____

4. Admiring his natural intelligence and honest character, his law practice became extremely successful. _____

_____

_____

5. Defending the British soldiers who had fired on some Massachusetts citizens in the Boston Massacre, his reputation and political future were risked. _____

_____

_____

_____

6. After proving that the British soldiers had fired in self-defense, the people of Boston were impressed with Adams's courage and integrity.

_____

_____

_____

6 WRITING

Using the words provided, write two sentences that imitate the pattern of each sentence below.

1. Standing by the edge of the sea, Gwendoline looked dreamily at the horizon.

(sitting) _____

_____

(lying) _____

_____

2. To succeed in the business world, a person must be bright, hardworking, and honest.

(to earn) _____

_____

(to learn) _____

_____

3. Warned of the approaching storm, the residents of the town took shelter.

(informed) _____

_____

(shocked) _____

_____

4. With his hand close to his gun, Black Barth glared at the sheriff.

(belt) _____

_____

(teeth) _____

_____

5. Elroy smiled as he talked, twirling his mustache suavely.

(bowing) _____

_____

(scratching) _____

_____

7 WRITING

Complete each of the following sentences with a modifying phrase or clause.

1. Most people attend college _to prepare themselves for careers._

_____

2. Many college graduates with degrees in business find jobs _____

_____

3. _____ a college degree is more important than ever.

4. However, many college students have to borrow money _____

_____

5. Frequently, too, college students hold down part-time or even full-time jobs _____

_____

_____

6. _____ the pressures on college students are intense.

8 WRITING   Go to a public place: the cafeteria, the student lounge, or the library in school; or a park, bus stop, or building away from school. Without calling attention to yourself, observe a stranger for a few moments and make notes about the person's appearance, clothing, and behavior. Later, when you are alone, write a paragraph summarizing what you saw.

9 EDITING   The following passage contains misplaced or dangling modifiers. Write your corrections on the lines after each sentence that should be changed. Some sentences need no changes.

Facts about the Dollar

1. Working for them, sometimes hoping for them, dollar bills are important to everyone. _Working for them, sometimes hoping for them, everyone thinks dollar bills are important._

2. However, have you ever taken a close look at a dollar bill? _____

3. Examining it carefully, it is a piece of paper which is 2-5/8 by 6-1/8 inches, with a thickness that is .0048 inches. _____

4. No one knows what is in the paper except the government. _____

5. In an inch you can stack 233 dollar bills. _____

6. The government spends $8.02 to print one thousand bills. _____

7. The average life span is eighteen months of a dollar bill. _____

8. In circulation at all times, you'll find over two billion bills. _____

9. Because their value changed so quickly during the colonial period, when the founders of our country formed the government, they didn't trust paper bills.

10. However, during the Civil War, Congress decided to print the first paper money, called *greenbacks* or *legal tender*. _____

11. The current dollar is the Federal Reserve Note, issued by the twelve Federal Reserve banks spread across the country which is printed by the U.S. government. _____

_____

_____

12. Unlike dollars backed by hard currency, you cannot exchange today's dollar bills for gold or silver. _____

_____

_____

SOME ADDITIONAL HELP IN CORRECTLY PLACING MODIFIERS

Look for Prepositions   Most misplaced or dangling modifiers are phrases, not clauses, so the first step is to recognize them. Prepositional phrases are the most common misplaced modifiers. They consist of two parts.

1. a preposition
2. a noun or an object-pronoun*

Prepositions are little words such as *in, on, off, by, with, between,* and *of.* (A list of the most important prepositions follows shortly.) Here are some examples of prepositional phrases.

by the refrigerator	from me
in the attic	to them
from my neighborhood	between you and me
with Judy	without us
like a bird	on a windy day

A phrase beginning with a preposition can function *only* as a descriptive phrase. It has no other use. When you see a prepositional phrase in a sentence, you know the phrase must describe something.

the man *with the big stomach* (describes *man*)

the government *of the people* (describes the type of *government*)

With great effort, he lifted the heavy carton. (describes how he *lifted* the carton)

He went *to Hawaii.* (describes where he *went*)

She left *after work.* (describes when she *left*)

The most important prepositions. The following lists include most of the prepositions you are likely to use.

*The noun or pronoun after a preposition is always an object word.

A. One-word prepositions

about	by	out(side)
above	concerning	over
across	despite	regarding
after	down	since
against	during	through(out)
along(side)	except	till
among	for	to
around	from	toward
at	in	under(neath)
before	inside	until
behind	into	up
below	like	upon
beneath	near	with
beside	of	within
between	on	without
beyond	onto	

B. Two-or-more-word prepositions*

as for	except for	in view of
as to	for the sake of	next to
aside from	in addition to	on account of
because of	in behalf of	regardless of
by means of	in case of	with regard to
by way of	in favor of	with respect to
contrary to	in regard to	with the exception of
due to	in spite of	

10 WARM-UP

Circle the prepositional phrases in the following sentences. Then draw a line from each prepositional phrase to the word it describes.

1. Since 1840 no president elected in a year ending in zero has lived out his full term of office. This coincidence is called the *zero factor*.

2. In 1840 William Henry Harrison was elected president, but within a month he caught pneumonia and died.

3. An Illinois man named Abraham Lincoln was the winner of the 1860 election, and he was reelected in 1864.

4. While Lincoln was watching a play in Washington, an actor named John Wilkes Booth crept up behind him and shot him in the head.

5. Slightly more than six months after his election in 1880, President James A. Garfield was assassinated by Charles J. Guiteau, who wanted to be an ambassador to Paris.

6. A man named Leon Czolgosz shot and killed president McKinley, the winner of the election of 1900.

*This list could be much longer. These are only samples.

7. Warren G. Harding, who won the election of 1920, died suddenly on a tour of the West. To this day many people think that Harding died from poisoning.

8. Franklin D. Roosevelt was also elected in a year ending in zero, although he was running for his third term in office.

9. On April 12, 1945, Roosevelt collapsed and died in his summer home.

10. Before the election of 1960, candidates were asked how they felt about the zero factor.

11. John F. Kennedy wrote that if the candidates worried about it, the landlord of the White House "would be left with a 'For Rent' sign hanging on the gate-house door."

12. The assassination of President Kennedy occurred three years later on November 22, 1963.

Look for *-ing* Words

Words that end in *-ing* can be verbs only when you combine them with some form of *be: am, is, are, was,* or *were.* (See Chapter 2.) Otherwise *-ing* words usually function as adjectives.*

a *smiling* man
a *moving* object
a *hanging* pot

They frequently begin modifying phrases.

a man *smiling at the crowd*
an object *moving as fast as a car*
a pot *hanging in the front window*

Therefore look at your sentences and spot all the *-ing* words that are not verbs. Then notice where you have placed the *-ing* words. They should come *directly before* or *directly after* the words they describe. If they don't, they may be misplaced or dangling.

11 EDITING

Each of the following groups of sentences contains one sentence with a misplaced or dangling *-ing* phrase. Underline the problem phrase. Then rewrite the sentence that contains the problem.

1. In 1773 Benjamin Franklin claimed that he had performed the first successful electrocution. <u>Writing to friends in France</u>, his letter

---

*Sometimes, however, an *-ing* word or the phrase it begins can function as a noun (that is, it will be a subject or an object in a sentence). Notice that the subject of the following sentence is the word *jogging.*

Jogging is good exercise.

Here are some more examples of *-ing* words or phrases used as nouns.

I like *walking to work each morning.* (object)
Swimming and hiking long distances will build up your endurance. (subject)

described how he had created an electrical current that killed several chickens and a ten-pound turkey. Writing to friends in France, he described how he had created an electrical current that killed several chickens and a ten-pound turkey.

2. By dropping the *u*'s, Noah Webster published the *American Spelling Book* (1783), which changed the spelling of words like *colour* and *labour*.

_____

_____

_____

3. Until 1785 the custom of *bundling* was popular in New England. It allowed engaged couples to share the same bed, if wearing clothes and separated by a bundling board. _____

_____

_____

_____

4. For fifty years John Chapman walked through the Ohio Valley and met many people giving out apple seeds and Bibles. He became known as Johnny Appleseed. _____

_____

_____

_____

5. When Thomas Jefferson became president, he greeted guests wearing plain working clothes. He wore an old brown coat, corduroy pants, and old slippers. _____

_____

_____

_____

_____

Look for Past Participles and Infinitives

Past participles (*gone, done, seen,* or *asked*) can begin modifying phrases. So can infinitives (*to go, to have,* or *to see*). Here are examples of each; notice that they can be placed before or after the words they describe.

Past Participles

A criminal *known through the country* escaped from jail.

Tired after a hard day's work, the man collapsed in his easy chair.

Infinitives

The person *to see* is Harry Stanford.

To open the can, you must lift the tab on top.

12 WARM-UP

Underline each past participle or infinitive in the following sentences.

1. <u>Tired</u> after many years of service to his country, President George Washington announced his decision <u>to retire</u> in 1796.

2. Soon afterwards the Federalist party candidate, John Adams, ran for president against the man nominated by the Republican party, Thomas Jefferson.

3. Adams was a man known to everyone because of his long and distinguished career, so he was the favorite to win the election.

4. However, complicated by divisions in the Federalist party and by an oddity in the election laws, the contest had a surprising outcome.

5. At that time, according to the Constitution, the person to receive the highest number of electoral votes became president; the person to receive the second highest number of votes became vice-president.

6. In a scheme to elect a man he could control more easily than Adams, Alexander Hamilton persuaded some Federalist electors to drop Adams's name from their ballots and to vote for the Federalist vice-presidential candidate, Thomas Pinckney.

7. Informed of the plot, Adams's supporters dropped Pinckney's name from their ballots in retaliation.

8. As a result Adams received seventy-one electoral votes, enough to win the presidency, but his opponent, Thomas Jefferson, received sixty-eight electoral votes, enough to win the vice-presidency.

9. After that election the Constitution was amended to avoid the problem of a president and a vice-president coming from different political parties.

13 WRITING

Write a complete sentence using each of the following past-participle or infinitive phrases.

1. seen from afar _Seen from afar, the city lights are beautiful._

   _____

2. to finish on time _____

   _____

3. exhausted from the workout _____

   _____

4. to complete college in four years _____

   _____

5. talked about most often by college students _____

   _____

14 EDITING   The following passage contains misplaced or dangling modifiers. Write your corrections on the lines after each sentence that should be changed. Some sentences need no changes. It may help to underline the problem phrases first.

The Real Dr. Jekyll and Mr. Hyde

1. A real man named William Brodie lived in Edinburgh, Scotland, between 1741 and 1788, who became the inspiration for the fictional Dr. Jekyll and Mr. Hyde. A real man named William Brodie, who became the inspiration for the fictional Dr. Jekyll and Mr. Hyde, lived in Edinburgh, Scotland, between 1741 and 1788.

2. Robert Louis Stevenson wrote *The Strange Case of Dr. Jekyll and Mr Hyde,* using Brodie as his model in a three-day period in 1885. _____

3. Brodie worked for his father in a very successful business, and, after his father's death, he inherited a large estate. _____

4. Later he became a town councilman, benefiting from his position to win city contracts for his business. _____

5. However, at night Brodie was the opposite of a respectable citizen with a few beers in his belly. _____

6. He would keep company with thieves and gamblers, and he supported two mistresses and their children. _____

7. As a result of gambling losses and the expenses involved in running three households, he had to search for other ways to get money. _____

8. Hanging inside their doors, Brodie's shopkeeper friends usually left their keys. _____

9. Brodie would make impressions of these keys, using a small wad of putty concealed in his hand. _____

_____

_____

10. Shortly afterwards he would burglarize the shops, and several times he was almost caught by the police although wearing a mask. _____

_____

_____

11. In July 1786, tired of small pickings, the idea of committing bigger robberies occurred to him. _____

_____

_____

12. He and his gang of three convicts looted several stores. _____

_____

_____

13. After one of his accomplices confessed to police hoping to escape from them, Brodie left the city. _____

_____

_____

14. Hiding in a cupboard in Amsterdam, the police found him and brought him back to Scotland for trial. _____

_____

_____

DEFINITION

A *definition* is an *explanation of a word's meaning*. The most common source of definitions is the dictionary, which usually defines words through synonyms and short explanations. However, another good way to define a word is to *illustrate* what it means to you. You can give an example of how to use the word or tell a story that reveals its significance.

Consider the word *mother*. The dictionary defines the word in biological terms, but most of us can provide our own personal, and much more human, definitions by describing the mother we knew as we were growing up. For some of us she could be a warm, loving woman whose natural domain was the kitchen and the PTA meeting. She always had cookies and milk on the table when we and our friends came home from school or play. For others among us she could be the superefficient mom—no less warm and loving—who rose early, got us dressed and fed, and packed us off to school before she left for her full-time job. She wasn't home to greet us after school, but she nonetheless had dinner on the table soon after she returned from work. We could draw either portrait through stories of her typical activities and through a few examples of what she did on special occasions.

Thus a good paragraph or theme of definition is both a carefully worded statement of meaning and a vivid narration that reveals meaning. It requires careful word choice, careful description, and careful placement of modifiers. Here is an example of a paragraph of definition.

As the search for alternative forms of energy continues, scientists are paying much more attention to *geothermal energy,* which is inexhaustible and potentially cheap. What, exactly, is geothermal energy? It is energy that comes from the natural heat of Mother Earth, which as its center, or core, reaches a temperature of perhaps 7200 degrees Fahrenheit! This heat travels toward the surface of the planet but cools down along the way. On the surface the energy appears in hot springs, geysers, or steam vents, which are usually located in areas of past volcanic activity. People have been harnessing this natural energy for thousands of years. For example, the early Romans heated their bathing pools with the water from hot springs. Hot well water has been used since the 1890s to heat some buildings in Boise, Idaho. In fact natural steam from the fields near Pisa, Italy, has been driving an electrical generator since 1913. Today the Soviet Union, Hungary, Iceland, New Zealand, and the United States use geothermal energy as a power source. In northern California the Geysers energy field—the world's largest—produces enough energy to satisfy the power needs of a city of five hundred thousand people. This kind of energy has great potential, for as long as there is an Earth, there will be geothermal energy.

Discussion Questions

1. Which sentence—or part of a sentence—actually defines the term *geothermal energy?* Which sentences further explain the term?
2. What follows the explanation of the term?
3. The paragraph begins and ends with a discussion of the interest in geothermal energy today. Why doesn't the paragraph discuss this interest only in one spot—either at the beginning or at the end?

PARAGRAPH WRITING AND REVISING ASSIGNMENT

Choose a holiday—Christmas, Thanksgiving, Valentine's Day, or any other one you wish—and write a paragraph defining what the holiday means to you. Assume that you are writing for a general audience, most of whom are familiar with American and Christian (and a few Jewish) holidays. Therefore you need not explain the usual meaning of a holiday such as Thanksgiving or Easter, but you probably should explain the religious significance and rituals associated with a holiday such as Mohammed's birthday, the Oriental New Year, or Purim.

Begin the process by exploring your ideas through free writing or brainstorming. In later drafts include a topic sentence that defines or summarizes the meaning of the holiday. Develop that topic sentence either through a short explanation or a little story about a typical celebration in your household. If the holiday has more than one meaning for you, explore and illustrate each one.

After waiting awhile, do the final revision of the paragraph, making sure you have made your definition clear and have developed and illustrated it fully. In the editing stage pay special attention to all of the following matters:

1. complete sentences and clauses;
2. correct use of coordination to join sentences;
3. correct use of subordination to join sentences;
4. correct noun-plural forms and subject-verb agreement;
5. correct past-tense and past-participle forms;
6. correctly placed modifiers; and
7. correctly spelled words.

Hand in a clean, proofread copy of your work.

SUPPLEMENTARY WRITING AND REVISING ASSIGNMENT

Every family or group of friends uses a few of its own *pet words*—made-up words or ordinary words that have a special meaning for members of that family or group. Write a paper that defines one of these pet words so that your classmates will understand its meaning. Use a little story to define the word, either to show how it originated or to show how you use it in your family or group.

As an alternative to this assignment, you can define one of the technical or jargon words used on your job. Make the word clear to an audience of people completely unfamiliar with its meaning and provide an illustration (an example or a story) for the word.

Revise and edit the paper according to the criteria mentioned in the "Paragraph Writing and Revising Assignment."

Here is an example of a short theme that narrates a series of little stories which might explain the origin of the word it defines.

Sweet Speculations

Everyone with a sweet tooth can tell us what the word *sundae* means, and we all have vivid memories of our favorite sundaes, complete with whipped cream, nuts, cherries, and all. But where did the word come from originally? The explanation is still a mystery.

Because of its spelling, many people have tried to link the word to the day of the week. According to one story, when the laws of Virginia prevented the sale of soda drinks on Sundays, a clever merchant served the ice cream and syrup alone, and there it was! Then again, another tale has a certain George Hallaver of Two Rivers, Wisconsin, ordering a dish of ice cream with chocolate syrup on top. News of the innovative dish spread to nearby Manitowoc, where George Giffy began to sell it in his ice cream parlor as a Sunday treat. On the other hand, some people claim that the students of Northwestern University named the dish after their baseball coach, Billy Sunday.

However, even if the word did come from *Sunday*, none of these stories can explain why a 1904 newspaper spelled it *Sundi* and why, as late as 1929, dictionaries listed *sondhi* as another version of the word, which they also called *college ice*. No one can explain where the *-dae* ending came from, either.

In short we don't know the true origin of the word. However, we all personally know the origin of the pleasure it brings us. As long as all those wonderful calories stimulate our taste buds, we won't worry too much about where the word came from. We'll just eat and enjoy—and worry about our waistlines.

Discussion Questions

1. Does the first paragraph provide a conventional definition of the word *sundae?* What is the function of the first sentence in the paragraph?
2. How many different explanations does the second paragraph offer for the origin of the name *sundae?* What words or phrases signal the beginning of each explanation?
3. How many problems with these explanations does the third paragraph discuss? What words help to identify each problem?

CHAPTER

8

Using Pronouns

The word *pronoun* literally means "for a noun," and pronouns are in fact substitutes for nouns. Like nouns, pronouns can function in many different *cases*—grammatical relationships to the other words in a sentence. Pronouns can function as subjects, objects, or possessive words. This chapter explains the rules for using *subject* and *object pronouns*, *reflexive pronouns*, and *pronouns in comparisons*. It will show you the rules by which pronouns refer to their *antecedents* (the words that precede pronouns): with *multiple antecedents*, *missing antecedents*, and *indefinite pronouns*, as well as *collective nouns* as antecedents. And it will discuss the rules for using the demonstrative words *this*, *that*, *these*, and *those*. Finally, this chapter will explore one more method of paragraph development: *classification*.

FOLLOWING THE RULES FOR PRONOUN USE

Subject and Object Pronouns

For review, here are the subject-case and object-case pronouns.

	Subject	*Object*
1st person		
singular	I ⟶	me
plural	we ⟶	us
2nd person		
singular	you ⟶	you
plural	you ⟶	you
3rd person		
singular	he ⟶	him
	she ⟶	her
	it ⟶	it
plural	they ⟶	them

In general you use subject-case pronouns only as the subjects of sentences.* However, you use object-case pronouns in two ways. *After action verbs (or after -ing words or infinitives formed from action verbs):*

after verbs	Sylvio saw *us*.
	Please help *me*.
	Did Tom give *her* the message?
after -ing words	After delaying *it* for hours, Ira finally began fixing *them*.
	Ann looked at the worm without touching *it*.
after infinitives	To understand *them*, you will have to ask *him*.
	Most people want to meet *her*.

After prepositions:

> one of *them*
> to *us*
> between *you* and *me*
> with *them*
> from *us* to *you*

When a sentence has only *one* subject or object, using the correct pronoun is no problem. For example, these sentences probably sound silly to you because they use the wrong pronoun case.

Him wants a job.

Nancy saw *I* yesterday.

Us are here.†

However, when a sentence contains more than one subject or object, using the right pronoun can be tricky. The following sentences, which contain pronoun-case errors, may sound correct to you.

Me and him have been friends for years.

Why don't you join *Mary and I* for dinner tonight?

You and me need to discuss the plans.

Supply the correct pronoun for these sentences.

_____ and _____ have been friends for years.

Why don't you join Mary and _____ for dinner tonight?

You and _____ need to discuss the plans.

You should have written *He* and *I, me,* and *I*. The simplest way to determine which pronoun case to use in a sentence with more than one subject or object is *to remove all but one* subject or object for a moment.

---

*You can also use subject-case pronouns after linking verbs. (See Chapter 2.) That is why in formal English you should say or write, "It is *I*," not "It is *me*."

†Some people do confuse *they* (subject) with *them* (object).

incorrect: *Them* are here.
correct: *They* are here.

Make sure the difference is clear to you.

incorrect: *Me* . . . have been friends for years.
correct: *I* . . . have been friends for years.
incorrect: Why don't you join . . . *I* for dinner tonight?
correct: Why don't you join . . *me* for dinner tonight?

Choosing the proper pronoun case can be confusing when *we* or *us* appears before a noun.

Before the lake became polluted, *us kids* always swam in it.

For *we folks*, nothing is too good.

To find out if you have used the proper pronoun case, temporarily remove the noun.

incorrect: Before the lake became polluted, *us* . . . always swam in it.
correct: Before the lake became polluted, *we* . . . always swam in it.
incorrect: For *we* . . ., nothing is too good.
correct: For *us* . . ., nothing is too good.

In Summary: To choose the proper pronoun case in a sentence with two or more subjects or objects,

1. temporarily remove all but one subject or object from the sentence;
2. if the remaining pronoun is not the proper case, change it.

To choose the proper pronoun case when *we* or *us* appears before the noun,

1. temporarily remove the noun from the sentence;
2. if the remaining pronoun is not the proper case, change it.

---

1 WARM-UP

Some—but not all—of the following sentences use improper pronoun cases. Above each incorrect pronoun form, write the proper one. If a sentence contains no errors, make no changes.

1. We have always said that for ∧ she and ∧ I, nothing is too good.
   (her above "she"; me above "I")

2. Us smokers would rather fight than switch.

3. We want to have a small party with just our friends and us.

4. Can you keep a secret between you and I?

5. Only four other students and him scored above ninety on the test.

6. Our pet boa constrictor is fond of Linda and I.

7. It loves to hug us humans.

8. Me and him shared a pizza, a banana, and an Alka-Seltzer.

9. Just send your money orders to her and me, but make them out to "cash."

10. Some people feel that them are the best kind.

Reflexive Pronouns   Sometimes the same person or thing is both the subject and the object in a sentence.

> *I* saw *myself* in the mirror.
> *He* bought *himself* a present.
> *The new oven* cleans *itself.*

The object pronouns in these sentences are special kinds, called *reflexive pronouns*, because they reflect back to their subjects like mirrors. Here is a full list of reflexive pronouns.

	Singular	*Plural*
1st person	myself	ourselves
2nd person	yourself	yourselves
3rd person	himself (*not* hisself)	themselves (*not* theirselves)
	herself	
	itself	

Notice that the singular pronouns end in *-self*, while the plural pronouns end in *-selves*.

A reflexive pronoun can be only an *object* in a sentence, but people sometimes confuse *myself* with the subject pronoun *I*, especially when a sentence contains more than one subject.

> *incorrect:*   *John and myself* are grateful for your help.
> *correct:*   *John and I* are grateful for your help.
> *incorrect:*   *Carlos, Bill, and myself* have much in common.
> *correct:*   *Carlos, Bill, and I* have much in common.

Again, the best way to determine the correct case is to remove the other subjects or objects temporarily (and change the verb, if necessary, to agree).

> *incorrect:*   . . . *myself* am grateful for your help.
> *correct:*   . . . *I* am grateful.
> *incorrect:*   . . . *myself* have much in common.
> *correct:*   . . . *I* have much in common.

In Summary: When you use reflexive pronouns,

1. end singular pronouns in *-self*; end plural pronouns in *-selves* (for example: *yourself* = singular, *yourselves* = plural);
2. use *himself*, not *hisself*, and use *themselves*, not *theirselves*;
3. never use reflexive pronouns as subjects; use them only as objects. To test for the correct case with multiple subjects or objects, remove the other subjects or objects, leaving only the reflexive pronoun. Replace it with a subject pronoun if it is incorrect.

2 WARM-UP   Write the correct pronoun in each of the following sentences.

1. I like to make repairs by _____myself_____.

2. By reading the Spanish text on his own, Mr. Harper has taught _____ Spanish.

3. You and John will have to make dinner for _____ tonight.

4. We think of _____ as thrifty, not cheap.

5. Angela, you should do _____ a favor.

6. My mother, my father, my sister, and _____ have our own apartment.

7. The Smiths like to go out on weekends by _____ .

8. All of you should make _____ at home.

Proper Pronoun Case in Comparisons*

Read the following comparisons.

Bob is a better tennis player *than I am.*
Cory runs as fast *as we do.*

Notice in these examples that a simple clause—a subject pronoun and a verb—comes after the words *than* or *as.*

. . . than *I am.*
. . . as *we do.*

You can often drop the verb from these simple clauses, but even so, you should use the subject pronouns, as if the verb still were there.

Bob is a better tennis player than *I* (am).
Cory runs as fast as *we* (do.)

Once in a while you write a sentence that should take an object pronoun after *than* or *as*—when the words you compare are objects.

Mother likes *him* as well as (she likes) *me.*
They saw *him* more often than (they saw) *us.*

Notice how these sentences differ in meaning from those with subject, pronouns after *than* or *as.*

Mother likes him as well as *I (do).*
They saw him more often than *we (did).*

*For more practice with comparisons, see Chapter 10.

The simplest way to determine the correct pronoun form after *than* or *as* is temporarily to insert the words you have dropped from the short clause; the pronoun form will then be obvious. However, in many sentences it is probably best to leave in the inserted words and avoid confusion.

Mother likes him as well as *she likes* me.

In Summary: To determine the proper pronoun case after *than* or *as* in a comparison,

1. insert the omitted words in the clause after *than* or *as*: He looks better than *her* = He looks better than *she does* (change *her* to *she*).
   Rudi knows them as well as *us* = Rudi knows them as well as *he knows us* (*us* is correct).
2. then, remove the words you inserted, or, to avoid possible confusion, leave them in.

---

3 WARM-UP

Circle the proper pronoun in parentheses.

1. They walked as quickly as (we/us).
2. You are probably smarter than (I/me).
3. The package was for us rather than (they/them).
4. Tony is taller than (she/her).
5. We said more to her than to (he/him).

4 WRITING

Write a sentence making a comparison based on the information in each of the following sentences.

1. Guy is 200 pounds, but she is 112 pounds.
   Guy is heavier than she (is).

2. Gloria is very pretty. Her mother is also very pretty.

3. Sam works hard. We don't work too hard.

4. Mr. Williams has three part-time jobs. She has only one job.

5. The counselor talks to you quite often. She hardly ever talks to me.

6. Albert ate seventeen hamburgers for lunch. I ate two.

PROBLEMS WITH ANTECEDENTS

The antecedent of a pronoun is the word or words that the pronoun *refers to* or *replaces.** Here are some examples.

Antecedent	*Pronoun*
the team	it
a person	he/she; him/her
John and I	we
John and me	us
John and you	you
John and she	they
John and her	them

Multiple or Missing Antecedents

A pronoun can sometimes have more than one possible antecedent, making its meaning unclear. For example, what does *he* refer to in the following sentence?

Roberto told his father that *he* was wrong.

The answer can be either *Roberto* or *his father*, and the only way to eliminate the confusion is to rewrite the sentence. Here are two possible revisions.

Roberto told his father, "I am wrong."
Roberto accused his father of being wrong.

Sometimes a pronoun does not have an antecedent, and the meaning of the pronoun is not clear. For example, what does *he* refer to in this sentence?

After I honked my horn at the cab that was blocking my way, *he* just honked his horn back and refused to move.

Apparently, *he* refers to *the cabdriver*, but the sentence doesn't mention a cabdriver. The best solution to the problem is to remove the pronoun and use a noun.

After I honked my horn at the cab that was blocking my way, *the cabdriver* just honked his horn back and refused to move.

Here is another example. In speaking, people sometimes use *they* or *them* without clear reference to an antecedent.

At work they (unstated antecedent: *the employees*) are receiving double-time pay right now.

*See Chapter 7 for more practice with antecedents.

What should I tell them (unstated antecedent: *my parents*) when I get home?

In writing, however, *they* and *them* should refer only to a *previously stated* antecedent. Therefore you should first state the antecedent and then use *them* or *they* to refer to it.

At work the *employees* are receiving double-time pay right now. *They* are obviously happy about the increase.

What should I tell *my parents* when I get home? I promised *them* that I would return hours ago.

In Summary: When the antecedent of a pronoun isn't clear,

rewrite the sentence, usually replacing the pronoun with a noun.

---

5 WARM-UP

Insert a noun to replace the pronoun in parentheses.

1. In the last ten years the micro-electronics industry has grown very fast and made better and less expensive products. (They) Micro-electronics companies make pocket calculators, digital watches, computers, video games, and word processors.

2. Ten years ago pocket calculators cost fifty to one hundred dollars, but now (they) _____ are selling them for five dollars.

3. The first digital watches were very expensive and hard to find, but now you find them in all kinds of stores. (They) _____ are cheap enough so that anyone can afford them.

4. Nowadays stores sell calculators and watches for such cheap prices that (they) _____ don't repair them but just throw them away and buy new ones.

5. Ten years ago nobody would have thought that computers would be in so many homes, but (they) _____ are so inexpensive now that many families own them.

6. The electronics industry is changing so fast that you have to wonder: What will (they) _____ think of next?

Indefinite Pronouns and Collective Nouns as Antecedents

Indefinite pronouns, as their name suggests, do not refer to a specific person, place, or thing. On the next page is a partial list of such pronouns.

For People		*For Things*	*For Places*	*For People, Things, or Places*	
everyone	everybody	everything	everywhere	each	either
anyone	anybody	anything	anywhere	any	neither
someone	somebody	something	somewhere	one	
no one	nobody	nothing	nowhere		

Indefinite pronouns present a particularly difficult problem. For example, which pronoun should refer to the antecedent *everyone* in the following sentence?

Everyone in the class does _____ homework.

Did you answer *their?* It is a common choice, but think about the sentence for a moment. *Everyone*, like all of the indefinite pronouns in the list above, is *grammatically singular*. (Notice that the verb after *everyone* is *does*.) *Their* isn't really logical or grammatically correct. The alternative choice is to use *his*, which is certainly singular but seems to exclude the women in the class. Of course *his* works fine when an indefinite pronoun represents only males.

Everybody in the men's gym class does *his* exercises regularly.

Her would work equally well in a sentence about females.

Each of the women on the tennis team practices her backhand.

However, when an indefinite pronoun represents both sexes, there is no easy answer to the problem. Some people refer to the pronoun with *his* because they feel that in this situation the meaning of *his* is neuter— neither male nor female. Other people use *his or her*, as in "Everyone in the class does *his or her* homework." Others have experimented with new pronoun forms such as *s/he* and *s/his*, but these new forms haven't been very popular. Still others decide to rewrite the sentence and make its subject plural.

All of the students in the class do *their* homework.

This last solution is probably the best, but it won't work in every situation. Since the handling of pronoun references after indefinite pronouns is controversial, you may want to discuss the issue in class and perhaps get your instructor's opinion.

*Collective nouns (a team, a band, an audience)** are usually singular, too. Therefore you must be careful to observe the following rules when you use either an indefinite pronoun or a collective noun.

1. The verb must agree grammatically with its singular subject.

Each of the students *is* from a good high school.
Neither of those movies *interests* me.
The band at the football game *was* loud but not very good.

*See Chapter 6 for more on collective nouns.

2. A pronoun must agree grammatically with its singular antecedent.

Someone has left *his* (or *his or her*) coat in the room.
The team has already won more games than *it* (not *they*) won all last year.

6 WARM-UP

Write appropriate pronouns—or nouns, if necessary—in the blank spaces provided below.

1. Ants have five different noses, and each of the noses has
   _____its_____ own function.

2. A human being has a longer life span than almost any other animal on the face of the earth. _____ can live at least 113 years and sometimes longer.

3. If a person sees a cobra snake, _____ should avoid it, for these snakes kill ten thousand people every year.

4. Every bird, proportionate to _____ size and weight, is 75 percent stronger than a human being.

5. One type of Asian fish can crawl out of water. _____ can live for a week on land.

6. Every kind of snake shakes _____ tail when emotionally upset, but only the rattlesnake has a noisemaker.

7. Hummingbirds are unusual; _____ can hover in one spot and also can fly backwards.

8. Piranhas can swim in a school of one thousand. A school will attack _____ own kind, and _____ can strip a horse down to a skeleton in minutes.

9. Someone should have no trouble keeping _____ eyes on a blue whale, which weighs one hundred tons.

10. Any one of the reptiles, because of _____ hinged jaws, can swallow an animal larger than _____.

7 TRANSFORMING

Rewrite each sentence in the following passage to avoid any apparent sexual bias. Change the male singular pronouns to plural pronouns or use *each,* and make other corresponding changes. Be careful. In some cases you may have to replace pronouns with nouns.

Suppose we were back in ancient Egypt. . . .

1. When someone dies, his soul has to go to Amenthe, the final resting place. _When people die, their souls go to Amenthe, the final_
   resting place.

2. His relatives leave food, certain necessities, and *The Book of the Dead* in the tomb to guide the deceased on his journey. _____

_____

_____

_____

3. The deceased has to evade any demon or monstrous monkey that tries to catch him with a net. _____

_____

_____

4. Then he has to ask a ferryman, Face-Behind (who always faces backwards), to take him across a body of water. _____

_____

_____

5. Next a monster—part crocodile, part lion, part hippopotamus— threatens that it will tear out the heart of the traveler if he has been sinful. (hint: use *each* and a *who* clause) _____

_____

_____

_____

6. Inside the gates of Amenthe, the traveler wanders until he comes to a place where forty-two judges decide on his right to be there. _____

_____

_____

_____

7. He must make a Declaration of Innocence, saying that he has not sinned. _____

_____

_____

8. Then during his final trial the heart of the traveler is weighed on a scale, balanced against a feather, which is the symbol of truth. (hint: use *each*) _____

_____

_____

_____

9. If the heart and the feather exactly balance, then his declaration of innocence was true. (hint: use a possessive noun) _____

_____

_____

10. When the scales do not balance, a traveler can be reincarnated on Earth as a disgusting animal or tortured until his sins are cleaned away and he can be reincarnated as a human being. _____

_____

_____

_____

_____

8 WRITING

The subjects of sentences are supplied below. Complete each sentence, referring back to the subject with an appropriate pronoun.

1. Everyone _must declare his or her major this semester._____

2. Nobody _____

_____

3. The team _____

_____

4. Anyone in the boys' choir _____

_____

5. A large department store _____

_____

6. One of the women in the room _____

_____

This/That; These/Those

This/that and *these/those* are called *demonstrative words* because they *demonstrate* which one or ones you are discussing. They can be placed before nouns as demonstrative adjectives *(this man, that story, these men, those stories);* or they can be used alone as demonstrative pronouns. (*This* is a nice place, but *that* is not.)

As you can see, demonstratives have both singular and plural forms.

Singular	*Plural*
this	these
that	those

You should generally use *this/these* to refer to things physically close to you and *that/those* to refer to things farther away.

These cookies (close by) look delicious, but *those* (over there) don't look as good.

9 TRANSFORMING

Supply the *singular* forms of the words in the right-hand column and the *plural* forms of the words in the left-hand column.

Singular	*Plural*
1. this child	1. _these children_____
2. _____	2. those men

3. that house   3. _____

4. this person   4. _____

5. _____   5. these things

6. _____   6. those mice

7. that deer   7. _____

8. _____   8. these women

9. this kind   9. _____

10 WARM-UP

Circle the correct word in parentheses.

1. Why don't you tell me (this/(these)) things?

2. When we were young, we used to go to the ball games with our parents. (This/That) was a lot of fun.

3. (This/That) plant next to the house looks healthy, but (these/those) by the fence don't.

4. (That/Those) kids are always getting into trouble.

5. Remember (this/that): cats don't have to be walked but dogs do.

6. (This/these) type of plants grow well indoors.

11 WARM-UP

Using the words supplied, write two sentences that imitate the pattern of each of the following sentences.

1. These women lost their handbags on the bus.

(people) _These people found their children in the park._

(gorillas) _____

_____

2. Do you want any of these desserts to take home?

(records) _____

_____

(hundred-dollar bills) _____

_____

3. I'll take some of these apples and a few of those bananas.

(pens/pencils) _____

_____

(snakes/worms) _____

_____

USING *WHO* AND *WHOM*

In Chapter 4 you saw that **who** serves as the subject of a clause in a combined sentence.

Please return this snake to the person *who lent it to you.*
The man *who lent the snake to me* took my skunk in exchange.

Many people insist that in formal writing you must use another relative pronoun—*whom*—as the object in a relative clause. Here are some examples.

O   S   V

Mr. Santana was the man *whom you borrowed the snake from.*

or

O   S   V

Mr. Santana was the man *from whom you borrowed the snake.*

However, you can usually eliminate *whom* from a clause entirely, except when *whom* comes after a preposition.

S   V

Mr. Santana was the man *(whom) you borrowed the snake from.*

but

P   O   S   V

Mr. Santana was the man *from whom you borrowed the snake.*

12 COMBINING

Combine each pair of sentences below into one sentence, using *who,* *whom,* or no relative pronoun.

1. Francesco A. Lentini was a man. People called him the Three-Legged Wonder. Francesco A. Lentini was a man whom people called the Three-Legged Wonder.

   or

   Francesco A. Lentini was a man people called the Three-Legged Wonder.

2. Lentini toured for many years with the Ringling Brothers and Barnum and Bailey Brothers Circus. He had an almost full-sized third leg extending from the right side of his body. Lentini, who had an almost full-sized third leg extending from the right side of his body, toured for many years with the Ringling Brothers and Barnum and Bailey Brothers Circus.

3. Born in Sicily in 1889, he was delivered by a midwife. She supposedly hid him under the bed and ran screaming from the room.

_____

_____

4. Lentini's third leg was actually part of an undeveloped body, or an incomplete Siamese twin. The twin was attached to his body at the base of the spine.

_____

_____

5. Doctors had determined that this extra leg could not be removed surgically without grave danger of death or paralysis for Lentini. He was doomed to live with this oddity.

_____

_____

6. Anxious to help their son adjust to his disability, Frank's parents took him to an institution for blind, crippled, and terribly deformed children. He saw they were in far worse condition than he was.

_____

_____

7. From that time on he never complained and felt he had advantages over other people. They did not have a built-in stool for sitting and a rudder for swimming._____

_____

8. Lentini married and had four normal children. He was very devoted to them until his death at the age of seventy-seven.

_____

_____

13 EDITING

The following passage contains many errors related to pronoun use. To correct these errors, make any changes that are necessary above the lines.

Thomas Alva Edison (1847–1931): An Unlikely Genius

(1) People all over the world find ∧theirselves living better lives because [themselves] of the inventions of one man, Thomas Alva Edison. (2) This man started three large laboratories where they invented and patented 1097 different

products—including the electric light bulb, the phonograph, the Dictaphone, and the motion picture camera and projector. (3) However, a more unlikely genius could never be found.

(4) When Edison was in first grade, his teacher told him to drop out of school because he was hopelessly stupid. (5) Edison soon became a dropout, and at the age of twelve he was working full-time selling candy and newspapers on railroad trains. (6) His hearing had been harmed earlier by scarlet fever, and when someone playfully lifted him by the ears onto a train, they made his hearing worse. (7) Without a formal education and largely deaf, Edison educated hisself while working on his inventions. (8) Unfortunately, one of his experiments were rather unsuccessful. (9) It set a train on fire, and they fired him.

(10) Soon afterwards he saved the life of a stationmaster's son, and he gave Edison a job as an apprentice telegraph operator. (11) In 1868 he filed for his first patent, for a vote-recording machine, but it was a business failure. (12) Nobody wanted a machine that recorded an accurate vote; they couldn't cheat when they counted the results with it. (13) Nonetheless Edison soon quit his job as a telegraph operator and devoted his time to inventing. (14) In 1871 he built a machine shop in Newark, New Jersey, that evolved into the present General Electric Company. (15) In the next few years he became financially secure when Western Union and Automatic Telegraph paid him seventy thousand dollars for the rights to inventions that his assistants and himself had perfected. (16) Soon another of his inventions—the phonograph—were earning him national fame. (17) Everyone was buying one for themselves. (18) With this sudden changes in his fortunes, Edison built hisself another laboratory in Menlo Park, New Jersey. (19) There they invented most of his most important products, including the electric light bulb. (20) In Menlo Park many more of Edison's dreams became reality—for him and the rest of the world.

SOME ADDITIONAL HELP IN USING PRONOUNS

Check Antecedents Carefully

People often make three common errors when using pronouns:

1. the pronoun doesn't have an antecedent;
2. the pronoun has more than one possible antecedent; or
3. the pronoun does not agree with its antecedent.

Therefore, when you proofread your papers, you must carefully check for the antecedents to each pronoun. Look for missing antecedents and supply them. Look for more than one antecedent and rewrite the sentence to avoid confusion. Look for a pronoun that does not agree with its antecedent; then change the pronoun so that it does agree.

14 WARM-UP   Circle the antecedent of each underlined pronoun in the following passage.

Arizona Clark "Ma" Barker (1871–1935): Notorious Criminal

(1) Arizona "Kate" Clark was born and raised in the outlaw tradition. (2) Her greatest thrill as a small girl was seeing Jesse James ride past, and she wept bitterly when Bob Ford shot him in 1882. (3) In 1892 Kate married a farm laborer named George Barker, and they soon begot four monsters: Herman, who committed suicide at thirty-three; Lloyd, who eventually served twenty-five years and then was killed by his wife; Arthur, who was shot while trying to escape from Alcatraz; and Freddie, the youngest and Ma's favorite. (4) By 1910 the boys started turning up on police blotters. (5) Sometimes Ma got them off by storming into the police station and screaming or weeping, whichever tactic she reckoned would work best.

(6) The boys went on to serious things such as bank robberies. (7) The FBI theory was that Ma planned the jobs, taught her sons getaway routes that she mapped out, and then stayed home and wept and prayed that they wouldn't get hurt. (8) However, in 1927 Herman was so badly shot up by police that he finished himself off with a bullet to the head. (9) This tragedy, according to J. Edgar Hoover, then in the early years of his reign, changed Ma "from an animal mother of a she-wolf to a veritable beast of prey." (10) On the other hand, Alvin "Creepy" Karpis—who joined the gang, became its leader, and finally was Public Enemy Number 1— always insisted that FBI publicity turned Ma into "Bloody Mama" after she was killed.

(11) If Ma was a criminal genius, then she was the one <u>who</u> switched the gang from robbery to kidnapping and decided to abduct millionaires William A. Hamm, Jr. and Edward George Bremer, which netted a total of three hundred thousand dollars in ransom. (12) If Ma ever killed anyone, <u>it</u> was probably her "loving man" Arthur Dunlop (a billboard painter), who ended up ventilated with bullets and dumped in a lake in 1932. (13) Then again, maybe the boys did it, unmindful of Ma's feelings, when <u>they</u> suspected <u>him</u> of ratting to the cops.

(14) Ma died with Freddie in a famous four-hour shoot-out with the FBI in a hideout cottage in Florida on January 16, 1935. (15) <u>She</u> was managing a machine gun and stopped one to three fatal bullets—or committed suicide, depending on which account one believes. (16) George Barker, who had left the family around 1927, afterwards said this of his wife and sons: "<u>She</u> never would let <u>me</u> do with <u>them</u> what I wanted to."

15 EDITING

In each of the following sentences one or more of the pronouns can have more than one logical antecedent, causing potential misunderstandings. Underline the problem pronouns and then substitute a noun that will clarify the sentence's meaning.

1. Felix Mendelssohn wrote music that another German composer, Richard Wagner, sometimes conducted, yet ∧<u>he</u> always wore gloves.
   <small>Wagner (or the conductor)</small>

2. After these performances Wagner took them off and threw them on the floor to be swept away by a janitor—because Mendelssohn was a Jew and Wagner was an anti-Semite.

3. Because King Otto, the ruler of Bavaria from 1886 to 1913, insisted on taking two of his attendants with him each morning to shoot a poor person, they made a practice of deceiving him. One gave him a rifle filled with blank bullets, and the other dressed as a peasant, strolled into view, and fell dead at the sound of a gunshot.

4. Hans Christian Anderson, the famous writer of fairy tales, was terrified that he would pass out, a policeman would find him, and he would be buried alive.

5. Anderson almost always carried a note in his pocket telling anyone who might discover him unconscious that he must not assume that he was dead unless he was examined again.

6. King Charles II, the ruler of Great Britain from 1660 to 1685, sometimes gathered up powder from the mummies of Egyptian Kings and, in hopes of acquiring "ancient greatness," would rub it on himself.

Make Sure You Know the Pronouns

Sometimes the easiest way to distinguish among the types of pronouns is to memorize the pronouns within each type. Then you can easily recall which pronoun to use.

Subject pronouns

	Singular	*Plural*
1st person	I	we
2nd person	you	you
3rd person	he, she, it	they

Object pronouns

	Singular	*Plural*
1st person	me	us
2nd person	you	you
3rd person	him, her, it	them

Reflexive pronouns

	Singular	*Plural*
1st person	myself	ourselves
2nd person	yourself	yourselves
3rd person	himself	themselves
	herself	
	itself	

Possessive adjectives (go before nouns; for example, *my coat*)

	Singular	*Plural*
1st person	my	our
2nd person	your	your
3rd person	his, her, its*	their*

Possessive pronouns (replace a possessive adjective and a noun; for example, *my coat = mine*)

	Singular	*Plural*
1st person	mine	our
2nd person	yours	yours
3rd person	his	theirs
	hers	
	its	

Indefinite pronouns (do not refer to a specific person)

*For practice in distinguishing between these pronouns and their sound-alikes (*it's*, *there*, or *they're*), see Chapters 5 and 15.

Singular	Plural
one	some
everyone	all
everybody	most
someone	a few
somebody	a couple
anyone	several
anybody	many
each	a number
much	
a thing	
something	
anything	
everything	
nothing	

Demonstrative pronouns and adjectives (can go before nouns or stand alone as pronouns)

Singular	Plural
this	these
that	those

Relative pronouns (used in adjective clauses; see Chapter 5)

who (subject)

whom (object)

that

which

16 EDITING   The following passage contains many errors related to pronoun use. To correct these errors, make any changes that are necessary above the lines.

Edison's Electric Light

(1) For years Edison regularly worked ∧ himself /hisself into a state of exhaustion because he never took a rest. (2) Finally, in the summer of 1878 his family forced him to take his first vacation. (3) He took a trip to Wyoming to witness a total eclipse of the sun, but it was hardly relaxing. (4) A traveling companion and him spent the entire time talking about the scientific and business aspects of electric light. (5) When he returned to his laboratory in Menlo Park, they put aside all their other projects and began working on a practical electric light.

(6) Edison needed money to pay for new equipment and to pay the salaries of his lab assistants, so he went to New York. (7) There on Wall Street an important conversation took place between he and the banker J. P. Morgan. (8) He told him that he could turn out a marketable electric light in six weeks and that the new invention would make a fortune. (9) As a result, Morgan talked other bankers into forming the Edison Electric Light Company in October of 1878. (10) They issued three thousand shares, but they did not sell. (11) Therefore, to stimulate business, Edison lied to the newspapers, saying that they had already invented an electric light. (12) Quickly everyone bought stock for themselves, and Morgan gave Edison fifty thousand dollars to conduct his research.

(13) For the next year Edison's five assistants and himself worked twenty hours a day. (14) One of the problems with the electric light were that the filament (the part that glowed) inside the bulb always burned up or melted after a few minutes. (15) Edison attacked it by enclosing the filament in a glass bulb and creating a vacuum inside of it. (16) They also tested a variety of materials as filaments, including types of bamboo.

(17) Finally, he manufactured a cotton thread coated with carbon and used them as a filament. (18) This filaments worked, and Edison turned on his light bulb on October 21, 1879. (19) It burned with a reddish light for over forty hours, and it quit only because Edison increased the voltage to see how much the filament could take before they burned out. (20) That small piece of thread in Menlo Park, New Jersey, turned night into day throughout the world.

CLASSIFICATION

Classification is the process of *grouping together people or things that are alike in some way*. You can classify college students into four groups: freshmen, sophomores, juniors, and seniors. You can classify automobiles into several groups: full-size cars, mid-size cars, compact cars, and subcompacts. These groups, or categories, are helpful in letting you see relationships among people or objects. They help you to organize and compare information.

However, these categories do not exist in the real world; they exist only in your mind. You create them using some *criterion* (or standard). The criterion for classifying students in the example above is the number of credit hours completed. The criterion for classifying cars is size. On the other hand, you can just as easily classify students by age, grade point average, or religion. You can just as easily classify cars by cost, gas mileage, or color.

Therefore, if you want your categories to be clear and consistent when you create a classification, make sure to follow these two rules:

1. *Use only one criterion for classifying.* Group people according to income, intelligence, or industriousness—but *not* according to income *and* intelligence or intelligence *and* industriousness. Otherwise you may discover that a person fits into more than one category. A rich student can also be bright; a bright student can be lazy or hardworking.
2. *Create categories that allow room for everyone or everything you are classifying.* Suppose, for example, that you are grouping your classmates according to age. If you make your youngest category people between the ages of eighteen and twenty, you exclude a classmate who is only seventeen. A better category might be students seventeen to twenty years old or students who are twenty years old or under.

The following paragraph includes a classification:

There are hundreds of thousands of words in the English language, but they have been painstakingly arranged into categories by one man, a British physician named Peter Mark Roget. He completed the undertaking in 1852, when, after fifty years of work, he published *Roget's International Thesaurus*. The book, which has been revised many times since then, is a dictionary of synonyms that helps people find exactly the right word to express a thought. The current edition of the *Thesaurus* contains eight general categories, which are then subdivided more specifically. The first category, *abstract relations*, includes such words as time, order, change, and power. The second category, *space*, lists such words as region, size, and bottom. The third category, *physics*, provides such words as heat, brightness, and fragrance. The remaining categories with some examples of words in each are (4) *matter* (chemicals, rain, and wind); (5) *sensation* (touch, sight, and silence); (6) *intellect* (knowledge, experiment, and doubt); (7) *volition* (choice, habit, and plan); and (8) *affections* (pride, wonder, and gratitude). A glance at these categories suggests that words in the book are classified according to the branch of science or philosophy in which they belong. Don't be misled, however. The *Thesaurus* isn't a scientific book; it is a tool for anyone interested in writing: a student, a poet, a secretary, a businessperson, or a homemaker. To use the book, simply look in the alphabetical index to find a word that at least slightly resembles the word you have in mind. Then turn immediately to the proper category to discover all the words related to this idea, right down to the smallest shade of meaning. No good home library should be without a copy.

Discussion Questions

1. Where is the sentence that introduces the categories in the *Thesaurus?* Why isn't this sentence the first one in the paragraph?
2. Is this paragraph merely a classification, or does it have another purpose? What other organizational devices does the paragraph use (description, narration, process analysis, causal analysis, or definition) to achieve that purpose?
3. Who is the audience for this paragraph? What does the writer of the paragraph assume the audience knows or does not know?

PARAGRAPH WRITING AND REVISING ASSIGNMENT

Your possessions often reveal a great deal about your personality and interests. Assume you are writing for a group of general readers who do not know you and, as a way of getting them to know you, describe a group of possessions that reveal something about yourself. You can write about the clothing in your closet, the objects in your room, the things in your pocket or your purse, the furniture in your living room, the albums in your record collection, or even the food in your refrigerator and pantry. Classify the items of the group into categories so that each category reveals a different aspect of your personality or interests. For example, you can write, "I am a very careless person by nature, so I force myself to be organized. The following items are therefore in my book bag: an address book; a small notebook for recording my daily assignments in school; and various scraps of paper with names, addresses, and lists on them." If you prefer not to discuss yourself, write about the possessions of a person you know very well, but do not use the person's real name.

You can begin by jotting down information in a list and then arrange all the information into categories. Discard details that don't fit into any category and add other details as they occur to you. Then write a first draft of the paper. As you revise, make sure the categories are clear and complete. Do all the items in each category develop the same theme? Have you omitted any important items?

Return to the paragraph later and revise it further, checking that your classification is clear and fully developed. Also check the paragraph for its use of pronouns. For example, have you begun any clause with a singular word such as *something* and then referred to it later with *they*? During the editing stage check all of the following matters:

1. complete sentences and clauses;
2. correct use of coordination to join sentences;
3. correct use of subordination to join sentences;
4. correct noun-plural forms and subject-verb agreement;
5. correct past-tense and past-participle forms;
6. correctly placed modifiers; and
7. correctly spelled words.

Make a clean, proofread copy of your work.

SUPPLEMENTARY WRITING AND REVISING ASSIGNMENT

Write a four- or five-paragraph paper that classifies any *one* of the following groups:

> automobile drivers
>
> students
>
> shoppers in a supermarket or department store
>
> guests at a party
>
> people at the beach or at a swimming pool
>
> people on a date

Choose your own topic if none of these appeal to you. In any case, though, assume that your audience is already familiar with the topic and that your purpose is primarily to be entertaining.

Be sure to choose only one criterion for classifying, and create at least three different categories within the classification. Describe the people in each category specifically and try to cite a few examples of the people.

When you revise, check your paper again for correct use of pronouns. Have you begun any sentence with a singular noun like *a person* and then referred to it later as *they?* Also, check your paper for the same matters mentioned in the "Paragraph Writing and Revising Assignment."

Read the following classification of alternative types of marriage and notice how it names and then describes each category.

To Have and to Hold

Today most men and women still honor the traditional marriage contract with its pledges of love, honor, and respect and with its legal obligations of alimony and child support if the marriage later dissolves. However, high divorce rates and changing times have caused many men and women to try alternative forms of marriage. Here are four of the most common forms.

The first, which dates back to the 1700s in England, is the *common-law marriage.* In it, a man and a woman do not undergo a wedding ceremony, but they agree to live together as husband and wife. After seven years they are considered legally married. This practice originated because at one time getting married (or divorced) was a complicated procedure. Now, however, only fourteen states and the District of Columbia recognize common-law marriages, and most people choose either to live together without claiming to be married or to go through the official wedding ceremony.

The second alternative marriage form is the *trial marriage*, which is very popular today. Many people are reluctant to commit themselves to a marriage contract before they are sure that their partners are really the ones for them. Therefore they agree to live together (and later, perhaps, separately) without marrying. This arrangement is especially popular with young people or with older people who have divorced and do not want to make another mistake.

A third, but far less common, form of alternative marriage is the *group marriage.* It gained some popularity in the flower-child protest days of the late 1960s but seems to be dying out now. In this arrangement the members of a group share several (but not necessarily all) the partners in the household, and any number of people can participate. While such groups may be liberating and exciting as long as they last, they almost always break up for nonsexual reasons, usually personality conflicts.

Finally, there is a form of legal marriage that has gained popularity over the last several years: *the contract marriage*. In it, couples attempt to make a formal civil agreement tailored to their individual needs and situations. Such contracts can run on for pages and deal with such items as sexual expectations, employment, and money (how much each partner has in a checking account). Reading them, you begin to think that what the partners gain in legal guarantees is lost in trust and love. Here, for example, are a few clauses in marriage contracts as reported by *Time* magazine.

1. Wife will not say she does not believe her husband loves her.
2. Ralph agrees not to pick at, nag, or comment about Wanda's skin blemishes.
3. Wanda will refrain from yelling about undone household chores until Sunday afternoon.

In addition to the four alternative forms of marriage just described, there are other forms. These include the homosexual marriage, the open marriage (with husband and wife free to experiment with different partners), and the renewable contract marriage (that must be renegotiated every few years). They are all signs of our ever-changing and complex life today.

Discussion Questions

1. What are the four categories of marriages discussed in this theme? The criterion for classifying them isn't explicitly stated, but what is it? Could the categories overlap?
2. Go through paragraphs two through four and identify each pronoun. What is the antecedent for each one? Does the theme discuss *people* in the second sense or *a man and a woman* in a singular sense?
3. The second paragraph violates the pattern of the rest of the theme. It begins by talking about a man and a woman and then switches to talking about people in general. Why does it switch? What would happen at the beginning of the paragraph if it were rewritten to discuss *men and women?*

CHAPTER 9

Being Consistent

As you read, you are annoyed if the writer confuses us.

Did that sentence seem confusing? It should have, for it contained an inconsistency. Here it is again, with the inconsistency corrected.

As you read, you are annoyed if the writer confuses you.

At best, inconsistencies in writing are only annoying. At worst, they make writing unclear. Therefore you should try to eliminate them from your writing. This chapter will focus on three types of inconsistencies: shifts *in person, in tense,* and *in parallel structure*. It will then examine ways to make the ideas in your writing hold together or *cohere*.

AVOIDING SHIFTS IN PERSON AND NUMBER

As you saw at the beginning of this chapter, shifts in person can confuse readers. Consistency in person (*first, second,* or *third*) and in number (*singular* or *plural*) will not only prevent that confusion but will add coherence to your writing. The most common shift is from first person (*I, we*) or third person (*he, she, it,* or *they*) to second person (*you*). For example, look at the following sentence:

We have to be careful when *we* go to the beach because *you* could get a sunburn.

The writer probably means: "*We* should be careful not to get sunburned." However, the sentence seems to be talking about *two different groups of people: we* and *you*. The shift in person is confusing.
Here is another muddled sentence.

People can see many wonderful things in New York, but *you* can spend a lot of money there quickly.

Are *people* and *you* the same, or are they meant to be different? Rewrite the sentence to avoid that confusion.

_____

_____

Finally, notice the illogical shift in this sentence.

A person can get a good seat at a rock concert if *they* know how to do it.

The subject of the sentence shifts from singular to plural. Rewrite this sentence to eliminate the inconsistency. You may use either singular or plural forms, but don't switch.

_____

_____

To be clear, be consistent. Choose one pronoun—*we, you,* or *everyone*—and stick with it all the way through your paper. Don't switch unless there is a logical reason to do so.

In Summary: To avoid confusing shifts in person,

decide which person—first, second, or third—is most appropriate for your paper and then use that person throughout.

---

1 WARM-UP

In each space write a pronoun that agrees with its antecedent. Do not make any illogical shifts in person. When the antecedent is third-person singular, use either *he* or *she* (or *his* or *her*).

1. We spend nearly one third of _____*our*_____ lives sleeping, and now scientists are beginning to understand what happens when _____ sleep.

2. During sleep the brain's electrical activity (or *brain-wave activity*) goes through a series of changes. The activity of the brain waves can increase or decrease in _____ strength and frequency.

3. The movement of the eyes behind _____ eyelids is quite rapid at times also, and scientists call _____ *rapid eye movement* or *REM*.

4. Rapid eye movement occurs regularly about every ninety minutes, and other activities of the body accompany _____.

5. Our breathing becomes irregular, the heartbeat increases, and the brain-wave pattern resembles the pattern during _____ waking state.

6. Most importantly, whenever this REM state happens, a sleeper does most of _____ dreaming.

7. Dreams are important to our emotional health. In one experiment that proved this, a scientist awakened some volunteers from _____ REM state each time _____ occurred.

8. As the experiment continued, _____ became harder to awaken, and _____ tempers were very short the next morning.

9. The following night these volunteers were undisturbed, and _____ dream activity was much greater than _____ normally was.

10. A person who takes sleeping pills regularly often does more harm than good because after a month or so, _____ reduce REM activity and make _____ irritable.

2 EDITING

The following passage contains many illogical shifts in person and number. Make the passage consistent in the *third person singular* whenever possible, writing your changes above the line. When you must substitute one pronoun for another, use the male pronoun *he.**

Searching for Buried Treasure in the United States

(1) At this moment more than four billion dollars in lost treasure is waiting for ⋀ you to discover it. *(someone)* (2) A person can find gold mines whose owners died before revealing the mines' locations. (3) We can also find loot buried by robbers such as Jesse James or Ma Barker before they were killed or sent to jail. (4) Getting information about the treasures may mean that you have to spend many hours in libraries as you go over ancient newspapers or books. (5) But a single coin can make one of us rich for a few years.

(6) To be a successful treasure hunter, one should have the heart and mind of Sherlock Holmes, but they should also have a piece of modern equipment called a metal detector. (7) It can cost you anywhere from twenty to one thousand dollars. (8) Even the less expensive ones will allow us to find lost coins and watches on a sandy beach. (9) However, the best detectors will help you find large deposits of deep metal in the earth. (10) Most treasure hunters have been unsuccessful, but you might be lucky.

*See Chapter 8 for a discussion of the sexism issue and how it relates to pronoun use.

3 WRITING

Complete each of the following sentences, maintaining the same person and number throughout.

1. When a teenager is urged to experiment with drugs, _he or she may_ find the peer pressure hard to resist._____

2. Every parent should _____

_____

3. An employer _____

_____

4. Most students _____

_____

5. One cannot excell in school unless _____

_____

AVOIDING SHIFTS IN TENSE

When you write, you can become so involved in the subject that you forget what tense you began your paper in and switch to another one. The results can be confusing and annoying, as in this example.

> A man boards the bus and sits beside me. He lights up a cigarette, even though the sign in the front says, "No smoking." I was really angry.

The last sentence says that you were angry *before* the man lit his cigarette. Obviously, you should have written, "I *am* really angry."

Therefore, as you proofread, note the tenses of your verbs. If you find illogical tense shifts, correct them. Here is a handy question to keep asking: Is this happening *now, in the past,* or *in the future?*

> **In Summary:**   To avoid illogical shifts in tense,
>
> 1. proofread your papers, paying close attention to your verbs;
> 2. keep asking yourself: Is this happening *now, in the past,* or *in the future?*

4 TRANSFORMING

Change the following sentences from present to past tense or from past to present tense.

Present Tense	*Past Tense*
1. He can answer you	1. He ___could___ answer you.
2. It _____ fine.	2. It seemed fine.
3. We talk for an hour each day.	3. We _____ for an hour each day.

4. He is supposed to come.

4. He _____ supposed to come.

5. I _____ been there before.

5. I had been there before.

6. I think it is all right.

6. I _____ it _____ all right.

7. He gets up, throws on some clothes, eats a quick breakfast, and leaves.

7. He _____ up, _____ on some clothes, _____ a quick breakfast, and _____ _____.

8. I wonder if I will be there later.

8. I _____ if I _____ be there later.

9. I _____ used to it.

9 I was used to it.

10. I know they will do it.

10. _____ they _____ do it.

5 EDITING The following passage contains illogical shifts in tense. Above each line, make whatever corrections are necessary to eliminate those shifts.

The Explosion of Krakatoa

(1) A volcano is a hole in the earth's crust that ∧served [serves] as a chimney for the fires burning in the earth's center. (2) As the inside of the earth cooled, it also contracts. (3) The result was that the gases and steam in the center are put under great pressure. (4) Therefore they try to escape. (5) They would travel up from the center through a series of cracks until they reached the surface 1800 miles above. (6) Then their heat melted the surface until it weakens, broke apart, and created a fiery explosion.

(7) In 1883 a small, uninhabited island called Krakatoa was the scene of the most destructive volcano eruption in history. (8) Three volcanoes on the island have slept for half a million years. (9) No one thought that they can erupt again. (10) However, early in the year they show signs of life. (11) For three months smoke appears in their craters. (12) Finally, all three explode in huge blasts that lasted twenty-two hours. (13) People all around the world can hear the sound of the explosion. (14) At least 36,417

people on nearby islands died, while 165 villages are completely destroyed.

(15) Many more villages are badly damaged.

AVOIDING FAULTY PARALLELISM

The following sentences probably don't sound good to you.

> He is 5′10″ tall, weight 185 pounds, and brown eyes.
> They loved telling stories, to dance, and sang.

The same sentences would sound better rewritten.

> He *is* 5′10″ tall, *weighs* 185 pounds, and *has* brown eyes.
> They loved *telling* stories, *dancing*, and *singing*.

The first two sentences move along as if they have lost their balance. In fact they are *unbalanced*. They join similar ideas but do not balance them with similar grammatical structures. Notice the rewritten sentences, however. The grammatical structures are the same.

> He *is* . . . *weighs* . . . and *has* (three present-tense verbs).
> They loved *telling* . . . *dancing*, and *singing* (three *-ing* words).

This repetition of grammatical structures is called **parallel construction,** or **parallelism.** You can see the advantage of using it—clearer and smoother sentences. You can use it to balance subjects with subjects, verbs with verbs, phrases with phrases, clauses with clauses—or any other grammatical structures. The important point to remember is that when you use parallelism, express similar ideas in the same grammatical structures.

Here are some more examples of parallelism.

> He is *a lover*, not *a fighter*. (a noun and a noun)
>
> We would *meet* downtown, *shop* for a few hours, *have* a bite to eat, and then *leave*. (four main verbs following *would*)
>
> I could have *gone* and *seen* it. (two past participles following *could have*)
>
> It is true that *you may fool all the people some of the time; you can even fool some of the people all of the time;* but *you can't fool all of the people all of the time.*
>
> —Abraham Lincoln (three clauses beginning with *you*)

In Summary: To join similar ideas,

use *parallel construction*. That is, repeat the same grammatical structure for each idea (a subject balanced with another subject, a past-tense verb balanced with another past-tense verb, and so forth).

6 **WARM-UP**

Underline the grammatical structure that is different from the others in each group.

1. shifting gears
   <u>avoid the accident</u>
   keeping control
   swerving left

2. saw it
   walked away
   goes for it
   returned to it

3. cooperation
   admiring
   respect
   reliability

4. cute
   friendly
   a good student
   athletic

5. works by night
   plays by dawn
   eats junk food
   sleeps by day

6. large onions
   seasoned with vinegar
   ripe tomatoes
   crisp lettuce

7. overtired
   swollen feet
   sore muscles
   aching back

8. a television set
   an expensive stereo
   radio programs
   a tape recorder

9. with wit
   with a smile
   happy with the news
   with sparkling eyes

10. sewn by hand
    decorated with ribbons
    embroidered in red
    an odd color

11. gone there
    done it
    ran back
    been finished

12. go in a large group
    sing silly songs
    told dirty jokes
    act like fools

7 **WRITING**

Take five of the groups of parallel phrases from Exercise 6 and write a sentence using each group. Do not use the phrase that is different from the others in the group.

Example. He saw it, walked away from it quickly and then returned to it because he was curious.

1. _____

_____

_____

2. _____

_____

_____

3. _____

_____

_____

4. _____

_____

_____

5. _____

_____

_____

8 WRITING

Complete the following sentences, using parallel construction.

1. At the party we _____ talked _____, _____ danced _____, and _____ ate _____.

2. In that new dress Maria looks _____, _____, and _____.

3. The man _____ his dog, _____ his son, and _____ his wife.

4. In summer _____, but in winter, _____.

5. The batter _____ the ball, _____ first base, and _____ second base.

6. I love _____ and _____ but not _____.

7. Don't forget to _____ and then _____.

8. My favorite pastimes are _____ and _____.

9. He was whistling a tune, _____, and _____.

10. I need _____ or _____.

9 EDITING

Each of the following groups of words contains an error in parallelism. Underline the section with the error and then rewrite it to make it parallel.

1. The great San Francisco earthquake of 1906 began with a rumble, then grew to a roar, and <u>knocking buildings to the ground.</u>
   Rewritten: ____ knocked buildings to the ground ____

2. First to go was the seven-million-dollar city hall, and next the glass dome of the Palace Hotel went.
   Rewritten: _____

3. Chunks of brick fell, and pieces of concrete were hitting half-awake people who ran in the streets.
   Rewritten: _____

4. The panic-stricken residents tried to find a place to hide or for resting, but there was nowhere to go.
   Rewritten: _____

5. Consequently, they watched broken water mains explode, sewer pipes leap from the ground, and fires broke out everywhere.
   Rewritten: _____

6. As night came thousands of people tried to sleep in the parks or lying down in the streets.

   Rewritten: _____

7. The earthquake was vicious, terrifying, and did much harm.

   Rewritten: _____

8. As a result the city was knocked down, split apart, and fire destroyed it.

   Rewritten: _____

9. When the earthquake ended, six hundred people were dead, thirty thousand were left homeless, and property damage of four hundred million dollars.

   Rewritten: _____

10. San Francisco immediately began to rebuild, developing new safety systems, and to construct stronger buildings.

    Rewritten: _____

10 EDITING   The following passage contains errors in parallelism, shifts in person, and shifts in tense. Above each line, make whatever corrections are necessary to eliminate those errors and shifts.

More About Krakatoa

(1) It was 10:55 A.M., Sunday, May 20, 1883, when the first warning of the disaster ⋀occurs. (2) A German ship sailed close to the island and its captain can notice a large black cloud above it. (3) The cloud sent out flashes of lightning, exploding, and ash showers also came out of it. (4) Then you could see the cloud go away. (5) It appeared again in June and July.

(6) On Sunday, August 26, the three volcanoes blew their tops. (7) The explosion was enormous. (8) Black clouds shoot seven miles into the sky. (9) For an hour people on the ships and islands nearby can see the clouds. (10) Then the ash from the volcanoes blacked out a 150-square-mile area and had turned day into night. (11) You will not see anything for the next three days. (12) Explosions continued and soon are two minutes apart.

(13) The sea turned violent, dark, and it was frightening. (14) It rose and was falling in huge waves. (15) You could not escape from the nearby

islands by boat. (16) At 7:55 P.M. a violent earthquake shakes the whole area, and rain and lightning are everywhere. (17) By midnight the beaches of the other islands are buried in huge waves. (18) At 1:00 A.M. an entire village is washed away, and the waves almost reaching people on top of a 125-foot hill.

(19) The next morning a wave would pick up a ship at sea, carried it more than a mile inland, and killing all of the crew. (20) Still the eruptions continued, the earth would shake, and the waves are taking more lives. (21) Finally, at 10:02 we could hear the largest roar yet. (22) Three-quarters of Krakatoa disappeared into the sea, and the sound carries for three thousand miles.

(23) The explosion created winds that circled the globe seven times. (24) A wall of water flooded beaches, burying villages, and was knocking down hilltops. (25) Gigantic tidal waves were traveling as far south as the bottom of Africa and to the English channel, which was very far north. (26) The waves hit an island thirty miles from Krakatoa and killing ten thousand people. (27) Other islands were submerged in water.

(28) After twenty-two hours the volcanoes disappear into the sea, and the greatest eruption ever has ended.

SOME ADDITIONAL HELP IN AVOIDING SHIFTS IN PERSON

Don't Use *You* Unless You Speak Directly to Your Readers

When speaking informally, you may use the pronoun *you* to mean three different things.

1. I
2. a person or people (in a general sense)
3. the person you are speaking to

Writing, however, is more precise than speaking. When you mean *I*, you should use the pronoun *I*.

poor: When I reached the top of the World Trade Center, I was amazed. *You* could see for miles.

better: When I reached the top of the World Trade Center, I was amazed. *I* could see for miles.

When you mean *a person* or *people*, use those words and the pronouns that refer to them.

poor: Once *a person* has been to California, *you* don't want to leave.
better: Once *people* have been to California, *they* don't want to leave.

or

Once *a person* has been to California, *he or she* doesn't want to leave.

Use *you* only when you speak directly to your readers (as in this sentence).

11 WARM-UP

Each of the following groups of sentences contains a shift in person. Cross out the inappropriate pronoun(s) and write in the appropriate one(s) above.

1. I find psychology class fascinating. ∧You can learn so much about ∧yourself.
   (above "You": I; above "yourself": myself)

2. When I come back to my dormitory after class, you never know what kind of funny things you'll find happening.

3. All my friends should eat at the new Thai restaurant. You will really like the food.

4. One should be cautioned against trying to write in a formal style if you are not sure how to use it.

5. I love the dress shop on Fremont Street. Everything you try looks good on you.

SOME ADDITIONAL HELP IN AVOIDING SHIFTS IN TENSE

Don't Be Fooled by Past Participles

Past participles (such as *done, seen, eaten,* and words ending in *-ed*) can be used in three different ways. (See Chapter 6.)

In perfect tenses
(present perfect)   I *have worked* for hours.
(past perfect)   I *had worked* for hours.
After linking verbs
(present tense)   He *looks exhausted.*
(past tense)   He *looked exhausted.*
In the passive voice
(present tense)   The prizes *are awarded* by the judges.
(past tense)   The prizes *were awarded* by the judges.

In each case note that the past participles *(worked, exhausted,* and *awarded)* have nothing to do with tense. The verbs before them *(have/had; looks/looked; are/were)* determine the tenses of the sentences.

As you proofread your sentences, look at the *first* word in the verb phrase after the subject. It—not the past participle that follows—determines the tense. Also, be sure to ask: Is this happening *now, in the past,* or *in the future?*

12 TRANSFORMING

Change each of the following sentences from present to past tense or from past to present tense.

Present Tense	*Past Tense*
1. He has seen it already.	1. He had seen it already.
2. They appear surprised.	2. _____
3. _____	3. Our car was serviced by an excellent mechanic.
4. The food is prepared in our special kitchens.	4. _____
5. _____	5. He seemed amused.
6. I have talked about this before.	6. _____
7. Their child is very spoiled.	7. _____
8. _____	8. Lisa felt excited.

Make Sure You Know the Past-Tense Forms of Special Verbs*

Compare the following verb forms.

Present Tense	*Past Tense*
I *am*	I *was*
you *are*	you *were*
she *is*	she *was*
I *have*	I *had*
he *has*	he *had*
I *can*	I *could*
I *will*	I *would*
I *say*	I *said*
she *says*	she *said*

*If you wish to review and practice these verbs further, see Chapter 6.

13 TRANSFORMING   Change each of the following sentences from present to past tense or from past to present tense.

Present Tense	*Past Tense*
1. I say that I can do it.	1. I said that I could do it.
2. _____ _____	2. We had to paint the living room walls.
3. I think that I will get all *A*'s.	3. _____ _____
4. _____ _____	4. I was pleased with my new purple rug.
5. You think that you are a handsome devil—and you are half right.	5. _____ _____ _____

SOME ADDITIONAL HELP IN USING PARALLELISM

Read Your Paper Aloud and Listen for Patterns to Repeat

You do not always have to identify grammatical structures to know when they should be repeated. You can often hear what should be repeated.

14 WARM-UP   Read aloud each sentence in the following passage and listen for the structures that are parallel. Then underline the parallel structures and number them above the line. Not every sentence will have parallel structures.

The Eruption of Mount Vesuvius

(1) August 24 A.D. 79, began like any other day in the resort town of Pompeii, Italy: window shutters banged, shopkeepers opened for business, and conversations buzzed about the upcoming elections. (2) But at 1:00 P.M., the volcano Mount Vesuvius ended 1500 years of sleep and roared with a mighty explosion. (3) A black cloud rose to cover the sky and blot out the sun. (4) Melted rock shot from the volcano's mouth, cooled quickly in the air, and fell back into the volcano. (5) Then came a second explosion and a rain of stones all over the mountainside.

(6) A few people ran from the city toward the sea and into boats. (7) They lived to tell about the disaster. (8) However, most people tried to

find safety in their homes, temples, or public baths. (9) They weren't as lucky as those who left by sea. (10) Hot stones piled on roofs, collapsing some and setting others on fire. (11) Poisonous gases killed many people, while thirty to fifty feet of volcanic ash buried the city and killed the rest.

(12) Within twenty-four hours, thirty thousand people were dead. (13) Their bodies and homes were to be preserved in the ash for almost 1700 years. (14) Then the city would be excavated, visitors would again come in large numbers, and Mount Vesuvius would lie asleep but be ready to erupt again at any time.

Look for Similarities in the Forms of Words

Another way to recognize parallel structures is to look for similarities in word endings and in the words that begin phrases. For example, do all the words end in *-ing?* Are all the verbs in the past tense? Do all the phrases begin with prepositions? Look for the pattern of similarities and then continue the pattern.

15 WRITING   Each of the following incomplete sentences develops a pattern. In the space following each sentence, complete the pattern.

1. The kids talked about hiking, sailing and _____ swimming _____

2. She was spoiled by her mother, bored by school, and _____
_____.

3. He talks big and puts on a good act, but _____
_____.

4. We have been doing our best, trying to get this done, and _____
_____.

5. You could have called me, written me, or _____
_____.

6. The cat searched for a comfortable spot, curled up, and _____
_____.

7. I liked its style, its shape, and _____
_____.

8. The movie has no story, only scenes. It has no characters, _____
_____.

9. The food was too ordinary, the portions too small, the price _____
_____.

10. He is long on conversation but _____
_____.

16 EDITING The following passage contains errors in parallelism, shifts in person, and shifts in tense. Above each line, make whatever corrections are necessary to eliminate those errors and shifts.

The Spanish Influenza Epidemic
(March–November, 1918)

(1) It all started one spring day during World War I when a United

States Army fort $\wedge$ᵂᵃˢ i̶s̶ hit with the first cases of Spanish influenza. (2)

Before the epidemic has run its course almost twenty-two million people

throughout the world will die.

(3) The disease struck first in Fort Riley, Kansas; it quickly was

spreading throughout other military camps from coast to coast. (4) Soon so

many sailors in Norfolk, Virginia, and Boston, Massachusetts, have high

fevers that you cannot go to sea. (5) In California one third of the

prisoners in the San Quentin jail became ill.

(6) The influenza soon spread to Europe. (7) Scotland began reporting

fifteen to twenty deaths daily, and three hundred deaths a week were

reported in London. (8) In Berlin, Germany, 160,000 stayed in bed; in

France, many soldiers cannot fight. (9) Then the killer disease hit China

and India; would hop the Pacific to Hawaii; and Alaska, Puerto Rico,

Iceland, and Norway were attacked. (10) It finally hit Spain, where doctors

call it *Spanish Influenza.*

(11) It swept across the United States, Canada, and Mexico; struck

millions; and killing hundreds of thousands of people. (12) In Pennsylvania

alone, 250,000 people are confined to bed. (13) There are not enough

coffins, graves, and undertakers were in short supply. (14) To prevent the

spread of the disease, churches closed on Sundays, businesses and stores

had gone on half-day schedules, and theaters would shut down.

(15) No one knew what caused the disease or how you could cure it. (16)

A public-health official in Virginia says a tiny poisonous plant called "the

germ of influenza" causes it. (17) A Boston doctor said, "Influenza is caused

chiefly by excessive clothing." (18) Another doctor suggested that you put

towels soaked in hot vinegar on your stomach to cure it.

(19) By early October the disease was completely out of control. (20) U.S. military camps reported one death every hour, and Britain was recording 2000 deaths a week. (21) India lost 12.5 million people; the United States lost 500,000. (22) Finally, in November the war ended, and the disease also came to an end.

(23) In the 1930s a microscope was invented that allowed people to see the virus responsible for the Spanish influenza. (24) The virus looked like a cottonball, and thirty million of them can be placed on the head of a pin.

(25) Since 1918, however, the virus has almost completely disappeared. (26) Where did it come from and what location is the place where it went to? (27) No one knows.

COHERENCE

Coherence literally means that things *stick together*. Coherence in a paragraph means that all the ideas and sentences stick together logically. The relationships among the ideas are clear, and every sentence flows smoothly into the next one so that the reader can follow along without confusion or hesitation.

A paragraph with poor coherence will not be clear, no matter how well developed it is. Therefore you should attempt to write coherent paragraphs and to check carefully for coherence as you revise. There are several ways to establish coherence among your ideas.

1. *Write your ideas in the most logical order.* If you are describing an object, describe it from top to bottom. Don't skip from the top to the side, then back to the top, and then to the bottom. If you are writing a narration, stay in chronological order. Don't skip from yesterday to last week and then back again to yesterday. If you are analyzing the causes of an event, establish an organization and stick to it. Don't name a cause, explain it, and then name three more causes before you begin to explain each one.

2. *Use* transitional *words and phrases to explain the relationships between ideas.* To show chronology, use such terms as *then*, *next*, *afterwards*, and *several hours later*. To show spatial relationships, use such terms as *on the top*, *below that*, and *a few inches to the right*. To list causes, use terms such as *first*, *second*, *third*, and *finally*. To show contrast, use terms such as *however*, or *on the other hand*. To show other relationships, use *if*, *because*, *in short*, and *in summary*. These are just a few examples of transitional expressions; the list is endless.

3. *Repeat the same sentence structure when listing ideas that are parallel.* Notice, for example, that in rule 1 the parallel ideas are in sentences beginning with *If*. Notice that in rule 2 the parallel ideas are in sentences beginning with *To show*. Notice in this rule that the parallel ideas are in sentences beginning with *Notice*.

4. *Repeat key words as you move from sentence to sentence.* In rule 3 notice the repetition of the words *parallel ideas* and *sentences*.

5. *Use pronouns to refer to key nouns in a paragraph.* When you discuss a singular subject, refer to it with such pronouns as *it, this,* or *that*. When you discuss a plural subject, refer to it with pronouns such as *they, them, these,* or *those*. However, if a pronoun can refer to more than one thing in a sentence, use a noun to avoid confusion. Notice, for example, that in the first sentence of this rule the pronoun "it" refers to *a singular subject*. On the other hand, notice the sentence beginning with "However, if a pronoun. . . ." Instead of using the word *it*, this sentence uses *pronoun* because *it* could refer to many things in the previous sentences.

Here is a paragraph that should serve as a good model of coherence.

Rubber as we know it was discovered as the result of a lucky accident that brought a mixture of India rubber and sulfur into contact with a hot stove. Before 1939 rubber was useless for practical purposes. When it got hot, it was too sticky. When it got cold, it was too stiff and brittle. For seven years Charles Goodyear had been experimenting with ways to overcome these problems. Then one day in 1939, he was brushing some powder off his hands. The powder, which consisted of rubber and some sulfur, fell onto a hot stove. The rubber naturally melted, as it always had, but this time it mixed with the sulfur and hardened. Goodyear was amazed. After he had let the mixture cool down slightly, he picked it up and discovered that it wasn't sticky. Now he was excited. He held the rubber near the fire, but the rubber neither softened nor became sticky. At this point Goodyear could barely control his emotions, but he tried one more test. That night he nailed the rubber to the outside of his kitchen door in the intense cold. The next morning he brought the rubber in. He felt it, he bent it, and he was overjoyed. The rubber was perfectly flexible, just as it had been the night before. A little sulfur, a little rubber, and a little heat had combined to form vulcanized rubber, the product that makes tires, rubber balls, and all the other rubber products that we use today.

Discussion Questions

1. Is this paragraph structured according to chronological order, spatial order, or some other organizing principle? The first sentence violates that organizing principle. Why is that sentence different from the rest of the paragraph?

2. What transitional devices create coherence in the paragraph? Where does repetition of structures create coherence?

3. The paragraph alternates between describing Goodyear's experiments and describing Goodyear's emotions. What devices make the switch between these two ideas easy to follow?

PARAGRAPH WRITING AND REVISING ASSIGNMENT

Write a paragraph about an important event in your life. The topic sentence should name the event and suggest why it was important, as in: "When I moved to a different city, my life changed in several ways." The rest of the paragraph should describe the event and the changes it caused. As you revise, be careful to provide coherence between ideas by organizing them logically, supplying transitional words and expressions, repeating sentence structures, repeating key words, and using pronouns to refer to key nouns.

Return to the paragraph later and make a final revision, checking once again for coherence. In editing the paper also look carefully for the following:

1. complete sentences and clauses;
2. correct use of coordination to join sentences;
3. correct use of subordination to join sentences;
4. correct noun-plural forms and subject-verb agreement;
5. correct past-tense and past-participle forms;
6. correctly placed modifiers;
7. correct use of pronouns; and
8. correctly spelled words.

As usual, make a clean, proofread copy of your work.

SUPPLEMENTARY WRITING AND REVISING ASSIGNMENT

Write a biography of a person you know very well: your mother or father, a close friend, a teacher, a minister, or some other person you respect. If necessary, interview the person to find out about important events in the person's past. Then structure the biography so that your classmates can appreciate why you respect, admire, or like the person strongly.

Write your biography in the third person. (That is, use only *he* or *she*.) Be consistent in tense, too. Write in the past tense when you discuss what the person did; write in the present tense when you discuss what the person still does (if the person is alive now). During revisions and while editing the paper, check it carefully for the matters listed in the "Paragraph Writing and Revising Assignment."

The following biography of a rock star uses all five of these rules to create coherence. As you read it, see if you can identify the type of organization in each paragraph. Also, see if you can identify specific transitional words and phrases, as well as the repetition of key words or the repetition of sentence structures.

The Father of Rock 'n' Roll

In 1926, when the Jazz Age was its height in the smoke-filled nightclubs of New York and Chicago, Charles Edward Anderson Berry—the pioneer of a new musical form—was lying in his cradle in San Jose, California.

Many years later Chuck Berry was to make use of jazz and other musical traditions in the development of his own special kind of music: rock 'n' roll.

Soon after his birth Berry's family moved to a suburb of St. Louis, Missouri. Although he was raised in a secure middle-class environment, Berry had his problems, including a three-year term in reform school for attempted robbery. After his release from reform school, he entered the blue-collar world. He got a job at the General Motors plant in St. Louis and attended night school to study hairstyling. In the 1950s he finally set up his own hairdressing business.

Now that his nights were free from study, he next turned to his real love—honky-tonk guitar. He played in all the local nightclubs until he had saved enough money for a trip to Chicago, the blues capital of the world, to hear and meet the legendary Muddy Waters. When Waters invited Berry to perform onstage, the electricity of Berry's new hard-beat blues and incredible performing style attracted immediate attention. He played the guitar in intricate patterns of sound. He duck-walked across the stage. He bowed his legs like vibrating rubber bands. He flung his guitar behind his legs or behind his head, all while he played to a hard, steady beat. Soon Berry had signed a recording contract and was on his way to fame.

His first record, "Maybelline," was a huge success and earned him a great deal of money. Now that he was financially secure, he set out to write and record a series of powerfully rhythmic songs, which carried some of the most creative lyrics of the era. In 1957 and 1958 his hits came in rapid succession: "School Days," "Rock and Roll Music," "Sweet Little Sixteen," and "Johnny B. Goode," to name just a few.

Taken together, Berry's hits are the best of early rock, and Berry himself was the best of the early rock performers. As both lead guitarist and songwriter, he became the most important influence on the major rock groups of the 1960s, including The Beach Boys, The Beatles, and The Rolling Stones.

While the careers of these groups rose quickly in the 1960s, Berry's career faded, largely because of some new personal problems. However, in the 1970s Berry resurfaced and began performing to sell-out crowds again. As one of the first men to blend jazz, country, and rhythm and blues into the music known as rock, Berry has returned to his rightful place at the top of the popular music world.

Discussion Questions

1. In the second paragraph what words or phrases show the passage of time?
2. In the third paragraph what is the purpose of the first sentence?
3. In the third paragraph what words or phrases are repeated to achieve coherence? What words or phrases are repeated in the fourth paragraph?
4. In the last paragraph what two ideas are opposed in the first sentence? What is the purpose of the word *However* at the beginning of the next sentence?

CHAPTER 10

Comparing Adjectives and Adverbs

Each day you make comparisons: this lesson was *easier* than the last one; traffic this morning ran *more smoothly* than traffic the day before. Whenever you compare people or things, you use adjectives *(tall, taller, tallest)* or adverbs *(gracefully, more gracefully, most gracefully)* to describe them. This chapter will demonstrate how to use adjectives and adverbs in comparisons by beginning with the *simple*, the *comparative*, and the *superlative* forms of *regular adjectives;* continuing with the same three forms for *regular adverbs;* and ending with the forms of *irregular adjectives and adverbs.* Once again the chapter will end by examining another method of paragraph development: *comparison and contrast.*

DISTINGUISHING BETWEEN ADJECTIVES AND ADVERBS

Remember that adjectives *describe nouns.* One-word adjectives usually come before the nouns they describe.

> the *red* balloon
> a *slight* chance
> a *pleasant* experience

One-word adjectives may also come after linking verbs and describe the noun-subjects or pronoun-subjects of those verbs.

> Henry is *nice.* (*Nice* describes *Henry.*)
> He appears *happy.* (*Happy* describes *He.*)
> Your ideas sound *interesting.* (*Interesting* describes *your ideas.*)*

*For more about linking verbs, see Chapter 2 and the end of this chapter.

You should recall that adverbs, as their name suggests, usually *describe verbs*.† One-word adverbs often tell *how* an action occurs or occurred, and most one-word adverbs end in *-ly*.

Henry dresses *neatly*. (*Neatly* describes how Henry dresses.)
The meat is cooking *slowly*. (*Slowly* describes how the meat is cooking.)

Compare some adjectives and adverbs within sentences.

Adjective	Adverb
Mr. Walters is a *quick* worker. (*Quick* describes *worker*.)	Mr. Walters works *quickly*. (*Quickly* describes *how* Mr. Walters *works*.)
Angela has a *beautiful* voice. (*Beautiful* describes *voice*.)	Angela sings *beautifully*. (*Beautifully* describes *how* she *sings*.)
The pigeon has an *odd* walk. (*Odd* describes *walk*.)	The pigeon walks *oddly*. (*Oddly* describes *how* it *walks*.)
The man's face looked *menacing*. (*Menacing* comes after a linking verb and describes *the man's face*.)	The man stared *menacingly* at me. (*menacingly* describes *how* the man *stared*.)

> **In Summary:** An adjective
>
> describes a noun and usually comes before the noun it describes. It may also come after a linking verb and describe the noun-subject of the verb.
>
> An adverb
>
> 1. describes a verb and usually tells *how* an action occurs or occurred. Most one-word adverbs end in *-ly*;
> 2. sometimes describes an adjective or another adverb. Then, it usually tells *how much* or *how often*.

1 TRANSFORMING

Change the adjectives in the left-hand sentences into adverbs in the right-hand sentences.

1. The wind is *fierce*.

1. The wind blew
   ___fiercely___.

2. The train is *slow*.

2. The train runs
   _____.

---

†One-word adverbs can also describe adjectives or other adverbs.

a *really* cool day (*Really* describes the adjective *cool*.)

an *embarrassingly* silly mistake (*Embarrassingly* describes the adjective *silly*.)

a *slightly* crooked picture (*Slightly* describes the adjective *crooked*.)

Sheila talks *very* loudly. (*Very* describes the adverb *loudly*.)

The horse ran *very* fast. (*Very* describes the adverb *fast*.)

When adverbs describe adjectives or adverbs, they usually explain *how much* or *how often*.

3. She has an *intelligent* mind.

3. She speaks

_____.

4. The motor seems *quiet*.

4. The motor runs

_____.

5. Tom is a *careful* worker.

5. Tom works

_____.

6. Her advice was *helpful*.

6. She _____

advised me.

7. The sea looks *peaceful*.

7. The waves rolled in

_____.

8. The search was *thorough*.

8. They searched the house

_____.

9. My instructor is *patient*.

9. My instructor explains things

_____.

10. The towels seem very *neat*.

10. The towels are folded

_____.

11. I have never seen a more *emotional* man.

11. The man cried

_____.

12. She has *bad* handwriting.

12. She writes

_____.

13. The test was *easy*.

13. I passed the test

_____.

14. The music is *loud*.

14. The music played

_____.

15. He was *quick*.

15. He reacted

_____.

16. They are *independent* people.

16. They acted

_____.

2 WARM-UP   In the following passage, circle the correct adjective or adverb form in parentheses.

Montezuma's Treasure

(1) When the Spanish arrived in Mexico in the sixteenth century, their greed conquered their common sense (complete/completely). (2) Rather than being (peaceful/peacefully) traders for gold, they made the Aztec Indians into slaves and forced them to work their own mines. (3) The Spanish stripped the Aztec temples of their ornaments of (solid/solidly)

gold, which they melted down and shipped back to Spain. (4) As a result, the Aztecs revolted (violent/violently), hid their gold, and escaped. (5) In 1520 the Aztec ruler Montezuma learned that Hernando Cortez and his troops were (greedy/greedily) again. (6) They were heading (quick/quickly) toward the Aztec capital, which, many years after the fall of the Aztecs, became Mexico City. (7) Montezuma ordered his buildings (total/totally) stripped of their gold, silver, and jewels. (8) A caravan then (secret/ secretly) took these valuables to the north and buried them. (9) However, Montezuma was (final/finally) killed by Cortez and died leaving no record of where his treasure was hidden. (10) It is (probable/probably) still where his men left it over 450 years ago. (11) The (real/really) question is, "Where?" (12) One story says that the treasure is hidden in a cave in a (real/really) large mountain canyon. (13) Other versions say that the treasure may (actual/actually) be stashed away as far north as Arizona, New Mexico, or Utah. (14) If you want to look for it, you have as (excellent/excellently) a chance as anyone else. (15) Although many people have claimed to have found it, all their stories have proved to be (false/falsely).

COMPARING REGULAR ADJECTIVES

The Simple Form

You can show equality between two things or people like this:

Harry is *as tall as* Mike [is].
The book is *as interesting as* the last book [was].
The window on the right is *as dirty as* the window on the left [is].

> **In Summary:** To show equality, use:
>
> *as* (adjective) *as*
>
> Note: Both *as* before and *as* after the adjective must be included.

The Comparative Form of Regular Adjectives

Here is how to compare two unequals.

This lesson is *longer than* the last one [was].
Bruce is *fatter than* he used to be.
Shelly is *more beautiful than* her mother [is].*

*For advice about using pronouns after *as* and *than*, see Chapter 8.

The words *longer, fatter,* and *more beautiful* are called the comparative forms of adjectives since you use them in comparisons of unequals. Notice the difference between comparative forms and simple adjective forms.

Simple	Comparative
tall	taller
fat	fatter
beautiful	more beautiful

Three rules determine whether you add *-er* or *more* to the simple form of a regular adjective.

1. Add *-er* to one-syllable adjectives.

Simple	Comparative
sweet	sweeter
cold	colder

If the adjective ends in a *single* consonant, you usually double the consonant before adding *-er.**

Simple	Comparative
thin	thinner
big	bigger

2. Add *-er* to two syllable adjectives ending in *-y* or *-ow.*

Simple	Comparative
pretty	prettier
hollow	hollower

Notice that *-y* changes to *-i* before adding *-er.*
Put *more* before most other two-syllable adjectives.

Simple	Comparative
awful	more awful
spacious	more spacious

(Exception: simple, simpler)

3. Always put *more* before adjectives of three or more syllables.

Simple	Comparative
beautiful	more beautiful
comfortable	more comfortable
necessary	more necessary
luxurious	more luxurious

*For additional advice about doubling final consonants, see Chapter 14.

Be Careful:

1. You cannot use *more* and *-er* with the same adjective.

Incorrect: Bill is more bigger than I am.
Correct: Bill is *bigger* than I am.

2. Always use *than* after a comparative adjective.

Bill is bigger *than* his brother.

Don't confuse *than* with *then*, which means "at a later time": First he asked her father's permission. *Then* he proposed to her.

In Summary: To use the comparative form of a regular adjective,

1. add *-er* to one-syllable adjectives (small → smaller);
2. add *-er* to two-syllable adjectives ending in *-y* or *-ow* (funny → funnier; yellow → yellower). Put *more* before most other two-syllable adjectives (fearful → more fearful);
3. put *more* before all adjectives of three or more syllables (unpredictable → more unpredictable);
4. follow each comparative adjective with *than* (not *then*).

3 WARM-UP

Fill in the correct form of each adjective in parentheses.

1. Michelangelo was a (talented) ____more talented____ artist than fighter. A fellow artist broke Michelangelo's nose in a fist fight one day, and as a result he had a (flat) _____ nose than any other artist.

2. On the other hand, Jimmy Durante had a (profitable) _____ nose than any other entertainer. The comedian's famous "schnozzola" made him instantly recognizable—and (rich) _____ than most other comics.

3. The sixteenth-century Danish astronomer Tycho Brahe had a (shiny) _____ nose than anyone else. He lost the tip of it in a sword fight and replaced it with a gold one—probably a (expensive) _____ operation than most people have.

4. Thomas Wedders, who worked in a circus in the eighteenth century, had a (long) _____ nose than anyone else in recorded history. It measured 7½ inches.

5. Albert Weber's nose is (useful) _____ than most people's noses. He's an official smeller for the U.S. Food and Drug Administration.

6. Finally, a Czech composer named Josef Mysliveček had a (noticeable) _____ problem with his nose than other people have. When he developed a disease in his nose, a doctor cut the nose off. That left him (healthy) _____ but a lot (sad) _____.

4 WRITING

Write a statement using the comparative form of an adjective to describe each pair of subjects in parentheses.

1. (two bicycles) _One bicycle is *newer* than the other one._

2. (two books) _____

_____

3. (two presidents) _____

_____

4. (two kittens) _____

_____

5. (two steaks) _____

_____

6. (two different sets of feet) _____

_____

The Superlative Form of Regular Adjectives

When you compare *more than two* things or people, use the superlative form of the adjective.

This lesson is *the longest* of the three (lessons).
The center is *the tallest* player on the basketball team.
Shelly is *the most beautiful* girl I have ever seen.

Superlative forms differ from comparative forms only in one way: the *-er* ending becomes *-est* in the superlative, and *more* becomes (the) *most* in the superlative. Note that *the* usually precedes superlative forms.

Simple	Comparative	Superlative
long	longer	(the) longest
fat	fatter	(the) fattest
loud	louder	(the) loudest
pretty	prettier	(the) prettiest
beautiful	more beautiful	(the) most beautiful

> **In Summary:** To use the superlative form of a regular adjective,
>
> 1. add *-est* to one-syllable adjectives (tall → tallest);
> 2. add *-est* to two-syllable adjectives ending in *-y* or *-ow* (happy → happiest; pretty → prettiest; narrow → narrowest). Add *most* to virtually all other two-syllable adjectives (gruesome → most gruesome);
> 3. put *most* before all adjectives of three or more syllables (unusual → most unusual);
> 4. generally, use *the* before superlatives.

5 WARM-UP

Fill in the correct superlative form of the adjective in parentheses.

1. In a survey published in the January 10, 1982, *Chicago Tribune*, leading historians, authors, and political scholars said that Abraham Lincoln was (great) ____the greatest____ American president in history.

2. The same survey determined that Warren G. Harding was (inept) _____ president.

3. The place with (long) _____ name is probably Krung Thep Mahanakhon Borvorn Ratanakosin Mahintharayutthaya Mahadilok pop Noparatratchathani Burirom Udumratchanivetmahasathan Amornpiman Avatarnsathit Sakkathattiyavisnukarmprasit, which is the poetic full name for the capital of Thailand. Foreigners call it Bangkok.

4. According to *Cat Fancy*, September, 1981, (popular) _____ name for a male cat is Tiger or Tigger.

5. (Small) _____ country on Earth is Vatican City, only 16 square miles with a population of 750. It is located inside Rome, Italy.

6. According to *The Hobo's Handbook*, (friendly) _____ freight yard for hopping trains is the Burlington Northern in Minot, North Dakota, while (unfriendly) _____ is the Union Pacific in Cheyenne, Wyoming.

7. As of 1983 (big) _____ money-losing movie of all time was *Heaven's Gate*, which lost at least thirty-four million dollars.

8. According to the Gallup Poll, (hated) _____ household task is washing dishes.

9. (Large) _____ country in the world by area is the Soviet Union.

10. (Tall) _____ building in the world is Sears Tower in Chicago.

6 WRITING   Write a statement using a superlative form of an adjective to describe one of three subjects from each group in parentheses.

1. (three fish) _The salmon is *the largest* of the three fish._

2. (three clowns) _____
   _____

3. (three turkeys) _____
   _____

4. (three old suits) _____
   _____

5. (three beautiful watches) _____
   _____

6. (three used cars) _____
   _____

COMPARING REGULAR ADVERBS

Regular adverbs always end in *-ly*, and you cannot add anything to this ending. (For example, you cannot compare *quickly* by using *quicklier* or *quickliest!*) Therefore, when you compare *-ly* adverbs, use the same patterns that you use when comparing three- and four-syllable adjectives: *as* _____ *as*, *more* _____ *than*, and *the most* _____. Here are a few examples of sentences that compare *-ly* adverbs.

(equality) She dances *as gracefully as* a ballerina.

(comparative) She did her work *more carefully than* Maria (did).

(superlative) Toni completed the assignment *the most rapidly* of anyone in the class.

In Summary: To use the comparative or superlative form of an adverb ending in *-ly,*

1. place *more* in front of the adverb to form the comparative. Follow the adverb with *than (more awkwardly than);*
2. place *(the) most* in front of the adverb to form the superlative *(the most awkwardly).*

7 WARM-UP Fill in the correct comparative or superlative form of the adverb in parentheses.

1. The population of Swaziland, Africa, is growing (quickly)

   _____ more quickly _____ than that of any other nation.

2. Calamity Jane, with twelve husbands, was at the altar (frequently)

   _____ than Pancho Villa, with nine wives.

3. The name Johnson appears (commonly) _____

   than the name Jones in the United States.

4. People have bought the Bible (steadily _____

   than *Quotations from the Works of Mao Tse-tung.* The Bible has sold 1.5

   billion copies; *Quotations* has sold 800 million copies.

5. According to the FBI, a murder is (likely) _____

   to happen between 6:00 P.M. and 6:00 A.M.

COMPARING IRREGULAR ADJECTIVES AND ADVERBS

Adjectives and Adverbs with the Same Form

A few words can serve as adjectives or adverbs. Here is a partial list.

early	hard	low
fast	late	straight

The comparative and superlative forms of these words are the same whether they are used as adjectives or adverbs.

Simple	*Comparative*	*Superlative*
early	earlier	(the) earliest
fast	faster	(the) fastest
hard	harder	(the) hardest
late	later	(the) latest
low	lower	(the) lowest
straight	straighter	(the) straightest

Good Versus Well*   People sometimes confuse these two words. *Good* is an adjective.

   a *good* job

   The steak is *good*.

Well is an adverb.

   He did the job *well*.

   The car runs *well*.

*Well can also be an adjective when it means "in good health" (I am feeling well).

However, the comparative and superlative forms of *good* and *well* are the same.

Simple	*Comparative*	*Superlative*
good	better	(the) best
well	better	(the) best

(adjectives) The salad is *good*. The soup is *better*. But the dessert is *the best* of all.

(adverbs) Juan draws *well*. Lourdes draws *better*. But Sixta draws *the best* of the three.

8 WARM-UP

Circle the proper adjective or adverb in parentheses.

1. Tom wrote a (good/well) paper.
2. Tom wrote (good/well).
3. Yolanda is (good/well) to small animals.
4. But she does not treat people (good/well).
5. The copper cleaner shined the bottom of the pot really (good/well).
6. It is a (good/well) product.
7. Angela is certainly (good/well)-looking in that dress.
8. When Terry had the flu, she didn't feel (good/well).

9 TRANSFORMING

Circle the correct adjective or adverb in parentheses in the left-hand column. Then use the correct comparative or superlative form of that word in the right-hand column.

1. Susan swims (good/well).

1. But Maria swims
   _____better_____ .

2. His painting looks (good/well).

2. But Renoir's painting looks
   _____ of all.

3. Nobody does it half as (good/well) as you.

3. Nobody does it
   _____ .

4. The team performed as (good/well) as could be expected.

4. But its opponents performed
   _____ .

5. I have seen some (good/well)-trained dogs.

5. But Lance is _____
   -trained dog that I have ever seen.

Bad Versus Badly

Bad is an adjective.

a *bad* actor
I feel *bad*.

Badly is an adverb.

He performs *badly*.

He took a *badly* needed vacation.

Like *good* and *well*, *bad* and *badly* have the same comparative and superlative forms.

Simple	*Comparative*	*Superlative*
bad	worse	the worst
badly	worse	the worst

10 WARM-UP

Circle the correct adjective or adverb form in parentheses.

1. With his sprained ankle, Henderson runs (bad/badly).
2. With his sprained ankle, Henderson is a (bad/badly) runner.
3. He felt (bad/badly) when he heard the news.
4. He made his presentation (bad/badly).
5. His suit is (bad/badly) worn.
6. That drink is (bad/badly) tasting.
7. The color has faded (bad/badly).
8. The faded color looks (bad/badly).

11 TRANSFORMING

Circle the correct adjective or adverb in parentheses in the left-hand column. Then use the correct comparative or superlative form of that word in the right-hand column.

1. The light in this room is (bad/badly).

   1. In fact, of the light in all the rooms, it is ___the worst___.

2. The old schoolhouse looks (bad/badly).

   2. But it looks _____ than it actually is.

3. Jerome plays tennis (bad/badly).

   3. But Juan plays _____ than Jerome.

4. He fell and broke his arm (bad/badly).

   4. It was broken _____ of any the doctor had seen in years.

5. The spoiled child behaves very (bad/badly).

   5. He always behaves _____ than my son.

Less and *Least*

So far you have seen how to use adjectives and adverbs to make things *bigger* or *greater* or *more*. Suppose, however, that you want to make them *smaller* or *less*. Here is how you do it.

Simple	Comparative	Superlative
tall	less tall	(the) least tall
beautiful	less beautiful	(the) least beautiful
quickly	less quickly	(the) least quickly

As you can see, the comparative and superlative forms are *the same for adjectives and adverbs.*

comparative = less   superlative = least

12 EDITING

The following passage contains many errors in the use of adjectives and adverbs. Cross out the errors and write in your corrections above each line.

The Loch Ness Monster

(1) Loch Ness is one of the ~~more~~ larger lakes in Scotland. (2) It is 750 feet deep, twice as deep than the North Sea. (3) It is more long than twenty-four miles and varies in width from one to three miles. (4) For 1500 years people have been seeing a monster in it. (5) The legend is that long ago, people saw "the most oddest looking beastie, something like a huge frog, only it isn't a frog."

(6) In 1933 several people saw the monster. (7) One man, who observed it good, said he saw a series of humps above the water, with a long thick neck on which there was a much more small, snakelike head. (8) Its skin was gray-black. (9) Two months more later a couple from London saw the monster even closer. (10) It was crossing a road. (11) They said its body was five feet high and as wide like the road. (12) It moved as jerky as a snail. (13) Later, when he was shown a picture of a prehistoric dinosaur called a *plesiosaur,* the man said that the two looked alike.

(14) During the early 1930s several people photographed the monster. (15) In fact Sir Edward Mountain, who lived near the lake, arranged for people with binoculars to watch for its appearance. (16) A few weeks later he was able to take the onliest movie of it.

(17) Since World War II the monster has been taken much more serious than other monsters. (18) In October 1954 the passengers on a bus driving

by the lake were able to get the most best look at the monster. (19) They observed it for ten minutes from a distance no farther than one hundred yards. (20) In December 1954 a fishing boat was crossing the lake when its radar began to chart something swimming at a depth more great than five hundred feet. (21) It was recorded as a creature with a small head on an enormouser neck, with eight short legs, and with a fifteen-foot tail. (22) It measured about fifty feet in length.

(23) Four years later the British Broadcasting Company attempted to produce a program about the monster. (24) Using radar, it recorded an object that moved twelve feet more deep than the boat's bottom. (25) Then, just as quick as it appeared, the object disappeared. (26) Two days later four men riding by on a bus saw humps come up in the same spot.

(27) People are real sure that there is something big living in Loch Ness. (28) The bestest guess is that it is a plesiosaur. (29) The monster could even be traveling between the lake and the ocean through an underground water route. (30) It might come to the lake to breed or to escape its enemies at sea. (31) Whatever it is, the monster still remains one of the most greatest mysteries in the world.

SOME ADDITIONAL HELP IN USING AND COMPARING ADJECTIVES AND ADVERBS

Don't Confuse an Adjective After a Linking Verb with an Adverb After an Action Verb

Chapter 2 distinguishes between action verbs and linking verbs. You may wish to review that material now. In it you will see that an *adjective* describing the subject of a sentence often follows a linking verb. Here are some examples.

Joe looks *happy*.
Joe sounds *happy*.
Joe appears *happy*.
Joe seems *happy*.
Joe is *happy*.

On the other hand, a descriptive word following an action verb is almost always an adverb.

Joe works *well* with small children.

Joe plays the piano *well*.

Joe entered the room *happily*.

13 WARM-UP   Circle the correct adjective or adverb form in parentheses.

1. After much practice Hernando became (proficient/proficiently) at tennis.

2. After much practice Hernando learned to play tennis (good/well).

3. He feels (bad/badly) about the error.

4. He performed (bad/badly) and made a mistake.

5. June sews very (careful/carefully).

6. June is very (careful/carefully) about the way she sews.

7. The dessert tastes (delicious/deliciously) to me.

8. The icing was (delicious/deliciously) sweet.

9. The solution to your problem is (obvious/obviously).

10. The answer seemed (obvious/obviously) to me.

Don't Use Both *more/most* and *-er/-est* When Comparing Adjectives

You can form the comparatives or superlatives of adjectives *either* by adding *more/most* or by adding *-er/-est*. Don't use both.

incorrect: One meal is *more* tasti*er* than another.
correct: One meal is tasti*er* than another.
incorrect: The blue dress looks *more* bett*er* than the yellow one.
correct: The blue dress looks bett*er* than the yellow one.

Don't Use Adjective Forms to Compare Adverbs

Many people confuse adjectives with adverbs in the comparative and superlative forms. Remember that an adverb explains *how* an action occurs or occurred—it describes a verb, not a noun.

incorrect: He did it *quicker* (adjective) than I did.
correct: He did it *more quickly* (adverb) than I did.
incorrect: The road work is going *slower* (adjective) than planned.
correct: The work is going *more slowly* (adverb) than planned.
incorrect: Cindy skated the *poorest* (adjective) of anyone in the skating rink.
correct: Cindy skated the *most poorly* (adverb) of anyone in the rink.

14 WARM-UP   Circle the correct adjective or adverb form in parentheses.

1. Cowboys in the movies always talk and act (slower/more slowly) than normal people.

2. Julio behaves (more serious/more seriously) than my other friends.

3. The music played (softer/more softly) than usual.

4. Of the ten people I met, Dick shook my hand the (firmest/most firmly).

5. His presentation was (more convincing/more convincingly) organized than his opponent's.

15 EDITING   The following passage contains many errors in the use of adjectives and adverbs. Write in your corrections above each line.

The Bermuda Triangle

(1) Flight 19 should have been as routine ∧ as ~~than~~ any normal training flight from the Naval Air Station at Fort Lauderdale, Florida. (2) On December 5, 1945, five torpedo bombers equipped with the bestest navigational and radio equipment took off and flew good at a speed of two hundred miles per hour.

(3) They should have returned to the base 1½ hours more later. (4) Instead there was a real weird radio message from the flight commander: "Calling tower. (5) This is an emergency. . . . (6) We seem to be off course. . . . (7) We cannot see land." (8) When the pilot was told to head due west, he radioed: "We do not know which way is west. (9) Everything looks badly . . . even the ocean doesn't look as it should."

(10) Fifteen minutes passed, and the personnel in the control tower heard the pilot say that he was turning over control of the flight to one of his men. (11) The pilot's action was unusual, but even unusualer was the next (and last) message: "Not certain where we are. . . . (12) Looks like we are—"

(13) A Martin flying boat with a crew of thirteen men took off as quick as it could to begin a search for the missing planes. (14) In five minutes it vanished more mysterious than Flight 19, without even sending back radio messages. (15) All night long Coast Guard planes searched, and in the morning an aircraft carrier sent up more planes than before. (16) In all, there were twenty-one ships, three hundred planes, and twelve land-based parties looking for the missing Flight 19 and the Martin flying boat. (17)

However, the missing planes had disappeared more completer than any others ever had. (18) There was no trace of them, not even an oil slick.

(19) Since 1945 many planes and ships have vanished, as did Flight 19, in the Bermuda Triangle, the area bounded by Florida, Bermuda, Puerto Rico, and Jamaica. (20) Perhaps it is simply coincidence that planes and ships there have vanished the most frequent. (21) Since the area is heavily traveled, accidents are more likelier to take place. (22) On the other hand, some scientists think that explanation is not the onliest one. (23) Perhaps the ocean there produces chemical reactions that make humans lose their sense of direction. (24) Then again, perhaps the Bermuda Triangle is the same like several areas of the world where gravity and magnetism are thought to work strange. (25) The planes might have fallen *up*. (26) Perhaps spaceships from another planet captured the planes and ships (or at least their crews). (27) Finally, and the most interestingest, perhaps the ships, planes, and people aboard them passed into a fourth dimension through a kind of gap in time.

COMPARISON AND CONTRAST

Comparison and contrast is *an examination of the similarities and differences among people, ideas, or things.* You sometimes make such an examination in order to evaluate: to decide which is best or most friendly or most valuable. Other times you compare and contrast in order to describe subjects more clearly. The contrast control on a television set makes the picture sharper, and a contrast between people or things often brings them into sharper focus than would a simple description.

To write a clear and logical comparison and contrast paper, keep these ideas in mind, especially during revisions.

1. *Don't oversimplify.* Few issues are as simple as black versus white or good versus evil. It's fine to say that Movie A is better than Movie B, but don't automatically assume that Movie B is a waste of time. Movie B may be pretty good—but not as good as Movie A.
2. *Don't use circular reasoning.* When explaining *why* Movie A is better than Movie B, give specific, concrete reasons to support your claim. Don't say merely that Movie A was better because it was better. For example, the statement, "Movie A was interesting because it held my attention," is circular reasoning because "interesting" and "held my

attention" mean the same thing. A better statement would be, "Movie A was interesting because it was quick-moving, full of surprises, and well acted."

3. *Be consistent in your organization.* There are two ways to organize a comparison and contrast of Movie A and Movie B.
   a. *Whole to whole.* In this organization describe Movie A completely, then Movie B completely. Draw comparisons and contrasts either after describing both movies or while describing Movie B.
   b. *Part to part.* In this organization describe one part of Movie A, such as its plot, and then draw a comparison to the plot of Movie B. Next return to Movie A to describe its acting and then draw another comparison to the acting in Movie B. Proceed in this manner until you have drawn all the comparisons between the two movies.

Here is an example of a paragraph that compares and contrasts two ideas.

In most parts of the world monogamy—the practice of one man marrying one woman—has been the rule for hundreds of years. However, outside the industrialized world, certain societies have practiced *polygyny* (marriage of one man to several wives), and other societies have practiced *polyandry* (marriage of one woman to several husbands). The reasons for one practice are quite different from the reasons for the other. Polygyny occurs most frequently in societies with a shortage of men and an oversupply of women. For the men, their multiple wives provide sexual benefits, a cheap source of household labor, and a way of obtaining status. The more wives a man has, the more powerful he appears to other men. For the women who consent to marriage, the practice merely allows them to survive with a small amount of dignity. Without a husband to support them, they die of starvation or become prostitutes. Although polygyny was (and is) most common in primitive societies in Australia, the South Pacific, and Africa, it has occurred in more advanced cultures as well. It even happened in the United States among the Mormons, but it was made illegal in 1900. On the other hand, polyandry occurs in far fewer societies of any sort, mainly because women have historically lacked the social and economic power of men. In fact polyandry, like polygyny, largely benefits men—not women. In some societies, when a man is too poor to afford a wife all for himself, he shares her with another man or men. Often the multiple husbands are brothers with still another motive—to keep their land in the family. For example, in Tibet a woman might marry a whole group of brothers. One of them will stay home with her while the others go to war, herd sheep, or go on trading expeditions. In fact unlike societies in which polygyny has been common, societies that have engaged in polyandry have not suffered from a natural shortage of one sex or the other. To hold down the percentage of women in the population, some primitive tribes have even killed off a number of the female babies. Groups that practice polyandry have been located in Tibet, Siberia, and other places not very hospitable to human beings. (The practice still continues in some of these places.) In sum, although polygyny should benefit men and polyandry should benefit women, both types of multiple marriage have actually benefited men.

Discussion Questions

1. Is this a whole-by-whole or a part-by-part comparison and contrast? What words and phrases are used to draw the contrasts?
2. What other organizational devices—narration, description, classification, cause-effect, definition, process analysis—does the paragraph use?
3. Is the purpose of the paragraph to inform, to persuade, or to entertain?
4. What is the topic sentence of the paragraph, the sentence that introduces the contrasts?
5. What is the similarity between polygyny and polyandry? Which sentence makes that point?

PARAGRAPH WRITING AND REVISING ASSIGNMENT

Choose two subjects that are similar in some ways: hockey and soccer, rock music and jazz, two teachers you have had (don't use their real names), two jobs you have had, two vacations you have taken, or any other subjects you can write about comfortably. Compare and contrast them to show why one is or was better than the other. Assume that your audience is a group of general readers who are somewhat familiar with one of the subjects (for example, rock music but not jazz) or who are unfamiliar with both (the two teachers, for example) and that your main purposes is either to inform or persuade.

During the prewriting stages list the points of similarity and difference, adding to and revising the list until you feel confident about your organization. Then write a first draft. The later revisions of the paragraph should include a topic sentence that makes your point clear, and it should draw at least three specific comparisons and contrasts.

In your final revisions and during the editing stage, check the paragraph carefully for the correct forms of adjectives and adverbs in comparisons. Also scrutinize the paper for these matters:

1. complete sentences and clauses;
2. correct use of coordination to join sentences;
3. correct use of subordination to join sentences;
4. correct noun-plural forms and subject-verb agreement;
5. correct past-tense and past-participle forms;
6. parallel structures, consistency in tense, and consistency in pronoun number and case;
7. correctly placed modifiers;
8. correct use of pronouns; and
9. correctly spelled words.

Once again, make a clean copy of your work and proofread it.

SUPPLEMENTARY WRITING AND REVISING ASSIGNMENT

Write a four- or five-paragraph paper that argues why one behavior in school, in society, or even at an informal gathering such as a party is better than another. For example, discuss why majoring in computer science is better than majoring in marketing (or vice versa). Discuss why having a small family is better than having a large family (or vice versa). Discuss why groups that don't take drugs are better than groups that do. Again, your audience should be general readers, and your purpose should be to persuade.

Whatever you choose to write about, make sure you know the subject well enough to make a convincing argument. (Also make sure you can and do explain ideas that are unfamiliar to your readers.) Since the paper will be drawing contrasts to support your argument, at some point in the writing process, divide the paper into paragraphs that develop each contrast separately.

During the editing stage be sure to check your paper for the same matters mentioned in the "Paragraph Writing and Revising Assignment."

Here is an example of a paper that draws several contrasts between two kinds of nuclear weapons. As you read it, note the specific contrasts it makes and the reasoning that supports each one.

The "Safe" Weapon

Everyone knows about the terrible power of the hydrogen bomb, or H-bomb. It can wipe out whole cities, kill millions of people, and leave clouds of radioactivity (called fallout) that linger for many years, making large areas of the globe unlivable. However, another type of atomic bomb, called the neutron bomb (or N-bomb), is less well known. Its effects may be quite different from those of the H-bomb—in some ways less terrible, but in other ways far worse.

For one thing, when an H-bomb explodes it flattens everything for miles—buildings, trees, and people—and burns everything and everyone in a much wider area. However, the N-bomb destroys far less property but kills people from intense radiation. So, in theory, a city could be reinhabited within a short time after an N-bomb was dropped. (This assumes, of course, that there are people left to return to the city.)

The neutron bomb is supposedly a more desirable weapon for a second reason. In theory, the N-bomb causes far less radioactive fallout than the H-bomb. Therefore the N-bomb would kill only the people directly in the target area and not any innocent people outside the area.

What then are the disadvantages of the N-bomb? The first answer to this question lies in the weapon's attractiveness. Unlike the H-bomb, which is so terrifying that no sane person would ever consider exploding it, the neutron bomb seems "safe." It could be used in a "limited" war since, theoretically, it kills only the people within a carefully defined area. Therefore the leaders of a country at war might actually be tempted to use such a weapon.

The second disadvantage hinges on the phrase "in theory." The bomb has never been tested, so no one knows its effects for sure. In theory, the weapon is "safer" than the H-bomb, but would the N-bomb be safer in practice? Would its radiation disappear within a short time? Would there be no fallout? Or would the explosion of several neutron bombs create a much larger cloud of radioactivity than anyone had thought? Could the whole world perish because a new weapon seemed theoretically sound but wasn't? Unfortunately, the only way to test the weapon is on a real population during a real war, and that's a risk we can't take.

Thus, while the neutron bomb may be more limited in destructive power than the hydrogen bomb, it may ultimately be more dangerous. Unlike the H-bomb, which only madmen would use, the N-bomb appears to be a weapon for "sane" leaders. They might drop it, and it might just destroy us all.

Discussion Questions

1. Which method of contrast—whole to whole or part to part—is used in this theme?
2. The first paragraph says that the N-bomb may be "less terrible" than the H-bomb "but in some ways far worse." Which paragraphs discuss the "less terrible" aspects of the N-bomb? Which paragraphs discuss the "far worse" aspects?
3. What words or phrases in the second and fourth paragraphs signal a contrast between ideas?
4. The fifth paragraph includes many questions. Does the author expect answers to these questions? What is the purpose of the questions?

CHAPTER 11

Punctuating Sentences

As you have already seen in Chapters 3 and 4, punctuation—commas, periods, semicolons, and the like—helps readers understand your sentences and thus avoid confusion. Some marks join ideas; other marks separate them. Punctuation incorrectly used can signal the end of a sentence that shouldn't end, join ideas that shouldn't be joined, or separate ideas that shouldn't be separated. To punctuate correctly, you must know the rules, which this chapter will explore in the following order: commas, periods, question marks, exclamation points, semicolons, colons, dashes, parentheses, and quotation marks.

USING THE COMMA

If you tend to place a comma wherever you hear a pause, don't do it. Commas have six specific uses—some to separate ideas, and others to enclose them. Learn those rules and you won't use too many commas, nor will you use too few.

Three or More Separate Items in a Series

When you write a series of three or more items, separate them by placing a comma after each item except the last one. Generally, *and* or another coordinating conjunction *(but, or, for, so, nor,* or *yet)* precedes the last item. A comma before this conjunction is optional; you can include the comma or not. But be consistent; include it each time or omit it each time.

(subjects)	*Anna, Maurice,* and *I*
(verbs)	They *came* late to the party, *threw* their coats on the bed, and *made* a dash for the refreshments.
(adjectives)	The field was *wet, muddy,* and *slippery.*
(phrases)	government *of the people, by the people,* and *for the people*

item in a series, item, and item

1 WARM-UP

Place commas where they are needed in the following groups of words. Some groups need no commas.

1. a dog‸ a cat‸ and a parakeet
2. an expensive diamond ring and a necklace
3. Would you please address this letter and mail it?
4. We always found Joe to be bright energetic and interesting.
5. in a few days or weeks
6. months years or decades away
7. We had to drive from the South Side to the North Side back to the South Side and then home.
8. She has blue eyes blonde hair and buckteeth.
9. Charles is going to finish his homework take a bath and go to sleep early tonight.
10. The telephone rang and rang until I picked it up.

2 WARM-UP

Place commas where they are needed in the following biography.

Henry VIII and His Six Wives

(1) King Henry VIII of England (1491–1547) had six wives: Catherine of Aragon‸ Anne Boleyn‸ Jane Seymore‸ Anne of Cleves‸ Catherine Howard‸ and Catherine Parr. (2) He divorced the first Catherine beheaded Anne lost Jane in a childbirth death annulled his marriage to Anne executed the second Catherine and stayed married to the last Catherine. (3) He was a busy—but unhappy—man.

(4) Why were there so many women who shared his crown? (5) The main reason was that he wanted to have a son, but in his last years he wanted a good woman as a political ally and a companion. (6) In fact he actually loved his first wife Catherine and wore her initials on his sleeve at tournaments.

(7) On January 1, 1511, Catherine of Aragon bore Henry a son. (8) People all through London lit bonfires drank wine and came to an elaborate pageant at Westminster Abbey. (9) Then seven weeks later the infant died. (10) In the following years Catherine became pregnant suffered numerous miscarriages and had many stillbirths. (11) The only child who lived to maturity was a daughter, Mary.

(12) Rumors of Henry's interest in other women started circulating within two years of his marriage to Catherine. (13) He had at least three mistresses: Mary Boleyn (Anne's sister) Bessie Blount and Anne Boleyn. (14) Eventually, he fell in love with Anne, who was a great flirt but no great beauty. (15) An Italian said this of her: "Mistress Anne is not one of the handsomest women in the world; she is of small height dark complexion long neck wide mouth and bosom not much raised." (16) Some people said that she had three breasts. (17) On her left hand she had a sixth finger that she hid in her dress folds, and many people considered it a mark of the devil.

(18) Henry wanted to marry Anne and asked the pope for a divorce from Catherine. (19) A long debate followed among Henry the pope and several English archbishops. (20) Meanwhile Anne became pregnant. (21) Henry desperately wanted a legitimate son, so he had an English archbishop declare his marriage to Catherine invalid, and then Henry married Anne. (22) Unfortunately, the baby was a girl, Elizabeth (who later became Queen Elizabeth I). (23) Henry was disappointed lost interest in Anne and began flirting with other women, including Jane Seymore. (24) Anne, desperate to keep her husband, decided to make him jealous. (25) She intensified her flirting with other men was accused of adultery and was sent to prison. (26) Eventually, Henry had her beheaded.

(27) Henry then married Jane. (28) She bore him a son named Edward, but she died twelve days later. (29) Henry was brokenhearted and began to search for a new wife. (30) Anne of Cleves was next, but Henry found her unattractive. (31) He bribed her to leave divorced her and executed the man who had recommended her.

(32) Henry's next queen was Catherine Howard. (33) By this time Henry was no prize. (34) He had an enormous belly slits for eyes and an ulcerated leg. (35) Catherine grew unhappy with him started to flirt took on some lovers and conducted a hot romance with a man named Thomas Culpeper. (36) This romance was a bad mistake and cost her her head in 1542.

(37) Catherine Parr was Henry's last wife. (38) Henry felt that she nursed him tenderly was kind to his children but tended to buy too many shoes and argue too much about religion. (39) Henry died while still married to her.

Two Independent Clauses Joined by Coordinating Conjunctions*

Separate Two Independent Clauses Joined by *and, but, or, for, so, or yet* with a Comma Before the Conjunction. Remember that an independent clause has a subject and a verb and can be a sentence by itself. Join two independent clauses with *and, but, or, for, so, nor* or *yet,* and place a comma before these conjunctions.

The Smiths' television set hasn't worked for a week, *so* they have been forced to talk to each other.

I love going to plays, *but* I can't afford them.

My history books cost twenty dollars, *and* my mathematics book costs fifteen.

Don't Use a Comma Between Two Verbs. Don't confuse two independent clauses with two *verbs,* which should have no comma before the *and* or *but* joining them.

incorrect:	Most college students work, and also have scholarships to pay tuition and housing expenses.
correct:	Most college students work *and also have* scholarships to pay tuition and housing expenses.
incorrect:	Puerto Rico is hot, but feels comfortable because of the constant breezes over the island.
correct:	Puerto Rico is *hot but* feels comfortable because of the constant breezes over the island.
correct:	Puerto Rico is hot, *but it feels* comfortable because of the constant breezes over the island.

> independent clause, *and* independent clause
> , *but*
> , *or*
> , *for*
> , *so*
> , *yet*
> , *nor*

*See Chapter 3 for further explanation of this rule.

3 EDITING

Some—but not all— of the sentences in the following biography contain two independent clauses and require commas. Place the commas where they are necessary.

"Diamond Jim" Brady (1856–1917): Millionaire and Food Lover

(1) James Buchanan ("Diamond Jim") Brady was a famous spender, and he was also the all-time U.S. eating champion. (2) He was born of poor Irish parents in New York but he worked his way up from a railroad porter to a salesperson for a railroad-equipment firm. (3) He was a very convincing salesperson and soon acquired a fortune.

(4) Hardly anyone has spent so much money nor has anyone spent it in worse taste than Diamond Jim. (5) He accumulated a wardrobe of two hundred custom-made suits and some fifty glossy silk hats and he bought jewelry worth at least two million dollars. (6) His diamond rings were the biggest ever seen in New York and his thirty watches included one valued after his death at seventeen thousand dollars. (7) He owned twelve gold-plated bicycles with diamonds and rubies on the handlebars and he spent great sums of money on girlfriends such as actress Lillian Russell.

(8) Jim had many loves but his greatest love was food. (9) He probably ate more than any other human being but never touched a drop of liquor. (10) For breakfast he would eat hominy grits, eggs, corn bread, muffins, flapjacks, chops, fried potatoes, a beefsteak, and a full gallon of orange juice. (11) However, such a light breakfast couldn't satisfy Jim's appetite so at 11:30, Jim would begin to feel hungry and he would snack on two or three dozen oysters and clams.

(12) His lunch at 12:30 consisted of more substantial food, such as more oysters and clams, several boiled lobsters, a slab of beef, and several pies so he was not hungry again until afternoon tea. (13) Then he would eat only a platter of seafood and chase it down with a gallon or so of lemon soda.

(14) Jim saved his appetite for dinner so that he could eat a really good meal. (15) For appetizers he consumed two or three dozen oysters and half

a dozen clams and then he gulped down two huge bowls of green-turtle soup. (16) The main course was more satisfying and consisted of six or seven lobsters, two whole ducks, two portions of turtle meat, a sirloin steak, vegetables, and an entire platter of pastries for dessert. (17) He washed all this down with more orange juice and gobbled a two-pound box of candy for a little after-dinner treat.

(18) Crowds would gather around his table in restaurants to cheer him on and to make bets on whether he would drop dead before dessert. (19) Jim did manage to live to be sixty-one but when he died an autopsy revealed that his stomach was six times larger than normal.

Interrupters

Place Two Commas Around Words, Phrases, or Clauses That Interrupt a Sentence. You often write words, phrases, or clauses that interrupt the flow of the sentence—that is, you insert them in the middle of a grammatically complete sentence. For example, read the following sentences, the first without the interrupter and the second with the interrupter:

> You will find that the water is cool.
> You will find, *however*, that the water is cool.

To show your readers that you have written a sentence interrupter, place two commas around the interrupter—in the same spots where parentheses would go if you used parentheses. Here are a few more examples.

> Jack Smith, your friend and mine, wants to borrow money again.
> Jack Smith (your friend and mine) wants to borrow money again.
> And I, who should know better, will probably lend it to him.
> And I (who should know better) will probably lend it to him.

Notice that the word(s) in parentheses could be removed from each sentence without seriously affecting its meaning. Thus there are two ways to test for sentence interrupters that should be enclosed in commas.

1. See if they fit logically within parentheses.
2. Temporarily remove them from the sentence.

The sentence interrupter is often an *appositive*, a word or phrase that renames a noun. Here are some examples of appositives.

> Henry David Thoreau, *a famous author*, lived for two years in a tiny cabin in the woods. (*Thoreau* and *a famous author* are the same person.)
> *Walden, his book about the experience*, is an American classic. (*Walden* and *his book* are the same thing.)

An appositive after a proper noun (that is, a capitalized noun) is generally a sentence interrupter.

Henry David Thoreau, *a famous author,* . . .

But an appositive after an uncapitalized noun may not be a sentence interrupter.

The famous author Henry David Thoreau . . .

Be careful to enclose an interrupter in *two* commas. When people write interrupters, they often hear just one pause and include only one comma. Notice the confusion that only one comma can cause.

incorrect: Jerry Brody, whom I think you know is going on to graduate school. (This looks like a sentence fragment.)

incorrect: Jerry Brody whom I think you know, is going on to graduate school. (This sentence seems to have a comma between its subject and verb: Jerry Brody, . . . is going . . . .)

correct: Jerry Brody, whom I think you know, is going on to graduate school.

> ,sentence interrupter,

4 **WARM-UP**

The following sentences contain only one comma before or after a sentence interrupter. Place the second comma where it is required.

1. Harry Smith the owner of the car you hit, is here with some friends to talk to you.
2. Remember however, that only one answer is correct.
3. I think that, after a few hours' sleep I will feel better.
4. Juan, you realize is learning English quickly.
5. The submarine races of course, go on as scheduled.
6. Tom's interesting table manners, such as drinking soup in his cupped hands make him a hit at parties.
7. John Keats, Percy Bysshe Shelley, and George Gordon Byron, the three youngest of the Romantic poets all died before the age of thirty-four.
8. Henry Crane, the author of *The Red Badge of Courage* an astonishingly realistic depiction of the Civil War, never served in the army and never saw a war.

Introductory Words and Phrases

Place a Comma After an Introductory Word, Phrase, or Clause.
Quite often, a sentence interrupter comes at the beginning of a sentence (like the phrase "quite often" in this sentence). When this happens, use only one comma since, of course, you cannot begin a sentence with a comma.

> However, you will find that the water is cool.
> In a few minutes, I will be leaving.

Often, by the way, these sentence interrupters are dependent clauses.*

> When you see me again, I will be a changed man.
> As she held packages in both arms and her keys in her teeth, she fumbled to open the door.

Notice that the words after each comma above make a complete sentence. The words before the comma interrupt the sentence.

> However, . . .
> In a few minutes, . . .
> When you see me again, . . .
> Holding her packages in both arms and her keys in her teeth, . . .

---

introductory words (or sentence interrupter), sentence

A sentence interrupter can also come at the end of a sentence.

> You will find that the water is cool, however.
> She fumbled to open the door, holding her packages in both arms and her keys in her teeth.

However, not every word or group of words at the end of a sentence interrupts the sentence.

> I will be leaving in *a few minutes*.
> I will be a changed man *when you see me again*.

Thus, as you can see, the comma before a word or group of words at the end of a sentence is optional. You can hear when it is necessary.

Finally, if you are not sure whether a word or a group of words interrupts a sentence—no matter where the word or group of words is placed—remember this simple rule:

When in doubt, leave the commas out.

---

*See Chapter 4 for more information on dependent clauses.

5 **TRANSFORMING**   Rewrite each of the following sentences, taking the sentence interrupter from the right-hand column and including it in the sentence on the left. Be sure to use commas where they are needed.

1. I couldn't believe my eyes.   nevertheless

Nevertheless, I couldn't believe my eyes.

2. There are only forty-six states.   contrary to popular opinion

_____

_____

3. The other four are officially   which are Kentucky,
called commonwealths.   Massachusetts, Pennsylvania, and
          Virginia

_____

_____

4. There are five Great Lakes,   Lake Michigan
but only one is entirely in the
United States.

_____

_____

5. Alaska and Louisiana have no   instead
counties but call separate areas
within themselves by other
names.

_____

_____

6. Louisiana calls these areas   however
parishes; Alaska calls them
divisions.

_____

_____

7. Only one state is named after a   although four state capitals bear
president.   the names of presidents

_____

_____

8. The state is Washington.   of course

_____

_____

9. Adolph Hitler owned 8960   while he was waging war against
   acres of land in Colorado.   the United States in 1942.

_____

_____

10. George Washington used to   thereafter
    refer to New York as "the seat
    of the Empire," so it was called
    "the Empire State."

_____

_____

_____

6 EDITING   Correctly punctuate the sentence interrupters in the following biography.

Carry Nation (1846–1911):
Anti-Drinking Crusader

(1) Carry Nation˄ the saloon-smashing giant around the turn of the century˄ was born in Kentucky. (2) At six feet and 175 pounds she was well equipped for the career of destruction to which the Lord summoned her. (3) After marrying a doctor when she was twenty-one she watched helplessly while he drank himself to death within two years. (4) Carry remarried in 1879 and dedicated herself to the fight against alcohol.

(5) David Nation her new husband was a traveling preacher and lawyer who took Carry to settle in Medicine Lodge, Kansas. (6) Soon Carry was elected chair of the local chapter of the Women's Christian Temperance Union. (7) At this point Kansas was technically a dry state although no one enforced the law. (8) To protest the existence of saloons all over town Carry wrote letters to everyone including the governor and the editors of the local papers. (9) When no one responded to her letters she decided to take matters into her own hands.

(10) She prayed for divine guidance and to her amazement heard a voice from above telling her to smash the saloons to pieces. (11) The next day June 5, 1900 she picked up bricks and stones from her backyard and wrapped them in old newspapers. (12) Walking into a saloon in a nearby town she began to heave stones at liquor bottles, a mirror, and two front windows as surprised men ducked for cover. (13) Not stopping there she invaded a bar in a famous hotel in Wichita, Kansas. (14) A huge mirror and a large picture of a nude woman entitled *Cleopatra at the Bath* hung over the bar. (15) When she saw the picture she flew into a rage shattering the mirror and ripping the canvas from the wall.

(16) Of course a policeman came to arrest her for defacing property. (17) Her reply to the charges was characteristic of her zeal: "Defacing? I am defacing nothing! I am destroying!" (18) Her trial attracted great publicity especially when embarrassed officials had to drop the charges since the bars she had attacked were themselves illegal.

(19) Carry now nationally famous set about destroying saloons everywhere. (20) She began however to use better weapons than stones: metal hatchets. (21) The hatchets soon became her trademark, and she published a weekly newspaper *The Hatchet*. (22) Women who before had been barred from all saloons began to imitate Carry and invade them. (23) Few though could match Carry's effectiveness and ability to terrify her victims the owners and the patrons of the saloons.

(24) At the age of sixty-three she made her greatest raid an attack on a famous barroom in the Union Depot in Washington, D.C. (25) With three hatchets named Faith, Hope, and Charity she ripped the bar apart attracting more publicity than ever. (26) Soon after as she was lecturing against the evils of alcohol she collapsed and was carried to a hospital where she died.

Two or More Adjectives

Place a Comma Between Adjectives in Places Where You Could Use *and*. If you can place *and* between two or more adjectives preceding a noun, you can use commas to separate them.

an ugly, disgusting wart
(an ugly *and* disgusting wart)

a thick, juicy, rare steak
(a thick *and* juicy *and* rare steak)

If you cannot place *and* between the adjectives preceding the noun, use no commas to separate them.

a bright red rubber ball
(*not* a bright *and* red *and* rubber ball)

a large frozen pizza
(*not* a large *and* frozen pizza)

> adjective (and), adjective

7 WARM-UP   Place commas where they are needed in the following groups of words.

1. a playful, friendly little puppy
2. an old gray elephant
3. a five-pound small-mouth bass
4. a towering glass and steel building
5. a worn torn and faded pair of blue jeans
6. a wise old man
7. a silent temperamental child
8. a turbo-charged high-powered engine
9. a graceful ballet dancer
10. a hustling competitive team

Dates and Addresses

Place a Comma After Each Element in a Date or Address, but Not Before a Zip Code.

May 12, 1978

On August 9, 1979, the building should be completed. (Note the comma after *1979*.)

Brookline, Massachusetts

1324 W. Juneway Street, Brookline, Massachusetts 01506 (Note that no comma comes before the zip code.)

We visited Texas last year. (A single element requires no comma.)

> element in date or address, element, element

8 WARM-UP

Punctuate the following dates or addresses.

1. 1522 E. Hartford Street, Elizabethtown, New York 12932
2. Have you been to New York before?
3. Jory began kindergarten on September 5 1972.
4. After June 5 1989 Kathy will be an attorney.
5. We expect 1988 to be a good year.
6. The Declaration of Independence was signed on July 4 1776 in Philadelphia Pennsylvania.

In Summary: Use commas

1. to separate three or more items in a series;
2. to separate two independent clauses joined by *and, but, or, for, so, nor,* or *yet;*
3. to enclose a sentence interrupter;
4. to separate introductory words or phrases from the rest of the sentence;
5. to separate two or more adjectives before a noun when *and* could be placed between the adjectives;
6. to separate elements in a date or an address.

---

9 EDITING

Place commas where they are needed in the following biography.

"Wild Bill" Hickok (1837–76): Famous Western Lawman

(1) He was born James Butler Hickok on a farm in La Salle County, Illinois. (2) After a fine career as an Indian scout for the army he turned up at Fort Riley Kansas where he was appointed U.S. deputy marshal in 1866. (3) Three years later in August 1869 Wild Bill was elected sheriff of Ellis County Kansas and he soon developed the reputation of being the best gunman and most colorful character in all of Kansas Territory.

(4) While most of his fellow lawmen wore plain durable clothes Wild Bill dressed like a prince. (5) He was fond of fine tailored suits with fancy satin

lapels and he liked to show off his collection of colorful silk ties. (6) He wore his hair below shoulder length carefully curled into ringlets kept in place with fragrant hair oil. (7) His long drooping moustache was waxed and it was twirled up at the ends.

(8) As early as 1866 Wild Bill boasted to a reporter that he had personally killed "considerably over one hundred men." (9) He soon improved on that total for as sheriff he had many opportunities. (10) Once for example two murderers fled from him in opposite directions down the street. (11) Bill pulled his two six-guns from his holsters and shot the two men simultaneously.

(12) In 1871 Wild Bill arrived in Abilene Kansas one of the most famous cow towns in the West. (13) All summer long hundreds of cowboys weary from months on the trail would spend a full year's pay in the brothels saloons gambling joints and other places of amusement around town. (14) Wild Bill already a legend was appointed marshal and told to clean up the town. (15) Nevertheless, Bill spent more time accepting bribes from local hustlers than making arrests—that is when he wasn't spending his time playing poker.

(16) Respectable people complained about Bill's behavior yet his reputation as a great lawman kept him on the job. (17) On the night of October 5 1871 however he went too far. (18) While playing poker he heard someone fire a shot outside rushed into the darkness and killed an innocent man named Phil Coe and then hearing someone coming up behind him turned around in time to shoot his own deputy. (19) The citizens of Abilene were fed up and fired him.

(20) Bill's career went downhill from then on and Bill was arrested several times for drunkenness. (21) Finally in 1876 he arrived in Deadwood South Dakota where he soon joined the local poker games. (22) On the afternoon of August 2 a young man named Jack McCall entered a saloon and shot Bill through the back of the head. (23) The bullet passed through

Bill's brain exited from his cheek and struck the left forearm of one Captain Massey a river boat pilot. (24) The cards Bill held in his hand as he died were two pairs aces and eights a combination known ever since as "the dead man's hand."

USING THE PERIOD

Statements

Use a Period to End All Statements. Do not use a period at the end of a question or exclamation.

It looks like a nice day.
Please help me move this chair.
I agree.

> *but*

Do you think it will rain?
Get out of here!

---

sentence. question? exclamation!

Abbreviations

Use a Period After Most Abbreviations. The following abbreviations require periods.

Mr., Mrs., Ms.
Dr.
Rev.
A.M., P.M.
etc.

You do not need periods within or after the abbreviations of some well-known organizations (CIA, AFL-CIO), television or radio stations (WBBM), and commonly used abbreviations (mph or scuba—self-contained underwater breathing apparatus). Consult your dictionary whenever you are not sure whether an abbreviation requires periods.

---

abbr. (but CIA)

You can use the abbreviations mentioned earlier in compositions. You should write out most other words rather than abbreviating them. *Do not* use the following abbreviations and symbols in your writing.

lb. (use *pounds*)
& (use *and*)
ft. (use *feet*)
Feb. (use *February*)
St. (use *street*)
w. (use *with*)

W. Va. (use *West Virginia*, except when addressing an envelope)
hr. (use *hour*)
yr. (use *year*)

10 WARM-UP

Place periods where they are needed in the following groups of words.

1. I don't care what you say⟨ I am not going to give a speech in front of all those people⟨

2. 121 W Third Ave, N Y, N Y

3. This party will cost us forty dollars

4. Mr and Mrs Jones

5. 6 ft 4 in and 178 lbs

6. Don't call me I'll call you

USING THE QUESTION MARK

Place a Question Mark at the End of All Direct Questions, but Not at the End of Indirect Questions.* All direct questions end in a question mark, but not indirect questions.

Where is the library?

> *but*

Please tell me where the library is.
Do you know the answer?

> *but*

He will ask you if you know the answer.

---

direct question? indirect question.

---

11 WARM-UP

Place a period or a question mark at the end of each of the following sentences.

1. When was the Revolutionary War ⟨?⟩

2. We have to know when the Revolutionary War was

---

*For more about indirect questions, see Chapter 12 and the section on quotation marks later in this chapter.

3. Could you baby-sit for her son tonight

4. She asked if you could baby-sit for her son tonight

5. How can he get downtown

6. He wants to find out how to get downtown

7. Why is the sky blue

8. My child asked me why the sky is blue

USING THE EXCLAMATION POINT

Place an Exclamation Point at the End of a Sentence, Word, or Phrase That Expresses Strong Emotion. An exclamation point signals excitement, anger, fear, and other strong emotions.

This is the last time I'll tell you!

Don't, please!

Help! Police!

Don't overuse exclamation points! They are intended only to show strong emotion! Too many of them will bombard your readers! (As do the three sentences you have just read.)

---

statement of strong emotion!

---

12 WARM-UP

End each of the following sentences with either a period or an exclamation point. Use an exclamation point only if the sentence expresses strong emotion.

1. Needless to say, I was surprised⌃

2. We don't need your help, I'm sure

3. *That* is what you call a large sandwich

4. I'm sick and tired of all this complaining

5. I'm being swallowed by a boa constrictor

6. Let's end this exercise

In Summary: Use periods

1. after each sentence that makes a statement;
2. after each abbreviated word, except those that stand for well-known organizations, television and radio stations, and commonly used groups of words.

> Use question marks
>
> after all direct questions but not after indirect questions.
>
> Use exclamation points
>
> after all sentences or sentence fragments expressing strong emotion.

USING THE SEMICOLON

Place a Semicolon Between Two Independent Clauses That Are Not Joined by a Conjunction.* Notice the semicolon between the independent clauses in each of the following sentences.

The lamp is working; it just needs a new bulb.

Pedro spoke only Spanish when he came to the United States; later, he learned to speak English well.

Teaching jobs are in short supply; however, Amelia still wants to teach.

Note that the joining word (the *conjunctive adverb*) after the semicolon is followed by a comma. It is punctuated just like a sentence interrupter at the beginning of a sentence.

> independent clause; independent clause

13 WARM-UP

Place semicolons and commas in the following sentences wherever necessary.

1. James wants to be a professional basketball player; therefore, he studies hard so he can continue to play ball.

2. Two is company three is a crowd

3. Use semicolons where they are necessary but don't use them before conjunctions.

4. If you think the last sentence was easy to punctuate you will have no trouble with this one.

5. He can't walk very well he sprained his ankle.

*For further explanation and examples, see Chapter 4.

6. Terry will do anything on a dare last week he swallowed a frog.

7. The craziest thing he ever did however was to eat four pizzas and chug a quart of beer.

8. This is the last sentence let's thank heaven for small favors.

Use Semicolons to Separate Items in a Series When the Items Contain Internal Commas. You will recall that commas separate three or more items in a series. However, the items in a series can also contain commas used for other purposes—such as commas separating city names from country names.

Shanghai, China
Seoul, South Korea
Calcutta, India
Mexico City, Mexico
Tokyo, Japan
Peking, China
Moscow, USSR

If you were to write these names in a series, separating them with commas, you would be using the commas for two purposes and would thus confuse your readers. Therefore retain the commas between the city and country names but use semicolons to separate the items in the series.

According to the 1987 Edition of *The World Almanac and Book of Facts*, the cities with the largest populations in the world are Shanghai, China; Seoul, South Korea; Calcutta, India; Mexico City, Mexico; Tokyo, Japan; Peking, China; and Moscow, USSR.

item, in a series; item, in a series; and item, in a series

14 WARM-UP

Place semicolons and commas where they are needed in the following sentences.

1. The officers of the organization are William Conley, president; Alice Steptoe, vice-president; Latoya Smith, treasurer; and Sandy Derwinski, secretary.

2. The novels you will read in the American literature course are Nathaniel Hawthorne *The Scarlet Letter* Mark Twain *Huckleberry Finn* Herman Melville *Moby-Dick* William Faulkner *The Sound and the Fury* F. Scott Fitzgerald *The Great Gatsby* and Ernest Hemingway *For Whom the Bell Tolls*.

3. If you are going south on your vacation, be sure to visit Bear Wallow Kentucky Pewee Kentucky Bulls Gap Tennessee Difficult Tennessee Hot House North Carolina Improve Mississippi Scratch Ankle Alabama and Dime Box Texas. (They are all on the map.)

4. The winners of the Academy Awards for 1985 were as follows: Best Picture *Out of Africa* Best Actor William Hurt in *Kiss of the Spider Woman* Best Actress Geraldine Page in *The Trip to Bountiful* Best Supporting Actor Don Ameche in *Cocoon* Best Supporting Actress Anjelica Houston in *Prizzi's Honor* and Best Director Sydney Pollack in *Out of Africa.*

5. Among the most important dates in World War II were September 1 1939 when Hitler invaded Poland December 7 1941 when the Japanese attacked Pearl Harbor Hawaii September 3 1943 when Italy surrendered to the Allies May 7 1945 when Germany surrendered unconditionally and September 2 1945 when Japan also surrendered.

USING THE COLON

Use a Colon After a Complete Statement That Introduces a List or a Long Quotation.

Please bring the following items: a spool of thread, several yards of material, a set of sewing needles, and a four-foot dueling sword.

After the group had debated the subject, Debra concluded the meeting with these words: "I've heard all sides of the question now from everyone involved. Obviously, no solution will please you all. So let's return here next week after you have had a chance to consider things more carefully. Then we can decide."

Don't use a colon every time you have a list. Use a colon only after a *complete* statement.

Please bring a spool of thread, several yards of material, a set of sewing needles, and a four-foot dueling sword. (*Please bring* is not a complete statement since the verb *bring* needs an object.)

Never place a colon after any form of *to be.*

incorrect: His favorite foods *are:* tacos, enchiladas, and chop suey.
correct: His favorite foods *are* tacos, enchiladas, and chop suey.

introductory statement: list or long quote

Don't Use Semicolons to Introduce Lists. Remember that semicolons join independent clauses.

These tacos are delicious; I'll take another seven.

Colons introduce lists.

This is a fine neighborhood to live in except for a few things: crime, dirt, and run-down buildings.

In Summary: Use a semicolon

1. to join two independent clauses not joined by *and, but, or, for, so, nor,* or *yet;*
2. to separate items in a series when the items have internal punctuation.

Use a Colon

after a complete statement introducing a list or a long quote.

---

15 WARM-UP

Use either a *colon* or a *semicolon*—whichever is required—in each of the following sentences.

1. For our trip to Central America we took only the essentials‸ suntan lotion, some light clothing, and a great deal of money.
2. We have always wanted to visit Ecuador many of our family live there.
3. I have to go to the grocery store I need some vegetables and fruit.
4. The climate must be changing winters have been unbearable the last few years.
5. Your car needs a major overhaul its motor, transmission, and brakes are worn out.
6. Your car needs many parts replaced a new motor, a new transmission, and new brakes.
7. The party had everything food, music, and the right kind of entertainment.
8. Vanessa likes helping people she wants to be a nurse.

16 WARM-UP

Place colons in the following sentences when necessary.

1. I want you to get me several things‸ two dozen eggs, three heads of lettuce, a pound of bananas, and a loaf of bread.
2. She is wearing the latest summer fashions a halter top, flowered shorts, orange and green spiked hair, and fourteen pounds of jewelry.
3. I just bought a new pair of tennis shoes, a tennis bag, and three cans of tennis balls.

4. Remember that you can take one from column A, two from column B, and your choice of two from column C or three from column D.

5. This is everything you should need a mosquito net, a tent, a set of fishing poles, and five cases of beer.

6. The requirements for graduation are 120 hours completed with a 3.0 average.

USING THE DASH

Use Two Dashes to Enclose Sentence Interrupters That You Want to Emphasize. Use the dash (—) in pairs, just like the two commas that enclose sentence interrupters. Most of the time, in fact, you can use dashes and commas interchangeably to enclose sentence interrupters. However, the dashes make an interrupter more dramatic; they call attention to it. When you want to emphasize an interrupter, use two dashes instead of two commas.

Some—but not all—of the work was easy.
The answer—I think—is obvious.
Jim Browne—that man over there—is the one you want to see.

Of course, an interrupter can come at the end of a sentence. When that happens, use only one dash.

The answer is obvious—I think.

Dashes usually aren't used for interrupters at the beginning of a sentence.

Sometimes you use dashes not only for emphasis but for clarity, for example, when an interrupter has internal commas that would confuse your readers. The following sentence, which began this chapter, illustrates the point:

Punctuation—commas, periods, semicolons, and the like—helps your readers understand your sentences.

—emphasized sentence interrupter—
—sentence interrupter, punctuated with commas—

USING PARENTHESES

Use Two Parentheses to Enclose a Sentence Interrupter That You Want to Deemphasize. Parentheses work in just the opposite way from dashes. Instead of calling attention to a sentence interrupter, they draw attention away from it. They enclose information that is merely incidental to a sentence (usually short explanations, definitions, or examples—like the material you are reading right now). Think of parentheses as footnotes within a sentence; almost anything that can go in a footnote can go in parentheses.

> The *wallaby* (a small- or medium-sized kangaroo) is found only in Australia and New Zealand.
>
> George Washington Gale Ferris (1859–96) built the Ferris wheel for the World's Columbian Exposition in Chicago in 1893.
>
> Only a few states (such as Wisconsin) border two of the Great Lakes.

Notice that the parentheses are part of the sentence in which they appear, so the period ending the sentence goes after the final parenthesis (like this).

Use parentheses sparingly, however. Too many parentheses are distracting or annoying to your readers.

(incidental information)

In Summary: Use dashes

to enclose a sentence interrupter that you want to emphasize.

Use parentheses

to enclose incidental information in a sentence.

---

17 WARM-UP

Each of the following sentences contains an interrupter. Enclose it in two dashes (or use one dash) if it should be emphasized; enclose it in parentheses if it provides incidental information.

1. Sizzling hot meteors ∧ some huge fireballs, others mere specks ∧ bombard the earth's atmosphere at the rate of one million per hour.

2. Five planets Mercury, Venus, Mars, Jupiter, and Saturn are visible to the naked eye.

3. Uranus the first planet beyond normal eyesight to be observed was discovered accidentally by William Herschel, who thought it was a comet.

4. For many years the best candidate among the planets for sustaining life other than Earth, of course was Mars.

5. Since the moon's gravity is too weak to capture and hold atmosphere, there is no weather at all on the moon in fact, there is no wind, no sound, no life.

6. The surface temperature of the sun is approximately 6000 degrees Kelvin 11,000 degrees Fahrenheit.

USING QUOTATION MARKS

Titles

Put Quotation Marks Around the Titles of Poems, Magazine Articles, Newspaper Articles, Songs, and Other Short Works. You should *underline* the titles of complete books, the names of magazines, the names of newspapers, and other complete longer works.

> <u>Time</u> (magazine)
> The <u>Washington Post</u> (newspaper name)
> <u>Airport</u> (book title)
> <u>Citizen Kane</u> (movie)

However, you should *quote* the titles of short works or works contained within longer ones.

> "Coming of Age" (chapter title within a book)
> "Raging Fire Kills Three" (newspaper headline)
> "Michelle" (song title contained within an album)
> "Ode on a Grecian Urn" (poem contained within a book of poems)

Note: Never put quotation marks around or underline the title of your own writing.

> "Title of Short Work"
> <u>Title of Long Work</u>

18 WARM-UP

Use underlining or quotation marks for the following titles.

1. <u>Newsweek</u> (magazine)
2. The Saint Louis Post Dispatch (newspaper)
3. War and Peace (novel)
4. The Undervalued Dollar (title of article) in U.S. News & World Report (magazine)
5. Grease (play) played on Broadway for years.
6. My favorite song from Flashdance (movie) is Maniac.
7. Dodgers Win 3–2 (headline)
8. Perhaps Robert Frost's most popular poem is The Road Not Taken.
9. Death of a Salesman (play)
10. The Sun Also Rises (book)

Definitions

Put Quotation Marks Around Words You Are Defining and Around Their Definitions. To call attention to a word you are defining, quote or underline the word and its definition.

"Agnostic" literally means "without knowledge" (of God), while "atheist" means "without belief in God."

<u>Recalcitrant</u> means <u>unwilling</u>; it comes from a Latin word that means <u>to kick back</u>.

"word to be defined" and "definition"
or
<u>word to be defined</u> and <u>definition</u>

Words Used in a Special Way

Quote Words That You Use in a Special Way. When you use words in an original or unusual way, put the words in quotation marks.

When Carry Nation was smashing saloons, Kansas was technically a "dry" state—that is, liquor was illegal.
Diamond Jim Brady was very fond of his "golden nectar," orange juice.

Do not overuse quotation marks, especially in quoting slang words. If you feel you must excuse your words by quoting them, use other words instead.

poor: I really "dig" his music. (Notice that *dig* isn't even an interesting or original word.)
better: I really love his music.

or

His music turns my spine to spaghetti.
poor: Sam is a real "punk."
better: Sam is worthless.

or

Sam will never win any awards as a model citizen.

"word used in a special way"

---

19 TRANSFORMING   Substitute another expression for each item in quotation marks or remove the quotation marks if the expression need not be excused.

1. I really "have a knack" for science.
   I'm really good at science.

2. Schmidt "blasted" a home run into the third deck.

3. Let's go and "boogie" tonight.

_____

4. I can't stand the "hassle" of registration.

_____

_____

5. Tomas is always "putting down" the people he meets.

_____

_____

6. George is always "cool."

_____

Speech

Once you know how to do it, quoting someone's speech or writing is easy. However, there are several principles to know.

Quote Only a Speaker's Exact Words. Quotation marks signal that you are using a speaker's or writer's exact words, so use them only for direct quotations. Do not put quotation marks around indirect quotations.

direct quotation:	Harry said, "I need a rest for a while."
indirect quotation:	Harry said _that_ he needed a rest for a while.
direct quotation:	Patty asked, "Are you studying for the exam with anyone?"
indirect quotation:	Patty asked _if_ I was studying for the exam with anyone.

Note that the words which identify a speaker are not in quotation marks. Note also that the words _that_ or _if_ introduce indirect quotations. (Both _if_ and _whether_ can introduce indirect questions.)

> "speaker's exact words"
> in a direct quotation

20 WARM-UP

Place quotation marks around _direct quotations only_ in the following sentences.

1. Tom said that he knew what he was doing. (no change)
2. Tom said, I know what I am doing.
3. Will you be going to the rock concert tonight? Stella asked.
4. Stella asked if you would be going to the rock concert tonight.
5. Brian yelled, Watch out for that open manhole!
6. Brain yelled to us to watch out for the open manhole.
7. My mother always asks me what I want for supper.
8. My mother always asks me, What do you want for supper?

9. Did you see a kangaroo come by carrying a pogo stick? the man inquired.

10. The man inquired if we had seen a kangaroo come by carrying a pogo stick.

Begin Direct Quotations with Capital Letters. Any time you begin a sentence with a direct quotation—even if it is just one word—you must capitalize the first word of the quotation.

"It makes no sense to me," Jason replied.

"Please," Tom begged.

Any time you quote a *whole sentence*—whether you begin with the quotation or not—you must capitalize the first word of the quotation.

Before he was shot by a firing squad, murderer Gary Gilmore shouted, "Do it!"

David asked, "What else do we need?"

> Introductory words, "Whole sentence."
> "Quotation," identifying words.

However, if you quote *part of a sentence* (but do not begin the sentence with that quotation), then you should not capitalize the first word of the quotation.

Janet told me that she was "surprised, but not shocked" by the news. According to Lillian, Janet was "torn in two."

> Introductory words, "part of a sentence"

Place a Comma After the Words That Introduce a Quotation. Notice that a comma goes after the introductory words that identify a quotation.

. . . Gary Gilmore said, "Do it."

David asked, "What else do we need?"

Of course, you can begin a sentence with a quotation and put the identifying words last. When this happens, end the quotation with a comma, unless it is a question or an exclamation.

"Do it," Gary Gilmore said.

"What else do we need?" David asked. (The quote and the words following it are considered to be one sentence, despite the question mark at the end of the quote.)

"Be careful!" the man shouted. (Notice that the first word after the quote is not capitalized.)

> "Quotation," identifying words.
> "Quoted question?" identifying words.
> "Quoted exclamation!" identifying words.

Place All Periods and Commas Inside the Final Quotation Mark. All periods and commas go inside the final quotation mark, whether they are part of the quotation or not.

He said, "That makes sense to me."
"We could do it that way," she replied.

Place Question Marks and Exclamation Points Inside the Final Quotation Mark If They Are Part of the Quotation. Place them outside the quotation mark only if they are not part of the quotation.

He asked, "Do you agree?"

but

What do you think of that song, "The Disco Kid"?
The crowd screamed, "More! More!"

but

You have got to read "The Forbidden Sea"!

> ," ." (but   ?" or "?   !" or "!)

If a Speaker Says More Than One Sentence, Place the Second Quotation Mark Only at the End of the Last Sentence. Quotation marks go around an *entire quotation*, not around each sentence within the quotation.

incorrect: Lupe said, "Let's get together after this class." "We can meet in the cafeteria."
correct: Lupe said, "Let's get together after this class. We can meet in the cafeteria."

Notice that in the first example—the incorrect one—it is hard to tell if Lupe is the person who says the second sentence.

> "Quoted sentence. Quoted sentence."

You can split a quotation from the same speaker, however. Notice the punctuation of the following quotations.

Once Diamond Jim Brady, the famous eater, found a box of delicious candy and ordered several hundred more boxes of the same kind. He was told that the candy was in short supply. *"Hell," said Brady, taking out his checkbook, "tell* them to build a candy foundry with twice their capacity. Here's the money." He proceeded to write out an advance of $150,000 to be taken out in trade.

When Carry Nation, the famous saloon-smasher, entered the hotel in Wichita in which a nude picture of Cleopatra hung over the bar, she was told that the saloon did not serve ladies.
"Serve me?" screamed Carry. "Do you think I'd drink your hellish *poison?" She waved a furious finger at Cleopatra. "Take* that filthy thing down and close this murder mill!"

In the first example why isn't the first word capitalized after the quotation resumes?

In the second example why is the first word capitalized each time the quotation resumes?

The answer, of course, is that when you split a quotation *in the middle of a sentence,* you do not capitalize the first word when the quotation resumes. However, when you split a quotation *between sentences,* you do capitalize the first word when the quotation resumes because *it is the beginning of a new sentence.*

> "Quoted sentence," he said. "Quoted sentence."
> "Part of a quoted sentence." he said, "other part of the quoted sentence."

Each Time You Quote a New Speaker, Begin a New Paragraph.
There are two changes of speaker in the following passage. Notice where the paragraph breaks occur.

After Carry Nation had overturned the saloon's tables, slashed chairs, smashed hundreds of bottles of whiskey, and wrecked the mirror and the picture of Cleopatra, a police officer arrived on the scene.
"Madam," said the officer, "I must arrest you for defacing property."
"Defacing?" she screamed. "I am defacing nothing! I am destroying!"

> "Quotation from one speaker." (full paragraph)
> (new paragraph) "Quotation from another speaker."

In Summary: Use summary marks

1. around the titles of short works or works contained within longer works;
2. around words you are defining and around their definitions;
3. around words that you use in a special way;
4. around a speaker's exact words when you quote them:

   a. Begin these quotations with a capital letter if they are complete sentences or if they are the first words of a sentence.

   b. Place a comma after words that introduce the quotation.

   c. If the identifying words come after the quotation, end quoted statements with a comma, quoted questions with a question mark, and quoted exclamations with an exclamation point. Do not capitalize the identifying words.

   d. Place all periods and commas inside the final quotation mark.

   e. Place question marks and exclamation points inside the final quotation mark if they are part of the quotation, outside the final quotation mark if they are not part of the quotation.

   f. Place quotation marks around the entire quotation, not around each sentence in the quotation.

   g. Each time you quote a new speaker, begin a new paragraph.

---

21 WARM-UP   Correctly punctuate and capitalize the following quotations.

Famous Last Words

1. As Ethan Allen, the famous revolutionary soldier, lay dying, his doctor said to him General, I fear the angels are waiting for you. Waiting, are they? he answered. Waiting, are they? Well—let 'em wait!

2. Just before her plane disappeared during her attempt to fly around the world, Amelia Earhart wrote to her husband please know that I am quite aware of the hazards. I want to do it because I want to do it. Women must try to do things as men have tried. When they fail, their failure must be but a challenge to others.

3. It is very beautiful over there said Thomas Edison as he lay in a near-coma.

4. Well, I must arrange my pillows for another weary night murmured Washington Irving, the famous American author When will this end?

5. As Marie Antoinette, the French queen, was being led to her execution, she stepped on the executioner's foot. Monsieur she exclaimed I beg your pardon.

6. Marie Antoinette's husband, King Louis XIV, bravely asked his servants why do you weep? Did you think I was immortal?

7. I have a terrific headache complained Franklin D. Roosevelt.

8. Please mumbled Theodore Roosevelt put out the lights.

9. Florenz Ziegfeld, the American theatrical producer, lay in a near-coma, saying curtain! Fast music! Lights! Ready for the last finale! Great! The show looks good. The show looks good!

10. Sister said playwright George Bernard Shaw to his nurse you're trying to keep me alive as an old curiosity, but I'm done, I'm finished, I'm going to die.

22 EDITING Check over the punctuation of two of your previous papers and make whatever changes necessary with a red-colored pen or pencil. If you must remove an incorrectly placed punctuation mark, use this symbol: ⟶ℛ

CHAPTER 12

Keeping Verbs in Order

You already know a great deal about verbs and the order of words in sentences, even if you don't know a great deal about grammar. For example, you would not say or write the following combination of words.

Friend my to the drove store groceries for me.

Rearranged, these words make a sentence. Try unscrambling them.

_____

_____ *

However, some of the finer points about grammar may be somewhat tricky and confusing, especially those related to verbs and the words associated with verbs—adverbs and direct and indirect objects. To help you sharpen the finer points as you revise your papers, this chapter will examine a few of the trickiest matters: how to use continuous tenses; how to form other two-word, three-word, and four-word verb phrases; how to write indirect questions; how to place objects after verbs; how to place adverbs; and how to make verbs negative.

USING THE CONTINUOUS TENSES

The Simple Present Tense and the Present Continuous Tense

There are *two* present tenses in English, but they are used in entirely different ways.

1. The *simple present tense* is used to discuss *habitual actions*—actions that happen all of the time, most of the time, or some of the time.

I *go* to my English class three days a week.
My instructor usually *assigns* a short composition on Friday.

*One possibility is "My friend drove to the store for some groceries."

It is also used to discuss *feelings* or *observations*, and with *verbs that do not show action*.

I *like* spinach, but I *hate* asparagus. (feelings)

I *hear* a noise, but I *don't see* anything. (observations)

We *don't have* a car. Do you know how much they *cost?* (verbs that do not show action)

All verbs in the simple present tense end in *-s* (for example, *he likes*) or *no -s* (for example, *I like*); and in questions or negative statements, they take the helping verbs *do* or *does*. (See pp. 278–279).

2. The *present continuous* (or *progressive*) tense is used to discuss *actions that are happening now or actions that will happen later.*

I'm *going* to my English class *now*.

We're *handing* in our compositions *on Monday*.

All verbs in the present continuous tense have two parts: *am, is,* or *are* + *-ing*. (See pp. 277–278.)

1 TRANSFORMING　　Rewrite each of the following sentences, changing it from the simple present tense to the present continuous tense, or vice versa.

Simple Present Tense	*Present Continuous Tense*
1. We often walk home after classes.	We're walking home after classes today.
2. My brother-in-law sleeps fourteen hours a day.	_____ _____ right now.
3. _____ _____ every week.	My father is washing the car now.
4. Jason often has a party on the weekend.	_____ _____ this Saturday.
5. _____ _____ all the time?	Is Albert eating again?
6. Mrs. Highnose doesn't watch television.	_____ _____ now.
7. _____ _____ on Sunday.	Bill isn't working this Sunday.
8. It gets cold in here once in a while.	_____ _____ today.

2 WRITING   Complete each of the following sentences, using suitable verbs in the simple present tense or in the present continuous tense. You may have to add other words besides verbs.

1. Every morning _____ I gobble my _____ breakfast and
   _____ hurry off _____ to school.

2. Nobody _____ how the brain _____ .

3. We _____ in a few minutes.

4. I _____ popular music, and I _____
   often.

5. Many students _____ the library, but some students
   _____ .

6. I _____ this weekend.

7. Mr. Gonzalez _____ at the moment, but his
   assistants _____ .

8. Who _____ tonight?

The Simple Past Tense and the Past Continuous Tense

There are also two past tenses in English, and they are also used in entirely different ways.

    1. The *simple past tense* is used to discuss *any completed action or situation in the past.*

Eunice *passed* her test and *felt* wonderful.
We *didn't see* the movie last night.

Most verbs in the simple past tense end in *-ed* (but many are irregular); and in questions or negative statements, they take the helping verb *did.* (See pp. 278–279.)

    2. The *past continuous* (or *progressive*) *tense* is used to discuss *actions that were continuing at a specific time or period of time in the past.*

I *was studying* at midnight yesterday.
They *were working* all day yesterday.

    The most common way to use the past continuous tense is in combined sentences joined by *when, while,* or *as.*

I *was taking* a shower *when* the telephone rang.
While my wife and I *were working,* my brother-in-law *was sleeping.*

All verbs in the past continuous tense have two parts: *was* or *were* + *-ing.* (See pp. 277–278.)

3 TRANSFORMING Rewrite each of the following sentences, changing the simple past tense to the past continuous tense, or vice versa.

Simple Past Tense	*Past Continuous Tense*
1. I studied for the test this morning.	I was studying for the test when you called.
2. _____ _____ yesterday.	Our telephone wasn't working for several hours.
3. _____ _____ every day last week.	They were doing the wash again this morning.
4. Bill got a haircut yesterday.	_____ when the barbershop caught on fire.
5. They didn't listen to the news last night.	_____ _____ during dinner.
6. _____ when _____ this morning?	Who was watching the children while you were shopping?
7. What did you do last night?	_____ _____ at eight o'clock?
8. _____ _____ late last night.	I was beginning my homework when you turned on the stereo.

4 COMBINING Combine each of the following pairs of sentences, using *when* or *while*. Change one or both of the clauses in the combined sentence to the past continuous tense.

1. Mario had dinner. His cat sat down in his spaghetti. _____

   Mario was having dinner when his cat sat down in his spaghetti.

2. I talked to my friend. A thousand-dollar bill dropped from my pocket. __

   _____

3. Mr. Gotbucks smoked a cigar. His chauffeur drove the car. _____

   _____

4. They fell in love. They danced cheek to cheek. _____

   _____

5. His wife washed the dishes, swept the floor, and threw out the garbage. Mr. Hogg read the paper. _____

   _____

   _____

WRITING MORE VERB PHRASES

As you have already seen in this chapter and in Chapter 2, a verb can be more than one word. It can be two words, as in continuous tenses. Or, it can be three or even four words. The last word in a verb phrase is called the *main verb;* all the other words in the phrase are called *helping verbs.* Although verb phrases may seem very complicated, they are not. The rules for forming them are entirely consistent. There are only four kinds of helping verbs: *to be, to have, to do,* and the fixed-form verbs. Each of these helping verbs can be followed only by certain verb forms.

Forming Two-Word Verb Phrases

Here is how to form verb phrases using each of the helping verbs mentioned above.

Category 1: the helping verb is *to be.*
Only two verb forms can follow *to be.*

1. An *-ing* word, which makes one of the continuous tenses you have seen earlier in this chapter.

he is
I am   } seeing (present continuous tense)
they are

she was   } seeing (past continuous tense)
you were

2. A *past participle*, which makes the *passive voice.* (See Chapter 6.)

she is
I am   } seen (present-tense passive voice)
we are

I was   } seen (past-tense passive voice)
they were

Category 2: the helping verb is *to have.*
Only two verb forms can follow *to have.*

1. A *past participle*, which makes the *perfect tense.* (See Chapter 6.)

he has   } seen (present-perfect tense)
they have

we had   seen (past-perfect tense)

2. An *infinitive*, which in the present tense creates the same meaning as *must.*

she has   } to see (must see)
they have

I had   to study (This past-tense idea cannot be expressed with *must.*)

5 WARM-UP   Complete each of the following sentences by including a verb phrase in the present-perfect or past-perfect tense.

1. I don't want to see that movie because _____ *I've seen it* _____

_____ before.

2. Bill apologized for being rude after ____ he had dumped a bowl of spaghetti ____ on top of my head. _____

3. I can't take a coffee break now because _____

already _____

4. I am happy that it's going to rain because _____

not _____ in three weeks.

5. It isn't necessary to go shopping because _____

just _____

6. Carmen felt terrible after _____

7. Wilbur couldn't drive a car after _____

8. All the students were overjoyed because _____

6 WARM-UP   Complete each of the following sentences by including a verb phrase with *have to, has to,* or *had to.*

1. I couldn't watch television last night because ____ I had to study for an ____ examination. _____

2. That is a very dangerous intersection, so any driver _____

_____ if he wants to avoid an accident.

3. Your brother just called and said that _____

as soon as you can.

4. Tomorrow is a holiday, so _____ n't _____

5. When you visit Europe, you _____

6. Mr. Simpson was very sick yesterday, so _____

Category 3: the helping verb is *to do.*

Use *to do* in questions, negative statements, and for emphasis in affirmative statements with any main verb except *to be.*

1. In questions:

Do you ⎫
Does he ⎬ like sports?

Did he   eat dinner?

2. In negative statements:

I *don't* like sports.
He *doesn't* like sports.
He *didn't* eat dinner.

3. For emphasis in affirmative statements:

I *do* like sports.
Oh yes, he *does* like sports.
You're wrong; he *did* eat dinner.

> Notice that in all three categories the *first verb*—the helping verb—*determines the tense and subject-verb agreement. The second verb—* the main verb—*never changes* for tense or subject-verb agreement.
>
> *Does* he *like* sports?
> He *didn't eat* dinner.

7 WRITING

Write an appropriate negative statement after each of the following statements.

1. I worked yesterday. ___I didn't get much rest.___

_____

2. Abraham Lincoln died in office. _____

_____

3. It rains in Florida during the winter. _____

_____

4. In Europe most children start school when they are seven. _____

_____

5. We got mail yesterday. _____

_____

6. Most college students these days hold part-time or full-time jobs. _____

_____

Category 4: the helping verb is a fixed-form verb.

These helping verbs use the same form, regardless of their subjects. The main verbs following them are partial infinitives (without *to*); they cannot change for tense or agreement.

I, we,
he, she, { will
they   would
            can
            could
            shall   } *go, have, be*
            should
            may
            might
            must

(Exception: *Ought* is followed by a complete infinitive—*ought to go, ought to have*, or *ought to be*.)

8 WRITING

Complete each of the following sentences, using an appropriate main verb.

1. I am ___composing great sentences___ now.

2. At 8:00 P.M. yesterday we were _____.

3. These clothes were _____ by someone else.

4. I've _____ many times.

5. Has our teacher _____ yet?

6. I had _____ before coming to school today.

7. I could _____ many years ago.

8. You should _____.

9. They'll _____.

10. We may _____ tomorrow.

Forming Three-Word Verb Phrases

Here is how to form three-word verb phrases. The first word in a three-word verb phrase is always a fixed-form helping verb. The second word must be another helping verb—the short infinitive of *have* or *be* (or the full infinitive after *ought*).

> might have
> might be

The third verb follows the rules for words after *have* or *be*. That is, after *have* the only possible verb forms are a past participle or an infinitive.

> might have gone
> might have to go

After *be* the only possible verb forms are an *-ing* word or a past participle.

> might be going
> might be gone

1. Three-word verb phrases with *have* are used to interpret past actions or circumstances.

Bill didn't feel well yesterday, so he
{
must have been sick.
could have had a cold.
might have had the flu.
may have had the flu.
should have stayed home.
}

They are also used to make statements about changing past actions or conditions—an impossible task—so these statements include the conditional word *if*.

If I had known that Bill was sick, I { would have called him.
could have taken him to the doctor.
might have gone to his house.

2. Three-word verb phrases with *be* discuss opinions or speculations about present or future actions or circumstances.

I don't know where Bill is now. He { could be working.
might be working.
ought to be working.
may be gone.

Bill isn't home now, so he   must be working.

By this time next week, Young   will be flying to Korea.

Forming Four-Word Verb Phrases

Four-word verb phrases are actually extensions of three-word phrases. The first word in a four-word phrase must be a fixed-form helping verb, and the second word must be *have*. Then comes *been*, the past participle of *be*.

might have been

Since only *-ing* words or past participles can follow any form of *be*, either one can complete the verb phrase.

might have been going
might have been gone

The meanings of these four-word verb phrases are similar to those of three-word verb phrases, except that four-word verb phrases discuss continuing actions.

Bill wasn't home yesterday. He { could have been working.
must have been working.
may have been working.
might have been working.

But Bill was sick yesterday. He   should have been resting.

If Bill had been smart, he   would have been resting.

9 WRITING

Complete each of the following sentences using an appropriate three- or four-word verb phrase.

1. It wasn't my brother who called you, but it could ___have been my___ father.

2. I took the bus today, but I should _____

   _____

3. I was watching television last night, but I could _____

   _____

4. We are eating right now, but we will _____

_____ soon.

5. I forgot my wallet, but I might _____

_____

6. Mr. Smith isn't at home now; he must _____

_____

7. I don't know if I can call you later; I may _____

_____

8. If I had known that you wanted to see a movie last night, I would _____

_____

9. This play wasn't written by Ben Jonson, but it might _____

_____ by Shakespeare.

10. I'm attending college now, and in a few years I will _____

_____

WRITING INDIRECT QUESTIONS*

Although writing an indirect question is easy, writing an indirect question can cause problems, for the question is actually part of a statement. Compare these direct questions with indirect questions.

> *(direct question)* How *can I get* to the train station?
> *(indirect question)* I want to know how *I can get* to the train station.
> *(direct question)* Where *is the office?*
> *(indirect question)* I wonder where *the office is.*
> *(direct question)* *Did Susan move* from her apartment?
> *(indirect question)* I asked if *Susan moved* from her apartment.

Now, answer these questions.

What punctuation mark ends a *direct question?*

_____

What punctuation mark ends an *indirect question?*

_____

In the *direct question*, where is the helping verb—before or after the subject?

_____

In the *indirect question*, where is the verb—before or after the subject?

_____

*For advice about direct and indirect *quotations*, see Chapter 11.

Notice that a direct question ends in a question mark and has the verb before the subject. However, an indirect question—since it is a statement—ends in a period and has the subject before the verb.

> **In Summary:**   A direct question
>
> ends with a question mark and uses this word order:
> *verb—subject—(verb)*
>
>   v s
>   *Example:*   Where is he?
>   v   s   v
>   Did you see him?
>
> An indirect question
>
> is a statement, so it ends in a period and uses statement word order:
> *subject—verb*
>
>   s   v
>   *Example:*   She wants to know where *he is.*
>   s   v   v
>   I wonder if *you have seen* him.

You can sometimes include an indirect question in a sentence that asks a direct question. Suppose you write a direct question.

Where is the registrar's office?

You can make it into an indirect question *contained in a statement.*

   (statement)   (indirect question)
Please tell me where the registrar's office is.

You can also change that statement into a question.

    (question)   (indirect question)
Can you tell me where the registrar's office is?

Note that even though this last sentence ends in a question mark, the indirect question *within* it uses statement word order: *subject—verb.*

Also note these differences in verb tenses within direct and indirect questions asked in the past.

Direct Question	*Indirect Question*
He asked me, *"Are you all right?"*	He asked me if I *was* all right.
He asked me, *"Were you working?"*	He asked me if I *had been working.*
He asked me, *"Will you come?"*	He asked me if I *would come.*
He asked me, *"Can you come?"*	He asked me if I *could come.*
He asked me, *"Did you come?"*	He asked me if I *had come.*
He asked me, *"Have you finished?"*	He asked me if I *had finished.*

10 TRANSFORMING   Rewrite each of the following direct questions as an indirect question, beginning with the words provided.

1. Do you need any help?

   I want to know *if you need* any help. _____

2. How are your parents?

   I would be interested to know _____

3. Are the strawberries fresh?

   The cook wants to know if _____

4. Where is room 814?

   Can you tell me _____

5. How many guests will you have?

   Do you know _____

6. When does the class begin?

   He asked me _____

7. Did you study for the final examination?

   I wanted to know if _____

8. Will the test be at the end of the month?

   He asked me if _____

9. When can I call the doctor?

   He inquired about _____

10. Where has all the money gone?

    He asked me _____

11. Is this the last question?

    The students wanted to know if _____

PLACING OBJECTS AFTER VERBS

Objects After (or Between) Phrasal Verbs

When you write a sentence using an action verb (a *does* verb), the normal word order is *subject-verb-object*. (See Chapter 1.)

   S   V   O
We picked some grapes.

   S   V   O
Bill dropped the plate.

   S V   O
I took the dishes.

These objects are direct objects since they directly receive the action of the preceding verbs.

We picked ——————→ some grapes.
Bill dropped ——————→ the plate.
I took ——————→ the dishes.

These objects can be nouns *(grapes, plate, dishes)* or pronouns *(them, it, them)*. Thus the same sentences would look like those below if you replaced the nouns with pronouns as objects.

We picked *them.*
Bill dropped *it.*
I took *them.*

Suppose, however, that you want to change the meaning of each verb in these sample sentences by adding another word to it.*

picked up
dropped off
took out

When you write one of these phrasal verbs, placing the object becomes more complicated. If the object is a *noun*, often—but not always—it can go before or after the second verb word.

I *picked up* some grapes at the store.
I *picked* some grapes *up* at the store.
Bill *dropped off* the plate at my house.
Bill *dropped* the plate *off* at my house.

Try writing the sentence "I _____ the dishes" in two ways, using *took away* as the verb.

_____

_____

If, however, the object is a *pronoun*, it usually goes before the second verb word.

I *picked* them *up.*
Bill *dropped* it *off.*
I *took* them *out.*

*Most of these added words are prepositions, but when they become *part of the verb*, they are not called prepositions.

> **In Summary:** Use an object with a phrasal verb as follows:
>
> *Noun object:*   verb—object—second verb word
>   (James *put* the work *off.*)
>
>   or
>
>   verb—second verb word—object
>   (James *put off* the work.)
>
> *Pronoun object:*   verb—object—second verb word
>   (James put *it* off.)

There are no hard-and-fast rules to explain when you can separate a phrasal verb and when you cannot, but there are some helpful generalizations. First, you usually *can* separate a two-word verb that *moves* or *changes the condition* of an object in some way. Notice these examples:

We *put* the dishes *away.* (The verb *put away* moved the dishes.)

I *did* my homework *over.* (The verb *did over* changed the homework—presumably, it made it better.)

The second generalization is that you usually *cannot* separate a phrasal verb when it does not move or change the condition of an object. In this case the object comes *after the second word* in the verb—not before it:

I *ran into* an old friend yesterday. (The verb *ran into* didn't move or change the object.)

Bill *went out* with Susan last night. (The verb *went out* didn't move Susan; she moved by herself.)

11 WRITING   Write a sentence using each of the following phrasal verbs and its object.

1. *(verb)* make up

   (object) the examination
   Alicia *made up the examination* she had missed.
   _____

2. *(verb)* put off

   (object) studying

   _____

3. *(verb)* look up

   (object) it

   _____

4. *(verb)* throw away

   (object) an old dress

   _____

5. *(verb)* try on

   (object) them

   _____

6. *(verb)* take out

   (object) the lettuce

   _____

7. *(verb)* do over

   (object) it

   _____

8. *(verb)* find out

   (object) the secret of long life

   _____

9. *(verb)* get back

   (object) him

   _____

10. *(verb)* take apart

    (object) the radio

    _____

11. *(verb)* give up

    (object) smoking

    _____

12. *(verb)* take off

    (object) hat

    _____

In Summary: To place an object after or between a phrasal verb;

1. If the verb *moves* or *changes the condition of the object*, you generally can put the object before or after the second word of the verb.

   They *set up* the chairs.
   They *set* the chairs *up*.

   Remember, though, that you *must* place pronoun-objects *before* the second verb word.

   They *set* them *up*.

2. If the verb does not move or change the object, you generally must put the object after the second word of the verb.

   He'll *get over* his disappointment.
   He'll *get over* it.

Direct and Indirect Objects After Verbs

A direct object follows a verb.

S   V   DO
1. A repairman fixed the broken *window.*

    S   V   DO
2. Soon the company will open a branch *store.*

   S   V   DO
3. Hank Aaron hit over 750 *home runs.*

However, suppose you were to write sentences with direct *and* indirect objects after their verbs.

   S   V   IO   DO
4. Later, the repairman sent *us* the *bill.*

     S   V   IO   DO
5. The branch store should offer its *customers* many *services.*

   S   V   IO   DO
6. Casey also hit the *infielders* many ground *balls.*

The direct object receives *the action of the verb,* and the indirect object receives *the direct object.* For example, in Sentence 5 the direct object tells what the store will offer—*services.* The indirect object—*customers*—tells who will receive the services. In Sentence 6 the direct object tells what Casey hit—*ground balls* (he certainly didn't hit the infielders). The indirect object—*infielders*—received the ground balls.

Notice the order of the objects in Sentences 4–6: *the indirect object comes before the direct object.*

> indirect object—direct object

There is a second way to write a direct object and an indirect object in a sentence. You may write the direct object *first* and then follow it with *to* (or sometimes *for*) plus the indirect object.

       DO   IO
7. Later, the repairman sent the *bill to us.*

          DO   IO
8. The branch store should offer many *services to* its *customers.*

       DO   IO
9. Casey also hit many ground *balls to* the *infielders.*

     DO   IO
10. Richie mixed a *drink for* his *guests.*

In this second pattern the indirect object is the object of the preposition *to* or *for.**

> direct object—*to* (or *for*)—object

*Technically, the object of a preposition is not an indirect object, although in these two patterns both have the same meaning.

There are only two ways to place direct and indirect objects in a sentence. They should *never* be placed in this order: *to* (or *for*)—object—direct object.

wrong:	I lent *to* Juan my pen.
right:	I lent Juan my pen.
right:	I lent my pen to Juan.
wrong:	Richie mixed *for* his guests a drink.
right:	Richie mixed a drink for his guests.
right:	Richie mixed his guests a drink.

In Summary: To place a direct object and an indirect object after a verb,

1. use this pattern: *indirect object—direct object* (The man handed *me a pamphlet.*);
2. or use this pattern: *direct object—to* (*or* for)—*(indirect) object* (The man handed *a pamphlet to me.*);
3. but *never* use this pattern: *to* (*or* for)—*(indirect) object—direct object.* (The man handed *to me a pamphlet.*)

---

12 TRANSFORMING

Rewrite the following sentences, reversing the order of the objects.

1. Tom gave the information to Judy. _____
   Tom gave Judy the information.

2. In 1837 the famous showman P. T. Barnum sold the public his first hoax. _____

   _____

3. Over 10,000 New Yorkers bought tickets for themselves. _____

   _____

4. And Barnum showed them a 161-year-old ex-slave. _____

   _____

5. After her death and an autopsy, the newspapers told her real age—eighty—to the public. _____

   _____

6. Naturally, Barnum did not give refunds to anyone. _____

   _____

13 WRITING

Using the verbs in parentheses, write sentences containing both direct and indirect objects. Be sure to vary the object word order.

1. (give) _Tom gave me a piece of paper. or Tom gave a piece of paper to_
   me.

2. (tell) _____

3. (make) _____

4. (sell) _____

5. (send) _____

6. (bring) _____

PLACING ADVERBS IN SENTENCES

As chapters 4 and 10 have shown, adverbs tell *when, where, why* or *how* an action occurs. *Whole clauses* can be adverbs. (See Chapter 4.)

After John Jacob Astor had made millions of dollars as a fur trader, he opened the Astor Hotel (later the famous Waldorf-Astoria) in New York.

Single words (usually ending in *-ly*) and *phrases* can be adverbs, too. Here are some examples of each.

Single Words

(how much)
Eighteenth-century clockmaker Levi Hutchins *intensely* disliked oversleeping.

(how)
He awoke *promptly* at 4:00 A.M. each day.

(when)
But *sometimes* he would sleep past his normal waking hour.

Phrases

(why)
As a result, Hutchins set out to invent the first alarm clock *in 1787*. (when)

(how)
He combined a clock and a bell *in a unique way*.

He wrote, "It was simplicity itself to arrange the bell to sound (when)
at the predetermined hour."

As you can see from these examples, an adverb can go in many places in a sentence, depending on what you want to emphasize.

Levi Hutchins *intensely* disliked. . . . (between the subject and the verb)

He awoke *promptly*. . . . (after the verb)

. . . *sometimes* he would sleep. . . . (before the subject)

or

. . . he would *sometimes* sleep. . . . (between the helping verb and the main verb)

However, an adverb *rarely* goes between a verb and its object or objects.

poor: Levi Hutchins disliked *intensely* oversleeping.

poor: He combined *in a unique way* a clock and a bell.

In Summary: Place an adverb

1. before the subject;
2. between the subject and the verb;
3. between the helping verb and main verb;
4. after the verb;
5. but *rarely* between the verb and its object or objects.

---

14 TRANSFORMING

Rewrite each of the following sentences, placing the adverb where its emphasis will be most logical.

1. *(adverb)* intensely

   (sentence) Eighteenth-century clockmaker Levi Hutchins disliked oversleeping.

   Eighteenth century clockmaker Levi Hutchins intensely disliked oversleeping.

2. *(adverb)* often

   (sentence) In past times people had depended on the sun to awaken them.

3. *(adverb)* at 4:00 A.M.

   (sentence) However, in New England there was no sun.

4. *(adverb)* one day

   (sentence) Hutchins looked at his shelves of clocks and got an idea.

5. *(adverb)* in a pine cabinet

   (sentence) He combined a clock mechanism, a bell, and a little pin.

6. *(adverb)* when the minute hand hit four o'clock

   (sentence) The hand would trip the little pin.

   _____

   _____

7. *(adverb)* immediately

   (sentence) The pin would set the bell in motion.

   _____

   _____

8. *(adverb)* as the bell rang

   (sentence) Hutchins would wake up.

   _____

   _____

9. *(adverb)* since he wasn't interested in money

   (sentence) Hutchins never patented or mass-produced his clock.

   _____

   _____

10. *(adverb)* primarily

    (sentence) He was interested in not oversleeping.

    _____

    _____

11. *(adverb)* perhaps as a result

    (sentence) He stayed so healthy that he lived to be ninety-four.

    _____

    _____

15 EDITING

Each of the following sentences contains an incorrectly placed adverb. Draw a line through the adverb and then place the adverb in a new location by writing it on the line above the sentence.

1. Three men and a giraffe_∧ shared ~~cheerfully~~ a box lunch. *(cheerfully)*

2. Throw Momma from the train a kiss.

3. Smoking a hand-rolled cigarette, the man turned on quickly the radio.

4. The man walked down the block his dog.

5. I gave to him the answer to the question.

6. Jonnie kissed on a moonlit night his girlfriend.

Placing More Than One Adverb in a Sentence

If you write a sentence with more than one adverb (that is, if you give more than one piece of information as to *how, where, when,* or *why* the action occurs), you may wish to spread the adverbs throughout the sentence for variety or emphasis. Here is one example.

(when) (where)
In 1843 a man *in Troy, Ohio,* was fined ten dollars
(why)
for kissing a married lady.

However, when you place more than one adverb at *the end* of a sentence, there are two common ways of doing it. In a sentence with no object after the verb, place the adverbs in this order:

verb—*how—where—when—(why)*

(how) (where)
1. President William Henry Harrison died *of pneumonia in Washington*
(when)
after only thirty days in office.

(where) (when)
2. The first U.S. bank robbery occurred *in New York in 1831.*

(where) (when)
3. Private bathtubs appeared *in a New York hotel in 1844,* perhaps
(why)
for sanitary reasons.

In a sentence that has an object after the verb, place the adverbs in this order:

how—verb—object—where—when—(why)

(how)
4. Robert M. Green *happily* invented the ice-cream soda
(where) (when)
in Philadelphia in 1874.

(how) (where) (when)
5. Walter Hunt *pointedly* designed the safety pin *in New York in 1825.*

(where) (when)
6. Whitcomb Judson put the first zipper *on boots in 1893*
(why)
so people would not have to tie their shoes.

> **In Summary:**   To place more than one adverb at the end of a sentence,
>
> 1. when there is no object after the verb, use this order: verb—*how—where—when—(why);*
> 2. when there is an object after the verb, use this order: *how—*verb—object—*where—when—(why).*

16 WRITING   Write five sentences that each include *at least two* adverbs from the following list.

happily   on several occasions
slyly   from one place to another
uneasily   to his high-rise apartment
smartly   fourteen hours a day
swiftly   in May of this year
drowsily   on the sidewalk
loudly   from Nevada to California
briskly   after the term ends
since he called his parents   although he walks like a three-
because he always is tired   legged turtle
in more than one way   at work
                                 when Manuel saw the ten-dollar
                                    bill

17 TRANSFORMING   Rewrite each of the following sentences, inserting two or more of your own adverbs.

1. The television set's picture faded.   (how)   (when)
Rewritten: The television set's picture faded *in and out all night.*

2. The policeman walked.

Rewritten: _____

_____

3. She slapped him.

Rewritten: _____

_____

4. We began to feel comfortable with each other.

Rewritten: _____

_____

5. The little girl cried.

Rewritten: _____

_____

6. I passed all my exams.

Rewritten: _____

_____

AVOIDING DOUBLE NEGATIVES

In most languages a sentence can have two, three, or even four negatives. In English, though, a negative sentence can have *only one* negative word. The word can be *not*, which is attached to the verb:

We did*n't* do anything last night.

Alternatively, the verb can be affirmative, with the negative word coming later in the sentence:

We did *nothing* last night.

However, you shouldn't use two negatives in the same sentence. They actually cancel each other out and create an affirmative idea:

We did*n't* do *nothing* last night. In fact we were quite busy.

Here is a list of the most common negative words, along with their affirmative versions.

Negatives	Affirmatives
no one	anyone
nobody	anybody
nothing	anything
nowhere	anywhere
no	any
none	any
never	ever

Two other words are negative in meaning: *hardly* and *scarcely*. They mean *almost* no, none, or ever.

I had *hardly any* homework this week. (almost no homework)
The Wilsons *scarcely ever* go out. (almost never)

Therefore, do not use *hardly* or *scarcely* with another negative.

incorrect:　We did*n't* have *hardly* any money.
correct:　　We had *hardly* any money.

18 EDITING

Eliminate the double negatives in each of the following sentences by crossing out a negative and writing any changes above the line.

1. Nobody ever says ^any ~~nothing~~ unkind to Bruno.

2. Reno never has no luck at cards.

3. When Mr. Swift explains something, it doesn't make no sense.

4. I've scarcely spent no money this week.

5. That's because I've hardly had none to spend.

6. I don't like to borrow nothing from other people.

7. We didn't go nowhere on our vacation.

8. You can't hardly find an honest man these days.

9. I didn't notice no difference between those two pizzas—I ate them both.

10. When you don't have no friends, you can't have no happiness.

CHAPTER

13

Mastering the Little Words: Articles and Prepositions

Two kinds of little words—articles and prepositions—can sometimes cause big problems for nonnative speakers of English—and even for some native speakers. No one notices these words when you use them correctly. But when you don't, your writing sounds odd, and sometimes your meaning can be unclear. Remember that good writing should allow readers to pay attention to what you have to say rather than forcing them to notice mistakes in the way you say it. This chapter will examine some solutions to typical problems with articles and prepositions.

USING ARTICLES

The articles—*a*, *an*, and *the*—help your reader understand whether you are using a noun in a general or a specific way. However, some people confuse *a* with *an*, and many nonnative speakers of English have difficulty distinguishing when to use *a/an*, *the*, or no article at all. Unfortunately, rules will not explain all uses of articles; some must simply be memorized. The following rules explain most uses, though.

A/An

Use *a* Before Consonant Sounds, *an* Before Vowel Sounds. The beginning sound—not the spelling—of a word determines whether you should use *a* or *an* before it. *A* goes before *consonant sounds*.

a lesson   a shoe
a chair   a doctor

An goes before *vowel sounds*. (For example, *an apple* is easier to pronounce than *a apple*.)*

an elephant   an awful experience
an enormous task   an overcharge

*Don't confuse *an* with the conjunction *and*:

an hour
I took a nap for an hour, *and* then I got up.

Note: The following two sounds are different from their spellings.

1. Long *u* is pronounced like the word *you*, so its *sound* begins with *y*, a consonant. Therefore use *a* before words beginning with long *u*.

a unit   *but:* an uncle
a unique experience   an unusual experience
a useful product

2. Words beginning with *silent h* have a vowel for their first sound. Therefore *an* comes before these words.

an hour   *but:* a happy moment
an honor   a humorous story
an heir

In Summary: To use *a/an*,

1. place *a* before consonant sounds, including long *u* (for example: a *b*ottle, a *u*niversal idea);
2. place *an* before vowel sounds and silent *h* (for example: *an* April day, *an* *h*onor).

---

1 WARM-UP   Place *a* or *an* before each of the following words or phrases.

1. __a__ child   10. _____ historic event
2. _____ hour   11. _____ carpenter
3. _____ eager beaver   12. _____ elephant
4. _____ lion tamer   13. _____ letter
5. _____ unit of instruction   14. _____ humid day
6. _____ hopeful moment   15. _____ alley
7. _____ sidewalk   16. _____ urban environment
8. _____ island   17. _____ unique environment
9. _____ open book   18. _____ ironing board

Singular Countable Nouns: *A/An* Versus *The*

With Singular Countable Nouns, Use *a* or *an* to Mean "Any One." There are two kinds of nouns in English.

1. countable nouns (you can put a number before them): *one day, three apples, five people*
2. uncountable nouns (you cannot put a number before them): *water, music, honesty, luggage*

The article *a/an* means the same thing as the number *one*. Therefore use *a/an* only before a *singular countable noun*. *A/an* means "any one" or "one of many."

> Don't use *a/an* before plural countable nouns.

Here are some examples of the use of *a/an*.

Take *a* pencil. (*any one* pencil; there are many choices)

I just ate *an* apple. (*one of many* possible apples)

A robin built its nest in that tree. (not a specific robin; it could be *any one* robin)

Use *a/an* for Identification. In many languages you can write "I am student" without the *a*. In English you must include the *a* since you mean, "I am *one of many* students." Here are some more sentences in which *a/an* identifies someone or something.

He is *a lawyer*.

It is *an adjective*.

She is only *a* little *girl*.

Mr. Buzhard is *a* municipal *worker*.

That was *a* funny *story*.

The

Use *the* to Point to a Specific One. Unlike *a*, which means "any one," *the* points out a *specific* one or a *particular* one. Here are some examples of the use of *the*.

What is *the assignment for Wednesday?* (specifies and distinguishes it from other assignments, such as those for Monday and Friday)

The new Chevrolet that Linda bought is beautiful. (specifies and distinguishes it from other cars or Chevrolets)

Let's eat *the apple pie*. (specifies and distinguishes it from other pies, such as peach or cherry pies)

The man standing over there asked to speak to the manager. (specifies *man* and distinguishes him from others who may be present)

Use *the* When You Mean the *Only* One. Sometimes there is only one of something in a room or in a house or in the whole world. When you refer to that thing, you cannot use the article *a*, for *a* implies that something comes from a group containing more than one. You must use the article *the*.

The roof of this house leaks. (The house has only one roof.)

I want to buy carpeting for *the floor*. (There is only one floor.)

What time does *the clock* say? (There is only one clock in the room.)

The sky is cloudy today. (There is only one sky.)

Use *the* to Refer to Nouns You Have Already Mentioned. Once you have mentioned a noun, you have specified which one you mean. When you mention it a second time, you should use *the* before it instead of *a*.

Would you buy *a used car* from that man?

Yes, but only if *the car* (now specified) had a five-year guarantee.

You will find *a pair* of earrings and *a necklace* in my drawer. *The necklace* (now specified) was my grandmother's.

In Summary: To use *a/an* or *the* with singular, countable nouns,

1. use *a/an* when you mean *any one* or *one of many* (for example: *a* tree = *any* tree; *a* hair = *one* hair);
2. use *a/an* for identification (for example: "Tom is *a* barber.");
3. use *the* to point out a *specific* or *particular* one (for example: *the chair* in *the corner*, or *the pen* with *the missing cap*);
4. use *the* when you mean *the only one* (for example: *the floor*, *the second floor*, *the attic*).
5. use *the* to refer to nouns you have already mentioned (for example: "I found *a* photograph and *a* painting in the attic. *The* painting [now specified] apparently was based on *the* photograph.").

---

2 WARM-UP

Write either *a/an* or *the* in each blank space.

1. In 1843 ___a___ gentleman from Abbeville, South Carolina, refused _____ challenge to _____ duel. As a result, his neighbors were so happy that they gave him _____ barbecue.

2. In 1844 New York got _____ police department, but no uniforms.

3. In 1849 Elizabeth Blackwell was _____ first woman doctor to practice in the United States.

4. In 1860 baseball's seventh-inning stretch began. It was _____ way to bring luck to _____ home team because "7" was _____ winning number in dice.

5. In 1861 Congress passed _____ first income-tax law. _____ rate was 3 percent of income over eight hundred dollars _____ year.

6. In 1862 _____ twenty-three-year-old man invested four thousand dollars of his life's savings in _____ oil refinery. His name was John D. Rockefeller.

7. In 1864 _____ motto In God We Trust appeared for _____ first time on _____ coin.

8. In 1865 _____ black chef introduced _____ potato chip to the United States.

9. In 1870 Mississippi sent _____ new senator to the U.S. Congress. He was Hiram R. Revels, _____ first black man ever to serve in _____ Senate.

10. In 1871 _____ fire started in _____ stable on _____ west side of Chicago. It swept through _____ city, destroying $200 million in property.

11. In 1873 John Henry, _____ black railroad worker whose unbelievable strength made him _____ legend in his lifetime, died while working on _____ railroad tunnel in West Virginia. _____ ballad based on his life quickly became popular.

12. In 1876 Alexander Graham Bell patented _____ telephone.

13. In 1878 Thomas Edison took out _____ patent on _____ phonograph.

14. In 1879 Frank W. Woolworth wanted to set up _____ low-priced shopping center. _____ result was _____ five-and-ten-cent store in Lancaster, Pennsylvania.

Plural Countable Nouns and Uncountable Nouns: *The* Versus *No Article*

Use *the* Before Specific Plural Countable and Specific Uncountable Nouns; Use No Article Before General Plural Countable and General Uncountable Nouns. As you know, you cannot place *a/an* before a plural noun. Therefore, when you use a plural noun, your choice is limited to *the* or no article at all. *The* makes the plural noun specific; no article makes the plural noun nonspecific, or general, in its meaning. Compare these examples.

The three birds on the windowsill (specific) are pigeons.

but

Birds (in general) are interesting animals.

The people on my block (specific) are friendly.

but

People (in general) are attending college in larger numbers.

The examinations this semester (specific) have been easier than the examinations last semester.

but

Examinations (in general) don't usually make me nervous.

If you use an *uncountable* noun in a general sense, don't use an article. Compare these examples.

The water in Lake Erie (specific) is polluted.

but

Water (in general) is plentiful.

The fruit this season (specific) has been expensive.

but

Fruit (general) is good for you.

In Summary: With plural nouns,

1. place *the* before specific plurals (for example: *the last three days, the lectures Professor Chin gave*);
2. place no article before plurals used in a general sense (for example: *many students, rock bands, prices*).

With uncountable nouns used in a general sense,

use no article (for example: *religion, exercise, air*).

---

3 WARM-UP

Write *the* only where it is needed in the blanks below; otherwise leave the space blank.

1. __The__ people I know like _____ movies.
2. I loved _____ two movies I saw this weekend.
3. _____ electric company is a legal monopoly.
4. _____ legal monopolies include the electric company and the gas company.
5. _____ police do not belong to _____ unions.
6. _____ police in our neighborhood seem to patrol each block regularly.
7. _____ refrigerators in Europe are smaller than _____ ones in the United States.
8. We saw _____ some beautiful refrigerators on sale.
9. I attend _____ church on Main Street.
10. I go to _____ church.
11. _____ good diet is important to _____ good health.
12. You ought to try _____ new high-protein diet.
13. _____ lunch at Chez Pierre costs _____ five dollars.
14. _____ five-dollar bill has Lincoln's picture on it.

Some Additional Advice About *A/An* and *The*

Some Names Require *the*. Use *the* before the names of countries that end in *-s* or contain the word *Republic*.

the Union of Soviet Socialist Republics (but just Russia)
the Netherlands (but just Holland)
the British Isles (but just Great Britain)
the People's Republic of China (but just China)
Exception: *the* Soviet Union

Use *the* before the names of rivers, oceans, and seas (but not lakes).

the Nile River   *the* Mediterranean Sea
the Atlantic Ocean   Lake Superior
Exception: *the* Great Salt Lake

Use *the* before the names of colleges and universities beginning with the words *College* or *University*.

the University of Illinois   Indiana University
the University of Southern California   Boston College
the College of Liberal Arts and Sciences

In Summary: Place *the* before capitalized nouns

1. that are country names that end in *-s* (*the* United States) or that contain the word *Republic* (*the* Republic of South Africa);
2. that are river, ocean, or sea names (*the* Atlantic Ocean). Do not place *the* before lake names (Lake Erie);
3. that are the names of colleges or universities beginning with the words *College* or *University* (*the* University of Iowa).

---

4 WARM-UP

Place *the* before the capitalized nouns that require it.

1. __the__ Caspian Sea
2. _____ University of Pittsburgh
3. _____ Lake Ontario
4. _____ Germany
5. _____ Northwestern University.
6. _____ Canada
7. _____ Socialist Republic of Vietnam
8. _____ Atlantic Ocean
9. _____ College of DuPage
10. _____ United Arab Republic

Some Words Replace Articles Before Nouns. When you place one of the following words before a noun, you cannot use an article.

every	any	much
each	no	which
either	enough	what
neither	many	his, her, their, and so forth
some	more	Bill's, Mary's, and so forth

Some Words Go Before Articles. Articles, of course, usually go before any adjectives describing a noun.

the large, round bowl
a dirty, old apartment

However, the following five adjectives go before articles.

both (the)   many (a)
half (the *or* a)   such (a)
all (the)

Examples: Both the men are here.
             I never saw such a fight before.

5 TRANSFORMING

Rewrite each of the following sentences so that it uses the article *the.*

1. People are very friendly. _The people in my English class are very_ _friendly._

2. We like modern furniture. _____

_____

3. Homework is usually difficult. _____

_____

4. Albert loves food. _____

_____

5. Love is hard to find. _____

_____

6. I like music. _____

_____

6 EDITING

The following passage is missing many articles. Insert articles where they are needed.

The Ford Model T (1908–28)

(1) The Model T Ford was ∧^{an} ugly, fragile-looking automobile, but it became ∧^{the} most popular American car ever made. (2) Henry Ford sold almost sixteen million Model T's between years 1908 and 1928, record that was not broken until equally plain and dependable car, Volkswagon Beetle, came along. (3) The Model T was introduced in 1908 at cost of $850. (4) It was immediate best-seller, not only because of its low price (there were other inexpensive cars on the market), but because it offered power, dependability, and simplicity of design to make it practical for average

American. (5) It offered transportation, not just amusement.

(6) Nicknamed the Tin Lizzie, the Model T sold well in rural and small-town market, which was previously hostile to automobile. (7) In 1908 half of country lived on farms or in towns of less than 2500 people. (8) To farmers who were enjoying period of prosperity, Henry Ford, farm boy from Dearborn, Michigan, provided automobile that could outperform team of horses and that was so simple in its design that almost anyone could repair it. (9) People could drive it almost anywhere—across streams, up steps, or down cow paths that served as roads in rural America in early 1900s. (10) And people could count on Model T. (11) As popular joke expressed it, there was a Model T owner who wanted to be buried with his Tin Lizzie. (12) When friends asked why, he replied, "Oh, because thing pulled me out of every hole I ever got into, and it ought to pull me out of this one."

(13) Henry Ford was not inventor of Model T; it was developed by team of engineers at his Ford Motor Company plant. (14) But his genius was responsible for bringing together such brilliant men and encouraging them to invent moving assembly line, superior one-piece parts, and use of new lightweight but sturdy metals. (15) His economic philosophy was to cut costs by building only one model and by developing creative new production methods. (16) Ford passed on his savings to consumer in lower prices, which increased sales. (17) Then he improved efficiency of production still further, produced more cars for less money, and lowered price again. (18) In 1923 Americans bought as many Tin Lizzies as all other types of cars combined, and next year the Model T sold for all-time low price of $290. (19) Of course people worshiped Henry Ford as businessman who passed on profits to buyers through lower prices and to workers through higher wages and who upheld important values of honesty, thrift, and hard work. (20) Ford gained even more admirers when he told Americans: "I am going to democratize automobile, and when I'm through,

everybody will be able to afford one and about everybody will have one."

(21) By time he died in 1947, he had fulfilled his promise.

USING PREPOSITIONS

There are many prepositions* and thousands of expressions that use them. You already know several of these expressions, but the following pages will present lists of those that are more common.

Prepositions to Indicate Time

1. *At* a specific or precise time

Class ends *at* 3:50 P.M.
At midnight the next day begins.
Most employees punch out for lunch *at* noon.

2. *By* a specific time (means *no later than* that time)

Tom will pick you up *by* 8:00.
Jill said she might be ready as early as 4:30 but certainly *by* 6:00.

3. *Until* a specific time (*continuing up to* that time)

Last night Juanita studied *until* 11:00.
I won't be able to see you *until* Monday.

4. *In* a specific time period (usually measured in hours, minutes, days, months, or years)

In five minutes I will be leaving.
In winter you see fewer people on the streets.
We are planning to go on vacation *in* July.
World War II ended *in* 1945.
in the morning, *in* the afternoon, or *in* the evening (but *at* night)

5. *For* a period of time

I have been a student *for* thirteen years.
We have been best friends *for* a long time.

6. *Since* a date or an hour

They have been living next door to us *since* 1973.
No one has eaten *since* 8:15.

*For a list of prepositions, see Chapter 7.

7. *On* a specific day or date

Most people are paid *on* Friday.
The doctor can see you *on* June 12.

8. *During* a continuing time period (or *within* the time period)

I was ill *during* the night.
We'll be away from the office *during* the next few hours.

9. Miscellaneous time expressions

on time (that is, promptly)
in a while
at the beginning (of a day, month, or year)
in the middle (of a day, month, or year)
at the end (of a day, month, or year)
from time to time (that is, occasionally)

7 WARM-UP

In each space below, write the appropriate preposition to indicate time.

1. _____ On _____ August 1, 1903, a Packard car arrived in New York, completing the first transcontinental automobile trip. It had been traveling _____ July 11, when it left San Francisco.

2. _____ June, 1905, the Pennsylvania Railroad's "fastest long-distance train in the world" began its route between New York and Chicago. It made its trip _____ eighteen hours. _____ the next week the New York Central Railroad started its own eighteen-hour service on its train, The Twentieth-Century Limited. Both trains operated _____ only two weeks, and then they had wrecks, killing nineteen people.

3. _____ January 22, 1907, the opera *Salome* opened at the Metropolitan Opera House in New York. The opera was called immoral because Salome did the "Dance of the Seven Veils" in exchange for the head of John the Baptist on a platter. The Metropolitan Opera House would not allow the opera's performance again _____ twenty-one years later.

4. _____ the end of 1908 Jack Johnson, a black man, won the heavyweight boxing championship of the world. This started a search for "the great white hope," a white boxer who could beat him. Johnson finally lost the championship _____ 1915. His boxing career lasted _____ thirty years, with only seven losses in 112 fights.

5. Most cars _____ the first years of the twentieth century were expensive, costing as much as $2800. Then came Henry Ford's "universal car," the Model T. _____ several years his cars were priced at $850, but later, the Model T sold for $290.

Prepositions to Indicate Place

1. *In* a country, area, state, city, or neighborhood

in France
in Michigan
in Boston
in Lincoln Square

2. *On* a street or block

We live *on* Wells Avenue.
They work *on* Main Street.

3. *At* a specific address

We live *at* 1621 Wells Avenue.
We work *at* 945 Main Street.

4. *At* an intersection of two streets

Let's meet *at* (the corner of) State Street and Madison.

8 WARM-UP   In each space below, write the appropriate preposition to indicate place.

The First Traffic Light

(1) On August 5, 1914, _____in_____ Cleveland, Ohio, drivers obeyed signals from the first traffic light _____ the United States. (2) It was installed _____ the corner of Euclid Avenue and East 105th Street. (3) Besides the red and green lights, the signal had a loud buzzer. Two buzzes directed traffic _____ Euclid to "Go," and one buzz meant "Go" _____ 105th Street.

Prepositions for Vehicles and Chairs

1. *In (to)* and *out of* for small vehicles (like cars) and chairs with arms

I got *in (to)* the cab as someone else was getting *out of* it.
My father likes to sit *in* his big, comfortable chair.

2. *On* and *off (of)* for large vehicles (like planes, trains, buses, and boats) and armless chairs or any long seat (like a bench or a sofa)

We rode *on* the subway and got *off* at our stop.
He's sitting *on* that bench over there.
The man *on* the wooden chair is his brother.

9 WARM-UP

Write the correct preposition in each space.

1. Years ago people came to the United States _____ on _____ boats. Now almost everyone comes here _____ on _____ a plane.

2. We took a ride _____ our new car. We got _____ it at the park and walked around for a while.

3. Some of the people are sitting _____ the couch, and some of them are sitting _____ armchairs.

4. Where do you usually get _____ the bus? Where do you get _____ it?

5. Would you please get _____ that table and sit _____ a chair?

Other Prepositions

1. *For* a reason or *for* someone who benefits

Bill went to the barber *for* a haircut.
Mr. Esposito asked me to mail this letter *for* him.
I bought a present *for* my sister.

2. *About* a subject (or *on* a subject)

We were talking *about* our plans for next week.
I recently read an article *about* (or *on*) space travel.

3. *Between* two; *among* three or more

We shared the sandwich *between* the two of us.
The five members of the board discussed it *among* themselves.

4. *From* a starting point; *to* a destination

We drove *from* Kansas *to* Alaska.

5. *Toward* (in the direction of) a place

I walked *toward* the beach but turned south before I arrived at the beach.

6. *Into* (entering) a place or space

He just went *into* that room through the back door.

7. *In* (inside of) a place or space

He's been running *in* the gym; he hasn't gone outside.

8. *On* a surface

The book is *on* the table.
The portrait is hanging *on* the wall.

9. *Off* a surface

I took the book *off* the table.
The painting fell *off* the wall.

10 WARM-UP   Write an appropriate preposition in each space below.

The United States Enters World War II

(1) Diplomacy _____between_____ Japan and the United States broke

down _____in_____ 1941 when Japan signed an agreement with

Germany and Italy. (2) Throughout 1941 the United States inched closer

and closer _____ war, but it didn't join the fighting. (3)

_____ March, 1941, the United States passed the Lend-Lease

Act, which allowed supplies to go _____ the United States

_____ Britain. (4) President Roosevelt began to make a

number of speeches _____ the possibility of war.

(5) _____ Sunday, December 7, 1941, General George C.

Marshall received an intercepted message _____ a Japanese

attack _____ the Pacific. (6) He sent messages of warning

_____ the Philippines, the Panama Canal Zone, and

San Francisco. (7) However, the message couldn't get _____

Pearl Harbor because bad atmospheric conditions prevented radio

transmissions. (8) _____ 7:55 that same morning, Japanese

planes flew _____ Pearl Harbor, filled with deadly presents

_____ American ships. (9) By 10:00 A.M., eighteen ships were

sunk or badly damaged and about 2500 people were killed. (10) When

President Roosevelt heard _____ the attack, he immediately

went on radio _____ the purpose _____

informing the American people that we were entering the Second

World War.

A SPECIAL CONTRAST: *ON* VERSUS *IN*

Two especially troublesome prepositions are *on* and *in*, especially if your first language is Spanish (in which only one preposition, *en*, means both *on* and *in*). Note the differences between the two prepositions.

1. To show place relationships:

   - *On* generally means "on the surface of" or "on top of."
     on the floor, *on* a street, *on* (top of) a bed (without sheets over one's body), *on* a large vehicle (a bus, a train, a plane, or a boat), *on* a chair (generally one without arms), *on* a long seat such as a sofa or couch, *on* (or *at*) a street corner, *on* a bicycle (or motorcycle), *on* (top of) a desk
   - *In* generally means "inside of" or "within."
     in a room, *in* the water, *in* a small vehicle (a car, a cab, or a small boat), *in* a bed (with the sheets over one's body), *in*(side) the corner of a room (the walls enclose the person or object), *in* a chair (generally one with arms) *in* a container, *in* a desk drawer

2. To show time relationships:

   - *On* refers to a day or a date.
     on Saturday, *on* July 5, 1990, *on* Thanksgiving
   - *In* generally means "within a period of time," including a month or a season.
     in January, *in* summer, *in* an hour or a minute, *in* a while

3. To express ideas within idioms:*

   - *on* foot, *on* time, every hour *on* the hour, *in* charge, *in* the mood

11 WARM-UP

Write *on* or *in* in each space below.

1. You will find the book _____on_____ the desk and the papers _____in_____ the drawer.
2. I will meet you _____ the corner of Fifth and Main.
3. The new table is _____ the corner of the room.
4. Please put your luggage _____ the trunk of the car.
5. They got _____ the bus, and then later they got _____ the cab.

*See the reference list on pp. 312–314 for more idioms with *on* and *in*.

6. I think I left my book _____ my bed.

7. Bill isn't feeling well; he is staying _____ bed today.

8. Several of the guests sat _____ the couch, but most of them had to sit _____ folding chairs.

9. We haven't gone to a movie _____ a month.

10. Very few stores are open _____ Christmas.

11. Sue is usually _____ time, so she should be here _____ a few minutes.

12. We always take a vacation _____ summer, and this year we will be going out of town _____ July 30.

13. I couldn't drive my car today, so I had to come _____ foot.

14. Who is _____ charge of this department?

15. Don't talk to Jim right now. He is _____ a bad mood.

Prepositions That Repeat the Meanings of Prefixes

A *prefix* is something attached to the beginning of a word. For example, the prefix *re-* means "again," so the word *review* literally means "view again." Many words in English came from Latin; here is a list of common Latin prefixes, along with their meanings.

Prefix	Meaning	Examples
ad-, ac-, ap-, a-	to	admit, acceptable, apply, agree
con-, com-	with	converse, communicate
ex-, e-	from	excuse, emigrate
in-, im-	in	involved, implicit

Many times—but not always—a word with one of these prefixes also repeats the meaning of the prefix in a preposition following the word.

*ad*mitted *to* a school; *ac*ceptable *to* me; *ap*ply *to* the school; *a*gree *to* a contract

*con*versed *with* me; *com*municated *with* a friend

*ex*cused *from* class; *e*migrate *from* a country

*in*volved *in* a crime; *im*plicit *in* his statement

12 WARM-UP   Write an appropriate preposition in each of the following spaces.

Was He, or Wasn't He?

(1) Because of his short height and hairless face, the French diplomat to England, Chevalier d'Éon de Beaumont (1728–1810) easily passed for a woman. (2) He was often involved _____in_____ spying activities in which

he dressed as a woman. (3) In fact he would never admit _____ the fact that he was a man. (4) Many people became interested _____ the controversy, and they made large wagers about d'Éon's sex. (5) Eventually, d'Éon placed an ad in a London newspaper saying that he was not concerned _____ resolving the issue and he would never admit _____ being either a man or a woman.

(6) By 1774 bets on d'Éon's sex, amounting _____ £120,000 (about $250,000), had been made. (7) A trial was held, during which a French doctor said that it was apparent _____ him that d'Éon was a woman. (8) An associate of the doctor concurred _____ him, and the judge legally declared d'Éon to be a female. (9) Nevertheless, d'Éon still would not allow any physical examination _____ him. (10) Many bettors were very angry at this refusal, but no one would make any approach _____ him because d'Éon was a fabulous swordsman who had beaten the finest opponents.

(11) However, in 1810 d'Éon died, and at last the truth was revealed in an examination. (12) Although he had certain female characteristics such as "remarkably full" breasts, something was not consistent _____ these female traits. (13) He had "male organs in every respect perfectly formed." (14) Thus d'Éon was declared a man, and there was a great exchange _____ money after the news.

A Reference List of Common Expressions Using Prepositions

Read through the following list to see if you know every expression. You may wish to memorize the ones you don't know or to use the list for reference when you write a paper.

accuse someone *of* something
acquaintance *with* someone or
   something
affection *for* someone
afraid *of* something
agree *with* someone *about*
   something
alarmed *at* something
a lot *of* something
amazed *at* something

ask someone *for* something
ask something *of* someone
associated *with* someone *in* some
   activity
assure someone *of* something
at the top *of*
aware *of* someone or something
bargain *with* someone *for*
   something
because *of* something or someone

amused *at* or *by* someone or something
angry *at* someone
angry *with* something
approve *of* someone or something
argue *about* something
argue *with* someone *for* (or *against*) something
arrive *at* a place *in* a city or country
ashamed *of* something
cheat someone *of* something
close *to* something or someone
comment *on* someone or something
communicate something *to* someone
comparable *to* something
complain *to* someone *about* something
composed *of* something
conceive *of* something
concerned *about* someone or something
confess *to* someone
confidence *in* someone or something
confident *of* something
congratulate someone *on* something
conscious *of* something
consideration *for* someone
contempt *for* someone or something
contribute *to* something
control *over* someone or something
convict someone *of* something
copy *from* someone
correspond *with* someone
count *on* someone *for* something
cure *for* something
cure someone *of* something
deal *with* someone or something
decide *on* something
dedicate something *to* someone
defend someone *from* something or *against* something
delighted *with* someone or something
delight *in* someone or something
demand something *of* someone
depend *on* someone *for* something
deprive someone *of* something
depend *on* someone *for* something

believe *in* something
blame someone *for* something
by means *of*
call *on* someone socially
call *to* someone from a distance
call *up* someone on the telephone
capable *of* something
certain *of* something
challenge someone *to* something
characteristic *of* something
displeased *with* someone or something
distrust *of* someone or something
do something *about* something
doubt *about* someone or something
dream *of* or *about* something
due *to* someone or something
duty *to* someone
engaged *to* someone
escape *from* something
excel *in* something
exception *to* something
excuse *for* something
excuse someone *from* something
explain something *to* someone
failure *of* someone *in* something
faithful *to* someone or something
fall *in* love *with* someone
fascinated *with* someone or something
fearful *of* something
fond *of* someone
for the purpose *of*
for the sake *of*
full *of* something
grateful *to* someone *for* something
guard *against* something
guess *at* something
hear *about* something
hear *of* something
hint *at* something
horrified *at* something
in case *of*
in common *with*
independent *of* someone or something
in favor *of*
influence *over* someone
inform someone *of* something
in place *of*
inquire *into* something
in search *of*
in spite *of*

designed *for* something
desire *for* something
die *of* a disease
different *from* someone or
    something
disagree *with* someone *about*
    something
disappointed *in* something
disappointed *with* someone
disgusted *with* someone or
    something
look *at* someone or something
look *for* something or someone
look *up* something *in* a reference
    book
made *of* something
make something *for* someone
mistaken *for* someone
need *for* something
obligation *to* someone
on account *of*
opportunity *for* someone or
    something
opposition *to* someone or
    something
pay someone *for* something
pay something *to* someone
pity *for* someone
point *at* someone or something
popularity *with* someone
prefer something *to* something
prejudice *against* someone or
    something
protect someone *from* something
provide something *for* someone
punish someone *for* something
qualification *for* a job
qualified *to* do something
quarrel *with* someone *over*
    something
quote something *from* someone
reason *for* something
reason *with* someone *about*
    something
recover *from* an illness
related *to* someone
rely *on* someone or something
remind someone *of* something
reply *to* someone *about* something

in the course *of*
intent *on* something
interfere *with* someone or
    something
introduce someone *to* someone
invite someone *to* something
irrelevant *to* something
knock *at* or *on* a door
laugh *at* something or someone
lecture *on* something
listen *to* someone or something
require something *of* someone
research *in* something
responsible *to* someone *for*
    something
result *from* a cause
result *in* a consequence
result *of* a cause
rob someone *of* something
satisfactory *to* someone
search *for* something
send *for* something
shocked *at* something
shocking *to* someone
similar *to* someone or something
smile *at* someone
stare *at* someone
start *with* something
supply someone *with* something
sure *of* something
sympathy *with* or *for* someone or
    something
take advantage *of* someone or
    something
take care *of* someone or something
talk *over* something *with* someone
talk *to* someone *about* something
tell someone *of* or *about* something
thankful *for* something
think *of* or *about* or *over*
    something
threaten someone *with* something
tired *of* something
trust *in* something or someone
trust someone *with* something
wait *for* someone or something
weary *of* something
work *for* someone or something
worry *about* something

13 WRITING In each space in the following passage, write an appropriate preposition. Consult the preceding list whenever necessary.

The Story Behind Lenin's Rise to Power in Russia

(1) Vladimir I. Ulyanov (later known as Lenin) was born ⎯⎯⎯on⎯⎯⎯ May 4, 1870, ⎯⎯⎯in⎯⎯⎯ the small city ⎯⎯⎯of⎯⎯⎯ Simbirsk, Russia. (2) Like many revolutionaries, he came ⎯⎯⎯⎯⎯ a solid, middle-class family. (3) There was very little indication ⎯⎯⎯⎯⎯ his childhood that when he grew up he would become fully involved ⎯⎯⎯⎯⎯ worldwide revolution and communism. (4) However, he was always full ⎯⎯⎯⎯⎯ contradictions. (5) He hated the authority of others but used it ruthlessly ⎯⎯⎯⎯⎯ people who opposed him. (6) On the other hand, he was often kind ⎯⎯⎯⎯⎯ people who agreed ⎯⎯⎯⎯⎯ his ideas.

(7) Vladimir's father was the inspector ⎯⎯⎯⎯⎯ public schools in Simbirsk. (8) His mother was the daughter ⎯⎯⎯⎯⎯ a physician. (9) Vladimir was a noisy and clumsy child, but he was brilliant. (10) He excelled ⎯⎯⎯⎯⎯ his schoolwork. (11) Although he was never quite comfortable ⎯⎯⎯⎯⎯ his classmates, he often helped them ⎯⎯⎯⎯⎯ their homework.

(12) ⎯⎯⎯⎯⎯ 1885 the first ⎯⎯⎯⎯⎯ two major tragedies struck his family. (13) Vladimir's father died of heart failure. (14) As a result, Vladimir lost all faith ⎯⎯⎯⎯⎯ God and developed a very strong affection ⎯⎯⎯⎯⎯ his older brother Alexander. (15) Nothing, it seemed, could ever come ⎯⎯⎯⎯⎯ the family except death, which happened to Alexander in 1887. (16) Alexander had become involved ⎯⎯⎯⎯⎯ a conspiracy to kill the Russian king, but it failed. (17) ⎯⎯⎯⎯⎯ May 20 Alexander was hanged.

(18) After his brother's death Vladimir tried to live a normal life, but that was impossible. (19) Because he was the brother ⎯⎯⎯⎯⎯ a revolutionary, he was not admitted ⎯⎯⎯⎯⎯ any schools. (20) Finally, his high school principal helped him to gain entrance ⎯⎯⎯⎯⎯ a law school. (21) However, ⎯⎯⎯⎯⎯ three months he was expelled

_____ attending a peaceful protest meeting. (22) No other school would accept him.

(23) So Vladimir tried gentleman farming and studied law on his own. (24) He took the law examination _____ November, 1891, and scored first _____ a group _____ 124 people.

(25) He moved _____ St. Petersburg _____ 1893 and dedicated himself _____ Marxism. (26) He conspired _____ other revolutionaries, who lived undercover and communicated _____ each other by codes written _____ invisible ink. (27) He visited factories, organized groups _____ workers, and wrote many pamphlets.

(28) _____ 1895 he went _____ Switzerland _____ more study _____ Marxism. (29) Then he returned _____ Russia _____ a printing machine and plans to print a revolutionary newspaper. (30) Before he could publish the first issue, he was arrested and accused _____ subversive activities. (31) He was _____ jail _____ the next fifteen months. (32) After his release he again traveled _____ Switzerland. (33) _____ the years he lived there, he began another newspaper that was shipped _____ Russia illegally. (34) _____ this newspaper he first used the name N. Lenin. (35) He also became deeply involved _____ the activities of a group he created called the *Bolsheviks*, who were extreme radicals. (36) Lenin returned _____ Russia _____ time _____ time, hoping _____ a revolution, but none occurred.

(37) Finally, during World War I, Lenin settled _____ Berne, Switzerland. (38) Meanwhile, _____ Russia, metal workers went on strike _____ a large city, and the strike spread rapidly. (39) The government of the tzar (the king) collapsed, and suddenly Russia was free. (40) Lenin, who was eager to return to Russia _____ his long-awaited revolution, had to make a deal _____ the Germans. (41) It

was understood that if he could take power in Russia, he would make

peace _____ Germany. (42) With this understanding German leaders

allowed Lenin to cross Germany _____ his trip _____ the

Russian border.

(43) Thus Lenin returned _____ Russia, _____ time

_____ the revolution—after it started, perhaps, but not too late to

take advantage _____ it. (44) That was the beginning _____

Lenin's rise _____ power.

CHAPTER

14

Checking Spelling, Apostrophes, Hyphens, and Capitals

Spelling, apostrophes, hyphens, and capitals are small things in writing. However, many people assume that a poor speller is "stupid," even though spelling ability and intelligence are completely unrelated. More important, misspellings, incorrect apostrophe use, incorrect hyphenation, and incorrect capitalization can annoy your readers or distract them from what you are saying. Therefore if you need to work on spelling, apostrophe usage, hyphenation, and capitalization, work on them.

SPELLING

You can eliminate many spelling problems if you follow some simple practices.

a. Carefully *pronounce* words you aren't sure how to spell. Most—but not all—words are spelled as they are pronounced.
b. *Use a dictionary* to look up spellings, especially if you aren't sure how to pronounce words or pronouncing them doesn't help.
c. *Don't confuse words that sound alike* (*their/there/they're, its/it's,* and so forth). Pronouncing these words won't help you. You just have to know how they are different.*
d. Carefully *proofread* your papers. That way you will discover and correct many careless errors.
e. *Keep your own spelling list* of words that give you trouble (preferably on flashcards so that you can study each one separately) and include a sentence that uses the word. Underline or capitalize the troublesome part of the word.
   difFERent   proBABly   choiCe.

*For practice in distinguishing between words that sound alike, see Chapter 15.

    f. *Use memory games* to remind you of tricky spellings.
       You always want two *deSSerts*, but you don't want to be in more than
       one hot *deSert*.
       Here is in other place words, *wHERE* and *tHERE*.
    g. When a word has a silent letter or a hard-to-recognize vowel,
       associate the word with a root word in which the letter is clearly
       pronounced.
       SiGn is in *siGnature*.   *LABOR* is in *LABORatory*.
    h. *Study only one rule at a time—but review it often—and study only*
       the words you need to learn.

The following rules should help improve your spelling.

ie/ei

Remember this rhyme.

> *I* before *e*
> Except after *c*
> Or when sounded like *a*
> As in *neighbor* or *weigh*

    a. *i* before *e*

    believe
    relief
    brief

    b. except after *c*

    receive
    conceive

    c. or when sounded like *a*

    eighty
    sleigh

    Some exceptions:

either   their   foreign   protein   leisure   weird   seize

1 WARM-UP

Circle the correct spelling.

1. (brief)/breif   5. chief/cheif
2. field/feild   6. reciept/receipt
3. conciet/conceit   7. decieve/deceive
4. frieght/freight   8. thier/their

-s/-es

Add *-s* or *-es* to form the plurals of most nouns and to form third-person-singular verb endings. Both nouns and verbs follow the same rules for taking *-s* or *-es*.

Add *-es* to Nouns or Verbs That Have These Endings: *ss, ch, sh, z,* or *x.*

boss + es = bosses
wax + es = waxes
reach + es = reaches
wish + es = wishes

Write three more of your own.

1. _____

2. _____

3. _____

Add *-es* to Most Nouns or Verbs Ending in *-o.*

tomato + es = tomatoes
potato + es = potatoes
echo + es = echoes
do + es = does

Some exceptions (all musical terms):

radio + s = radios
piano + s = pianos
stereo + s = stereos

Write two more words ending in *-oes.*

1. _____

2. _____

When a Consonant Comes Before Final *-y,* Change the *-y* to *-i* and Add *-es.*

study *y* becomes *i* + es = studies
try *y* becomes *i* + es = tries
sky *y* becomes *i* + es = skies

Write two more of your own.

1. _____

2. _____

When a Vowel Comes Before Final -*y*, Do Not Change the -*y*; Merely Add -*s*.

boy   + s = boys
play   + s = plays
buy   + s = buys

Change Noun (But Not Verb) Endings from -*f* or -*fe* to -*ve*; Then Add -*s*.

leaf   *f* becomes *ve* + s   = leaves
loaf   (noun) *f* becomes *ve* + s = loaves
wife   *fe* becomes *ve* + s   = wives

Some exceptions:

belief + s = beliefs
chief   + s = chiefs
safe   + s = safes
chef   + s = chefs

2 TRANSFORMING

Make the following nouns plural.

1. knife _____knives_____   4. hoof _____
2. half _____   5. shelf _____
3. self _____   6. chief _____

Add -*s* to Most Other Nouns and Verbs.

lamp   + s = lamps
pie   + s = pies
make   + s = makes
walk   + s = walks

Some exceptions:

child ⟶ children
man ⟶ men

3 WARM-UP

Add -*s* or -*es*—whichever is correct—to these words.

1. ride ^s _____   6. key _____
2. beach _____   7. ton _____
3. beauty _____   8. mess _____
4. rush _____   9. flower _____
5. tax _____   10. rose _____

11. witch _____   14. tidy _____

12. breath _____   15. day _____

13. breeze _____

In Summary: To choose whether to add *-s* or *-es* to nouns and verbs,

1. add *-es* to nouns or verbs ending in *s* sounds (such as *ss*, *ch*, *sh*, *z*, or *x*);
2. add *-es* to most nouns or verbs ending in *-o*;
3. when a *consonant* comes before final *-y*, change the *-y* to *-i* and add *-es*;
4. change *nouns* (but not verbs) ending in *-f* or *-fe* to *-ve*; then add *s*;
5. simply add *-s* to all other nouns and verbs.

Suffixes

A *root word* (such as *agree*) is a word to which you can attach additional syllables. A syllable attached to the *end* of a word is a *suffix*. (The suffix *-ing* added to *agree* makes *agreeing*). Since many spelling errors occur when suffixes are added to root words, here are some rules to help prevent those errors.

Change Final *-y* to *-i* Before a Suffix. When final *-y* is preceded by a *consonant*, change the *-y* to *-i* and add a suffix.

Root Word	Change and Suffix	New Word
busy	*y* to *i* + -ness	business
try	*y* to *i* + -ed	tried
happy	*y* to *i* + -er	happier
pretty	*y* to *i* + -est	prettiest
merry	*y* to *i* + -ment	merriment
angry	*y* to *i* + -ly	angrily
deny	*y* to *i* + -al	denial
beauty	*y* to *i* + -ful	beautiful

Note: Never change final *-y* to *-i* before the suffix *-ing*.

denying   trying

When Final *-y* Is Preceded by a Vowel, Do Not Change the *-y*; Merely Add a Suffix.

Root Word	Suffix	New Word
play	-ed	played
lay	-er	layer
employ	-ment	employment
joy	-ful	joyful
say	-ing	saying

4 TRANSFORMING   Combine the following root words and suffixes, making whatever changes are necessary.

1. destroy + er ___destroyer___   6. witty + ness _____

2. stay + ed _____   7. fly + er _____

3. apply + cation _____   8. fly + ing _____

4. ugly + est _____   9. happy + ly _____

5. pay + ment _____   10. petty + ness _____

Determine Whether to Drop or Keep Final *-e* Before a Suffix. Drop final *-e* before a suffix beginning with a vowel.

Root Word	Change and Suffix	New Word
ridicule	drop *e* + -ous	ridiculous
argue	drop *e* + -ing	arguing
strangle	drop *e* + -ing	strangling

Some exceptions:

hoeing   canoeing

Most words ending in *-ce* or *-ge* do not drop the final *-e*.

coura*ge*ous   noti*ce*able

Write three words of your own that drop final *-e*.

1. _____   2. _____   3. _____

Write two words of your own that do not drop final *-e* before a vowel.

4. _____   5. _____

Keep Final *-e* Before a Suffix Beginning with a Consonant.

Root Word	Suffix	New Word
hope	-ful	hopeful
complete	-ly	completely
time	-less	timeless

Some exceptions:

acknowledgment   argument   judgment
truly   awful

5 TRANSFORMING   Combine the following root words and suffixes, making whatever changes are necessary.

1. hate + ful ___hateful___   4. sincere + ly _____

2. awe + ful _____   5. stare + ing _____

3. dance + ing _____   6. note + ation _____

7. dine + ing _____   12. admire + ation _____

8. shine + ing _____   13. fame + ous _____

9. write + ing _____   14. store + ing _____

10. amuse + ment _____   15. civilize + ation _____

11. like + ing _____

A Note About -ly. As you know, you can add -*ly* to many words to make them adverbs. When you add -*ly*, however, look at the root word carefully. Do not change it (except to change final -*y* to -*i*). This is especially important with root words ending in -*l* (making -*lly*) or root words ending in -*e* (making -*ely*). Note these examples.

Root Word	*New Word*
rea*l*	rea*lly*
sur*e*	sur*ely*
sincer*e*	sincer*ely*
carefu*l*	carefu*lly*

One exception:

true   tru*ly*

6 WARM-UP

Add -*ly* to the following root words.

1. ideal _____*ideally*_____   6. angry _____

2. bare _____   7. fundamental _____

3. usual _____   8. real _____

4. sure _____   9. accidental _____

5. necessary _____   10. true _____

Double Final Consonants Before Suffixes Beginning with Vowels. Almost always, a combination of *vowel—consonant—vowel* (such as -*ate*, -*ine*, and -*ope*) creates a "long" vowel sound in the first vowel in the combination. A long vowel sound sounds just like the name of the vowel.

ā	hāte
ē	Pēte
ī	bīte
ō	hōpe
ū	cūte

On the other hand, a combination of *vowel—consonant—(no vowel)* or *vowel—consonant—consonant* creates a "short" vowel sound, as in the following examples:

hăt	hătter
pĕt	pĕtted
bĭt	bĭtten
hŏp	hŏpping
cŭt	cŭtting

$$v—c—v \; = \; \text{long vowel sound}$$
$$\left.\begin{array}{l} v—c \\ v—c—c \end{array}\right\} = \text{short vowel sound}$$

As you can see, you *double the consonant* to create a *short* vowel sound. However, you *do not double the consonant* to create a *long* vowel sound.

bite (*v—c—v = long* sound)
biting (still *v—c—v = long* sound)
bitten (now *v—c—c = short* sound)

Contrast these words.

(to frighten)	scāre	scāring	scāred
(to cause a scar)	scăr	scărring	scărred
(to get rid of)	rĭd	rĭdding	
(to ride, as in a car)	rīde	rīding	
(to hop, like a bunny)	hŏp	hŏpping	hŏpped
(to wish)	hōpe	hōping	hōped
(to slice)	cŭt	cŭtting	
(attractive)	cūte	cūter	

7 TRANSFORMING

Combine the following root words and suffixes, doubling the final consonant of the root word when necessary.

1. win + ing _____winning_____   9. run + ing _____

2. wine + ing _____   10. tune + ing _____

3. slope + ed _____   11. rot + ing _____

4. slop + ed _____   12. root + ing _____

5. tire + ing _____   13. hit + ing _____

6. stir + ing _____   14. heat + ing _____

7. cop + ed _____   15. cream + ed _____

8. cope + ed _____   16. cram + ed _____

There is one exception to the rule of doubling the final consonant before a suffix beginning with a vowel.

When a word has *more than one syllable,* double the final consonant only if the accent falls on the syllable *immediately before the suffix.*

commítted	occúrred	(tránsferred is an exception)
begínning	submítted	
preférred	expélled	

Note what happens when the accent falls on any syllable but the one immediately before the suffix.

háppened	lístened
ánswered	coúnselor
préference	tráveled

8 TRANSFORMING

Combine the following root words and suffixes, doubling the final consonant of the root word when necessary. Be careful to note where the accent falls.

1. defer + ed _____deferred_____   4. compel + ed _____

2. unravel + ing _____   5. prefer + ence _____

3. parallel + ing _____

Notice that this rule about doubling final consonants before vowels also helps in determining when to double consonants in other situations.

ăpple but āpe

bĕggar but bēgin

rŭmmage but ūnion

9 WARM-UP

Circle the correct spelling.

1. runing/running

2. forgetable/forgettable

3. stuborn/stubborn

4. refered/referred

5. writing/writting

6. pited/pitted

7. comming/coming

8. dining/dinning (as in *eating*)

9. biten/bitten

10. diferent/different

11. swimer/swimmer

12. happen/hapen

13. suning/sunning

14. deleted/deletted

15. sitting/siting

16. dificult/difficult

17. writen/written

18. gramar/grammar

19. trafic/traffic

20. occured/occurred

In Summary: When you add a suffix to a root word,

1. change *consonant-y* to *consonant-i* and then add the suffix. Do not change *vowel-y;*
2. drop final *-e* before a suffix beginning with a vowel. Keep final *-e* before a suffix beginning with a consonant;
3. to keep a short vowel sound within the root word, double the final consonant before a suffix beginning with a vowel. To keep a long vowel sound within the root word, do not double the final consonant before a suffix beginning with a vowel.

Prefixes

A *prefix* is a group of letters added to the beginning of a word. (For example, the prefix *re-* added to the root word *do* makes *redo*.) The rule for adding prefixes is simple: When you add a prefix, do not change the root word in any way. Keep the root word just as it is; do not drop any letters from it or double any letters.

Prefix	*Root Word*	*New Word*
un-	natural	un*n*atural
dis-	integrate	dis*i*ntegrate
mis-	spell	mis*s*pell
il-	logical	il*l*ogical
in-	accurate	in*a*ccurate
im-	moral	im*m*oral
co-	operate	co*o*perate
ad-	dress	ad*d*ress

10 WARM-UP

Circle the correct spellings.

1. (disinterested)/dissinterested
2. unnable/unable
3. inumerable/innumerable
4. unnerve/unerve
5. disatisfied/dissatisfied
6. ilegal/illegal
7. immaterial/imaterial
8. missapply/misapply
9. misstake/mistake
10. disagree/dissagree

11 EDITING

Correct each of the following misspelled words. When the spelling rules won't help you, use a dictionary or look at the list of commonly misspelled words on the inside back cover of this book.

1. accross _____ across _____
2. adress _____
3. alot _____
4. arguement _____
5. athelete _____
6. basicly _____
7. begining _____
8. beleive _____
9. brillient _____
10. buisness _____
11. carefuly _____
12. childrens _____
13. choosen _____
14. comming _____
15. competion _____
16. definate _____
17. delt _____
18. diffrent _____
19. dinning _____
20. disapoint _____
21. discribe _____
22. dosen't _____
23. eigth _____
24. entrence _____

25. enviroment ＿＿＿＿＿＿＿＿

26. existance ＿＿＿＿＿＿＿＿

27. explaination ＿＿＿＿＿＿＿

28. extremly ＿＿＿＿＿＿＿＿

29. finaly ＿＿＿＿＿＿＿＿＿

30. freind ＿＿＿＿＿＿＿＿＿

31. goverment ＿＿＿＿＿＿＿＿

32. grammer ＿＿＿＿＿＿＿＿＿

33. heigth ＿＿＿＿＿＿＿＿＿

34. hisself ＿＿＿＿＿＿＿＿＿

35. hopeing ＿＿＿＿＿＿＿＿

36. imediately ＿＿＿＿＿＿＿＿

37. interlectual ＿＿＿＿＿＿＿

38. intresting ＿＿＿＿＿＿＿＿

39. jewlry ＿＿＿＿＿＿＿＿＿

40. knowlege ＿＿＿＿＿＿＿＿

41. localy ＿＿＿＿＿＿＿＿＿

42. lonly ＿＿＿＿＿＿＿＿＿＿

43. mispell ＿＿＿＿＿＿＿＿＿

44. necesary ＿＿＿＿＿＿＿＿

45. ocasion ＿＿＿＿＿＿＿＿＿

46. occurance ＿＿＿＿＿＿＿＿

47. perfer ＿＿＿＿＿＿＿＿＿

48. possble ＿＿＿＿＿＿＿＿

49. potatoe ＿＿＿＿＿＿＿＿

50. preceed ＿＿＿＿＿＿＿＿

51. priviledge ＿＿＿＿＿＿＿

52. probly ＿＿＿＿＿＿＿＿＿

53. recieved ＿＿＿＿＿＿＿＿

54. rember ＿＿＿＿＿＿＿＿＿

55. sacrafice ＿＿＿＿＿＿＿＿

56. sence ＿＿＿＿＿＿＿＿＿

57. seperate ＿＿＿＿＿＿＿＿

58. shinning ＿＿＿＿＿＿＿＿

59. sincerly ＿＿＿＿＿＿＿＿

60. studing ＿＿＿＿＿＿＿＿

61. suceed ＿＿＿＿＿＿＿＿＿

62. suprise ＿＿＿＿＿＿＿＿＿

63. temperture ＿＿＿＿＿＿＿

64. themselfs ＿＿＿＿＿＿＿＿

65. tomatoe ＿＿＿＿＿＿＿＿

66. truely ＿＿＿＿＿＿＿＿＿

67. trys ＿＿＿＿＿＿＿＿＿＿

68. usualy ＿＿＿＿＿＿＿＿＿

69. writen ＿＿＿＿＿＿＿＿＿

70. writting ＿＿＿＿＿＿＿＿

USING THE APOSTROPHE

Apostrophes need not be confusing; the rules for using them are actually rather simple. Apostrophes have only three functions: to make nouns possessive, to form contractions, and to make letters plural.

Apostrophes to Show Possession

1. To Make a Singular Noun Possessive, Add _'s_. When something belongs to someone, that person _possesses_ it. There are several ways to express possession or ownership.

the house that belongs to Jerry

the car my neighbor owns

the room of my brother

However, a simple *apostrophe (')* + *s* added to a noun signals the same relationship in a shorter and more direct way.

Jerry's house
my neighbor's car
my brother's room

Although a house, a car, and a room are concrete and easy to visualize, a person can also possess things you can't see. Look at the following examples:

my friend's idea
the teacher's explanation
Rafael's ambition

The words *idea, explanation,* and *ambition* are abstract; they represent concepts or ideas. Although people don't own these qualities, people do possess them. "My friend's idea" really means "the idea *of* my friend." "The teacher's explanation" really means "the explanation made by the teacher."

In Summary: Form the possessive of a singular noun by adding *apostrophe (')* + *s* to

1. concrete nouns

   the coats that belong to the women = the women's coats
   the store that Mr. Smith owns = Mr. Smith's store

2. abstract nouns

   the work of Julia = Julia's work
   the smile made by Mickey = Mickey's smile

---

12 TRANSFORMING

Rewrite each of the following expressions, using *'s.*

1. the book that belongs to Tom _____ Tom's book _____

2. the coat that Judy has _____

3. the work done by Willie _____

4. the personality of Karen _____

5. the apartment that belongs to Maria _____

   _____

6. the bicycle that the boy owns _____

7. the temperament of the cat _____

8. the statement made by Mr. Johnson _____

   _____

9. the photographs made by Susie _____

_____

10. the good humor of Hector _____

2. **To Make a Noun That Already Ends in -*s* Possessive, Add '.** So far you have been working with nouns that do not end in -*s:* Jerr*y*, neighbo*r*, frien*d*, teache*r*, Rafae*l*, wome*n*, Mr. Smit*h*, and so forth. You add -*s* to these words to make them possessive. However, as you know, many nouns end in -*s*, especially plural nouns.

friend*s*	boy*s*	class*es*	the Smith*s*
teacher*s*	student*s*	parent*s*	the Gonzalez*es*

Even some singular nouns end in -*s* or -*ss*.

Mr. Jone*s*	busines*s*
Carlo*s*	bu*s*

Since these words already have a final -*s*, you make them possessive by adding ' *after* the -*s*.

the books that belong to the boy*s* = the boy*s*' books

the car that belongs to my neighbor*s* = my neighbor*s*' car

the smile made by Carlo*s* = Carlo*s*' smile*

the attitudes of my parent*s* = my parent*s*' attitude

Placing the apostrophe correctly is important. It tells the reader whether you mean that the possessive noun is singular or plural.

the boy's house (singular)

the boys' house (plural)

In Summary: To make a noun possessive,

1. add '*s* to nouns that do not end in -*s:*

   Bill'*s* hat,

   the men'*s* room,

   the doctor'*s* office.

2. add ' to nouns that already end in -*s* or -*ss:*

   the three boy*s*' bicycles;

   Thomas' brother;

   The Smith*s*' apartment;

   my boss' office.

---

*Some people prefer that you add '*s* to *all* singular nouns, even if they already end in -*s:* Keats'*s* poems, Mr. Jone*s*'*s* class, the busines*s*'*s* stationary. You may wish to discuss this matter with your instructor to see what he or she prefers.

13 TRANSFORMING   Rewrite each of the following expressions, using *'s* or *'*.

1. the lounge for women _____ the women's lounge _____

2. the idea of my boss _____

3. the house that belongs to Ramos _____

4. the room that belongs to the children _____

_____

5. the day for every mother _____

6. the schedules of the professors _____

_____

7. the laws of Texas _____

8. the smile made by Fides _____

9. the best restaurant in the city _____

10. the toys that belong to the dogs _____

_____

3. Use *'s* or *'* to Express Possession with Objects and Time. Not just people possess things; objects possess things, too. Note these examples.

the bicycle*'s* front tire = the front tire *of* the bicycle
the lamps*'* new shades = the new shades *of* the lamps.

Even some time expressions use *'s* or *'s*. Compare these examples; you will notice that the ones with *'s* or *s'* sound better than the ones with *of*.

a week*'s* pay = the pay *of* a week
a years*'* work = the work *of* a year

Finally, note that this way to show possession applies to nouns only. It does not apply to personal pronouns.

his house (not *hi's* house)
its instructions (not *it's* instructions)
her fence (not *her's* fence)
but: someone's work (*Someone* is not a personal pronoun.)

14 EDITING   Insert the omitted apostrophes in each of the following sentences.

1. I'm taking a weekˏs vacation soon.

2. The rooms air conditioner needs to be repaired.

3. A few hours work should take care of the problem.

4. This years schedule allows more time off than last years schedule.

5. The cars front fenders were dented in two separate accidents.

6. I'll be off on New Years Day.

Be Careful: When learning to use apostrophes, some people start putting them before every final -*s* they write. Don't confuse '*s/s*' for possession with the final -*s* on plural nouns or third-person-singular verbs.

incorrect: I have two *pen's.* Bill *want's* one.
correct: I have two pe*ns.* Bill wan*ts* one.

possessives
the *cat's* litter box
the *family's* secret
Judy's brother
plurals
Several *cats* use that litter box (not *cat's*).
The building houses eight *families* (not *family's*).
verb endings
He *wants* to meet you (not *want's*).
The team *plays* today (not *play's*).

15 WARM-UP

Circle the correct spelling in parentheses.

1. It was the (companies/company's) responsibility.

2. The Mets scored five (runs/run's) in the ninth.

3. He (runs/run's) a large business.

4. In the (movies/movie's) opening scene, four men were shot.

5. I ate at the (cities/city's) best restaurant.

6. She (lights/light's) the fire each night.

7. The trees have lost their (leaves/leaf's).

8. He (says/say's) that the coat doesn't fit.

Apostrophes to Form Contractions

To Make a Contraction, Use an Apostrophe to Replace the Missing Letters. A *contraction* is a shortened word that is missing a letter or several letters. An apostrophe goes in the spot where the letters are missing.

do not = don't (' replaces *o*)
can not = can't (' replaces *no*)
it is = it's (' replaces *i*)
they are = they're (' replaces *a*)*
they would = they'd (' replaces *woul*)

*For advice about distinguishing *it's* from *its*, *they're* from *their/there*, and about distinguishing the other sound-alike words from one another, see Chapter 15.

16 TRANSFORMING   Make the following pairs of words into contractions, placing apostrophes properly.

1. he is = ___he's___

2. we will = _____

3. it has (as in, "It has been a long time.") = _____

4. we are = _____

5. it is = _____

6. does not = _____

7. they are = _____

8. has not = _____

9. you are = _____

10. have not = _____

11. it is = _____

12. does not = _____

13. can not = _____

14. has not = _____

17 EDITING   Add apostrophes where necessary in the following sentences.

1. It ∧'s cold today.

2. Were going to get it done.

3. Well have to see what she says.

4. What do you think hell do?

5. Its purpose is clear.

6. I dont know what youre asking me.

7. Whos there?

8. Theyre always getting in trouble.

Apostrophes to Make Letters Plural

Add 's to Form the Plurals of Letters and Groups of Letters. Occasionally, you need to make a letter or group of letters plural. Use an apostrophe before the final -s so that your readers don't think that the -s is one of the letters.

Watch your p's and q's.
Billy already knows his ABC's.

In Summary: When you use an apostrophe,

1. add 's to nouns (but not pronouns) to show possession;
2. add ' to nouns already ending in -s or an s sound to show possession;
3. use ' to replace the missing letters in a contraction;
4. add 's to form the plurals of letters used as words.

18 EDITING   The following passage contains errors in the use of apostrophes. In some places apostrophes have been omitted; in other places unnecessary apostrophes have been included. Make all necessary corrections above each line.

James Gordon Bennett (1841–1918): The World's Greatest Spender

(1) In the history of the very rich, there have been many extravagant spender's or eccentric characters, but the most extravagant and eccentric has to be James Gordon Bennett. (2) He became rich when he inherited his fathers newspaper, the *New York Herald*, which he managed so well that it made him at least one million dollars a year after taxes. (3) (Thats at least six million dollars in todays currency.) (4) He spent most of the money—and in some very strange way's. (5) In *The Big Spenders*, Lucius Beebe describes some of Bennetts most notorious escapades.

(6) Heres one example. (7) Bennett was a notorious playboy, but after he became engaged to a beautiful socialite, Caroline May, he promised her that he would reform. (8) On New Years Day, 1877, he attended a party at her familys Manhattan home. (9) He soon got very drunk and mistook the fireplace for the toilet, whereupon he relieved himself of the evenings alcoholic consumption. (10) This piece of bad manner's caused such a scandal that after fighting a duel with Carolines brother (both men intentionally misfired their pistol's), Bennett headed for France.

(11) Bennett became a familiar sight in Paris's best restaurant's, where stumbling in drunk, he would walk between the elegant tables and pull on the tablecloths' to send food, wine, and all crashing to the floor. (12) Then he would insist that the costly china, crystal, and food be replaced, send expensive bottle's of wine to the tables of the astonished customer's, and order that all the cleaning bills be sent to him. (13) After the meal he would offer a wad of money to the owner's, letting them take as much as they considered sufficient to cover their losses.

(14) Bennett was famous for throwing his money around—in more than one way. (15) One night he tipped a train porter fourteen thousand dollars.

(16) The lucky man resigned from his job and opened his own hotel. (17) Another time, Bennett was interviewing a young man who wanted a job on Bennetts paper. (18) Throughout the conversation Bennett appeared physically uncomfortable as he squirmed in hi's chair. (19) Finally, he pulled a huge wad of money out of the back pocket of his pant's and tossed it into the fireplace. (20) Bennetts visitor leapt from his seat, grabbed the bill's from the fire, and handed them back to Bennett. (21) The publisher immediately threw them back into the flames, saying, "Thats where I wanted them in the first place."

(22) The storie's of Bennett's wastefulness with the forty million dollars he spent in his lifetime could go on and on, but there is one in particular that perhaps best illustrates the mans eccentricities. (23) It begins with his passion for good mutton chops, for which he searched far and wide. (24) In a small family restaurant in Monte Carlo he found the mutton chops of his dream's. (25) Bennett lunched their daily. (26) One day he arrived to find his regular table occupied by a large group of drinker's. (27) He approached the establishment's owner and said that he wanted to buy the restaurant. (28) He informed the owner that the owner could name his price but that he must sell on the spot. (29) The transaction was completed for forty thousand dollars, the drinking party was asked to leave, and Bennett sat down to his mutton chop's. (30) After the meal Bennett gave the restaurant to the waiter who had served him—under two conditions'—that a place be reserved for Bennett each day and that the mutton chops be prepared by the same chef. (31) Bennett didn't even know the waiters name, which in fact was Ciro, and the three *Ciro's* restaurants eventually became among the most famous in the world. (32) There was never an odder or more extravagant man than Charles Gordon Bennett.

USING HYPHENS

Hyphens have two purposes: *to join* and *to divide*. They join two or more words to make them one, or they divide one word into two parts when it must be split at the end of a line.

Hyphens to Join

Hyphenate All Two-Word Numbers from Twenty-One Through Ninety-Nine.

thirty-five

fifty-one

  but

one hundred

321 (use numerals for numbers that would require three or more words if they were written out)

Do not hyphenate fractions.

two thirds

five eighths

19 WARM-UP

Hyphenate the following numbers where necessary.

1. twenty∧one

2. three hundred

3. forty six

4. one thousand

5. three fourths

6. eighty two

Hyphenate a Word Consisting of a Prefix and a Capitalized Noun.

pro-American   anti-Chinese

Hyphenate between the prefixes *self-*, *all-*, and *ex-* (meaning "former") and all nouns.

self-confidence   ex-husband   all-world

Hyphenate words with *-in-law.*

mother-in-law   sister-in-law
father-in-law   brothers-in-law (note how the plural is formed)

Hyphenate two or more words acting as one adjective before a noun.

a three-piece suit   a three-star movie
a good-for-nothing guy   a two-thirds majority

However, do not hyphenate these groups of words when they appear after linking verbs.

That guy has always been good for nothing.
The required majority vote was two thirds.

20 WARM-UP   Hyphenate the following groups of words where necessary.

1. an ex officer of the group
2. two sisters in law
3. a self made woman
4. two man job
5. a pro Soviet speech
6. a hard to get out of bed morning

Consult a Dictionary About Hyphenating Compound Words. A compound word is a word made up of two or more complete root words (like *underground*). There are three different ways to write compound words.

1. As one word

Root Word	Root Word	New Word
back	ground	background
count	less	countless
fruit	less	fruitless
there	about	thereabout
through	out	throughout
school	house	schoolhouse

Notice that these compound words do not drop any letters from their root words.

2. As hyphenated words

Root Word	Root Word	New Word
heavy	duty	heavy-duty
go	between	a go-between
give (and)	take	give-and-take
follow	through	follow-through

3. As two separate words (these are not really compound words)

monkey wrench

heat wave

grand piano

Whenever you are unsure about the hyphenation or spelling of a compound word, check a dictionary.

21 TRANSFORMING   Combine a second root word with each root word below, using hyphens when necessary. Check the dictionary if you have any doubts about how to join the root words.

1. day _____ daylight _____   9. _____ ground

2. run _____   10. chair _____

3. _____ bitten   11. _____ maker

4. house _____   12. half _____

5. news _____   13. under _____

6. _____ worker   14. _____ book

7. _____ take   15. _____ car

8. water _____

> **In Summary:**   Use hyphens to join
>
> 1. all two-word numbers from twenty-one to ninety-nine;
> 2. a prefix and a capitalized noun;
> 3. the prefixes *self-*, *all-*, or *ex-* and a noun;
> 4. all words with *-in-law;*
> 5. many—but not all—compound words. Consult your dictionary when you are not sure whether to use a hyphen.

Hyphens to Divide

Hyphenate Only Between Syllables (and Never Hyphenate a One-Syllable Word). A syllable is a complete sound, which must include a vowel. For example, the word *understand* has three complete sounds: *un der stand*. Of course many words have only one syllable: *go, make, seen.* When you run out of space at the end of a line and must hyphenate a word, do so only between syllables. If a word has only one syllable, you cannot hyphenate it.

_____ accu-
rate _____

_____ intel-
lectual _____

_____ com-
munity _____

   but not

_____ swi-
ft _____ (one syllable)

_____ ho-
me _____ (one syllable)

_____ pict-
ure _____ (hyphenated in the middle of a syllable; should be *pic-ture*)

Some Hints About Breaking Words into Syllables. Since so many words have root words within them, one way to check for syllable breaks is to find the breaks after a complete root word.

transfer- able

spell- ing

play- er

Syllable breaks also occur after prefixes or before suffixes.

un- interesting

trans- port

sad -ly

govern -ment

And syllable breaks often occur between two consonants—unless the consonants form one sound, such as *-th*, *-sh*, *-sc*, or *-ch*.

cap- tain

volun- tary

hus- band

    but

sou*th* -ern

rea*ch* -ing

Whenever you are unsure where syllable breaks occur, look in the dictionary.

Break Hyphenated Words Only at the Hyphen. Since two hyphens in one word will confuse your reader, break a hyphenated word only at its hyphen.

poor: _____ un-Amer-

ican _____

better: _____ un-

American _____

poor: _____ self-con-

trol _____

better: _____ self-

control _____

If you can avoid writing an already hyphenated word on two lines, do so. Do not hyphenate a contraction.

wrong: _____ does-

n't _____

wrong: _____ is-

n't _____

wrong: _____ ca-

n't _____

Do Not Leave Only One or Two Letters at the End of a Line, and Do Not Carry Over Fewer Than Three Letters.

poor: _____ a-

live _____

better: alive

poor: _____ want-

ed _____

better: wanted

22 TRANSFORMING

Rewrite the following words, using a hyphen to show where they would be divided at the end of a line. If a word cannot be divided, do not write anything in the blank space.

1. unnecessary _____un-_____

_____necessary_____

2. repeat _____

_____

3. stepped _____

_____

4. waited _____

_____

5. watered _____

_____

6. rated _____

_____

7. ex-president _____

_____

8. aren't _____

_____

9. guardhouse _____

_____

10. attention _____

_____

In Summary: Use a hyphen to divide a word at the end of a line

1. only between the syllables of the word;
2. only where a word is already hyphenated.

Do not use a hyphen to divide a word

1. if the word is a contraction;
2. if you leave only one or two letters at the end of a line, or if you carry over fewer than three letters to the next line.

USING CAPITALS

First Word of a Sentence

Capitalize the First Word of Every Sentence.

In the beginning the book was slow reading.
He said he felt fine.

The Pronoun *I*

Capitalize the Pronoun *I* (But No Other Pronoun).

I   we   you   he   she   it   they   his   myself

Names

Capitalize the Names of People, Places, Courses, Organizations, Languages, and Words Formed from Them.

Howard
Elizabeth *or* Beth (nicknames are
    also capitalized)
Susan *or* Sue
New York
New Yorker
China
Biology 111 (the name of a course)
    but biology (not a course name)
Fleet Street
Seventh Avenue
The National Audubon Society
English
French
Main High School (*but* high school)

23 WARM-UP

Capitalize the following words when necessary.

1. russian _____ Russian

2. george herman "babe" ruth _____

_____

3. the corner of prairie road and central street _____

_____

4. mathematics 101 _____

5. mathematics _____

6. california wine _____

7. i, you, him _____

8. the american civil liberties union _____

_____

9. spanish _____

_____

Capitalize a Person's Title Before His or Her Name.

Mr. Juarez   **Dr.** Williams
Ms. Hwang
President Carter   *but*

but   She is a doctor.

the president   **Professor** Kosmenski

but

Who is your English professor?

Capitalize Words Such As North, South, East, Northeast, and West When They Are Names of Specific Areas of the Country or of the World. Do not capitalize these terms when they mean only a direction.

The **North** won the Civil War.

but

We are traveling north.

She is from the **Far East.**

but

Which way is east?

Capitalize the Names of Days, Months, Holidays, and Specific Events (But Not of Seasons of the Year).

Tuesday   **World War** II
March
Independence Day   *but*

summer
fall

Titles   **Capitalize the Title or Subtitle of a Book, Movie, Song, Play, Poem, Article, Newspaper, or Magazine.** Don't capitalize little words—short prepositions, conjunctions, and articles—unless they are the first words in the title or subtitle.

For **Wh**om the **B**ell **T**olls
Star **W**ars
"Johnnie **B.** Goode"
The **J**ournal of the **A**merican **M**edical **A**ssociation
Ms.

24 WARM-UP   Capitalize the following words if necessary.

1. tuesday _____ Tuesday _____

2. winter _____

3. august _____

4. the wild west _____

5. a reverend _____

6. the reverend mr. haley _____

7. the wind is coming from the east. _____

_____

8. *close encounters of the third kind* _____

_____

9. *webster's collegiate dictionary* _____

10. "the birth of the yuppies" _____

_____

In Summary: Capitalize

1. the first word of every sentence;
2. the pronoun *I* (but no other pronoun, except in titles);
3. the names of people, places, organizations, languages, and words formed from them;
4. the names of days, months, holidays, and special events (but not seasons of the year);
5. a person's title before his or her name;
6. *North, South, East,* or *West* when they refer to a specific area of the country or world (but not when they mean only a direction);
7. the title or subtitle of a book, movie, song, play, poem, article, newspaper, or magazine.

CHAPTER 15

Writing the Right Word

Words that look alike or sound alike create problems for many writers who confuse the words or accidentally write one when they mean the other. Most often these problems occur in first drafts and can be eliminated during revisions. To help you tell the difference between the most common look-alikes and sound-alikes, this chapter examines many of them. You may want to study all of the chapter or just the words that are most troublesome for you. The chapter lists and contrasts a great many sound-alikes and look-alikes. But as you study any of these word pairs or triplets, focus whenever possible on *one word* in the group—the one that occurs most often or gives you the most trouble. Doing so will prevent you from further confusing the words.

AVOIDING THE FOUR MOST COMMON LOOK- AND SOUND-ALIKE ERRORS

The following four categories of errors deserve special attention. They probably show up in more papers than do any other errors.

The Contractions Versus Their Sound-Alikes (and Look-Alikes)

The Contractions. The following words are all contractions of *is* or *are*.

it's	=	it is (and also *it has*)
who's	=	who is (and also *who has*)
they're	=	they are
you're	=	you are
he's	=	he is (and also *he has*)

Since these contractions contain *both a subject pronoun and a verb*, each contraction is always the subject *and* verb of a sentence or clause.

The Possessive Words. People often confuse these contractions with the following possessive words:

its   whose   their   your   his

If you are unsure whether to use a contraction or its sound-alike or look-alike, simply ask yourself whether the meaning you intend contains *is*, *has*, or *are*. Use the contraction only if it does.

The Verb *were*. One of the past-tense forms of *to be* is *were*. However, it is sometimes confused with the contraction of *we are*, *we're*.

were   =   past tense of *to be*   *we're*   =   *we are*

The Place Words. Similarly, *they're/their* and *we're/were* are sometimes confused with the *place words*.

there   where

You can remember that these two words refer to a place because both contain the word *here*.

t *here*   w *here*

As a way of summarizing and of compiling your own list of sound-alikes and look-alikes, label all of the words below. After each, write either *contraction*, *possessive*, *place*, or *past*.

1. it's _____

2. its _____

3. who's _____

4. whose _____

5. they're _____

6. their _____

7. there _____

8. you're _____

9. your _____

10. we're _____

11. were _____

12. where _____

13. he's _____

14. his _____

1 WARM-UP   Circle the correct word in parentheses.

1. (There/Their/They're) are two inventions responsible for many of the needless calories (where/were/we're) always consuming: the ice-cream soda and the sundae.

2. But first we should know about (there/their/they're) ancestor, the soda fountain.

3. (Its/It's) inventor was John Matthews. (He's/His) great discovery occurred in 1832.

4. Much later, in 1874, the ice-cream soda got (its/it's) start in Philadelphia, (where/were/we're) Robert M. Green demonstrated it at a fair.

5. Preachers immediately thought that it was sinful to "suck soda" on the Sabbath, so druggists served just half of (its/it's) ingredients on Sunday—the ice cream and syrup without the soda.

6. According to one theory, (there/their/they're) name became the Sunday—later spelled *sundae*—because these two ingredients (where/were/we're) served on Sunday.

7. Now that (your/you're) aware of whom to blame, relax and have (your/you're) sodas and sundaes.

8. After all, (there/their/they're) still good even if (there/their/they're) fattening.

2 WARM-UP   Circle the correct word in parentheses.

1. If (your/you're) used to thinking of zippers as something for (your/you're) pants or skirt, you'll be surprised to learn that they (where/were/we're) originally designed for fastening shoes.

2. (There/Their/They're) inventor was Whitcomb L. Judson, (whose/who's) company started in business in 1893.

3. Judson's partner soon decided that any place (where/were/we're) buttons or hooks could be used was also a place for these shoe fasteners.

4. The two men renamed (there/their/they're) invention the "universal fastener," but (its/it's) success was limited.

5. Judson then developed a simpler fastener called C-Curity, but (there/their/they're) was little market for it, either.

6. Finally a third partner entered the business and designed a still simpler fastener (whose/who's) success was guaranteed when the United States military ordered a large quantity.

7. From then on, (its/it's) been a standard feature on many pants and skirts.

8. The fastener got (its/it's) modern name, incidentally, when an executive from the B. F. Goodrich Company was so impressed with (its/it's) speed in opening that he said it was "quite a zipper."

3 WRITING

Write two sentences of your own for each of the words in this lesson.

1. (it's) _It's a nice day for going to school._____
2. (it's) _____
3. (its) _____
4. (its) _____
5. (who's) _____
6. (who's) _____
7. (whose) _____
8. (whose) _____
9. (they're) _____
10. (they're) _____
11. (their) _____
12. (their) _____
13. (there) _____
14. (there) _____
15. (you're) _____
16. (you're) _____
17. (your) _____
18. (your) _____
19. (we're) _____
20. (we're) _____
21. (were) _____
22. (were) _____
23. (where) _____
24. (where) _____
25. (he's) _____
26. (he's) _____
27. (his) _____
28. (his) _____

too/two/to

Here are three more frequently confused sound-alikes.
Too means *also* or *more than enough*.

We are coming, *too* (also).
We have *too* much money (more than enough).

This sentence should help you remember those meanings: The *zoo* was *too* crowded *too.*

Two means the number 2.

To is used in all other cases.

4 WARM-UP

Circle the correct word in parentheses.

1. Back in 1886, John S. Pemberton used an iron pot (too/(to)/two) mix a batch of a drink later (too/(to)/two) be called Coca-Cola.

2. Pemberton had returned (too/to/two) Atlanta, Georgia, after the Civil War (too/to/two) open a drugstore.

3. A friend named the drink after its (too/to/two) main ingredients: coca, the dried leaf of a plant, and cola from the kola nut.

4. (Too/To/Two) years later Pemberton died, and ownership of the soft drink was sold (too/to/two) a company for $2300.

5. Soon the public began (too/to/two) call the drink Coke, which the company felt was (too/to/two) informal a name.

6. In 1920 the company gave in (too/to/two) public practice and registered the name Coke as a trademark.

7. Today Coca-Cola is not only the most popular soft drink in America but is widely sold throughout the world, (too/to/two).

8. Nevertheless, (too/to/two) this day the formula of the syrup from which Coke is made is a closely guarded secret.

5 WRITING

Write two sentences of your own that use *too,* two that use *to,* and two more that use *two.*

1. I'm too rich, so I have to give away money. _____

2. _____

3. _____

4. _____

5. _____

6. _____

7. _____

The "of" Error After *Could, Should, Would,* and *Might*

When you speak, you probably use the following contractions.

could've	=	could have	would've	=	would have
should've	=	should have	might've	=	might have

The *-'ve* ending in each contraction sounds just like the preposition *of*. Consequently, many people write *could of* when they mean *could have*, and so forth.

incorrect:	He *should of* done it.
correct:	He *should have* done it.
incorrect:	I *might of* gone.
correct:	I *might have* gone.
incorrect:	We *would of* seen it.
correct:	We *would have* seen it.

Remember that *of* cannot follow the words *could*, *should*, *would*, and *might*.

6 WARM-UP

Circle the correct word in parentheses.

1. Ivory Soap's famous ability to float might never (of/have) happened if it had not been for a lucky accident.

2. In 1878 an employee of Proctor & Gamble should (of/have) turned off the soap-mixing machine before he went to lunch.

3. Anything could (of/have) resulted from his leaving the machine on too long.

4. Someone could easily have gotten rid (of/have) the soap, but no one did.

5. Consequently, the employee, who should (of/have) told his bosses, merely packaged it like any other batch.

6. The lengthy mixing process must have put a great deal (of/have) air in the soap, and as a result it floated.

7. People loved it, and so an employee who might otherwise (of/have) been fired was a company hero.

7 WRITING

Write one sentence of your own with *might have*, one with *could have*, one with *should have*, and one with *would have*.

1. I should have been a movie star. _____
2. _____
3. _____
4. _____
5. _____

Three Words Ending in -*d*

suppose*d* (to)

use*d* (to)

prejudice*d*

The sounds of the letters *d* and *t* are almost identical. As a result, when people write *supposed to* or *used to*, they sometimes drop the final *-d* before *to*. Remember that when *to* follows *supposed* or *used*, these words *must* end in *-d*.

We are suppose*d* *to* call later.
We use*d* *to* vacation in Michigan.

In many other cases, however, *suppose* or *use* may not end in *-d*.

I *suppose* that you are right.
I *use* my car for business.

People often incorrectly write one other word, the adjective *prejudiced*, without its final *-d*.

incorrect:	He is *prejudice* against me.
correct:	He is *prejudiced* against me.
incorrect:	They are *prejudice* people.
correct:	They are *prejudiced* people.

However, the noun *prejudice* does not end in *-d*.

Racial *prejudice* gets me angry.

When you use *prejudiced* as an adjective, be careful to add final *-d* to it.

8 WARM-UP

Circle the correct word in parentheses.

1. Coffee (use/used) to be served in the Maxwell House Hotel in Nashville, Tennessee.

2. The inventor of the coffee (use/used) a special blend of beans to make it.

3. Its (use/used) in the hotel led to its brand name, Maxwell House Coffee.

4. Years later President Theodore Roosevelt drank some and was asked if he wanted another cup. He is (suppose/supposed) to have replied, "Will I have another? Delighted! It's good to the last drop."

5. You might (suppose/supposed) that such an endorsement from a president might make many people (prejudice/prejudiced) in favor of the coffee.

6. At any rate, people are (use/used) to asking for a second cup of the coffee that is good to the last drop.

9 WRITING

Write two sentences of your own that use *used to,* two that use *supposed to,* and two that use *prejudiced.*

1. _I used to ride my bicycle a lot._

2. _____

3. _____

4. _____

5. _____

6. _____

7. _____

CORRECTLY USING OTHER COMMONLY CONFUSED WORDS

accept/except

Accept means *to receive*.

He *accepted* the reward.

Except means *excluding* or *but*.

Everyone *except* him is here.

Memory Trick. *Except* and *excluding* both begin with *ex-*.

10 WARM-UP

Circle the correct word in parentheses.

1. George Eastman, inventor of the Kodak camera, felt that a trademark should be short, strong, and unusual to be (accepted/excepted) by the general public.

2. His new camera had many good selling points, (accept/except) that it had no trademark.

3. He made up a nonsense word, Kodak, which he thought was (acceptable/exceptable).

4. Today everyone knows the word, (accept/except), perhaps, people in Siberia.

11 WRITING

Write two sentences of your own that use *accept* and two more that use *except*.

1. The winner accepted the award in person.

2. _____

3. _____

4. _____

5. _____

advice/advise

Advice is a noun.

We got *advice*.

Advise is a verb.

He *advised* us.

Memory Trick. *Advice* is *nice*, but only the *wise advise*.

12 WARM-UP

Circle the correct word in parentheses.

1. The ice-cream cone was invented at a fair in 1904 when Abe Doumar overheard an ice-cream seller complain that he had run out of ice-cream dishes. Doumar (adviced/(advised)) him to make a cone from a waffle, fill it with ice cream, and double his price.

2. It was good (advice/advise). The seller followed it and had a popular attraction at the fair.

3. Two years later Doumar followed his own (advice/advise) and set up an ice-cream stand, first on Coney Island, later in Norfolk, Virginia.

4. Today, many years after Doumar's death, his sons still operate the same ice-cream stand. Perhaps the moral is that it is better to take than to give (advice/advise).

13 WRITING

Write two sentences of your own that use *advice* and two more that use *advise.*

1.   My advice is always reliable. _____

2. _____

3. _____

4. _____

5. _____

affect/effect

Affect, a verb, means *to influence or change.*

Old age *affected* his ability to walk.

Effect, a noun, is *the result of a cause.*

What will be the *effect* of the new law?

Memory Trick. an ex*c*ellent *effect*
His *age affected* his *actions.*

14 WARM-UP

Circle the correct word in parentheses.

1. From 626 to 582 B.C., when he died, the Hebrew prophet Jeremiah warned that unless the Israelites reformed their ways, God would punish the people and destroy their temple, but his warnings had little (affect/(effect)).

2. In fact the only (affects/effects) of his predictions were the anger of the king and threats against Jeremiah's life.

3. Nothing (affected/effected) his courage, however, and while living in hiding, he dictated his prophecies to a disciple.

4. One day Jeremiah met a shepherdess and pleaded that she give up her sinful ways, warning that Jerusalem would soon be attacked by people from the north. His pleas had no (affect/effect).

5. Realizing the near impossibility of (affecting/effecting) human behavior, he uttered his famous words: "Can the . . . leopard change his spots? Then may ye also do good, that are accustomed to evil."

15 WRITING

Write a sentence of your own that correctly uses *affect* and another that correctly uses *effect*.

1. _____

2. _____

an/and

An is the article used before a vowel sound. (See Chapter 13.)

> *an* egg   *an* opportunity   *an* hour

And is a joining word. (See Chapter 3.)

> He huffed *and* he puffed *and* he blew the house down.
> Henry *and* I
> rich *and* famous

Memory Trick. *An* apple *and* a pear.

16 WARM-UP

Circle the correct word in parentheses.

1. Mrs. Caroline Astor, one of the richest women in the world, regularly gave (an/and) expensive (an/and) boring dinner party for her friends.

2. Each person's dinner was served on (an/and) elaborate gold plate.

3. Following dinner, Mrs. Astor left the room (an/and) then returned, sitting on (an/and) elegant silk chair placed on top of (an/and) ornate platform. In effect, she was sitting on a throne.

4. She sat up very straight, mainly because she wore jewelry even down to the waist across her back, (an/and) it was too painful to sit back in her chair.

5. Mr. Astor rarely attended these parties (an/and) stayed instead on his fancy yacht.

17 WRITING

Write three sentences of your own that use *an* and two more that use *and.*

1. I just ate an enormous banana.
2. _____
3. _____
4. _____
5. _____
6. _____

breath/breathe

Breath is a *noun.*

   She caught her *breath.*

Breathe is a *verb.*

   She *breathed* deeply.

Memory Trick. If the vowel sound is ē, there is silent -*e* at the end.

18 WARM-UP

Circle the correct word in parentheses.

1. Life Savers were originally advertised as "Crane's Peppermint Life Savers—5¢—For That Stormy (Breath/Breathe)."
2. Smith Brothers Cough Drops have been a favorite since the mid-nineteenth century with people who coughed or couldn't (breath/breathe) because of a cold.
3. The first submarine was invented in 1620 by a Dutchman named Cornelis J. Drebbel, who converted saltpeter into oxygen, allowing fifteen rowers to (breath/breathe) under water.
4. The men could stay under for fifteen hours—a long time to go with no (breaths/breathes) of fresh air.

19 WRITING

Write one sentence of your own that uses *breath,* another that uses *breaths,* one that uses *breathe,* and one that uses *breathes.*

1. I lost my breath when I fell.
2. _____
3. _____
4. _____
5. _____

buy/by

Buy means *to purchase.*

   Where did you *buy* that hat?

By, a preposition, has several meanings.

We placed the plants *by* the window.
I was finished with my homework *by* ten o'clock.
Bill paid for his college education *by* working every summer.

Memory Trick. You should *buy* it *by* credit card.

20 WARM-UP

Circle the correct word in parentheses.

1. William Collins Whitney (1841–1904), an American millionaire, would (buy/by) expensive things for the most frivolous reasons.

2. For example, in order to give a lavish ball for his friends, he decided to (buy/by) a brownstone building on Fifth Avenue in New York.

3. He then furnished it (buy/by) going on a four-year tour of Europe to (buy/by) antiques, stained glass windows, and fireplaces.

4. (Buy/By) the end of his tour, however, he had made his most outrageous purchase, (buying/bying) an entire ballroom from a castle in France and shipping it back to New York (buy/by) boat.

5. The ball he gave for his five hundred guests was an enormous hit, highlighted (buy/by) the fountain that gushed 1200 bottles of champagne.

21 WRITING

Write a sentence of your own that correctly uses *buy* and another that correctly uses *by*.

1. _____

2. _____

clothes/cloths

Clothes are what people wear. *Cloths* is the plural of *cloth—a piece of fabric*.

Memory Trick. *Clothes* sounds like *close*, which also contains an *-e*. *Cloths* has no *-e*.

22 WARM-UP

Circle the correct word in parentheses.

1. When we think of good (clothes/cloths), we don't usually think of underwear.

2. But three men did think about making (underclothes/undercloths).

3. Their names have not become household words associated with (clothes/cloths), but their product, *B.V.D.*, has.

4. The initials represent the last names of the three men—Bradley, Voorhees, and Day—who turned millions of (clothes/cloths) into underpants and undershirts.

23 WRITING

Write two sentences of your own that use *clothes.*

1. I wear old clothes when I paint.

2. _____

3. _____

conscience/conscious

Conscience tells you that you are being bad or good. *Conscious* means that you are awake and aware.

Memory Trick. *Science* is in *conscience*, and both teach you something.

24 WARM-UP

Circle the correct word in parentheses.

1. In 1895 King C. Gillette, a traveling salesperson, set out (consciously/ consciencely) to invent something that would be used and then thrown away so that people would continually buy more.

2. Apparently the idea of planned obsolescence did not bother Gillette's (conscious/conscience).

3. One day as he was shaving, he (unconsciously/unconsciencely) thought of the first disposable blade to be inserted in a razor. It became known as the Gillette blade.

25 WRITING

Write two sentences of your own that use *conscious* and two more that use *conscience.*

1. I was conscious during my operation.

2. _____

3. _____

4. _____

5. _____

-ence/-ent; -ance/-ant

-Ence and *-ance* are noun endings.

The *difference* was amazing.
The *significance* of the event was great.

-Ent and *-ant* are adjective endings.

It has a *different* meaning.
It has a *significant* meaning.

Memory Trick. The *rent* is *different*. The *dance* had *elegance*.

26 WARM-UP

Circle the correct word in parentheses.

1. Until 1884 all clerks and accountants added figures with a pencil and paper, but then a man named Door Eugene Felt decided to try a (difference/different) method.

2. He designed the first adding machine, putting it in a wooden macaroni box and making its parts from such (elegance/elegant) materials as staples, elastic bands, and meat skewers.

3. He marketed the invention in 1887 as the "Comptometer." Its accuracy in adding was (excellence/excellent).

4. Meanwhile, (independencely/independently) of Felt, another man, named Seward Burroughs, invented his "Adding and Listing Machine" in 1885.

5. Unfortunately, everyone but Burroughs and one salesperson was (ignorance/ignorant) of how to operate the complicated machine.

6. Finally, Burroughs made an (importance/important) change that simplified the machines, and to celebrate he threw all fifty of his old machines out the window.

27 WRITING

Write three sentences of your own that use words ending in *-ence* or *-ance* and three more that use words ending in *-ent* or *-ant*.

1. The significance of Einstein to modern science is enormous.

2. _____

3. _____

4. _____

5. _____

6. _____

7. _____

fine/find

Fine, as an adjective, means *acceptable* or *excellent*. As a noun, it means *a penalty you must pay*.

You did a *fine* job on this assignment.
If you get caught speeding, you must pay a *fine*.

Find means *to discover or locate*.

We never *find* a place to park near school.

Memory Trick. How can I *find* a *fine* job?

28 WARM-UP

Circle the correct word in parentheses.

1. You'll never (find/fine) a more influential book than Dale Carnegie's *How to Win Friends and Influence People*.

2. Although it was originally published in 1936, people can still (find/fine) the hardcover or paperback editions in just about any bookstore.

3. Carnegie will never have to pay a (find/fine) for vagrancy; as of 1980 his book had sold well over 10 million copies and had gone through 117 printings.

4. The book offers some (find/fine) advice. No one succeeds alone, and our success is measured by our ability to get along with and influence others to do what we want them to do.

5. Read the book, and you'll (find/fine) these words: "There is only one way under high heaven to get anybody to do anything. Did you ever stop to think of that? Yes, just one way. And that is by making the other person want to do it."

29 WRITING

Write a sentence of your own that correctly uses *fine* and another that correctly uses *find*.

1. _____

2. _____

know/no; knew/new

Know means *to be familiar with* or *understand*. Its past tense is *knew*.

I *know* your brother, and I *knew* your sister in high school.

No is a negative word. And *new* is *the opposite of old*.

Our old car had *no* radio, but we're buying a *new* car soon.

Memory Trick. The *knight knew* he had *no nose*.

30 WARM-UP

Circle the correct word in parentheses.

1. You may not (know/no) the origin of the phrase, "Don't look a gift horse in the mouth."

2. It has (know/no) relation to the gift of the Trojan horse but comes instead from St. Jerome in around 400 A.D.

3. The man (knew/new) that a gift should be appreciated for the thought and spirit behind it, not for its value.

4. Since a (knewborn/newborn) horse is worth more than an old one, people generally examine the horse's teeth to determine its age.

5. Therefore Jerome, who accepted (know/no) payment for his writing, first used the phrase in defense of this practice when he said, "Never inspect the teeth of a gift horse."

31 WRITING

Write a sentence of your own that correctly uses each of the following words.

1. (know) _____

2. (knew) _____

3. (no) _____

4. (new) _____

led/lead

Led (pronounced like *head*) is the past tense of *lead* (pronounced like *need*). *Lead* is a heavy metal.

   Memory Trick. A *head* like *lead*. I *fed* (past) him and *led* (past) him.

32 WARM-UP

Circle the correct word in parentheses.

1. In 1914 Carl Eric Wickman's failure to sell his Hupmobile—a seven-passenger automobile—(lead/led) him to start a bus service with it.

2. The bus (lead/led) its passengers on a short two-mile journey between two small towns in Minnesota.

3. After Wickman added more and larger buses, their long sleek appearance and (lead/led) grey color caused someone to say that they looked like "greyhounds streaking by."

4. The comment, of course, (lead/led) to the name "Greyhound Bus."

33 WRITING

Write two sentences of your own that use *lead* and two more that use *led*.

1. His carelessness led to problems. _____

2. _____

3. _____

4. _____

5. _____

lie/lay

Lie doesn't take an object.

   I'm going to *lie* down.
   The pen is *lying* on top of the book.

The forms of *lie* are as follows:

Present Tense	Past Tense	Past Participle
lie, lies	lay	lain

Lay is something you do to an object.

   I'm going to *lay this book* on the table.

Its forms are as follows:

Present Tense	Past Tense	Past Participle
lay, lays	laid	laid

   Memory Trick. The chicken *laid* an egg, and then it *lay* down to sleep.

34 WARM-UP

Circle the correct word in parentheses.

1. The continents of the earth (lie/lay) on enormous slabs of rock—or plates—that slide over the earth's core very slowly, at a rate of one to eight inches a year.

2. Sometimes this movement of the continents causes earthquakes, which result from the pressure of one plate (lying/laying) itself against another as they move.

3. Other times this movement of two plates causes a gap between them, and the earth's molten core that has (laid/lain) beneath the plates shoots through in the form of a volcano.

4. Geologists believe that the continents all (lay/laid) on one large land mass, called Pangaea, about 230 million years ago.

5. The continent of North America, like the other continents, is not (lying/ laying) still. It drifts away from Europe at a rate of three inches a year.

6. As a result, North America now (lies/lays) 120 feet farther away from Europe than when Columbus sailed here in 1492.

35 WRITING

Write one sentence using *lie* in the present tense, and one using it in the past tense. Then write one sentence using *lay* in the present tense, and one using it in the past tense.

1. (present tense) ___Bill normally lies down for a nap in the afternoon.___

2. (past tense) _____

_____

3. (present tense) _____

_____

4. (past tense) _____

_____

Now write one sentence in the present perfect tense using either *lie* or *lay.*

5. _____

lose/loose

To lose means to misplace or *not to win.*

Did you lose your book?

Loose is an adjective that means *not tight.*

My pants are *loose.*

Memory Trick. *Loose* as a *goose.*

36 WARM-UP

Circle the correct word in parentheses.

1. If you were to bet that the Baby Ruth candy bar was named after the baseball player Babe Ruth, you would (lose/loose).

2. That story of the candy bar's name has been (losely/loosely) told and believed for many years.

3. Don't (lose/loose) track of the actual facts: the candy was named after the oldest daughter of President Grover Cleveland.

4. Tell somebody the true story. What do you have to (lose/loose)?

37 WRITING

Write two sentences of your own using *lose* and two more sentences using *loose*.

1. I never lose at checkers.

2. _____

3. _____

4. _____

5. _____

mine/mind

Mine is a possessive word.

This pen is *mine*.

Mind as a noun means *your intellect*. As a verb, it means *to object*.

Einstein had a brilliant *mind*.
Do you *mind* if I close this window?

Memory Trick. A good *mind* is hard to *find*.

38 WARM-UP

Circle the correct word in parentheses.

1. Nowadays it's common to think that you should look out for your best interests, and I'll look out for (mine/mind).

2. This brings to (mine/mind) the expression, "Charity begins at home."

3. Ironically, the phrase, first written in 1642 by Sir Thomas Browne, was not an endorsement of selfishness. Browne was discouraged that so many people didn't (mind/mine) their poverty or ignorance and would not try to better themselves.

4. Therefore he (reminded/remined) his readers, "How shall we expect charity toward others when we are so uncharitable to ourselves? 'Charity begins at home' is the voice of the world; yet is every man his greatest enemy, and, as it were, his own executioner."

39 WRITING

Write a sentence of your own that correctly uses *mine* and another that correctly uses *mind.*

1. _____

2. _____

passed/past

Passed is the past tense and past participle of the verb *to pass.*

We *passed* the house.

Past can be a preposition meaning *beyond.* It can also be a noun or adjective meaning *before the present.*

We went *past* (beyond) that house.
That is *past* (before the present) history.

Memory Trick. The verb *pass* is in *passed.*

40 WARM-UP

Circle the correct word in parentheses.

1. In the (passed/past) Henry J. Heinz had failed to make money on his first attempt to sell a food product, horseradish.

2. But he (passed/past) that obstacle in 1876 and began to sell many more food products, although business could still have been better.

3. Then, one day in 1876, Heinz rode the elevated train (passed/past) an advertisement claiming a store sold "21 styles" of shoes.

4. The idea (passed/past) through his mind that he might create a slogan claiming that he had 57 varieties of food products, including catsup.

5. Actually, he had already gone (passed/past) that number of products for sale but he liked the sound of 57, and apparently so did other people— who still buy his products.

41 WRITING

Write two sentences of your own that used *passed* and two more that use *past.*

1. I passed the park this morning. _____

2. _____

3. _____

4. _____

5. _____

rise/raise

Rise means *to get up without help.*

The sun *rises* in the east.

Raise as a verb means *to lift something* or *to increase something*. As a noun, it means *an increase in pay*.

Raise your hand if you know the answer.
Susan just got a *raise*, so she can afford a larger apartment.

Memory Trick. He always *pays* when he gets a *raise*.

42 WARM-UP

Circle the correct word in parentheses.

1. The origin of the expression "steal my thunder" might (rise/raise) a few eyebrows.

2. John Dennis, an English playwright at the beginning of the eighteenth century, invented a new method of (raising/rising) a noise like a thunderclap and used it in his new play, *Appius and Virginia*.

3. The thunder was a great success, but the play didn't (raise/rise) enough money to continue beyond a few performances.

4. A short time later Dennis returned to the theater to see Shakespeare's *Macbeth*, only to discover that his method of making thunder was being used. He (raised/rose) to his feet and proceeded to (raise/rise) a ruckus.

5. "That's my thunder, by God!" he said, with his voice (raising/rising) louder and louder. "The villians will not play my play but they steal my thunder."

43 WRITING

Write a sentence of your own that correctly uses *rise* and another that correctly uses *raise*.

1. _____

2. _____

quiet/quite

Quiet means *not noisy*. (Notice the ending: *-iet*.)

It was a *quiet* night.

Quite means *very*. (Notice the ending: *-ite*.)

He's *quite* tall.

Memory Trick. It was *quite a bite*.

44 WARM-UP

Circle the correct word in parentheses.

1. The man who invented Birds Eye frozen foods was, (quiet/quite) naturally, named Clarence Birdseye.

2. He was an explorer, who, in 1916, was able to keep meat and vegetables (quiet/quite) fresh by storing them in freezing water.

3. Back in the United States he started a frozen-food company which became (quiet/quite) a success and was sold in 1929 to the Postum Company.

4. When Postum split the trademark into two words—Birds Eye—Clarence Birdseye kept (quiet/quite) about the change, for his family had originally spelled the name that way.

45 WRITING

Write two sentences of your own that use *quiet* and another two that use *quite.*

1. It's quiet in my room now._____

2. _____

3. _____

4. _____

5. _____

sit/set

Sit means *to seat yourself.*

    Please *sit* down.

Set means to *put something down.*

    Please *set* the glass on the table.

Memory Trick. *Set* the *bet* down.

46 WARM-UP

Circle the correct word in parentheses.

1. The first photograph was made in 1826 when Joseph Niepce of France coated a metal sheet with a special solution, exposed it to light, and (sit/set) it on a windowsill to dry.

2. Of course, that was a picture of an object, since the long exposure time made it impossible for someone to (sit/set) still for a photograph.

3. Motion pictures began in America sometime between 1867 and 1871 when two men made a bet that when a horse ran, its legs couldn't all be off the ground at once. So they (sit/set) up a series of cameras along a racetrack, and, using timing devices, they photographed the horse as it galloped past—with, at various points, all four legs off the ground.

4. Not until 1947 did Edwin Land invent the Polaroid camera. He wanted to take a picture of his daughter and develop it while she was still (sitting/setting).

47 WRITING

Write two sentences of your own that use *sit* and two more that use *set*.

1. <u>I'm sitting on top of a desk right now.</u>
2. _____
3. _____
4. _____
5. _____

then/than

Then is a time expression meaning *afterward* or *later*.

I studied for two hours and *then* took a break.

Than is used in a comparison.

Juan gets higher grades *than* anyone in class.

Memory Trick. *Then* tells you *when*.

48 WARM-UP

Circle the correct word in parentheses.

1. In the music world a terrible curse is to write nine symphonies. Six composers have done so and (then/than) died.

2. Ludwig Van Beethoven (1770–1827) is more famous (then/than) the other five. The German-born composer had just completed his ninth symphony and promised the London Philharmonic Society a tenth, but (then/than) he caught a cold on a trip to Vienna. He died a few months later.

3. Anton Bruckner (1824–1896), an Austrian, was virtually unknown until the end of his life; (then/than) he was recognized as a great composer. He died while working on the final sketches of his ninth symphony.

4. (Then/Than) came Anton Dvořák (1841–1904), the first composer of Bohemian ancestry to achieve worldwide fame. His Symphony Number 9 in E Minor, *From the New World*, was performed in New York in 1893, but he died a little more (then/than) eleven years later of a kidney disease without completing another symphony.

5. The other three composers were first, the Russian A. K. Glazunov (1865–1936); (then/than) the Bohemian Gustav Mahler (1860–1911); and finally the British Ralph Vaughan Williams (1872–1958).

6. Suffering from heart disease, Mahler was terrified of the curse of the ninth symphony. Therefore he completed his ninth and (then/than) feverishly set to work on a tenth, but the effort was more (then/than) his heart could take. Before he died Mahler raised his finger and (then/than) moved it back and forth like a conductor's baton. His last word was "Mozart."

49 WRITING

Write a sentence of your own that correctly uses *then* and another that correctly uses *than.*

1. _____

2. _____

whether/weather

Whether suggests a choice; it is used in the same way as *if* in indirect questions.

I don't know *whether* he can afford a vacation.
He wanted to know *whether* the test was hard.

Weather refers to the temperature and atmospheric conditions.

The *weather* has been mild this year.

Memory Trick. *Wet weather*

50 WARM-UP

Circle the correct word in parentheses.

1. Historians generally attribute the saying "War is Hell" to General William T. Sherman, but he was never sure (*whether*/weather) he really said it.

2. Before his death in 1891 the general searched through all his private papers to determine (whether/weather) the words were actually his.

3. There are several accounts of when the words were said. The earliest version goes back to 1863 during the Civil War, when Sherman's troops were crossing a pontoon bridge in bad (whether/weather). According to an eyewitness, the commander said to the passing soldiers, "War is hell, boys."

4. It's debatable (whether/weather) he made the statement then, for another account has Sherman delivering the line in an address during a military academy graduation in 1879, and a third account places it in a speech to Union veterans in 1880.

5. In fact no one can prove (whether/weather) Sherman ever said "War is hell," although at other times he did state, "War is cruel and you cannot refine it" and "War at best is barbarism."

51 WRITING

Write a sentence of your own that correctly uses *whether* and another that correctly uses *weather.*

1. _____

2. _____

CHAPTER 16

Writing a Powerful Paragraph

This chapter examines what makes a powerful paragraph and how you can go about writing one—either as part of a larger composition or as a separate and complete theme in itself. First you will see the purpose, form, and limits of a paragraph. Then you will examine the topic sentence and its relationship to the other sentences in a paragraph. Later you will take a look at the body of a paragraph: its specific development and unity. And all through the chapter, you will explore how each part of a paragraph can be written, revised, and revised again.

EXAMINING THE PARAGRAPH'S PURPOSE AND FORM

Throughout your college and working career you will need to write single paragraphs on various subjects. Essay examination questions require one-paragraph answers. Homework assignments require one-paragraph definitions or explanations. Many companies and organizations require one-paragraph memorandums or reports. Therefore learning to write a clear, well-organized, and well-developed paragraph is a valuable skill.

Furthermore writing effective paragraphs is an important first step in learning to write an effective composition. A *composition* is an *organized and complete discussion of one main subject or idea*. Paragraphs break the main idea down into smaller, easily understood parts, each of which is related logically to the next one. Without these smaller divisions, ideas appear to be nothing more than page after page of unrelated, uninterrupted sentences.

Defining the Paragraph

In fact you might think of the paragraph as a *composition in miniature*. While a composition is a group of paragraphs that discuss one main idea, or thesis, a *paragraph* is a *group of sentences that discuss one main idea, or topic*. The paragraph has *unity;* each sentence contributes to the development of that single topic. And the paragraph generally has an *introduction*, a *body*, and a *conclusion*.

- The *introduction* usually accomplishes two goals: (1) it catches your readers' interest, enticing them to read on; and (2) it states the paragraph's main point in a *topic sentence* (although the topic sentence doesn't always appear at the beginning of the paragraph).
- The *body* specifically supports the main point and is the longest part of the paragraph—three, four, or even ten sentences long.
- The *conclusion*—the last one or two sentences of the paragraph—summarizes or ties together the paragraph's ideas while bringing them to a graceful end. Many concluding sentences of short paragraphs omit an explicit summary because it sounds repetitive. But in any case, a good conclusion *never* introduces new ideas.

Another way to think of the three parts of a paragraph is to remember this old advice: "Tell them what you are going to say (the introduction); say it (the body); and then tell what you said (the conclusion)."

A paragraph such as the one you are reading typically begins with an *indented line*—that is, it begins with a line that is about a half inch (or about five spaces on a typewriter) to the right of the other lines. Second, each new sentence follows the preceding one *on the same line*, not on a new line. Third, the sentences in the paragraph are *logically related* to each other (in this paragraph through the words *First, Second, and Third*). In short a paragraph has a certain form that clarifies its ideas and makes them easy to follow.

Limiting a Paragraph's Topic

Although every paragraph discusses a single topic, that topic cannot be too broad. It must be something you can discuss fully in a small amount of space. Whether you are assigned a topic for a paragraph or choose the topic yourself, you usually start with a general idea that should be limited or made more specific. For example, suppose you chose the following topic for a one-paragraph composition:

The influence of television

This subject can fill a lengthy book, for you can discuss television quiz shows, talk shows, cop shows, cartoon shows, comedies, documentaries, miniseries, movies, soap operas, news broadcasts, sports events, or commercials. Furthermore you can discuss the influence of any one of these on young children, older children, teenagers, adults, or the elderly. You would have to narrow the topic to something much smaller and more manageable. Begin by listing a few possibilities.

How soap operas portray relationships between the sexes

How Saturday morning cartoons are warping the minds of young children

How the instant replay has changed the way we watch sports

Why light beer commercials are dangerous

What a documentary on child abuse taught me

Next select one of the topics—perhaps "How soap operas portray relationships between the sexes"—and then explore your ideas on the subject through brainstorming or free writing. This exploration might uncover too many ideas for a single paragraph, so you would have to narrow the topic further: how soap operas glamorize casual sex instead of lasting relationships.

In Summary: A paragraph

1. is a group of sentences that discuss *one main point, or topic,* which must be limited enough to discuss in a short amount of space;
2. often states the main point in a *topic sentence,* which usually—but not always—comes at the beginning of the paragraph;
3. has *unity*—all sentences develop the main point;
4. develops its main idea in the largest section called the *body;*
5. begins with the *first line indented;*
6. requires that each sentence follow *directly after* the previous sentence, not on a separate line;
7. often concludes with a sentence that ties together ideas and gracefully ends the paragraph.

1 WARM-UP

Limit each of the following broad topics to one that can be developed in a single paragraph.

1. A problem in the schools ___Some results of high absenteeism in the___ ___primary grades___

2. Living in the cities or suburbs _____

3. A popular trend today _____

4. Women's roles and men's roles _____

5. A favorite activity _____

6. The best jobs _____

EXAMINING THE TOPIC SENTENCE

What is the purpose of the topic sentence? You can answer this question best if you approach a paragraph from the reader's viewpoint. When you read, you don't just receive ideas from a page. Instead, you actively attempt to understand the writer's ideas, predicting what will come on the basis of what you have already seen. For example, suppose you encounter this sentence at the beginning of a paragraph: *Slavery was not the only cause of the Civil War in 1861*. What would you expect the rest of the paragraph to discuss? You would probably respond: an explanation of the other causes of the Civil War. Thus the topic sentence serves as your guide, helping you identify the main point and understand how the remaining sentences relate to that point.

Therefore a topic sentence usually—but not always—comes at the beginning of a paragraph (sometimes after an attention-getting opening sentence). It may occasionally end a paragraph and summarize ideas (as you will discover when you look for topic sentences in "Warm-Up Exercise 2.") And once in a while it may be omitted entirely when a paragraph's main point is clearly *implied* and need not be stated.

For the time being, however, concentrate on writing a topic sentence near the beginning of each paragraph. Doing so will help you and your readers. It will help you focus on a single idea and structure and organize your thoughts. It will help your readers perceive your main idea and organization.

Comparing General and Specific Statements in a Paragraph

The topic sentence is the most general sentence in a paragraph. The other sentences are more specific and develop the idea of the topic sentence. As you saw a moment ago when you practiced limiting a topic,

- *general* ideas are the largest ones; and
- *specific* ideas are smaller and *can be included within* the general ones.

For example, when you compare these two words, which is more general?

sports

football

Of course *sports* is more general because it *includes* football, baseball, and all the other sports. But which of these two words is more general?

football

quarterback

In this case *football* is more general because it *includes* quarterback.

Therefore general and specific are *comparative* terms; one idea is general when compared to others that can be included within it. Which of the following two sentences is more general?

Our quarterback has some unusual abilities.

He can pass with either hand.

You probably decided on the first sentence, which can serve as the topic sentence of a paragraph about several more of the quarterback's abilities. The second sentence, a specific statement of fact, couldn't easily serve as the topic sentence because it can't easily be developed. (Try to develop the statement, "He can pass with either hand," and you will have to write: "He can pass with his right hand, and he can pass with his left hand." That is a great way to put your readers to sleep.)

- Therefore a topic sentence *should be general enough to lead to specific development of its ideas in the rest of the paragraph.* The topic sentence *should not be so specific that it leaves little else to say.*

Here is how a full paragraph based on the previous topic sentence might look.

> Our quarterback has some unusual abilities. He can pass with either hand. He can run faster than most halfbacks, so he often carries the ball himself. He can run over defensemen better than most fullbacks, and he has done it several times for key first downs or touchdowns. He can block well for the other backs after he hands off the ball. He can even catch passes, as he proved during our last game when he scored the winning touchdown on a surprise pass from our fullback. With his abilities, he ought to receive offers from some professional teams after he graduates.

To summarize, a paragraph is a combination of general and specific statements. The most general statement is the topic sentence, while the remaining statements specifically explain or prove its claims.

2 WARM-UP

Underline the topic sentences in the following paragraphs. Be careful: not every topic sentence comes at the beginning of its paragraph.

Paragraph A. (1) *Few people realize that the most widely used form of mass transportation in the United States is the elevator.* (2) The more than 340,000 elevators in this country travel more than 1.5 billion miles a year and make more than 500 billion trips. (3) One manufacturer boasts that its elevators alone carry the equivalent of the world's population every nine days.

Paragraph B. (1) The average trip takes less than a minute, but some have been known to last longer. (2) A wealthy Chicago woman was trapped in her mansion's elevator for five days before someone found her. (3) At that point she was somewhat thinner but alive and relatively healthy. (4) And she felt even better when she received a hefty out-of-court settlement from the elevator company. (5) A not-so-wealthy hospital employee was trapped in an elevator of a busy Long Island hospital for twenty-two hours before she was discovered. (6) Her benevolent employer paid her overtime and gave her the next day off.

Paragraph C. (1) However, getting trapped in an elevator is the exception rather than the rule. (2) For in addition to being the most widely used form of mass transportation, elevators are also the safest, thanks to a man named Elisha Graves Otis. (3) He invented a safety spring device that sprang into action when the cable broke and its tension slackened. (4) He demonstrated this marvel at the Crystal Palace Exposition in New York City in 1853, when he rode the elevator above the heads of the spectators and then called for the cables to be cut. (5) Everyone expected him to plunge to the ground, but the Otis elevator stood fast and its inventor said, "All safe, gentlemen."

Paragraph D. (1) His relatively simple mechanism changed the architecture of the modern world. (2) Buildings began reaching for the sky. (3) The first passenger elevator began operating at the Haughwout Department Store in New York City in 1857, making the five-story trip in less than a minute. (4) Today elevators are much quicker and buildings much taller. (5) Sears Tower in Chicago, the world's tallest building, also houses the world's fastest elevators. (6) Their speed reaches 1800 feet per minute (about twenty miles per hour), taking passengers to the 103d floor in less than a minute.

Paragraph E. (1) The real safety of elevators was demonstrated in the most bizarre elevator accident of all time. (2) In July, 1945, an army bomber became lost in the fog and rammed the 79th floor of the Empire State Building. (3) The impact ripped the elevator cables, and an elevator with two passengers aboard fell from the 75th floor into the subbasement. (4) No one held hope for the passengers, but—thanks to a safety device that had slowed the plunge—they were alive. (5) A Coast Guard medic who happened to be at the scene was the first to crawl into the elevator. (6) A badly injured woman mistook him for a sailor and thanked God the navy had come to rescue her.

Paragraph F. (1) If you worry about riding elevators, one time to do so is when the doors open and close. (2) That is when most of the fewer than a thousand yearly elevator accidents occur, with people catching their hands, feet, or clothing in the doors. (3) The other time you might worry is if you happen to be riding an elevator in an earthquake. (4) During a brief quake in southern California, some of the counterweights that move along with the cabs swung erratically and smashed through the cabs. (5) These are the only serious dangers in elevators.

Paragraph G. (1) Today elevators throughout the world have profoundly changed our lives. (2) You will find them everywhere: in apartment buildings, in public buildings, in some private homes, and even in jumbo jets. (3) They transport people, furniture, goods, and cargo quickly and effortlessly up and down in all sorts of structures. (4) The next time you are in a big city, take a good look around. (5) Try to imagine what it would look like if elevators weren't there.

3 EDITING   Each of the following sentences is unsuitable as a topic sentence, either because it is too specific or too general. Label each sentence *S* (for specific) or *G* (for general) and then rewrite the sentence to correct the problem.

___S___   1. The United States declared its independence on July 4, 1776.

On July 4, 1776, the United States declared its independence for several

reasons.

_____   2. Technology is changing the United States.

_____   3. Sears Tower in Chicago is 1450 feet high.

_____   4. Many students attend college today.

_____   5. Unemployment is a big problem.

_____   6. The moon is over a quarter of a million miles from the earth.

_____   7. I visited some of my relatives last year.

_____   8. Abraham Lincoln was a famous president.

_____   9. Each morning I start my exercises by touching my toes ten times.

_____   10. I want to tell you about my job.

Stating Your Point in the Topic Sentence

The *topic* of a paragraph is different from its *topic sentence*. The topic is what the paragraph is "about," but the topic sentence *makes a point* about the topic. For example, you may recall the sample paragraph in Chapter 1, a paragraph about the writer's part-time job as a sales clerk in a shoe store. What point does the paragraph make about that part-time job? The writer's topic sentence in his first draft doesn't answer that question.

I have a part-time job as a sales clerk in a shoe store.

This sentence only announces a broad topic for the paragraph. You don't know if the writer will discuss the type of shoes he sells, his working conditions, his customers, his coworkers, his commissions, or even the layout of the store. A revised version of the topic sentence in the second draft still doesn't solve the problem.

> I want to explain the commission system for clerks in a shoe store.

This sentence is more specific; it mentions the commission system, not just the job. But it still doesn't make a point; it still doesn't answer the question, "What about the commission system?" It doesn't state or even suggest the *writer's viewpoint toward the subject:* that the commission system is complex or simple, profitable or unprofitable, a benefit or a harm to customers. The sentence simply *doesn't tell you what to think about the system.* Here is the final version of the topic sentence, this time making a point.

> In many stores the commission system is good for the clerks but unfortunate for the customers.

Notice that in this last draft the pronoun *I* disappeared. That is also part of the point, for the paragraph discusses the commission system—not the writer. The rest of the paragraph can now specifically explain how the commission system may benefit the clerks but not the customers.

A topic sentence, and the paragraph it is in, should answer the question, "So what." If the topic sentence can't answer that question, the paragraph is probably aimless, pointless, and merely a collection of vaguely related facts. Therefore you should expect to write and revise the topic sentence a number of times during the writing process. Very few writers are ultimately satisfied with their first or even second versions.

Another way to view the topic sentence is to think of its point as an *attitude toward the topic.* In the example above *good* and *unfortunate* express attitudes. Compare the following sentences:

No attitude:	Mr. Williams teaches chemistry.
Attitude:	Mr. Williams is a *terrific* chemistry teacher.
No attitude:	Most high school graduates go on to college.
Attitude:	A person without a college degree today is *at a disadvantage.*
No attitude:	I've had a cat for several years.
Attitude:	My cat *outsmarts* me all the time.

Many topic sentences, therefore, follow this pattern: *subject + stated attitude.* Note these examples.

Subject		*Attitude*
Our quarterback	has some	*unusual abilities.*
Betty	is	*an efficient secretary.*
Fishing	in the Halifax River is	*fun and relaxing.*
Mathematics courses		*bore me.*

In Summary: The topic sentence

1. is the most general sentence in a paragraph, and the remaining sentences specifically develop that idea;
2. usually comes at the beginning of a paragraph, although it can appear after an introductory statement or at the end of a paragraph;
3. does not simply announce the topic but makes a point about— or expresses an attitude toward—the topic of the paragraph;
4. can be implied (omitted from the paragraph), provided that the point of the paragraph is clear.

4 WARM-UP

Put a check next to the best topic sentence in each group below—the one that makes a point or expresses an attitude rather than merely stating the subject. Then underline the word or phrase in the sentence that expresses the point or attitude.

1. _____ This paragraph will compare living on campus and going to a commuter college.

   ✓ _____ Living on campus <u>affords students opportunities</u> that going to a commuter college cannot.

2. _____ Today's pop music is heading in several exciting directions.

   _____ The topic that I want to discuss is today's pop music.

3. _____ California has a number of pet cemeteries.

   _____ Nothing could be more offensive than a cemetery for pets.

4. _____ I have two young children.

   _____ Children today are growing up too fast.

5. _____ I work in a large clothing store near campus.

   _____ My job is giving me valuable experience in retailing.

6. _____ An issue in today's world is the nuclear arms race.

   _____ Unless the spread of nuclear arms can be controlled, there may be no countries left to defend.

7. _____ This paper will discuss learning in college.

   _____ Most learning in college happens outside the classroom, not in it.

8. _____ Sports are boring.

   _____ There are many different kinds of sports in the United States.

9. _____ Modern zoos create comfortable environments for their animals.

   _____ A lot of animals live in zoos today.

10. _____ Many people today argue about legalized abortion.

    _____ Why do many people favor legalized abortion?

Writing a Topic Sentence

Always think of your first attempt at a topic sentence as preliminary; you will probably revise it several times later. Also, you don't have to begin the writing process with a formal topic sentence; you can write it whenever your point becomes clear.

- If you prefer to formulate ideas through brainstorming or free writing, you can add the topic sentence afterwards and then organize the supporting ideas as you write the first draft of the paragraph.
- If your point is clear to you when you begin, you can write the topic sentence first and then add the supporting sentences.
- If you want to write and revise the entire paragraph without worrying about the topic sentence, you can add it to the paragraph after you have determined your point and feel comfortable with the order of the supporting ideas.

Furthermore you don't have to use the same method each time; most writers vary their procedures according to what works best at the moment. Remember that only the finished product counts; the process of achieving it varies from person to person and from task to task.

5 WRITING

For each of the following subjects, write a first version of a topic sentence that makes a point or expresses an attitude.

1. cats and dogs   People own dogs, but cats own people.

2. good teachers _____
   _____

3. the legal drinking (or driving age) _____
   _____

4. friendship _____
   _____

5. a popular place _____
   _____

6. public transportation _____
   _____

6 WRITING

Add a first version of a topic sentence to each of the following paragraphs.

Paragraph A.   The dog has had a long and important association with

mankind.   The *Canis familiaris*, or faithful dog, became the first

trained animal and the only beast willing to be domesticated by humans.

Stone Age cave paintings in Spain demonstrate that huntsmen and trained

dogs were stalking game together as early as 10,000 B.C. Many thousands of years before that date, however, dogs were undoubtedly working partners with earlier prehistoric men in Europe—lurking around campfires, surviving on discarded garbage, and guarding their human "pack."

Paragraph B. _____

_____ The ancient Egyptians used their greyhoundlike dogs to hunt antelope. Some Egyptian kings and nobles kept the dogs as pets—the first nonworking animals. In fact one Egyptian pharoah employed two thousand slaves to attend his sacred dogs. Later on the early Greeks used powerful mastifflike dogs to track lions in Africa. Then with the development of agriculture, dogs were taught to guard and herd livestock.

Paragraph C. _____

_____ Both dogs and cats share an ancient common lineage: the *miacid*, an animal that lived sixty million years ago. However, while there is ample evidence of the early domestication of dogs, there are no definitive drawings of domestic cats in prehistoric paintings or rock carvings. Not until around 2000 B.C. did cats appear in written and historical records.

Paragraph D. _____

_____ The Egyptians were the first to tame the African wild cat, which was similar in appearance to the modern Abyssinian. They closely associated this cat with their cat-headed goddess Bast. The cat was a working diety, however, and had to earn its keep by ridding the grain-storage areas of rodents. In fact it was such an important defense against famine and disease in Egypt that the punishment for killing a feline—even by accident—was death.

Paragraph E. _____

_____ Although exporting Egyptian cats was illegal, by 900 B.C. they had been smuggled out to all parts of Europe. There they were bred with local wild cats and produced two other basic feline body types, the sturdy British short-haired tabby and the flat-nosed longhair. These animals were idolized in the fourteenth century when they killed rodents that spread the Bubonic plague throughout the continent. Unfortunately, the same felines were also brutally tortured and murdered during the witch-hunting Middle Ages.

EXAMINING THE BODY OF THE PARAGRAPH

The topic sentence states the point of the paragraph, and the remaining sentences develop that point with *specific detail*—facts, explanations, examples, and stories. *Facts* are statistics and statements that can be proved. Suppose, for example, that a topic sentence in one of your paragraphs states: "Canada is a very large country, but not many people live there." You can develop both points of this main idea with statistics about its size (3,851,809 square miles) and its population (a little over twenty-five million people in 1984). *Explanations* give reasons. For example, you can explain why Canada doesn't have a large population: much of Canada is too cold for people to live in. *Examples* give specific illustrations—such as the ones beginning with the words "for example" in this paragraph. *Stories*, of course, are little bits of narration that tell what happened or is happening.

All of this supporting detail serves two very important purposes: it makes ideas clear, and it makes ideas interesting. Specifics are almost always easier to understand and livelier to read than generalizations. For example, the following paragraph is weak in specific development.

> Probably one of the biggest and most expensive meals of all time took place in 1905, when "Diamond Jim" Brady gave a party. Brady spent a lot of money to feed his guests, but, as usual, he ate most of the food himself. His guests drank a lot of expensive champagne, and everyone agreed that it was a very nice party.

The paragraph isn't very successful because you don't learn very much about the party, nor do you care very much about it. The paragraph leaves too many questions unanswered. How big was the meal? How much money did it cost? Who was "Diamond Jim" Brady, and why did he give the party? How many people were there, and what did they eat? How much food did the biggest eater, Brady himself, consume? How much champagne did everyone drink? In short what really made this meal so big and expensive? You don't know the answers because you weren't at the party, so the writer of the paragraph must provide them.

Here is the same paragraph, this time developed specifically. See if you like it better.

> Probably one of the biggest and most expensive meals of all time took place at a hotel in New York City in 1905 when the famous millionaire and the world's greatest eater, "Diamond Jim" Brady, gave a party in honor of his racehorse, Gold Heels. Brady invited only fifty guests, but together they ate at least forty thousand dollars worth of food. (That is eight hundred dollars a person!) Since nobody could ever eat more than

Brady himself, Diamond Jim's own meal probably came to several thousand dollars' worth. Here is what he had, which was a typical meal—for him. He started with three dozen oysters, followed with a half a dozen crabs, two bowls of soup, seven lobsters, two ducks, two huge portions of turtle, a sirloin steak, and large helpings of assorted vegetables. For dessert he consumed a platter of cakes, pies, cookies, and tarts, and topped that off with a two-pound box of chocolates. Of course all that food made him thirsty, so he guzzled a gallon or two of orange juice. Although Brady didn't drink any alcohol (he never did), he served his guests five hundred bottles of very expensive Mumm's champagne. When the meal was over, his guests said that they couldn't recall a nicer party given for a horse.

Notice that this second version of the paragraph is much longer than the first version. However, don't jump to the conclusion that paragraphs are powerful because they contain a lot of words. They are powerful when they contain clear, convincing, and lively supporting detail. The detail takes up the space.

How much supporting detail do you include? The answer to that question is really the answer to three separate questions. First, how complicated is the topic idea? The more complicated it is, the more you must explain and illustrate the idea. Second, how much do your readers know about the topic idea? The less they know, the more information you must supply. Finally, how interesting do you want to make the paragraph? An example or two can provide interest. There are no "rules" on how much you must say to develop the topic idea, but you must say enough so that your audience understands and accepts the claims you make in the topic sentence.

7 WRITING

Return to one of the topic sentences you wrote in Exercise 6 and do some brainstorming or free writing to develop its point. Assume that the audience for the paragraph will be your classmates, and try to generate at least five specific ideas that clarify and make the main point interesting for them. You needn't write in complete sentences since you are merely discovering and sorting out ideas.

_____

_____

_____

_____

_____

_____

_____

_____

_____

_____

8 WRITING   Return to the material you prepared in Exercise 7 and write a first and second draft of a paragraph based on it. Take a break between drafts and then carefully read the first version, criticizing it from your readers' viewpoint. Is the topic sentence clear and specific? What ideas need more explanation? What facts, examples, or stories will make the paragraph more interesting? Which sentences or parts of sentences need restating or rewording? Are the connections between ideas logical? Does the paragraph end gracefully? Revise the topic sentence if necessary and change or discard anything in the body that doesn't meet the criteria of these questions.

Unifying the Body of the Paragraph and Revising the Topic Sentence

Remember that a good paragraph has unity—all the sentences in the final version of the paragraph should develop one main point, usually stated in the topic sentence. However, during brainstorming, free writing, or outlining, you may include some information that is related to the subject of the paragraph but that doesn't develop its topic sentence. Your job during revisions is to find and eliminate this irrelevant information. For instance, which sentence probably doesn't belong in this early version of a paragraph?

(1) On November 19, 1915, the state of Utah created a legend. (2) It took a penniless migrant worker and turned him into one of the great martyrs of the American labor movement. (3) It achieved this transformation by executing a man named Joe Hill for a murder he was widely believed not to have committed. (4) Joe Hill was also a songwriter and union organizer.

The main point of the paragraph is how the state of Utah created a legend, so sentence (4) doesn't belong. Although it discusses Joe Hill, the information about him has nothing to do with Utah's action or Hill's martyrdom. The writer can remedy the problem in two ways: eliminating this sentence (perhaps including it in another paragraph) or revising the paragraph to make the sentence fit. Here is a revised version of the paragraph in which the material in sentence (4) has been incorporated to create unity.

(1) On November 19, 1915, the state of Utah created a legend. (2) It took a penniless migrant worker, *songwriter, and union organizer* and turned him into one of the great martyrs of the American labor movement. (3) It achieved this transformation by executing a man named Joe Hill for a murder he was widely believed not to have committed.

As you attempt to unify the paragraph, look at the topic sentence again. A sentence that is too general won't provide the readers with a clear understanding of the relationship between the main point and the specifics that develop this point. For example, in the following paragraph, the topic sentence suggests too much:

(1) *Joe Hill had an adventurous life.* (2) It began in Sweden in 1879, where he was born as Joel Emmanuel Haagland. (3) His father died

when Joel was eight, and after his mother's death in 1902, he emigrated to the United States in search of work. (4) Haagland was a quiet and uneducated man, but apparently he had a gift for organizing workers. (5) Shortly after his arrival in the United States he attempted to form a union among his fellow laborers in a machine shop and was promptly fired for his actions. (6) To escape the blacklist that resulted from the incident, he changed his name to Joseph Hillstrom, which was shortened by his acquaintances to Joe Hill.

This topic sentence suggests that the paragraph will discuss *all* of Joe Hill's life, a subject requiring much more than a paragraph to explore.

But remember that a topic sentence should not be too specific, as is the following example:

Joe Hill began his life in Sweden as Joel Emmanuel Haagland in 1879.

Although it suggests that the paragraph will discuss only the circumstances of Joe Hill's birth, the actual paragraph discusses several events after that time. Here is a better version of the topic sentence, accounting for all the information in the paragraph.

Joe Hill began his life in Sweden as Joel Emmanuel Haagland in 1879, *but a series of unfortunate events changed both his country and his name.*

In Summary: A well-developed and well-unified paragraph

1. should include a topic sentence that is not so general that the point of the paragraph is unclear but is not so specific that it doesn't account for all the information in the paragraph;
2. should include enough information so that readers understand, are convinced of, and are interested in the point;
3. should include only the information that develops or supports the point.

---

9 WARM-UP

Circle the number of the topic sentence of each paragraph below. Then draw a line through the sentence or sentences that do not support the topic sentence.

Paragraph A. (1) ~~Hill wandered around the country working at a wide range of jobs over the next few years.~~ (2) He found a true home in 1910 among the Industrial Workers of the World (the IWW, or Wobblies), a radical organization that wanted to destroy capitalism through a series of general strikes. (3) Hill helped the Wobblies organize workers up and down the West Coast. (4) But his main contribution to the IWW was the songs he wrote for the *Little Red Song Book*, the organization's most effective propaganda tool. (5) Such songs as "Casey Jones—The Union Scab," "Mr.

Block," and "The Preacher and the Slave" (which coined the phrase "pie in the sky") inspired workers throughout the country and helped contribute to the growth of Hill's legend.

Paragraph B. (1) While Hill was living in Salt Lake City, Utah, a double murder occurred on January 10, 1914, but not all the facts of the case were clear. (2) That particular Saturday night, two armed masked men entered the grocery store of John G. Morrison, who was closing up with his teenage sons. (3) According to the thirteen-year-old son, the men rushed toward the grocer shouting, "We've got you now." (4) One of the men then shot Morrison, after which his seventeen-year-old son grabbed a revolver and fired back. (5) The gun he used had been hidden under the counter. (6) Although the younger boy wasn't sure, he thought that one of the intruders had been hit. (7) However, he couldn't say for certain that his brother's gunfire was returned and that both his father and brother were killed. (8) The men fled without taking anything.

Paragraph C. (1) Joe Hill, who had come to Utah in 1913, soon became a suspect. (2) He appeared with a bullet wound at a local doctor's office on the night of the murders. (3) He claimed that he had been shot in a quarrel over a woman and that, since he was partly responsible for the incident, he didn't want the authorities brought in. (4) Accepting Hill's explanation, the physician dressed the wound and sent Hill home. (5) Then he had second thoughts about his patient's request for silence, and three days later he told the Salt Lake City police about Hill's visit. (6) The police went to Hill's boardinghouse and arrested him. (7) There were four other suspects in jail when Hill was picked up, but they were all released soon afterwards.

Paragraph D. (1) The general feeling in Salt Lake City was that the murder of the Morrisons was a crime of revenge—which should have ruled out Hill as a prime suspect but didn't. (2) More than once Morrison had been involved in a skirmish with criminals at his store. (3) Additionally, he was a former member of the Salt Lake City police, and a few days before the murder he had stated that he was afraid of being attacked by some men he'd arrested. (4) As far as anyone could tell, Hill had never met the grocer. (5) Suspicion focused on Hill probably because of the hostility toward the IWW. (6) In Utah the Wobblies had been involved in some very bitter labor disputes, which had triggered intense hostility. (7) Joe Hill's membership in this organization didn't enhance his image in the eyes of the local authorities. (8) Hill also was from outside the state.

Paragraph E. (1) The law's attitude toward Hill certainly wasn't based on the overwhelming strength of its case. (2) In his opening statement at the trial, the district attorney said that his evidence was circumstantial. (3) His major witnesses were Morrison's thirteen-year-old son and three women who had seen a man resembling Hill near the store at the time of the killings. (4) Not one of these four people, however, had definitely identified Hill as the man. (5) Then two of the women significantly altered their testimony from what they had said at the preliminary hearing, somehow becoming more confident—despite the passage of half a year's time—that the man they had seen was Hill. (6) Incidentally, the second attacker was never identified. (7) Furthermore the state's case had other holes. (8) It was never proved that one of Morrison's attackers had been wounded. (9) And the police were unable to find any spent bullets that could have passed through a human body, even though the bullet that wounded Hill had done just that.

Paragraph F. (1) The state's biased case wasn't the only factor working against Hill. (2) What gave his accusers added credibility was Hill's attitude, specifically his consistent refusal to reveal his whereabouts on the night of the murders. (3) Perhaps there really was a quarrel over a woman, and Hill was protecting her reputation. (4) Although he never married, Hill apparently was considered attractive to women. (5) Or perhaps he was guilty and decided to become a martyr. (6) Whatever the reason for his silence, he made other mistakes that hurt his case. (7) During the trial, for example, he tried to fire his defense attorneys. (8) Hill disliked their lack of aggressiveness when cross-examining prosecution witnesses and exposing inconsistencies in their testimony. (9) Finally, his attorneys were allowed to remain in the courtroom and question witnesses, but Hill conducted some of his own defense. (10) Overall, the jury was not impressed with Hill's behavior.

Paragraph G. (1) Hill's sentencing and subsequent execution turned him into an international hero and martyr of the labor movement. (2) On June 27, 1914, the jury found Hill guilty, and two weeks later he was sentenced to death. (3) The judge gave Joe Hill the option of hanging or facing the firing squad, and Hill replied, "I'll take shooting. I'm used to that. I've been shot a few times in the past and I guess I can stand it again." (4) During the year of the appeal process the IWW publicized the case, picturing their songwriter as an innocent victim of capitalist oppression. (5) As Hill's execution day approached, hundreds of letters and telegrams poured into the governor's office. (6) Many famous people pleaded for a pardon, including Helen Keller. (7) She was blind and deaf and later became the subject of a famous movie called *The Miracle Worker*. (8) Since Hill was a Swedish citizen, the Swedish ambassador also became involved. (9) He persuaded President Woodrow Wilson to write the governor of Utah, which won Hill a temporary reprieve. (10) But Hill stubbornly refused to reveal how he was wounded, and on November 19, 1915, he was shot by a firing squad. (11) His legend became an inspiration to radical labor movements around the world, and the message he wired to IWW founder "Big Bill" Haywood the night before the execution became famous. (12) It read, "Don't waste any time in mourning. Organize."

In Summary: A paragraph

1. is a group of sentences that discuss one main point, or topic;
2. often includes a statement of that main point in a topic sentence;
3. develops the point in a number of sentences called the body;
4. begins with the first line indented;
5. requires that each sentence follow directly after the previous sentence, not on a separate line;
6. has unity—all information supports the main idea;
7. is limited to a topic that can be developed in a short space.

In Summary: A topic sentence

1. is the most general statement in the paragraph, while the more specific statements in the paragraph develop that general statement;
2. usually comes at the beginning of the paragraph but can appear after an introductory statement or even at the end of the paragraph;
3. can be implied (omitted from the paragraph) if the main idea is clear without it;
4. should make a point about or express an attitude toward the subject of the paragraph, not simply announce the subject;
5. should be limited—made neither too general nor too specific.

10 REVISING

Return to the paragraph you wrote in Exercise 9 and criticize it again, paying special attention to the topic sentence and the unity of the paragraph. Rewrite the topic sentence if it is too general or too specific and omit or revise any parts that do not support the topic idea. Then write a final draft of the paragraph, strengthening the wording; correcting grammatical, spelling, and punctuation errors; and making a clean copy of your work.

CHAPTER 17

Writing Concretely and Concisely

Writing with confidence means writing clearly, directly, and vividly. It begins with listening to your writing voice as you compose and then revising your writing to strengthen that voice. This chapter will help you develop and polish your style by showing you how to choose *strong verbs and adjectives*, to *eliminate weak repetition* and *wordiness*, and to *avoid clichés*.

EXAMINING THE TRAITS OF STRONG WRITING

Good writing is direct and concise; it puts each word to work. It is specific, concrete, and lively. Bad writing is imprecise, abstract, dull, and repetitious. Compare these sentences.

1. In the modern-day world of today, there are many important problems that concern each and every one of us, and one of the most important of these problems is the problem concerning the danger of nuclear war.
2. Everyone fears nuclear war.

You probably prefer the second version, which makes its point in just four words. The first version, consisting of thirty-eight words, is bloated and repetitious. *Important* is used twice; *one* twice; *problems*, three times; and *concern* is not only repeated but is used in two different ways. The linking verb *be* is used twice (in *are* and *is*) versus the single-action verb *fears* in the second version, which implies the idea of *danger*. And the first version wastes both words and time by saying the obvious in *clichés*—lifeless and overused expressions.

In the modern-day world of today . . . (Isn't *today* a day, and isn't it modern? Why mention the *world* unless we expect a discussion of the moon?) there are many problems that concern each and every one of us. . . . (Don't we know that? And what is the difference between *each* and *every?*)

This version, in short, is filled with *deadwood:* lifeless and useless language.

As you write, don't waste any words. Be direct and specific while pruning the deadwood. In the first drafts listen to the sounds and rhythms of your sentences and then strengthen them during revisions, paying close attention to word choice. Here are some guidelines to aid you during the process.

WRITING STRONG VERBS

Don't worry about each word in your early drafts. Let your ideas and words flow freely. But as you revise, look carefully at the verbs. Commonly used (and overused) verbs such as *is/are/am, go, get, have, make, do, run, put, take, see, use,* and *talk* are vague and lifeless. The verb *take,* for example, can have countless meanings.

take medicine, take a vacation, take a nap, take a shower, take a bow, take care, take a walk, take an interest in, take a liking to, take a breath, take the cake, take effect, take up, take over, take charge, take on, take off, take from, take away, take down, take after, take back, take out, take a pick, take safety, take a side, take account of, take apart, take care of, take hold, take part in, take heart, take a break, take for granted, take your time, take the floor, take to, take shape, take-home pay, be on the take, take it easy, take a fancy to, and take a powder

Some of these expressions are fresh; some aren't. Don't try to eliminate all common verbs, but don't overuse them. As you revise, circle weak verbs and substitute more concrete (but not fancy) verbs or phrases that more precisely express your meaning.

took back   I ⎰ *returned* the shirt.
                ⎱ *retracted* my hasty words.
                  withdrew my application.

took down   The secretary ⎰ *recorded* the information.
                            ⎱ *removed* the drapes.
                              lengthened the hem on her skirt.

took   He ⎰ *accepted*
            snatched   the money.
            grabbed
            ran off with

> **In Summary:** To write strong verbs,
>
> 1. during revisions, circle weak verbs such as *is/are/am, go, get, have, make, do, run, put, take, see, use* and *talk;* and
> 2. if possible, substitute a verb or phrase that more precisely and vividly expresses your meaning.

Notice that using the verb *have* to express possession not only wastes words but sometimes whole sentences. A single word such as *my* can express the same idea.

Poor: I have an old car. It barely runs anymore.
Better: My old car barely runs anymore.

1 WARM-UP

Write three to five different verbs or phrases that express the idea in parentheses, but don't rely on common verbs. Be prepared to discuss the differences in meaning among the verbs.

1. (fast movement) The big cat _shot, darted, raced, tore, scooted_ into the room.

2. (talk loudly) The woman _____ at the salesman.

3. (make) Chef Alberto _____ a delicious cake.

4. (build) The workers _____ the garage in just a few hours.

5. (go) LaVelle _____ to work looking worried.

6. (slow movement) The sheriff _____ through the room, staring at each man at the poker tables.

7. (get) Wilfredo _____ the money.

8. (eat) Albert _____ a whole pie in just minutes.

2 COMBINING

Combine each of the following pairs of sentences or clauses, eliminating the verb *have*.

1. Ralph has a dog. It constantly begs at the table.
   Ralph's dog constantly begs at the table.

2. I have a brother. He's a foot taller than I am.

   _____

3. Laura has a new job that pays very well.

   _____

4. The university has a library that has every book you can imagine.

   _____

5. The dentist has an x-ray machine that she uses to find cavities.

   _____

6. I have an insane friend named Susan. She makes everyone laugh.

_____

7. The city has some laws that are very unfair.

_____

3 EDITING

The following passage overrelies on the verbs _do_ and _get._ Rewrite the passage, supplying verbs that are more exact and vivid. (In some cases replacing a verb will not work, and you should rewrite the sentence completely.)

When I get home from school each day, I have a lot of chores to do. I do the laundry and the housecleaning, I do the dishes from breakfast and lunch, and I get dinner ready for my family. We eat dinner at around 5:30, and after we get finished, I do the dishes again. I usually don't get any help from my children or husband, so I have to do everything myself. I get the kids in bed around nine o'clock, which is when I can do my homework. I do my math assignments first because I can do problems while the TV is on. Then I do the rest of the assignments I've got for the next day. I usually get to bed around midnight so that I can get up at 6:00 A.M.

_____

_____

_____

_____

_____

_____

_____

_____

_____

_____

_____

_____

_____

CHOOSING VIVID LANGUAGE

Scrutinize your adjectives as you revise; the most overused adjectives are often flat and imprecise. Circle common adjectives such as _good, bad, nice, different, interesting,_ and _fun_ and try to substitute words or phrases that are more vivid.

Weak	Better	
The Steven King novel was *very interesting*.	The Steven King novel was	*riveting.* *fascinating.* *terrifying.*
	Some especially frightening parts of the Steven King novel made the hairs on my legs curl.	

Also look for vague words and expressions. The words *things*, *ways*, *methods*, and *factors* and expressions such as *what he said* are so general that they are almost meaningless. Try replacing them with specifics.

Weak	Better
Everybody likes Susan because of all the funny things she does.	Susan makes everyone laugh when she says, "This test will be no problem," and then fakes a heart attack.
What the teacher said was interesting.	Everyone in class was surprised at the teacher's argument that high prices for imported oil are in the best interests of the United States.

In Summary: To write strong adjectives and expressions,

1. during revisions, circle vague adjectives such as *good, bad, nice, different, interesting, fun,* and *pretty;* and vague words or expressions such as *things, ways, what he does* or *the things he says;* and
2. substitute words and phrases that more vividly and exactly express your meaning.

---

4 EDITING

Rewrite each of the following sentences using language that is more vivid and exact.

1. Tom's behavior is annoying. ___When Tom borrows my clothes and___ returns them dirty, eats half a gallon of ice cream from my freezer without asking, or calls me at 2:00 A.M. to find out the next day's homework assignment, I seriously consider stabbing him in the heart with an ice pick.

2. I saw a good movie. _____
   _____
   _____

3. I had a really bad cold. _____

_____

_____

4. What the acrobat did was interesting. _____

_____

_____

5. Pedro has nice clothes. _____

_____

_____

6. My friend sometimes does odd things. _____

_____

_____

7. Celia's new dress is really pretty. _____

_____

8. There are some things we do in college that I don't like. _____

_____

_____

9. I really try hard to get good grades. _____

_____

_____

10. The United States is a good country in several ways. _____

_____

_____

ELIMINATING UNNECESSARY REPETITION

Not all repetition weakens writing. Intentional repetition can build to a climax.

Each day Brian studies the sports section, studies the movie listings, and occasionally even studies his assignments.

Or it can provide coherence.

We waited for an explanation, an excuse or any kind of answer, but *no answer* ever came.

But a word accidentally repeated (even in a different form or with a different meaning) can thud against your readers' ears like fenders crunching in a parking lot.

Weak	_Stronger_
Ball State _University_ is a _university_ that provides a complete program of undergraduate and graduate study.	Ball State University provides a complete program of undergraduate and graduate study.
The _playground_ is a good place for children to _play_.	The facilities in the playground are excellent.
Juan is _active_ in most school _activities_.	Juan thrives on school activities.
He had a _reasonably_ good _reason_ to be absent.	His absence was justifiable.
I just read a fascinating book. The book was about the U.S. space program.	I just read a fascinating book about the U.S. space program.

In Summary: To avoid weak repetition,

1. during revisions, circle repeated words, including those used in different forms or with different meanings;
2. decide whether their repetition strengthens or weakens the passage; and
3. rewrite the passage, substituting for or eliminating the weak repetition.

5 EDITING

Rewrite each of the following sentences to eliminate unnecessary repetition. In some cases you may wish to combine sentences.

1. Some of the algebra problems gave me problems. _Some of the algebra problems were difficult._

2. Park Place is an expensive place to live. _____

3. Our new house is a large house. _____

4. Bus fare is fairly high in this city. _____

5. Please note what the footnote says. _____

6. Jill's teacher is not like my teacher. My teacher is very understanding.

7. I always read the directions on an examination first. After I read the directions, I know exactly what's expected of me. _____

8. Many people like to get up early in the morning and run. Running makes them feel awake. Running also helps them stay alert. _____

_____

_____

ELIMINATING WORDINESS

Bad writing wastes words, saying in ten what could be said in four or five. Compare these flabby and tight expressions.

Wordy	*Tight*
As far as looks are concerned, Susan is very pretty.	Susan is beautiful.
at this point in time	now
He has the ability to swim.	He can swim.
She shouted at him in a very loud voice.	She screamed at him.
in my opinion	I think
in the near future	soon

Bad writing also insults a reader's intelligence, needlessly explaining what is already implied.

Poor
My mother is *the kind of woman who* cleans the house five times a day. (Why say that your mother is a *woman?* And why say that she is a *kind?* Both categories are obvious.)

Better
My mother cleans the house five times a day.

Poor
Calculus is a branch of mathematics that presents many different types of challenges to students. (Why say that calculus is a *branch of mathematics?* And why mention both *different* and *types* since one implies the other? In fact why mention either word since *challenges* is plural and means more than one?)

Better
Calculus presents many challenges to students.

Poor
Professional basketball players are very tall in height. (Why mention *in height* since *tall* includes that idea? And why say *very tall* when a single word expresses that idea?)

Better
Professional basketball players are giants.

Poor
The reason why rock music is so popular is *because* it appeals to the rebel in all of us. (Why say *the reason*, *why*, and *because*, since all three mean the same thing? And why say that rock music is popular, since that is obvious?)

Better
Rock music appeals to the rebel in all of us.

You should expect flabbiness in early drafts, so look for and tighten such phrasing as you revise. But be careful: never write a sentence that sounds awkward or distorts your meaning.

> **In Summary:** To avoid wordiness,
>
> 1. during revisions, look for and eliminate words whose meanings are already included in other words;
> 2. eliminate empty categorizing words such as *type of, kind of, way, area,* and *method;* but
> 3. violate this advice when the revision is unclear or awkward.

6 EDITING

Rewrite and tighten each of the following sentences.

1. The pie had an unusual taste to it. _The pie tasted unusual._

2. Horace Johnson is the kind of person who performs well under pressure.

3. The reason why I like art is because it allows me to be creative.

4. The getaway car was large in size and red in color.

5. Anita seems to have a lot of self-confidence in herself.

6. I'm the type of student who does not do well on tests or examinations at 8:00 A.M. in the morning.

7. Summer is the time of year when I enjoy the outdoors more than any other time.

8. Everett has the ability to think faster than just about any other kind of person that he is personally likely to meet.

9. When my instructor returned back my paper to me today, I saw that it had several different types of errors that were mistakes that came from being careless.

10. In my opinion I feel that in this modern day and age, too many people from all different walks of life and races, creeds, and religions are too selfish and care only about themselves.

_____

_____

ELIMINATING UNNECESSARY CLAUSES

Chapters 4 and 7 showed you how to write dependent clauses that serve as adjectives or adverbs. Such clauses are necessary and often effective, but why waste all the extra words on a clause when you can express the same idea in a short phrase? For example, you can write these combined sentences.

The tall man _who is wearing gym shorts_ must be a basketball player.
The tall man _who is in gym shorts_ must be a basketball player.

However, you can also remove the subject and verb—_who is_—from the dependent clauses in these sentences.

The tall man _wearing gym shorts_ must be a basketball player.
The tall man _in gym shorts_ must be a basketball player.

The italicized words that remain function as _adjective phrases_—they describe the man. You probably agree that the sentences with the phrases sound stronger and more emphatic than the ones with the _who_ clauses.

Here is another sentence containing both a _which_ clause and a _that_ clause. Rewrite it, changing the clauses to phrases.

Many people still read _Great Expectations_, which is a novel that was written by Charles Dickens over 120 years ago.

_____

_____

Is this what you wrote?

Many people still read _Great Expectations_, a novel written by Charles Dickens over 120 years ago.

Take a look at the phrases in the previous examples, and you will notice that there were four types—all of which described or renamed nouns:

1. phrases beginning with an _-ing_ word (_wearing_ gym shorts);
2. phrases beginning with a preposition (_in_ gym shorts);
3. phrases beginning with a noun (_a novel);_ and
4. phrases beginning with a past participle (_written_ by Charles Dickens).

As you can see, these phrases express the same meanings as clauses that begin with _who, which,_ or _that_ + _be_ (_am, is, are, was,_ or _were_). However, you cannot always remove these words from a clause and leave a descriptive phrase that is just as clear as the clause. Take, for example, the last part of the previous sentence: ". . . and leave a descriptive phrase that is just as clear as the clause." Does it make sense with *that is* removed? Nevertheless, as a general rule, if you can write a phrase instead of a clause, do it.

Similarly, you can shorten many adverb (*when, why, where*) dependent clauses into phrases. Here is a sentence with an adverb dependent clause.

Before Robert Wadlow reached the age of eight, he was six feet tall.

Notice that you can change this dependent clause into a phrase. Simply remove the subject from the clause and change the verb *reached* into an *-ing* word.

Before reaching the age of eight, Robert Wadlow was six feet tall.

Rewrite the following sentence by removing the subject from the dependent clause and making the clause into a phrase.

When Wadlow went through a doorway, he had to duck his head.

_____

_____

Is this what you wrote?

When going through a doorway, Wadlow had to duck his head.

Did you move the word *Wadlow* to the independent clause so that the subject of the sentence is clear?

WARNING: You can generally change a time clause (a *when, while, before,* or *after* clause) into a phrase—provided that the subject of the time clause and the subject of the independent clause are the same *(Wadlow . . . he)*. You *cannot* make the dependent clause into a phrase if the two subjects are different. Notice what happens in this sentence.

Clause
After *Wadlow* grew too big for the desks in school, *his teachers* had to find him other places to sit.

Phrase
After growing too big for his desks in school, *his teachers*. . . .

The second version seems to say that *his teachers* grew too big for the desks, not Wadlow. Therefore the sentence with the dependent clause "After Wadlow grew too big . . ." is preferable.

7 EDITING   Whenever possible, draw a line through *who, which,* or *that* and any form of *be* in the following sentences. In some cases you may decide not to eliminate these words from a sentence.

1. Robert Wadlow's life stands as a warning to any child who is interested in being a giant.

2. At his birth in 1918, his weight, which was 8½ pounds, didn't seem abnormal, and no one suspected a problem.

3. But he grew to a height that is the tallest ever verified in history.

4. After six months he weighed 30 pounds, and within eighteen months, his weight, which was now at 62 pounds, had more than doubled.

5. At the age of five, he reached a height that was 5 feet, 4 inches, and at the age of eight, he was 6 feet tall.

6. Wadlow continued to grow about 3 inches every year until he died, which was in 1940.

7. He passed 7 feet before he turned thirteen, and at nineteen years of age he became the tallest person who was ever measured, at 8 feet, 5½ inches.

8. When Wadlow was twelve, doctors diagnosed the cause of his rapid growth, which was a malfunctioning pituitary gland.

9. They knew that his bodily organs could not support such a large frame, which was 8 feet, 11 inches in 1940, and that eventually he would die from the strain placed on his body.

10. Several weeks before his death in 1940, Wadlow weighed 439 pounds, which was not excessive for his height, but his body had simply grown beyond its ability to function properly.

8 COMBINING

Combine each of the following groups of sentences by changing one of the sentences into a descriptive phrase and inserting it in the appropriate place. If you cannot change a sentence into a phrase, change it into a relative clause (a *who-which-that* clause). You may need to insert some commas in the combined sentences.

1. Robert Wadlow's first physical problem happened when he was two. It was a double hernia. _Robert Wadlow's first physical problem, a double hernia, happened when he was two._

2. As Wadlow's body quickly grew, it created many problems. These problems were associated with living in a normal-sized world. _____
_____
_____

3. For example, Wadlow had to sit at tiny desks in third grade. He was already six feet tall. _____
_____
_____
_____

4. He was a teenager. He was outgrowing even the adult world's furniture, cars, and doorways. _____

_____

_____

5. Walking damaged his ankles. They were fitted with braces when he was twenty-two. _____

_____

_____

6. The braces cut into his ankles and caused an infection. It was so serious that it eventually killed him. _____

_____

_____

7. Wadlow was an intelligent man. He was as much aware of the tragedy of his life as anyone else. _____

_____

_____

_____

8. Nevertheless he impressed everyone he met with his charm, and he never became a bitter person. Such a person was always complaining about his problems. _____

_____

_____

_____

9 EDITING   When it is possible, change the dependent clause to a phrase in each of the following sentences. Cross out the subject in the dependent clause and write your changes above the line. Some of the dependent clauses cannot be changed.

1. After ∧~~Wadlow reached~~ ^{reaching} his ninth birthday, ∧~~he~~ ^{Wadlow} became a national celebrity when his picture appeared in the newspapers.

2. When he celebrated any birthday after that, he was surrounded by newspaper reporters and newsreel photographers.

3. Nevertheless, while he grew older, he continued to have physical problems.

4. After he had a series of foot injuries, doctors advised him to walk a lot to build up strength in his legs.

5. However, when he walked too much, he actually damaged his legs more seriously.

6. Soon after Shurtleff College admitted him to a prelaw program, he had to drop out because walking to classrooms was too painful for him.

Examining More Ways to Change Clauses into Phrases

There are other ways of changing dependent clauses into phrases. Look for example, at this sentence.

As he was approaching the end of his life, Wadlow traveled often and met many famous people.

Here are just a few of the ways to change the clause to a phrase.

Approaching the end of his life,
Near the end of his life, } Wadlow traveled. . . .
Before his death,

Take a look at this sentence, also.

A shoe company in St. Louis supplied Wadlow with specially made shoes and paid him a fee *because the company wanted him to represent it in public appearances.*

Here is the revision.

A shoe company in St. Louis supplied Wadlow with specially made shoes and paid him a fee *to represent the company in public appearances.*

Notice the similarity between adjective descriptive phrases and adverb descriptive phrases. In both cases many of the phrases can begin with a preposition, an *-ing* word, or a past participle. In addition they can sometimes begin with an infinitive, such as *to represent* in the last example.

> **In Summary:** Any descriptive phrase can begin with
>
> 1. a **preposition** such as *from, in, with, after,* or *on;*
> 2. an *-ing word* such as *approaching, sitting,* or *knowing;*
> 3. a *past participle* such as *known, taken,* or *fitted;*
> 4. an **infinitive** such as *to know, to see,* or *to take.*
>   And a phrase after a noun can include another noun that renames it (Robert Wadlow, *the world's tallest man,* . . .).

10 TRANSFORMING Rewrite the dependent clause in each of the following sentences, changing it to a phrase. Use the words in parentheses to begin the phrase.

1. *As Robert went from his childhood to adulthood*, he had little trouble coping with the publicity surrounding him. (from) From his childhood to adulthood, Robert had little trouble coping with the publicity surrounding him.

2. Robert's father, the mayor of Alton, helped Robert *because he steered him away from all the publicity that followed.* (by + -ing) _____

_____

3. All sorts of people came to Wadlow *because they wanted stories, scientific information, or theatrical bookings.* (to ask for) _____

_____

4. Theatrical agents applied the most pressure *when they made large offers for his services.* (with) _____

_____

5. His parents rejected most opportunities to cash in on his size, *although there were two exceptions.* (with) _____

_____

6. The Peters Shoe Company offered to give him specially made shoes and a fee *if he would make public appearances as their representative.* (in exchange for his) _____

_____

7. He traveled more and more for the company over the years *because he hoped to go into the shoe business on his own later.* (-ing) _____

_____

8. In 1937 Wadlow worked briefly for the Ringling Brothers' Circus, but he appeared on stage *while he was wearing regular street clothes.* (in) ____

_____

_____

11 COMBINING

Combine the following groups of sentences into one sentence. Use descriptive phrases whenever possible.

1. Wadlow quit college. He traveled. He went around the country. He wanted to promote Peters Shoes. _After quitting college, Wadlow traveled around the country promoting Peters Shoes._

2. Wadlow was ten. He was 6 feet, 5 inches tall. He weighed 210. He wore clothes. They were made by tailors. _____

_____

_____

3. Wadlow made public appearances. They were for churches and charities. He did them without being paid. _____

_____

_____

4. He sold autographed pictures. He wanted to help the Methodist Church. It was located in Alton. It needed to buy a new pipe organ. _____

_____

_____

5. Wadlow was on summer vacations. He worked at state fairs. He sold soft drinks. _____

_____

_____

AVOIDING CLICHÉS

A *cliché* is an *overused and tired expression* that has lost its power and meaning. Because clichés are so familiar, you will probably write several in your early drafts. Look for them when you revise and try to substitute fresher expressions.

Cliché	Better
It was raining cats and dogs.	The rain quickly flooded the streets and basements.
as quick as a wink	instantly
as sharp as a tack	as sharp as a ninety-degree turn

The following (incomplete) list of clichés should serve as examples:

a chip off the old block	in this day and age
after all was said and done	it goes without saying
the break of day	last but not least
as cold as ice	let bygones be bygones
as happy as a lark	make my blood boil
at this point in time	more fun than a barrel of monkeys
avoid it like the plague	once in a blue moon
barely scratches the surface	one in a million
beat around the bush	over and done with
bite the bullet	the picture of health
blow my top	sadder but wiser
bored to tears	selling like hot cakes
easier said than done	shoot from the hip
few and far between	sleep like a log
from sunup to sundown	stick like glue
have a ball	stick to my guns
have the time of my life	straight shooter
in one ear and out the other	tell it like it is

the thrill of a lifetime
the time of my life
tried and true
true blue
up at the crack of dawn
waiting in the wings

water under the bridge
water over the dam
where it's at
where you're coming from
work like a horse

> **In Summary:** To avoid clichés,
>
> look for them during revisions and substitute your own words.

12 EDITING

Rewrite each of the following sentences to eliminate clichés.

1. The Electric Tool's new album is selling like hotcakes. _The Electric Tool's new album is selling like firecrackers on the fourth of July._

2. He was as happy as a lark.

3. Getting rid of every cliché is easier said than done.

4. The day of the exam I was up at the crack of dawn so I'd be good and ready.

5. The drill instructor told the men to toe the line or there would be hell to pay.

6. Billy's mother tries to keep a rein on him, but her scolding goes in one ear and out the other.

7. I had a ball at the party, and afterwards we were so tired that I slept like a baby.

8. Orlando really does his own thing on the dance floor.

9. In this day and age honest politicians are few and far between.

10. This exercise barely scratches the surface of clichés; you must work like a horse to get rid of them in your writing.

Index

Copy 1

Meyers Alene

AUTHOR

Writing With

TITLE

Confidence

DATE DUE	BORROWER'S NAME
	Carol Beimborn

Copy 1